Reel Change:
A History of British Cinema from the Projection Box

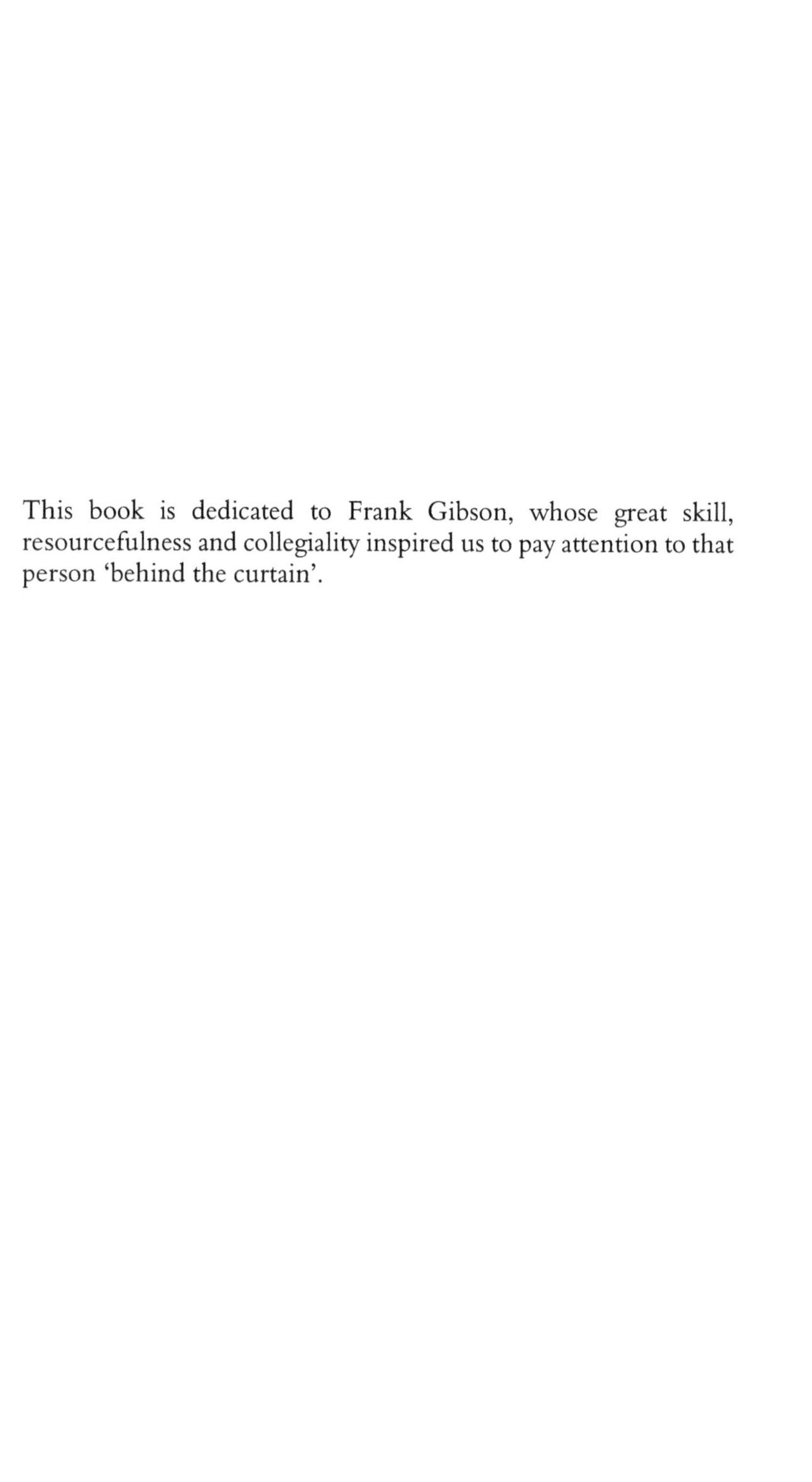

This book is dedicated to Frank Gibson, whose great skill, resourcefulness and collegiality inspired us to pay attention to that person 'behind the curtain'.

Reel Change: A History of British Cinema from the Projection Box

Richard Wallace and Jon Burrows

Afterword by Charlotte Brunsdon

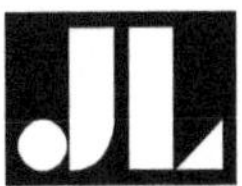

British Library Cataloguing in Publication Data

Reel Change:
A History of British Cinema from the Projection Box

A catalogue entry for this book is available from the British Library

ISBN: 9780 86196 751 3 (Paperback)
ISBN: 9780 86196 983 8 (ebook-EPUB)
ISBN: 9780 86196 984 5 (ebook-EPDF)

Front cover: Allan Foster in the projection box at the Hyde Park Picture House Cinema, Leeds. Image © Richard Nicholson.

Published by
John Libbey Publishing Ltd, 205 Crescent Road, New Barnet, Herts EN4 8SB, United Kingdom   e-mail: john.libbey@orange.fr; web site: www.johnlibbey.com

Distributed Worldwide by
Indiana University Press, Herman B Wells Library—350, 1320 E. 10th St., Bloomington, IN 47405, USA. www.iupress.indiana.edu

Printed and bound in the United States of America

Contents

	Preface	**1**
	Introduction	**3**
Chapter One	**Job Descriptions**	**13**
	The Mobile Array	15
	The Nitrate Array	17
	The Xenon Array	35
	The Multi-Screen Array	43
	A 'Jack-of-All-Trades'	56
Chapter Two	**The Art of Cinema Projection**	**67**
	Projection as an Element of Film Production	68
	Presentation and Showmanship	83
	Changing Standards	98
Chapter Three	**Terms and Conditions**	**101**
	The British Film Industry's First Union	103
	Short-lived Militancy	113
	Organisation Without Unions	123
	Industrial Conflict	130
	National Agreements	139
	Certification and Apprenticeships	149
Chapter Four	**Digital Projection(s)**	**169**
	Digital Developments: Image, Standards, Finance	171
	Discourses of Instability	175
	Redundancy	183
	Loss of Agency	191
	Deskilling	195
	The Cinema Experience in the Digital Age	199
Afterword	**In Love with Film Projection by Charlotte Brunsdon**	**207**
Appendix	**Details of Projectionists Interviewed for this Book**	**215**
	Bibliography	**217**
	Index	**227**

Acknowledgements

The research upon which this book is based was conducted for the AHRC-funded research project 'The Projection Project' (grant reference AH/L008033/1), which ran from 2014 to 2018. Additional funding for project-related activities that have benefited the research, writing and production of this book also came from the University of Warwick's Humanities Research Fund and from the university's Connecting Cultures Global Research Priority fund.

The project would not have been possible without the involvement of our partners Richard Paterson at the British Film Institute, Ian Francis, the director of Birmingham's Flatpack Festival, and Richard Nicholson, whose 'The Projectionists' exhibition held as part of Flatpack's 2016 festival was a highlight of the project. The project was also expertly steered by our brilliant advisory board: Charlotte Crofts, Allen Eyles, Ann Gray, Peter J Knight, Lawrence Napper, Roger Shannon, and Ken Worpole. The board made numerous suggestions that had an important bearing on how the project and its outputs developed.

There are two other members of the project's research team – Michael Pigott and Claire Jesson – who did not directly contribute to this book, but played a significant role in shaping some of its arguments through their contributions to the project reading group. The project was also expertly supported by our administrators, Elaine Robinson, Anne Birchall, Sabina Ahmed and Tracey McVey, and the team from Research Support Services at Warwick, especially Katie Klaasen, Liese Perrin, Harriet Hine and Colette Kelly. We should also like to thank former undergraduate students Thom Clipsom, who assisted in the early development of the project, and Elliott Howarth, who gathered portions of the research materials included in Chapter 4.

Much of the research for this book took place in a range of archives across the UK and we are very grateful for the support and dedication of the following people: Michelle Gait and Jan Smith of the Wolfson Reading Room, Special Collections Centre, The Sir

Duncan Rice Library, Aberdeen University; Carolyn Ewing at the Coventry History Centre; Lynette Cawthra at the Working Class Movement Library, Salford; Liz Wood, Martin Sanders and Helen Ford at the Modern Records Centre, University of Warwick; and the staff at the National Archives and the British Library.

In presenting elements of this research publicly, we also benefitted from collaborations with Rebecca Harrison, Karen Alexander, Alexa Raisbeck, Haidee Wasson, Lucie Èesálková, Eva Balogh, Virginia Crisp and Gabriel Menotti.

Finally our thanks go to all of those projectionists, technicians, programmers, and curators who agreed to be interviewed for the project or photographed for 'The Projectionists'. Thank you for your time, your enthusiasm, your views and your memories: Simon Allen, James Anderson, Brad Atwill, Ken Bagnall, Peter Bell, Sam Bishop, Chris Blower, Martyn Butler, Luke Capitani, Mick Corfield, Mark Cosgrove, John Douglas, Peter Douglas, Rachel Dukes, Ewan Dunford, Paul Edmunds, Phil Fawke, Allan Foster, Ian Francis, Frank Gibson, John Gore, Richard Horner, Peter Howden, Amanda Ireland, Abdul Kaher, Sam Lavington, Tom Lawes, Andrew MacLean, Ewen MacLeod, Chandra Makwana, Mike Marshall, Umit Mesut, Ross More, John Neal, Chris O'Kane, Adrian Pearce, Joan Pearson, Bill Pearson, David Powell, Alexa Raisbeck, Ray Reed, Neil Thompson, Chris Tweddell, Mike Williams, John Young, Roger Young.

Preface

At the time of writing, cinemas in Britain have been closed for most of 2020, and 2021 has commenced under renewed lockdown. Going to the cinema, a regular habit for millions during much of the 20th century, has, for the moment, dropped out of daily life. The COVID-19 pandemic has significantly accelerated the ascent to prominence of digital streaming as a means of watching films, whether on phones, laptops, tablets or television screens. In time, this may conceivably come to be seen as the beginning of a new era in the history of moving image media. But, however these events are subsequently viewed, it is important to remember that they have taken place within a broader context, in which nearly everything to do with film making and exhibition had already been transformed by digital technology. Since the end of the first decade of the 21st century, the films seen in cinemas have predominantly not been films in the original sense of that word, but digital files similar to the ones that bring audio-visual content to a mobile phone. As part of this wider process of transformation, it was not only analogue film projectors that were stripped out of multiplexes, but also key forms of human labour that had underpinned the cinema experience for over 110 years. Charlotte Brunsdon, at the University of Warwick, saw a need to take steps to ensure that this particular momentous change – largely concealed from public view – was documented and studied whilst it was still fresh in the minds of those most profoundly affected by it. She thus put together The Projection Project, a team of researchers funded by the Arts and Humanities Research Council between 2014 and 2018 to investigate why projectionists had been made redundant in such a swift and ruthless fashion by the advent of digitalisation in cinemas, how this might change our understanding of what cinema is, and also to properly evaluate and commemorate the role played by projectionists throughout the history of the medium.[1]

This book is one of the outputs of the Projection Project, written by two members of the project team. It seeks to document the entire history of cinema in Britain, from the late 19th century to the present day, from the perspective of one of its most hidden

1 The Projection Project, 2014-18, AH/L008033. For more on the project, see the Afterword to this book and the project's website: https://cinemaprojectionist.co.uk.

figures: the projectionist. We hope to make clear that the practical factors pertaining to the basic question of how the image gets onto the screen are significantly more complex, and demanded more arduous effort, than most of us have typically realised.

The sources used to write this alternative history are of two main types. Firstly, written documents, such as film industry trade journals, and the unpublished archival records of trade unions, local authorities and government departments like the Ministry of Labour, through which the history of the evolution of the job of 'projectionist' and the regulation of cinema exhibition can be traced. And secondly, interviews with people working in, or retired from, or made redundant from, that job. The interviews give a vivid, sensuous account of what the work was like and how it changed over the last fifty years in particular, and reveal the strenuous labour behind the magic of film projection. Many projectionists and former projectionists thus contributed to the book, and many other cinema workers and scholars helped us gather the material that is presented here, and also in other publications, exhibitions and events associated with the Projection Project.[2] We hope that this book will be of interest to a broad constituency of people associated with/interested in the film exhibition business, and not simply other academics. However, non-academic readers may prefer to skip the introduction – which explains how this project relates to previous work published by other cinema scholars – and dive straight into the main chapters. Chapter One, 'Job Descriptions', documents the changing forms of work involved in putting a picture on the screen at various stages in the technological evolution of cinema. Chapter Two, 'The Art of Cinema Projection', explores various aesthetic facets of cinema projection; not merely showing a film, but 'putting on a show' through precise and careful realising of particular codes of cinema 'presentation' that projectionists adhered to. Chapter Three, 'Terms and Conditions', examines the conditions of employment that projectionists experienced across the 20th century, and the complex and contentious history of their representation by trade unions. The final chapter, 'Digital Projection(s)', provides an overview of British cinema's transition to digital during the 21st century, capturing the experience of that change by those who worked through it, as well as examining the complex implications that digital projection technologies have for the experience of cinemagoing.

2 See the special issue of *The Journal of British Cinema and Television*, 15:1 (January 2018), edited by Brunsdon, Burrows and Wallace; Richard Nicholson, *The Projectionists*, exhibition, The Gas Hall, Birmingham Museums and Art Gallery, 19-24 April 2016; Michael Pigott and Richard Wallace, 'A New "Wild West" of Projection', in Virginia Crisp and Gabriel Menotti, (eds) *Practices of Projection: Histories and Technologies* (New York: Oxford University Press, 2020), pp. 19-35; Michael Lightbourne, *Sounds of the Projection Box* (Gruenrekorder, 2018), vinyl and digital audio release.

Introduction

In the introduction to their 2019 'introductory manual' *The Art of Film Projection*, Paolo Cherchi Usai, Spencer Christiano, Catherine A. Surowiec and Timothy J. Wagner suggest that their work 'is emphatically *not* a compendium on the history and technology of film projection' because 'There is a wealth of specialized literature on the subject'.[3] One of the reasons why we have written this book is because we would say that the opposite is actually true!

Although there have been technical manuals and trade publications addressing practitioners for almost as long as there have been practitioners to address, Usai and his fellow editors do acknowledge that 'projection was rarely a focus of attention in the academic world'.[4] In part they attribute this neglect to the tendency of scholars, historians, curators and the film industry itself to characterise the role of the projectionist as being 'to make visible what others had previously done', as if this is a trivial and unimportant thing.[5] It is, therefore, only recently that it has been recognised

> that cinema is neither made of 'content' nor of mere 'objects,' but is a complex performance involving a creative work (the film), its carrier (the print), an apparatus (the projector), a physical environment (the theatre and its screen), and the people in charge of exhibiting the work (the projectionists).[6]

In part, this reorientation has come about due to the arrival of all-digital workflows within the film industry, which has led to the virtual obsolescence of 35mm film as a mainstream exhibition format, and the concomitant near-obsolescence of the individuals necessary to care for and screen prints to cinema audiences. The

3 Paolo Cherchi Usai, Spencer Christiano, Catherine A. Surowiec and Timothy J. Wagner (eds), *Art of Film Projection: A Beginner's Guide* (New York: George Eastman Museum, 2019), pp. 19-20.

4 *Ibid.*, p. 21. For literature aimed *at* the projectionist see, for example, the trade papers *Ideal Kinema* (1927-1966), *International Projectionist* (1931-1965), *The Projectionists' Journal* (1932-1939) and its successor *The Projectionist's Bulletin* (1940-41) and *Cinema Technology* (1987-) as well as the seminal handbook for UK projectionists *The Complete Projectionist: A Textbook for all who Handle Sound and Pictures in the Kinema,* which was written by R. Howard Cricks and published by Odhams Press in four editions between 1933 and 1949, and Charles S. Swartz's (ed.) more recent (though less ubiquitous) book *Understanding Digital Cinema: A Professional Handbook* (Oxford; Burlington, MA: Focal Press, 2005).

5 Usai *et al.*, *Art of Film Projection*, p. 21.

6 *Ibid.* We will show in Chapter Two that projectionists have long understood their job in these terms.

format (the film print), the process (film projection) and the practitioner (the projectionist) have all become rare, and this has transfigured the art of film projection into a historical – even an archival – process. As Usai *et al.* argue, rather than being an everyday condition of the mainstream exhibition of movies, film projection has instead become 'the ultimate achievement of film preservation.'[7]

Although existing histories of cinema exhibition have tended to either focus on the history and development of cinema venues or the changing experiences of audiences within them, that is not to say that there has been no reflection at all on the work of projectionists.[8] Rather, scholarship that has brought cinema projection directly into view has tended to do so in order to enlighten an aspect of cinema history or theory, in relation to which projection or the projectionist (but rarely both) are a useful case study. There is a wealth of theoretical work that includes discussion of the projection of light (and often celluloid and/or digital files) within arguments about the specificities of cinema as a medium (and/or an experience), or which conceptualises 'projection' unbounded by its association with cinema.[9] Sean Cubitt, for example, makes brief mention of projectionists in *The Practice of Light* when outlining the process of filing aperture plates, and he characterises them as

7 *Ibid.*, p. 19.

8 For work on the infrastructure of cinema exhibition see, for example, Stuart Hanson, *From Silent Screen to Multi-Screen: A History of Cinema Exhibition in Britain Since 1896* (Manchester: Manchester University Press, 2007); Stuart Hanson, *Screening the World: Global Development of the Multiplex Cinema* (Cham: Palgrave Macmillan, 2019) and Allen Eyles's histories of the British cinema chains: *ABC: The First Name in Entertainment* (Burgess Hill: Cinema Theatre Association, 1993); *Gaumont British Cinemas* (Burgess Hill: Cinema Theatre Association, 1996); *The Granada Theatres* (London: Cinema Theatre Association, 1998); *Odeon Cinemas 1: Oscar Deutsch Entertains Our Nation* (London: Cinema Theatre Association, 2002); and *Odeon Cinemas 2: From J. Arthur Rank to the Multiplex* (London: Cinema Theatre Association, 2005). For work on the experience of cinema-going, see: Richard Farmer, *Cinemas and Cinemagoing in Wartime Britain 1939-45: The Utility Dream Palace* (Manchester: Manchester University Press, 2016); Matthew Jones, 'Memories of British Cinema', in I.Q. Hunter, Laraine Porter and Justin Smith (eds), *The Routledge Companion to British Cinema History* (London; New York: Routledge, 2017), pp. 397-405; Matthew Jones, Melvyn Stokes and Emma Pett, *Cinema Memories: A People's History of Cinema-going in 1960s Britain* (London: Bloomsbury, 2022); Annette Kuhn, *An Everyday Magic: Cinema and Cultural Memory* (London: I.B. Tauris, 2002); Jackie Stacey, *Star Gazing* (London: Routledge, 1994); Melvyn Stokes and Richard Maltby (eds), *Identifying Hollywood's Audiences: Cultural Identity and the Movies* (London: BFI, 2013); Lies Van de Vijer, 'The Cinema is Dead, Long Live the Cinema!: Understanding the Social Experience of Cinema-going Today', *Participations: Journal of Audience & Reception Studies*, 14:1 (May 2017), pp. 129-144.

9 See, for example, Dudley Andrews, *What Cinema Is!: Bazin's Quest and its Charge* (Chichester; Malden, MA: Wiley-Blackwell, 2010), pp. 66-97; Charlotte Brunsdon, '"This is Not a Cinema": The Projectionist's Tale', *Screen*, 60:4 (Winter 2019), pp. 527-547; Francesco Casetti, *The Lumière Galaxy: Seven Key Words for the Cinema to Come* (New York: Columbia University Press, 2015), pp. 21, 37; Sean Cubitt, *The Practice of Light: A Genealogy of Visual Technologies from Prints to Pixels* (London; Cambridge, MA: The MIT Press, 2007), pp. 202-234; Sean Cubitt 'Projection: Vanishing and Becoming', in Oliver Grau (ed.), *MediaArtHistories* (London; Cambridge, MA: The MIT Press, 2014), pp. 407-422; Mary Ann Doane, 'The Location of the Image: Cinematic Projection and Scale in Modernity', in Stan Douglas and Christopher Eamon (eds), *Art of Projection* (Ostfildern: Hatje Cantz Verlag, 2009), pp. 151-166; André Gaudreault and Philippe Marion (trans. Timothy Barnard), *The End of Cinema? A Medium in Crisis in the Digital Age* (New York: Columbia University Press, 2015), pp. 5-7.

'lighthouse keepers guarding the flame'. However, his key argument is that whatever configuration of projection technology one might imagine, 'the fundamentals [of cinema projection] remain the same: force light through a small aperture onto a vast screen across a vast hall'.[10] Cubitt's overall arguments about cinema being just one iteration of 'the long history of humanity's struggle to control light' might be evocative, but it does little to cast light upon the changing labour of the projectionist in relation to those differing technologies; the actual work that goes into that control.[11]

Instead, writing that focuses specifically on the labour, history and experiences of those who mediate the cinemagoing experience is surprisingly rare and often takes the form of an exploration of particular historical moments, technological developments or wider institutional transitions. Timothy Barnard has theorised the ways in which the labour of the projectionist was rendered invisible – if not actually reduced – as a result of the institutionalisation of narrative film in the early 20th century and John Izod has examined the impact that the arrival of sound had on projection work.[12] Rebecca Harrison and David R. Williams have published interesting articles outlining the role that women played in combatting wartime labour shortages in projection boxes, and Lawrence Napper has addressed a short-lived projectionist training scheme for disabled soldiers returning to civilian life after the Great War.[13] More recently, Charlotte Brunsdon has used detailed accounts of historically-situated labour processes within the projection box to '[disturb] some of the retrospective assumptions about medium specificity entailed in discussion of the transition to digital'.[14] There have also been a number of recent documentary films that attempt to address the work of the projectionist in the face of the job's obsolescence, including *The Last Projectionist* (UK, Thomas Lawes, 2011), *Side by Side* (USA, Chris Kenneally, 2012) and *The Dying of the Light* (USA, Peter Flynn, 2015).

10 Cubitt, *The Practice of Light*, p. 219.

11 *Ibid.*, p. 1.

12 Timothy Barnard, 'The "Machine Operator": *Deus Ex Machina* of the Storefront Cinema', *Framework*, 43:1 (Spring 2002), pp. 40-75; John Izod, 'Empowering Cinema Operators in the USA and UK, 1927-1933', *Music, Sound, and the Moving Image*, 12:2 (Autumn 2018), pp. 217-240.

13 Rebecca Harrison, 'The Coming of the Projectionettes: Women's Work in Film Projection and Changing Modes of Spectatorship in World War II British Cinema', *Feminist Media Histories*, 2:2 (Spring 2016), pp. 47-70; David R. Williams, 'Ladies of the Lamp: The Employment of Women in the British Film Trade During World War 1', *Film History*, 9:1 (1997), pp. 116-127 (see also Richard Wallace, Rebecca Harrison and Charlotte Brunsdon, 'Women in the Box: Female Projectionists in Post-War British Cinemas', *Journal of British Cinema and Television*, 15:1 [2018], pp. 46-65); Lawrence Napper, 'Disabled Operators: Training Disabled Ex-Servicemen as Projectionists During the Great War', *Journal of British Cinema and Television*, 15:1 (2018), pp. 94-114.

14 Brunsdon, '"This is Not a Cinema"', p. 529.

Discussions of the digital transition itself have tended to leave those most directly affected by these changes out of the picture. Instead, the focus has been on the development of the technology or the industrial and political machinations that have led to its adoption.[15] Another line of enquiry has been to examine the potential perils posed to the longevity of cinema images in the digital age, as Charlotte Crofts has done in her work on 'digital decay'. In posing a number of challenges faced by archivists, curators and exhibitors in preserving digital files for posterity, Crofts offers a digital counterpoint to the kinds of analogue loss that Usai *et al.* are attempting to avoid.[16] Questions about digital and analogue projection are also explored in scholarship that addresses the relocation of film projection from the cinema into spaces as diverse as the gallery, the town square, the night club and the classroom.[17]

These are all examples of scholarship that add sizeable fragments to the overall picture of what cinema projection has been and continues to be, and of key moments when the everyday routines of the projection box were reconfigured in response to wider industrial challenges. What has been less common is any focus on what took place between these reconfigurations, of the 'normality' that was disrupted by the seismic changes. We see a morsel of such writing in David Rosenbaum's short article 'Trysting with Trolls', and more emotively in the introduction to Ben Highmore's book *Cultural Feelings: Mood, Mediation and Cultural Politics*.[18] Here the orchestration of the film performance is characterised as 'mood work', and Highmore gives an overview of his own experience as a projectionist in a regional arts cinema in the late 1980s:

15 David Bordwell, *Pandora's Digitial Box: Films, Files, and the Future of Movies* (Madison, WI: Irvington Way Institute Press, 2012); Raymond Boyle, 'Digital Divides? UK Film Council Strategy and the Digital Screen Network', *International Journal of Media & Cultural Politics*, 11:1 (2015), pp. 3-20; Charlotte Crofts, 'Cinema Distribution in the Age of Digital Projection', *Post Script: Essays in Film and the Humanities*, 30:2 (Winter-Spring 2011), pp. 82-98; Gillian Doyle, Philip Schlesinger, Raymond Boyle and Lisa W. Kelly, *The Rise and Fall of the UK Film Council* (Edinburgh: Edinburgh University Press, 2015), pp. 107-126; Janet Wasko, 'The Future of Film Distribution and Exhibition', in Dan Harries (ed.), *The New Media Book* (London: BFI, 2002), pp. 195-206.

16 Charlotte Crofts, 'Digital Decay', *The Moving Image*, 8:2 (Fall 2008), pp. xiii-35.

17 See, for examples: Charles R. Acland and Haidee Wasson (eds), *Useful Cinema* (Durham, NC: Duke University Press, 2011); Virginia Crisp and Gabriel Menotti Gonring (eds), *Besides the Screen: Moving Images Through Distribution, Promotion and Curation* (Basingstoke: Palgrave Macmillan, 2015); Virginia Crisp and Gabriel Menotti Gonring (eds), *Practices of Projection: Histories and Technologies* (Oxford: Oxford University Press, 2020); Stan Douglas and Christopher Eamon (eds), *Art of Projection* (Ostfildern: Hatje Cantz Verlag, 2009); Alison Griffiths, *Shivers Down Your Spine: Cinema, Museums, and the Immersive View* (New York: Columnbia University Press, 2008); Chrissie Iles, *Into the Light: The Projected Image in American Art 1964-1977* (New York: Whitney Museum of American Art, 2001); Andrew V. Uroskie, *Between the Black Box and the White Cube: Expanded Cinema and Postwar Art* (Chicago: University of Chicago Press, 2014).

18 David Rosenbaum, 'Trysting with Trolls', *Film Comment*, 11:3 (May-June 1975), pp. 36-37; Ben Highmore, *Cultural Feelings: Mood, Mediation and Cultural Politics* (London; New York: Routledge, 2017), pp. 4-7.

> The trick was synchronicity. The trick was fading out the background music just as you're bringing down the house lights and opening up the curtains and starting the projector running, so that at the key moment when the house lights are nearly out and when the curtains are over halfway open and when the silence is just beginning, you can flip the switch that allows that intense beam of light to be thrown from the projector onto the screen and connects the speaker system to the soundtrack of the film. It took a bit of practice.[19]

There are a handful of articles that deal with the status of the profession and the terms and conditions under which projectionists were employed in the very first fixed-site cinemas. These articles deal with legislation and institutional policy that had a direct and material impact on the daily work of projectionists.[20] The Canadian website Planetary Projection, operated by the independent publisher caboose, is home to short first-person portraits of projectionists from around the world, each offering a brief overview of their career and their opinion of the digital transformation.[21]

However, such accounts are relatively rare, and this book is the first to directly attempt a comprehensive history of the job in the UK, from the earliest years of cinema in the 1890s through to the modern era, where the arrival of digital projection technologies has seen the majority of projectionists removed from cinema buildings through redundancy or retirement. It is the result of a three-year research project called 'The Projection Project', which ran from October 2014 to January 2018 and was funded by the Arts and Humanities Research Council. In particular, this book draws on archival research and interviews with projectionists undertaken by its authors as part of the project (see Appendix 1). As such, its focus is specifically on those responsible for operating the projection equipment and for putting on a show for cinema audiences across the entire history of cinema. This is, therefore, a book about projectionists more than it is a book about projection, though it is impossible to talk about one without the other.

Oral sources have been used before to explore cinema projection, by Brunsdon, by Lucie Česálková, and by one of the present authors, in three of the few articles that do include description of the minutiae of the work undertaken by projectionists in the

19 Highmore, *Cultural Feelings*, p. 4.

20 Barnard, 'The "machine operator"'; Jon Burrows, '"Certified Operators" versus "Handle-Turners": The British Film Industry's First Trade Union', *Journal of British Cinema and Television*, 15:1 (January 2018), pp. 73-93; Roberta E. Pearson and William Uricchio, 'Coming to Terms with New York City's Moving Picture Operators, 1906-1913', *The Moving Image: The Journal of the Association of Moving Image Archivists*, 2:2 (Fall 2002), pp 73-93.

21 'Planetary Projection', *caboose books*, https://www.caboosebooks.net/planetary-projection, accessed 25 January 2021.

mid-20th century (in the UK generally; in Brno in the Czech Republic; and in Glasgow, Scotland respectively).[22] In the latter two cases, the focus is on the intersection of work processes and memory, and *how* the specificities of the job are remembered and communicated as much as *what* is being communicated. Although this book is not primarily concerned with the process of remembering and all of the concomitant issues raised around the use of interviews as historical evidence, it *is* informed by debates around memory work.[23] In explaining her choice of methodology, Česálková argues that:

> The concept of professional memory is useful in understanding professions in history because it allows for examination of historical changes in professional identity in terms of the complex relationship between agency and structure. A focus on 'rhythms of professional discourse' in both oral histories and written texts makes it possible to uncover the shared routines, as well as the convictions and values, of a profession.[24]

The use of interviews has become commonplace within scholarship on cinema exhibition, such as Annette Kuhn's work on cinemagoing in the 1930s, and taking such an approach to cinema projection allows the individual projectionists to be placed at the centre of the discussion.[25] It offers an insightful way of understanding the position of projection within the industry, but it has also been a key aim of the project that we capture the techniques, skills and sensory experiences of a key job within the cinema industry as it passes into history. As Česálková acknowledges, oral accounts allow the continuities and discontinuities between different eras, different institutional settings and different personal approaches to the job to come to the fore: the art cinema vs the multiplex, for example, or the independent exhibitor vs the circuit. The combination of archival documents with personal testimony allows us to do this in a powerful and evocative way, that also happens to chime with G. M. Young's view that 'The real, central theme of History is not what happened, but what people felt about it when it was happening.'[26] The subjective accounts of life in the

22 Lucie Česálková, '"Feel the Film": Film Projectionists and Professional Memory', *Memory Studies*, 10:1 (January 2017), pp. 49-62; Richard Wallace, '"We Might Go into Double Act Mode": "Professional Recollectors", Rehearsed Memory and its Uses', *Oral History*, 45:1 (2017), pp. 55-66.

23 See, for example, Alessandro Portelli, 'What Makes Oral History Different', in Robert Perks and Alister Thomson (eds), *The Oral History Reader*, 3rd edn (London; New York: Routledge, 2016), pp. 48-58 and Paul Thompson, *The Voice of the Past: Oral History*, 3rd edn (Oxford: Oxford University Press, 2000) for an overview of key methodological issues related to oral history interviews.

24 Česálková, 'Feel the Film', p. 54.

25 Kuhn, *An Everyday Magic*.

26 G.M. Young (Annotated by George Kitson Clark), *Portrait of an Age: Victorian England* (London: Oxford University Press, 1977), p. 18.

projection box, therefore, speak towards a wider scholarly tradition of 'history from below' as epitomised by the work of Eric Hobsbawm, Studs Terkel and E.P. Thompson, amongst others.[27]

Since the very earliest years of cinema, projection has been classed as a hidden activity. An early filmgoer in Paris in 1897 noted of the newest mode of image reproduction that 'It is not generally appreciated how much research and labour is sometimes expended, in the industrial sector, to produce results that are often quite ephemeral.'[28] Andrew Uroskie makes a similar association between the laborious nature of projection work and the ephemerality that is the result of that work in arguing that, when we pay attention to the presence of the projector in the cinema auditorium,

> The difference between the materiality of the process and the immateriality of the resulting image becomes newly evident. Who knew that projectors were so noisy, so laborious? The process suddenly seems so material, so tangible, so corrosive. ... It becomes difficult to reconcile the ethereal cinematic image, so directly geared into the body of the viewer, with this clumsily mechanical process of screening, the churning gears, the friction, the light and the heat that together constitute the physical labor of projection.[29]

The projectionist is transfigured into the (invisible) mediator who transforms one side of this equation into the other. As we have already noted, Highmore suggests that this process constitutes a sustained orchestration of mood on the part of the projectionist. However, like the Parisian cinemagoer, Highmore recognises that 'The work of mood very often requires the obscuring of work'.[30] It is precisely the mechanics of this mood work that we are interested in outlining in this book.

It is a common claim of such labour (and the systems that are underpinned by it) that it remains invisible until something goes wrong, that, as Jussi Parikka suggests, 'only once things fail, *then* you start to see their complexity'.[31] However, Brian Larkin refutes this in his writing about how infrastructures function, arguing instead that 'all visibility is situated and what is background for one person is a daily object of concern for another'.[32] This book hopes

27 Miles Taylor, 'The Beginnings of Modern British Social History', *History Workshop Journal*, 43 (Spring 1997), pp. 155-176; Studs Terkel, *Working: People Talk About What They Do All Day and How They Feel About What They Do* (New York: New Press, 2004); E. P. Thompson, *The Making of the English Working Class* (London: Gollancz, 1963).

28 Anon., 'La vie utile des vues cinématographiques', *La Nature*, 2ème semester (1897), p. 302, trans. Paolo Cherchi Usai and Martin Sopocy; quoted in Paolo Cherchi Usai, *The Death of Cinema* (London: BFI, 2001), p. 5.

29 Uroskie, *Between the Black Box and the White Cube*, p. 30.

30 Highmore, *Cultural Feelings*, p. 6.

31 Jussi Parikka, *A Geology of Media* (Minneapolis; London: University of Minnesota Press, 2015), p. 98.

32 Brian Larkin, 'The Politics and Poetics of Infrastructure', *Annual Review of Anthropology*, 42 (2013), p. 336.

to reposition the reader in a similar way, using the testimony of those for whom projection work was 'a daily object of concern' to excavate a history of projection labour. It is a history that has, for the large part, not been clearly set out in one place before, and our aim is to provide a detailed overview of the working practices and experiences of those who worked as cinema projectionists in the UK between the 1890s and the 2010s.

The book focuses on four key aspects of the job that encompass the experiences of projectionists from the birth of cinema to the present day. In Chapter One we address the day-to-day minutiae of the work undertaken by projectionists inside and out of the projection box. We look at the ways in which institutional and technological changes materially amended what the job entailed. This includes how apparatus such as sound projection, platter projectors and automation systems altered the type of work undertaken and the number of projectionists employed to ensure that a picture got – and stayed – on the screen. This chapter also shows that much of the work expected of those employed to project films actually had little to do with the task of projection and often occurred outside of the projection box itself.

The work that did go into projecting films can generally be split into two separate, but linked processes: the physical labour of making-up prints and running the projector, and the psychological labour of attending to the aesthetic components of the show. Although the latter process is enacted through the former, it is clear that when projectionists project they are doing more than straightforwardly repeating learned physical processes. Rather, they are considering the impact that these processes – and their choices around how to enact them – are having on the material experiences of those in the auditorium. Chapter Two focuses on these considerations and draws out a history of what was known in the industry as 'presentation' and 'showmanship'. We will show that, before the multiplex era, the corporeal presence of human projectionists was indirectly impressed upon audiences through various forms of showmanship that were considered fundamentally important means of helping viewers to navigate the potentially disorienting and awkward perceptual experience involved in shifting attention from the three-dimensional world to an image projected on a flat screen.

Chapter Three offers an account of the terms and conditions under which projectionists were required to work. This is a complicated story in which the manual processes outlined in Chapter One and the aesthetic processes of Chapter Two converge around discussions as to how the job should be defined: were projectionists skilled or unskilled; tradesmen or artists? This had significant ramifications for projectionists' trade union representation and this chapter details the history of the profession's struggles for recognition in the face of social, cultural, institutional and technological change.

The concluding chapter returns to the topics of the earlier chapters to explore how the labour, aesthetics and conditions of the job changed with the introduction of digital technologies. Here, we outline the processes by which digital projectors were introduced into UK cinemas, the effect that this had on those working in operating boxes and the response of the Broadcasting, Entertainment, Communications and Theatre Union (BECTU) to these changes.

Returning to where we began, then, although it might be possible to endorse Cubitt's argument that all of cinema – at an ontological level – has the same essence, when it comes to the actual labour processes and the lived experiences of those doing the work, this is not the case. What it meant to be a cinema projectionist changed across the 20th century, and what the job entailed is historically inscribed in relation to a variety of factors including, but not limited to: technology; legislation; economics; and institutional policy. To return to the opposition outlined by Uroskie, these factors have very little in common with the spectral ephemerality of the cinema image in terms of the type of labour it required and the conditions under which this labour was carried out. We can, then, conceive of the projectionist as holding in tension these two ideas, and this is an account whereby, as well as embodying romantic notions like Cubitt's 'keepers of the flame', the experiences of the projectionists found here speak to an entirely different conceptualisation of the projectionist – often articulated by those that did the job – as 'slaves to the lamp'.[33]

33 We have found several uses of this phrase by frustrated projectionists characterising the nature of their labour: 'Operators' Hours and Conditions', *Kinematograph Weekly*, 20 November 1930, p. 66; 'Chief Operator's log book, Gaumont Cinema (Odeon Cinema), Jordan Well, Coventry', PA118/1-1-4, Coventry History Centre; Rosenbaum, 'Trysting With Trolls', p. 36. (The intended point of reference is to the Genie of the Lamp in the story of Aladdin.)

Chapter One

Job Descriptions

Full species documentation is a standard response to any imminent extinction event, but the task of describing the kind of work involved in projecting commercial film releases over the past 120 years or so is nearly as complicated as chronicling the constituent features of cinema itself. Although certain basic characteristics of the role have remained fairly consistent over time – such as lacing films onto the projector, mending broken sections of prints, adjusting focus and racking (i.e. making sure the image frame is centred on screen) – it has undergone significant shifts throughout multiple phases of film history, in response to major institutional and technological changes. Not even the job title has remained the same. The word 'projectionist' was first coined in 1917 by the American trade journalist F.[rank] H.[erbert] Richardson, but did not enter regular usage in Britain until the early 1930s.[34] For over thirty years, the people we would now describe as projectionists were known throughout the English-speaking world as 'operators'.

This chapter attempts to explain the key forms of labour undertaken by those employed to project feature films in UK cinemas – from the birth of the medium up to the end of the analogue projection era in the early 2010s – as the variable product of chronologically distinct technological systems. Thomas P. Hughes has influentially argued that technological systems are made up of a number of components (apparatus, organizations, legislation, operators) that interact with one another and adapt their characteristics to the addition, removal or alteration of other system components.[35] They are, as Markus Stauff puts it, 'unstable constellations of technologies including practices and discourses' that are 'characterized by constant transformation'.[36] Hughes argues

34 F.H. Richardson, 'Projection Standards To-day – and the Term "Projectionist"', text of speech reprinted in *Projectionists' Journal*, April 1937, p. 17.

35 Thomas P. Hughes, 'The Evolution of Large Technological Systems', in Wiebe E. Bijker, Thomas P. Hughes, and Trevor J. Pinch (eds), *The Social Construction of Technological Systems: New Directions in the Sociology and History of Technology* (Cambridge, Mass.: MIT Press, 1993), pp. 51-82.

36 Markus Stauff, 'Television's Many Technologies: Domesticity, Governmentality, Genealogy', in Annie van den Oever (ed.), *Techné/Technology* (Amsterdam: Amsterdam University Press, 2014), p. 137.

that these transformations occur by overcoming 'reverse salients' within the system: components 'that have fallen behind or are out of phase with the others'.[37] As each reverse salient is overcome, the system adapts until further development is hindered by the next reverse salient. Cinema projection can be seen as a technological system in these terms. However, we are not proposing a teleological view, with each technological advance leading to an improvement in projection processes and standards. The adaptations and developments in the system can be as much about improving the bottom line on a financial balance sheet as they are about improving the working conditions of the operator or the quality of experience for the cinema patron.

The work of projectionists was contingent upon the particular constellation of apparatus – or an 'array', to use the term adopted by researchers working on television production technologies – in use in any specific projection context.[38] We have identified four primary and chronologically distinct technological arrays that existed across the history of this profession: the mobile array, the nitrate array, the xenon array and the multi-screen array.[39] In each of the work regimes associated with these arrays, we argue, the nature of the job was largely determined by a particular set of technological affordances and the organisational practices created around them. Our attempt to document projection work is therefore divided into four separate sections dealing with each array. One exception to this structural arrangement concerns the fact that a significant portion of a projectionist's daily routine in all periods was dedicated to labour that was neither directly concerned with screening films nor located within the space of the projection box. The projectionist has been repeatedly described – by journalists,

37 Hughes, 'Evolution of Large Technological Systems', p. 73.

38 John Ellis, 'Filming for Television: How a 16mm Film Crew Worked Together', *VIEW: Journal of European Television History & Culture*, 8:15 (2019), pp. 91-110; John Ellis, 'Why Hands on History Matters', in Nick Hall and John Ellis (eds), *Hands on Media History: A New Methodology in the Humanities and Social Sciences* (London; New York: Routledge, 2020), pp. 11-25.

39 It should be noted that such transformations are rarely straightforward, and the generally robust mechanical qualities of 35mm cinema projectors, combined with the financial implications of a costly refit meant that in general projectors were not replaced without good reason. It is not the case, therefore, that wider advances in projection systems would be reflected in the projection arrays of all cinemas. The transitions to sound and digital projection are, perhaps, the exceptions, though in each case these processes were not immediate, and in the case of digital took around a decade to complete. Some other technological developments, such as colour and certain widescreen technologies were more easily adopted by exhibitors because they did not require a full refit, only the grafting of new components (an anamorphic lens, for example) onto existing projection technology. The majority of projection boxes would consist of a mix of apparatus from current and previous periods in the development of the wider projection system, retained until the need arose for an alteration to be made. The prompt adoption of major technological advances would, for the most part, be reserved for the projection suites of prestigious city centre cinemas, or when fitting entirely new cinema buildings, or where legislation demanded it.

scholars and projectionists themselves – as a 'jack of all trades',[40] and this aspect of the job will be explored at the end of the chapter.

The Mobile Array

Right from their inception and through to the middle of the 20th century, photographic moving pictures produced for the purposes of mainstream entertainment were carried on a highly flammable cellulose nitrate base. We feel, nonetheless, that it is appropriate to clearly distinguish the first common work regime for projectionists from what we are calling the period of the nitrate array, because in this early phase of the medium's development (1895-1909) the serious fire risk that 35mm film prints presented was not yet regulated by national safety legislation, and therefore did not dictate the formulation of projection practices in the way that it would do for the next forty years of film history.

Projectionists were exclusively referred to as 'operators' during this period. The greater vagueness of this earlier term suited the fact that the very first projectionists frequently operated cinematographic equipment other than the projector. Writing in 1906, Emile Lauste defined an operator as 'A man who can photograph, develop, print and project, with an exceptional experience of electricity and oxy-hydrogen work, and able to repair or make his own machines.'[41] Moving picture shows in the 1890s and 1900s would commonly feature locally-filmed actuality material, and it might be the operator who was tasked with shooting and developing, as well as projecting, this footage. The second part of Lauste's description of an operator pertains to the fact that it was predominantly an itinerant occupation when he wrote these words. Although some venues – such as the larger music halls – had projection equipment installed on a permanent basis, most early film shows in Britain relied upon mobile personnel who journeyed round the country for temporary engagements. The travelling operator would often encounter situations in which they arrived at a venue with little time to spare before the show, and had to perform a complete equipment installation from scratch, erecting a screen and setting up the projector to produce optimum image dimensions and clarity in an auditorium that might present a radically different shape and size compared to their last engagement. Mastery of a variety of illumination technologies was essential: differ-

40 'Early Bird', 'Letter: The Jack of All Trades', *Ideal Kinema*, 29 July 1926, p. 57; Charlotte Brunsdon, '"This is Not a Cinema": The Projectionist's Tale', *Screen*, 60:4 (Winter 2019), pp. 542-544.

41 Emile Louis Lauste, 'What is an Operator?', *Optical Lantern and Cinematograph Journal*, February 1906, p. 81. (Lauste himself worked simultaneously as a distinguished cameraman and projectionist throughout this period, thus typifying the hybridised nature of the role.)

ent venues would have different forms of electricity supply; some would have no electricity at all.[42]

The vast majority of travelling operators would not have personally manufactured their projector, as Lauste implied, but many were essentially freelance agents and possessed their own equipment and stock of films, which they furnished in addition to their labour.[43] Despite the known dangers of cellulose nitrate prints, throughout the first fourteen years of film history a large number of local authorities in the UK allowed projectors to be positioned within the space of the auditorium.[44] The operator would thus sometimes be visible to the audience, and, in the initial novelty years of photographic moving pictures, was a figure of some curiosity, contributing to the exhibitionistic tendencies of what Tom Gunning has famously described as the 'cinema of attractions'.[45] Timothy Barnard suggests that we should think of some of the early operators as 'both performer and entrepreneur'.[46] They were often named in newspaper advertisements, or even in the titles of their shows, and it is documented that, in some cases, operators simultaneously delivered a verbal commentary on the films whilst they cranked the projector.[47]

By 1910, however, the typical operator bore very little resemblance to Lauste's characterisation. From this point onwards, film exhibition in Britain was dominated by fixed-site cinemas and regulated by national safety legislation in the form of the Cinematograph Act (1909). In this new era, films were predominantly sourced from

42 For a detailed account of the tribulations of the travelling operator, see 'Ulster Scot', 'Itinerating in Erin', *Kinematograph and Lantern Weekly*, 28 March 1912, pp. 1205, 1207.

43 The pre-1910 entertainment press listings of vacant engagements for operators frequently specify that the successful applicant must supply their own projector; see, for example, 'Music Hall Artistes Wanted', *The Era*, 2 May 1903, p. 30; 'Miscellaneous Advertisements', *The Bioscope,* 2 October 1908, p. 22.

44 A tragic fire which occurred at a film show at the Town Hall, Newmarket, in 1907 was specifically caused by members of the audience bumping into the projector and its gas cylinder illuminant on their way out of the auditorium. Gas escaping from the cylinder caught fire and ignited the film, and a young woman was crushed to death in the ensuing panic; see 'Fatal Accident at a Picture Show', *Kinematograph and Lantern Weekly*, 12 September 1907, p. 277. It has been suggested that in the era before projection boxes became mandatory everywhere, back-projection was probably the most common arrangement, with the operator positioned out of sight behind a wettened translucent screen; see John Barnes, *The Beginnings of the Cinema in England Vol. 2: 1897* (Exeter: University of Exeter Press, 1996), p. 176.

45 Tom Gunning, 'The Cinema of Attractions: Early Film, Its Spectator and the Avant-Garde', *Wide Angle*, 8:3 (1986), pp. 63-70.

46 Timothy Barnard, 'Projectionists', in Richard Abel (ed.), *Encyclopedia of Early Cinema* (London; New York: Routledge, 2005), p. 536.

47 One regularly finds the name of the operator credited in newspaper publicity for travelling cinematograph exhibitions, such as the adverts for a New Year's Day film screening at the Peterhead Music Hall in *Buchan Observer and East Aberdeenshire Advertiser*, 27 December 1898, p. 1, and for Arthur B. Malden's 'Cinematograph Lectures' at the West Hartlepool Town Hall in *Hartlepool Northern Mail*, 27 October 1906, p. 2. There are accounts of verbal accompaniment being delivered by operators in Judith Buchanan, '"Now Where Are We?": Ideal and Actual Early Cinema Lecturing Practices in Britain, Germany and the United States', in Julie Brown and Annette Davidson (eds), *The Sounds of the Silents in Britain* (Oxford; New York: Oxford University Press, 2013), pp. 38-39, 41.

centralised rental exchanges, and most operators were hired as the permanent employee of a specific cinema with its own pre-installed machinery; only electrical illumination was permitted (in urban areas), and the projection enclosure had to be physically separated, and thus largely concealed, from the auditorium.[48] Cinema was transformed in this period from an occasional temporary attraction and/or supplementary adjunct to existing entertainment institutions, into a discrete mass medium with its own national network of dedicated exhibition venues. By the end of 1914 there were around 3,365 full-time cinemas operating in England, Scotland and Wales.[49] It is fair to say that this momentous expansion process involved a delimitation and marginalisation of the role of operators in comparison with the more public and conspicuous part they played during the initial phase of exploitation of the technology in the 1890s and 1900s, and, as we will subsequently show in Chapter Three, average salaries within the profession plummeted accordingly.

The Nitrate Array

A consistent, broadly-defined technological system determined working practices for all cinema projectionists from the 1910s through to the end of the 1940s. This certainly does not mean that no significant mechanical change occurred across this formative period of film history, however. A couple of innovations that were introduced within the silent period were particularly noteworthy and consequential. One relatively early modification in silent-era projector design must have made a substantial difference to the working lives of projectionists, although – surprisingly – it is discussed very infrequently in the industry trade papers. The first film projectors were manual devices, and the movement of the film through the machine at a sufficiently rapid rate to achieve the illusion of motion on screen was achieved by continuous hand cranking of a lever. The projectionist was thus physically wedded to the equipment for the duration of each presentation. One searches in vain for clues as to when exactly the point of wholesale transition to motorised projection was reached, and what specific effects this had upon the staffing of the projection box and the performance of operating duties. The editor of a leading trade paper's weekly projection column implied in 1919 that handle-turned projectors were a thing of the past by this date,[50] but reliable

48 For a detailed account of the scope of the Cinematograph Act (1909), see Jon Burrows, 'The 1909 Cinematograph Act: Some Myths Debunked', *Picture House*, 35 (2010), pp. 3-11.

49 Jon Burrows, *The British Cinema Boom, 1909-1914: A Commercial History* (Basingstoke: Palgrave Macmillan, 2017), p. 2.

50 Colin N. Bennett, 'Projection Points', *Kinematograph and Lantern Weekly*, 28 August 1919, p. 108.

motor-driven projectors had actually been introduced to the market twelve years earlier in 1907. It is unquestionably the case that purely hand-cranked machines continued to be commonly used in cinemas throughout the early 1910s, however.[51]

This all suggests that the adoption of motorised projectors was so gradual as to have gone unremarked upon. Why should this have been the case? British commentators seem to have had no doubts that the newer technology delivered a higher standard of projection:

> Without question, a motor-driven projector gives a steadier picture, on account of the very even turning, and because the drive is fixed to the machine, and not, like the human drive, actuated by a leverage from the floor. ... The motor drive enables the careful operator, in addition to projecting a steadier picture, to pay more attention to his light and the details of focussing and masking.[52]

The use of motor-driven projectors was prohibited in most of the larger cities of the United States in the 1910s, on the grounds that they allowed the operator to neglect his post, or temporarily leave it unattended, increasing the risk of films firing.[53] No such interdiction was ever introduced by licensing authorities in the UK, though concerns were voiced 'that the operator can, if he be that class of man, give less attention to the machine than he would were he obliged to turn by hand'.[54] The most likely explanation for the seemingly hesitant adoption of motorised projectors is therefore that cinema owners were reluctant to give up a technology that 'disciplined' operators by preventing them from leaving their workstation.[55] In this respect, the arrival of a more advanced apparatus conferred upon the crank handle a new function, as 'one of the missing masses of our society' influentially theorised by Bruno Latour.[56]

51 A rare photograph of the inside of a British cinema projection box from this period is reproduced in Frederick A. Talbot, *Moving Pictures: How They are Made and Worked* (London: William Heinemann, 1912), facing p. 135. It is the enclosure at the Picture House, Leeds, opened in April 1911 by Provincial Cinematograph Theatres Ltd. The two projectors in the picture are Butchers' Empire No. 12 models, which could only be cranked by hand. Motor-driven projectors were more expensive, but this would not have been an issue for the large chain that owned this cinema: Provincial Cinematograph Theatres Ltd invested over 2½ times more capital on building and equipping their cinemas than the average spend on purpose-built cinemas in this period (Burrows, *The British Cinema Boom*, pp. 120-122).

52 'Help in Trouble', *The Bioscope*, 19 December 1912, pp. 899, 901.

53 John B. Rathbun, *Motion Picture Making and Exhibiting* (Chicago: Charles C. Thompson, 1914), p. 27.

54 'Help in Trouble', *The Bioscope*, 2 July 1914, p. 75.

55 A supplementary explanation for the slow uptake of motorised projectors is that some projectionists and cinema managers/proprietors may have preferred the greater flexibility to make frequent adjustments to projection speed 'on the fly' during screenings that hand cranking permitted. This issue will be discussed in more detail in Chapter Three.

56 Bruno Latour, 'Where are the Missing Masses? The Sociology of a Few Mundane Artifacts', in Wiebe E. Bijker and John Law (eds), *Shaping Technology/Building Society: Studies in Sociotechnical Change* (Cambridge, Mass.: MIT Press, 1992), pp. 225-258.

The end of the silent period witnessed one of the most considerable changes in the nature, and organisation, of projection labour in the history of the profession when synchronised sound was universally adopted in British cinemas in the space of three years between 1929 and 1932.[57] R. [eginald] Howard Cricks, the author of *The Complete Projectionist* – the leading manual for projectionists – suggested that the addition of sound had straightforwardly doubled the number of elements that required close attention when projecting a film; where previously operators had to keep an eye on the screen, the machine and the arc light, they now had to simultaneously focus upon their sound monitor, fader (volume) cue-sheet and fader controls. (Sound-on-disc – initially the most common system installed – required, in addition, constant interaction with a gramophone record attachment, but Cricks excluded this from his list, because 'in this case, three operators are necessary in the box, the duties of one being solely to look after records, and see that they start and run correctly'.) Cricks also suggested that sound demanded a supplementary array of theoretical expertise and sensorial competencies:

> The silent operator is expected to be able to thread his machine, to feed his arc, to do minor repairs, to keep his plant in order, and to have a certain knowledge of electricity and mechanics. The talkie operator in addition, needs a very thorough knowledge of amplification, care of valves and accumulators, and so forth; he must have a good musical ear, a strong sense of drama, a certain knowledge of acoustics – in fact, the attributes of a dozen professions.[58]

A 28-year-old operator from Liverpool was reported to have suffered a debilitating stroke in 1930 as a direct result of 'the nervous strain of operating the sound pictures'.[59] Some of the more exasperating challenges – particularly those involving regular equipment breakdowns and loss of synchronisation with, and quick deterioration of, the shellac records used in the short-lived sound-on-disc systems – would prove to be temporary.[60] But sound had numerous long-term effects upon various aspects of the job performed before, during and after projection. Films needed to be handled with much greater care, given that, on prints with an optical soundtrack, bad joins, missing frames and scratches had a

57 Robert Murphy, 'Coming of Sound to the Cinema in Britain', *Historical Journal of Film, Radio and Television*, 4:2 (1984), p. 151.

58 R. Howard Cricks, 'Talkies and the Projectionist', *Kinematograph Weekly*, 15 August 1929, p. 55. The cue sheets that Cricks refers to were a short-lived expediency necessitated by problems with extreme variations in volume levels from shot to shot in early sound features, as explained in R. Pitchford and F. Coombs, *The Projectionist's Handbook: A Complete Guide to Cinema Operating* (London: Watkins-Pitchford, 1933), pp. 60-61.

59 'Liverpool Operators', *Kinematograph Weekly*, 23 October 1930, p. 23.

60 A.L. Carter, 'Talkie Failures', *ibid*., 26 September 1929, p. 47; R. Howard Cricks, 'Disc Synchronisation', *ibid*., 6 November 1930, p. 87;

particularly jarring and uncomfortable impact on the ears. (Prints simultaneously became more vulnerable to injury because the standard silent-era practice of coating them with a protective layer of wax became impractical, since it led to disastrous wax build-up in the projector sound head.[61]) Stricter regimes of cleanliness in projection boxes were similarly introduced to avoid the audibly deleterious consequences of dirt and dust passing through the projector's sound head.[62] It also became necessary to run rehearsal screenings when programmes changed to check for problems with the sound track, which could not necessarily be identified by eye during the inspection of prints on the rewind bench.[63]

Perceptions of the status and importance of the operator were significantly modified by the advent of sound. The chief projectionist at the Empire, Leicester Square, reflected in 1933 upon the fact that 'as soon as the "talkies" sign went up outside their cinema, the projectionist at once became the show, and the results of his efforts, good, bad or indifferent, represented what the public paid, and still pays, to see'.[64] Previously, the musical director at a cinema had been the most conspicuous (and best paid) employee, but, as John Izod has pointed out, 'after musicians were expelled from orchestra pits, projectionists ... became the principal human link between screen and audience'.[65] James Benson, the editor of the *Kinematograph Weekly*'s 'Kine Theatre Section', argued ten years down the line that

> With the advent of talkies, the projectionist moved out of the obscurity in which he had dwelt during the silent years and came to be recognised as a person of importance in the kinema. Before, he was only in the public eye when he failed to correct a divided picture on the screen, and cries of 'rack' awakened him from his somnolence. The talkies advanced him much and justified his assuming the better-sounding 'projectionist' instead of the older term 'operator'...[66]

As Benson suggests, it was the increased challenge, complexity and responsibility involved with the use of sound equipment that led to a symbolic change in job title. Calling the men in the box 'projectionists' rather than 'operators' was advocated on the basis that it sounded grander and conveyed a greater sense of the wide remit of the job, compared with the implication that 'operating'

61 R. Howard Cricks, 'Causes of Film Mutilation', *Ideal Kinema*, 5 January 1933, p. 59.

62 'How to Handle Sound Films', *Kinematograph Weekly*, 19 September 1929, p. 67.

63 'The Need for Rehearsals', *ibid.*, 28 August 1930, p. 55; R. Howard Cricks, 'Staffing the Projection Room', *ibid.*, 5 November 1931, p. 61.

64 Stanley T. Perry, 'Status Plus Prestige', *Ideal Kinema*, 5 January 1933, p. 60.

65 John Izod, 'Empowering Cinema Operators in the USA and UK, 1927-1933', *Music, Sound, and the Moving Image*, 12:2 (Autumn 2018), p. 217.

66 J.[ames] Benson, 'Projectionist as Key Man', *Kinematograph Weekly*, 26 June 1941, p. 26.

simply involved subserviently working a machine.[67] Usage of the term 'operators' largely disappeared over time, though some clung on to it in the belief that 'projectionist' had 'supercilious' and 'less manly' connotations.[68]

Sound also led directly to the enlargement of projection staffs within most cinemas. When certain wage agreements with the unions that represented operators were renegotiated in 1930, a standard clause was added that there must be at least three full-time projection staff in cinemas using talkie equipment.[69] One important consideration to bear in mind when attempting to understand what projectionists did during the nitrate era is that the role could vary enormously depending upon the size and location of a cinema, whether it was an independent venue or part of a circuit, and which circuit it belonged to. In fact, there was considerable variance in working routines for projectionists employed within the *same* cinema. In the late 1930s, when it reached its peak lifetime size, the British film exhibition industry consisted of 4,585 cinemas. Twenty per cent of these venues had less than 500 seats, whilst 35% had accommodation for more than 1,000 patrons. These figures come from a detailed statistical survey conducted by the Ministry of Labour in October 1937, which also revealed that around 12,700 men (and they were, at this particular moment in time, almost exclusively men) were employed as projectionists.[70] There were nearly three times as many projectionists as there were cinemas because, during the years in which cinema was the nation's dominant popular entertainment medium, film projection was a team-based activity.

In a few parts of the country, the practice of employing multiple operators in the service of a single screen pre-dated the emergence of permanent cinemas. Entertainment venues in which music occupied a prominent role, such as music halls, required the sanction of a local authority music licence to conduct their business. And because, right from the inception of photographic moving pictures, many such theatres consistently featured cinematograph 'turns', in 1898 the London County Council (LCC) added a set of safety regulations governing the use of celluloid film to its music licence conditions. One of these stipu-

67 Colin N. Bennett, 'Projection Points', *ibid*., 28 August 1924, p. 68.

68 R. Howard Cricks, 'Projectionist or Operator?', *Ideal Kinema*, 8 January 1948, p. 17.

69 Electrical Trades Union (Manchester District) Working Rules for Cinema Operators and Assistants, 18 October 1930, NA LAB/83/3320.

70 The Ministry elicited this information via a compulsory questionnaire, and enforced its completion with follow-up visits to cinemas. Nonetheless, 159 cinemas could not be compelled to submit a return. The 4,426 cinemas which did comply employed 12,274 projectionists, so we have extrapolated a figure that encompasses the missing venues on the basis that British cinemas employed 2.68 projectionists on average. The report was never published, but is preserved in the National Archives: NA LAB/10/83.

lated that two operators had to be present in the projection enclosure at all times when the equipment was in use – to avoid the possibility that a single operator might get momentarily distracted and fail to spot ignition of the film with sufficient promptitude.[71] Rather than paying two men the same wage, theatre owners observed this legal obligation by employing a junior 'assistant' operator alongside a senior 'chief'. When the Cinematograph Act (1909) came into force, the LCC retained the dual-operator rule for its cinematograph licences, and this regulation was widely copied throughout the rest of the country. A Ministry of Labour report written in 1917 suggested that around 60% of British cinemas employed a chief and an assistant.[72]

In the 1930s, the progressive expansion of the demands of the job was reflected in the increased sizes of projection teams. Cinemas staffed with a chief, second, third and fourth projectionist were common (Fig. 1.1). An additional projectionist-engineer might be needed if the cinema used its own electrical generating plant, and some of the larger super-cinemas, particularly those that featured live variety acts, had as many as seven.[73] A projectionist's numerical designation signified their place in a hierarchical chain of command, which was organised according to age and experience, with differing responsibilities allocated to each grade. One of the major circuits tasked seconds with making up the programme (transferring individual reels from shipping cans to sturdy show reels) and maintaining auditorium fittings, whilst the third was given responsibility for breaking the programme down and arranging its despatch.[74] Fourth projectionists would typically spend little or no time directly involved in the projection of films, or indeed within the projection box, occupying much of their working day in a separate room rewinding film reels in preparation for their next screening. (Before the era of safety film, many local authorities insisted that rewinding should take place outside the projection enclosure, to avoid having 'naked' nitrate film in close proximity to the searingly hot, ash-generating carbon arc lamps that beamed the image to the screen.)

Phil Fawke began his career as the fifth projectionist at the Regal Cinema, Leamington Spa in 1940 and makes it clear that in that lowly position

71 'L.C.C. Regulations' *Kinematograph and Lantern Weekly*, 2 January 1908, p. 131.

72 J. St. G. Heath, 'Reports Upon Openings in Industry Suitable for Disabled Soldiers and Sailors. No. III. The Cinematograph Industry', April 1917, NA LAB/2/624/TDS5896/1919.

73 R. Howard Cricks, *The Complete Projectionist: A Textbook for all who Handle Sound and Pictures in the Kinema* (London: Kinematograph Publications, 1933), p. 164.

74 R. Howard Cricks, *The Complete Projectionist: A Textbook for all who Handle Sound and Pictures in the Kinema*, 3rd edn (London: Kinematograph Publications, 1943), p. 217.

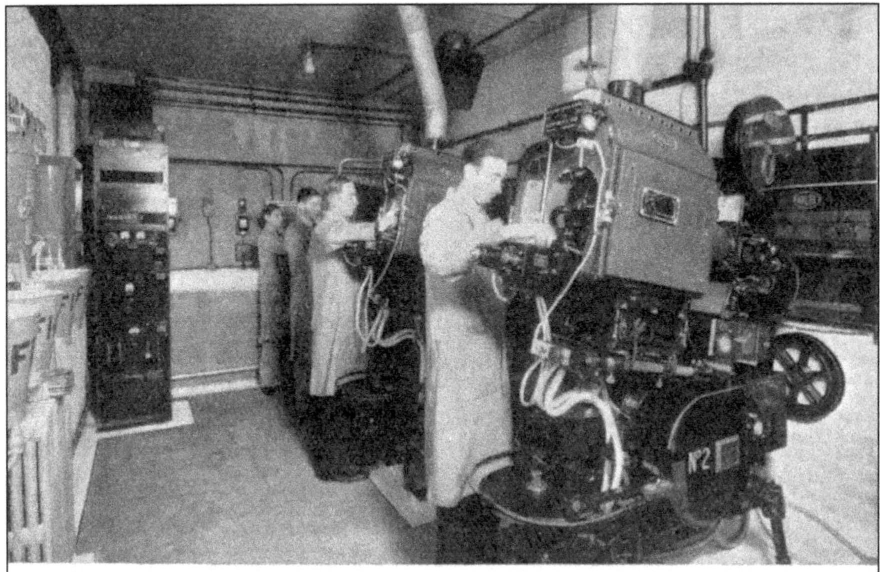

Fig. 1.1: The four-man projection team at the Adelphi, Slough in 1934.[75]

> we weren't allowed to touch a machine. We weren't allowed to do much really except clean up and make tea for the chief projectionist. We used to have to stand at the back ... and watch the other people. Then you were allowed to take a spool out of the bottom and take it into the rewind room. Then you were eventually told how to rewind it. ... And then eventually in about 1942 I was allowed to take my first changeover.[76]

Escalation up the ranks would usually be gradual and often required a move between cinemas, or else a long wait for those in more senior positions to move on – or die.[77] Martyn Butler characterises this process as 'waiting for dead men's shoes' and suggests that in general 'the rewind boy would end up going for the second projectionist, he'd eventually become a first projectionist and if he lived long enough he might become the chief, and that was your career option.' Butler recalls recognising at an early stage that his aspiration to be chief could only be accomplished through

75 'This Week's Projection Room', *Kinematograph Weekly*, 15 November 1934, p. 39

76 Interview with Phil Fawke, conducted by Richard Wallace, 4 December 2014. Although the two-year gap between starting the job and being allowed to handle changeovers described here is surely an exaggeration, this hands-off approach was not isolated to the nitrate era of film projection. As late as the 1970s it was not uncommon for junior projectionists to have scant experience of actually running film through projectors. John Young, who started in 1973, recalls that 'the first year I did nothing but sweep the place out' (interview with John Young, conducted by Richard Wallace, 5 February 2015).

77 We say 'usually', here, because in certain circumstances boys were promoted more quickly, such as during wartime when younger projectionists were required to fill the ranks vacated by their conscripted colleagues.

strategic redeployment: 'I did know that I had to leave Newport, even at the age of 16.'[78]

The duties of the chief projectionist could vary significantly depending on the size of both the cinema and the team. One common feature was that it was, in part, a managerial role with responsibility for organising, motivating and training the subordinate projectionists and overseeing the projection work, with responsibility for recording and reporting problems and ordering replacement supplies; one commentator compared the job to that of a factory works manager.[79] Their status created both fear and resentment; Martyn Butler, who worked in a number of prestigious West End cinemas, recalls that 'the chief was terrifying' but that 'I don't think I ever saw him lace up a reel of film ever ... he was in the chief's office. And that was the way of the West End ... I very rarely ever saw the chief there, they were office jobs. ... I *really* don't know what those chiefs did.'

The proprietor of a small West Country cinema alleged in 1929 that his larger rivals tended to handle films less carefully than his own men because the chief at a super-cinema would typically spend relatively little of their time manning the projectors.[80] The chief's designation as a managerial role was sometimes reflected in their attire. John Douglas recalls that on his first day on the job the chief arrived after the rest of the team, coming in 'at ten o'clock with a smart coat, soft hat, briefcase, rolled up umbrella [and] a newspaper under the arm'.[81] Butler notes that the elusive West End chiefs would often 'come out on a premiere in a dress suit and wander round looking important'. This is a far cry from the typical uniform of the projectionist, who at this point in time would generally be dressed in a white overcoat, and suggests that the demarcation of roles wasn't simply premised upon distinct working routines.

The main tasks pertaining to the 'live' operation of the projectors (e.g. lacing prints, adjusting focus and racking, correcting sound synchronisation problems, performing reel changeovers) would be principally handled by those of intermediate ranking within the bigger teams. A more detailed published account of the division of labour suggested that the chief might take charge of the first and last screening of each programme for the purpose of compiling reports on the condition in which the prints arrived at, and then departed, the cinema.[82] Monitoring and maintaining the working

78 Interview with Martyn Butler, conducted by Richard Wallace, 25 August 2015.

79 R. Howard Cricks, 'The Projectionist and His Career', *Ideal Kinema*, 13 August 1936, p. 42.

80 'C.E.A. Proceedings', *Kinematograph Weekly*, 7 March 1929, p. 41.

81 Interview with John and Peter Douglas, conducted by Richard Wallace, 24 June 2015.

82 J. Whitnall, 'Running the Show – I', *Ideal Kinema*, 9 October 1941, p. ix.

order of the equipment, in the manner of a supervising engineer, was another key responsibility of the head projectionist.[83]

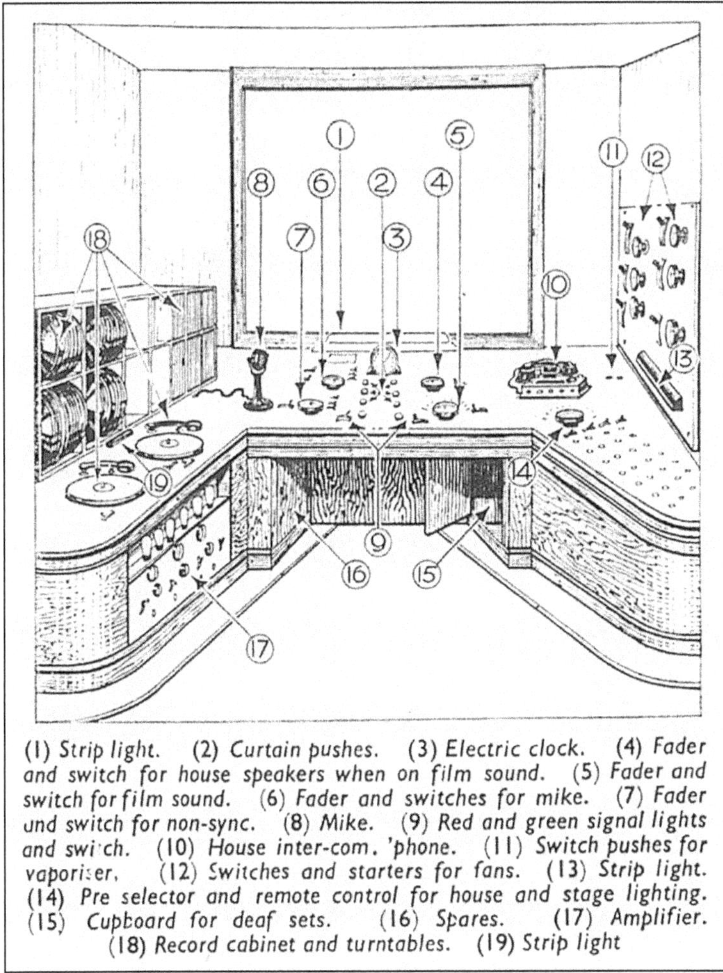

Fig. 1.2: Key responsibilities of the chief projectionist expressed in architectural form.[84]

It is also frequently documented that the theatrical showmanship element of the projection workflow was principally the chief's domain. Selection of the interval music, for example, was normally handled by the chief.[85] In 1945 the *Ideal Kinema* magazine publish-

83 As described in detail in A.B., 'Put Cleanliness First', *ibid.*, 9 August 1945, p. xiv.

84 Sketch by H. Ponchery, *ibid.*, 14 June 1945, p. xi. This is a vision of the future of cinema design that was never ultimately adopted by any British cinema architects, though we note in the next chapter comparable experiments in the early 1960s using a presentational control console intended for installation within the space of the auditorium.

85 'Getting the Best Out of the Non-Sync', *ibid.*, 16 April 1942, p. iv.

ed an image suggesting how the chief's workstation might be more effectively configured to their needs and responsibilities in the post-war design of cinemas – see Fig. 1.2. It proposed that the proper place for the person with overall technical responsibility for the show should be a new booth, separate altogether from the projection box. It would allow them to carefully observe the impact of the presentation upon the cinema audience, without the competing aural distractions of the projectors. They would adjust soundtrack volume levels in response to the reactions of spectators and be able to concentrate upon the control of the non-sync turntable, the screen curtains, or tabs, and the house lights from their dedicated console.

For all of these significant variations in projection responsibilities that characterise the nitrate film era, the dangerous flammability of 35mm prints resulted in the enforcement – via the Cinematograph Act (1909) – of a core set of technological, architectural and labouring practices that transcended many of the differences between silent and sound film projection. Throughout this period, it was consistently the case that multiple operators had to be present in the box at any one time, rewind rooms had to be separated from the main projection enclosure, the spool capacity on all projectors was restricted to 2,000 feet (roughly twenty minutes at twenty-four frames per second) so as to limit the opportunity for an accidental fire, and these reels had to be enclosed in metal spool boxes to limit the severity of any fire that did break out.[86]

There were a number of practical ways in which fires could be avoided. 'No smoking' rules were strictly enforced, and Frank Gibson recalls that 'you'd never ever open those spool boxes when [the projector] was running because ... it used to go like petrol'.[87] Projection boxes were required to include a fire blanket, two buckets of water and a bucket of sand as part of their inventory.[88] Despite these precautions, film fires (usually small ones) were semi-regular occurrences, with the projectionists finding themselves in the front line of any attempt to raise the alarm or extinguish the blaze. Although R. Howard Cricks advised that 'sand should be used only as a last resort, since it will probably ruin the projector', Phil Fawke recalls his chief responding to the 'whoosh' of a nitrate fire in precisely this way.[89] The film jammed in the

86 Films would arrive at cinemas in metal film cans as reels of approximately 1,000 feet in length and would be joined together to make larger reels of 2,000 feet.

87 Interview with Frank Gibson, conducted by Richard Wallace, 14 October 2014.

88 R. Howard Cricks, *The Complete Projectionist*, 4th edn (London: Odhams Press Ltd., 1949), p. 310.

89 *Ibid.*, p. 221.

gate of the projector and ignited and the chief 'threw some blasted sand bucket on it which didn't do the projector any good. We had to get another intermittent part from London.' There are numerous accounts of nitrate fires in the news and trade press of differing levels of severity.[90] A blaze at the Scala Cinema, Sheffield in November 1928 was described as not being 'of a serious character', but still resulted in the operator being 'overcome by the fumes ... and removed to hospital'.[91] At the other extreme, a fire in the operating box at the Welling Kinema on 16 July 1929 resulted in the deaths of the 19 year-old operator and his 14 year-old assistant when film jammed in the gate, ignited and spread to other reels during attempts to extinguish it. The cinema was a converted church, and the operating box had only a single point of entry – an iron ladder through a hatch.[92] Reports on the incident note that although the arrangement of the box was successful in 'confining the fire and preventing its spread to the auditorium' the stepladder exit became 'little better than a death trap'.[93] In the aftermath of this tragedy, W. Stanley-Aldrich argued that

> The responsibilities of the operator become greater and greater as the intricacies of the Trade increase, and now, with the advent of talkies, his job has become one which requires his every attention, necessitating alertness and alacrity from which there is no relief until the 'King slide' is thrown on the screen. Therefore, he is working under a tension of nerve strain which renders him almost unequal to resist a further call upon his resources should any mishap occur ... When a fire does occur, it is immediately asked, 'What was the operator doing?' Ask yourself, 'What wasn't he doing.'[94]

The projectionist's job as fire-watchman was aided by a range of devices that were built into or could be added onto film projectors in order to offer an automated element of fire safety. Phil Fawke recalls that the BTH Super projectors included a blade at the opening of each spool box that would automatically slice through the nitrate film if it got stuck in the gate and John and Peter Douglas recall the same make of projector including a cut-out if the spool box was opened mid-operation. A range of fire extinguishers were also developed that could be affixed to the projector. Walturdaw U.F.A.'s Moist Compressed Air Film Cooling Apparatus could be

90 See, for example: 'Film Blaze – Panic Averted at Sheffield', *Kinematograph Weekly*, 17 December 1925, p. iii; 'Bradford Fire – Manager and Operator Fight the Flames', *ibid.*, 8 July 1926, p. 46; 'Firescares at Manchester & Catford', *ibid.*, 6 January 1927, p. 71; 'Two Film Fires', *ibid.*, 17 February 1927, p. 49; 'Operating Box Blaze Still Unsolved', *ibid.,* 12 April 1934, pp. 51, 56.

91 *Ibid.*, 15 November 1923, p. 73

92 'Film Fire Tragedy – Two Operators Fatally Burned', *ibid.*, 18 July 1929, p. 63; A. L. Carter, 'The Lesson of Welling', *ibid.*, 18 July 1929, p. 53; 'Welling Kinema Fire – Home Office Not to Prosecute', *ibid.*, 23 January 1930, p. 25.

93 'Film Fire Tragedy – Two Operators Fatally Burned', *ibid.*, 18 July 1929, p. 63.

94 W. Stanley-Aldrich, 'Safety Sense', *ibid.*, 18 July 1929, p. 58.

fitted to their Ernemann projectors and was designed to blow a continuous blast of cold air onto the film as it passed through the gate, thus minimising the chance of combustion. Adverts for the device claim that 'all danger of fire is entirely eliminated, even if the film remains stationary in the gate for 20 to 30 minutes' and offer the cinema proprietor the opportunity to 'Insure your patrons, your operators' lives and your own peace of mind'.[95]

One device with particular longevity was the Pyrene Automatic Fire Extinguisher, which was described as being 'unique among the devices for dealing with fire in the projector in that it is an actual fire-fighter, entirely automatic and set in motion by the fire itself, should it break out.'[96] The device – triggered automatically – cut out the motor and the arc lamp and extinguished the fire with compressed carbon dioxide gas, meaning that no damage was done to the projector and that theoretically the film could be resumed within moments of the fire being extinguished.[97] The Pyrene system became a standard component of Kalee projectors and was still being advertised into the 1950s.[98]

Aside from attending to inflagration risks, much of the projectionist's time during the course of the programme was spent manning the projector. A significant part of this effort was dedicated to the quality of the presentation, and these working principles will be addressed in more detail in Chapter Two. But the basic functioning of the machines also required significant care and attention. The regulatory stipulation for projectors to have a limited-capacity spool box meant that entire feature films could not fit on a single projector. This necessitated the use of a second 35mm projector to enable a feature-length film to be screened without interruption. The operation of two projectors demanded particular rhythms of working, and the process of changing over from one machine to another was a carefully orchestrated routine. The approaching end of the current reel could be monitored in a number of ways. Mike Williams recalls with a certain amount of envy that 'Some cinemas had bells on the projectors that would start vibrating a couple of minutes before the end. We never had anything luxurious like that, you just used to look at the film in the spool box and decide you were near the end.'[99] In October 1952 the *Ideal Kinema* printed a 'running chart' to act as a guide to translate the volume of film left

95 'Fire! Fire!! Fire!!! And How to Prevent It – Walturdaw U.F.A. Patent Moist Compressed Air Film Cooling Apparatus', *ibid.*, 25 November 1926, pp. 16-17.

96 'Killing Fire – How the Pyrene Device Works.', *ibid.*, 25 June 1931, p. 95.

97 'Fire-Fighters Cross Swords - Rival Systems Warmly Debated', *ibid.*, 21 January 1932, p. 58; 'Pyrene Put to the Test', *ibid.*, 21 January 1932, p. 58.

98 *The Kinematograph Year Book 1950* (London: Odhams Press, Ltd., 1950), p. 6.

99 Interview with Mike Williams, conducted by Richard Wallace, 24 August 2015.

on a spool into the time remaining (Fig. 1.3). However, estimating the length of the film on a reel was one of a projectionist's key skills, as Andrew MacLean notes: 'You'd look at a reel and you could tell down to about a hundred foot how much [was left]. You used your eyes to do it and you would come up with a total running time ... you build up an instinct for doing [that kind of thing] ... and it never really leaves you.'[100]

RUNNING CHART

CORE DIAMETER	2 ins.	4 ins.
OUTER DIAMETER INCHES	MINUTES	MINUTES
4	1.4	—
4½	1.9	—
5	2.5	1.1
5½	3.1	1.7
6	3.8	2.4
6½	4.5	3.1
7	5.3	3.9
7½	6.2	4.8
8	7.1	5.7
8½	8.1	6.7
9	9.1	7.7
9½	10.2	8.8
10	11.4	10.0
10½	12.6	11.2
11	13.9	12.4
11½	15.2	13.7
12	16.6	15.1
12½	18.1	16.6
13	19.6	18.1
13½	21.2	19.7
14	22.8	21.4

Fig. 1.3: Chart correlating the amount of film left on a reel with its remaining running time.[101]

In the case of films that screened for many weeks, the movie's soundtrack could be used as a signal for an impending change-over, as Neil Thompson suggests: 'you know exactly where the change-over cues are because you've seen them that many times you could change over without looking. You just listen to the soundtrack and think, "Aye, there's a changeover coming up".'[102]

The approaching end of the reel signalled that the second machine needed to be readied. The film would have been laced up already and the lamp would be lit in anticipation. Simon Allen notes that this would be done a minute or two before because the carbon arc lamps would 'flicker and fluctuate a little bit for the first minute until they've heated up', so that when changeover time came the light would have become steady and the projectionist would then begin looking for cues that guided the precision timing of the switch.[103] 'On the end of each part you had the changeover cues',

100 Interview with Andrew MacLean, conducted by Richard Wallace, 25 August 2015.

101 *Ideal Kinema*, 9 October 1952, p. 11.

102 Interview with Neil Thompson, conducted by Richard Wallace, 11 November 2014.

103 Interview with Simon Allen, conducted by Richard Wallace, 8 March 2016.

Thompson recalls. 'First there used to be what you call the "motor dot" which was placed on four frames, about eleven feet from the end [of the reel], so you had to be ready ... [You'd] have your finger ready on the motor.' Martyn Butler takes up the process in a particularly vivid and compelling account:

> One minute to go and you'd be on standby and you'd have one finger on the 'start' button, or it was a switch in some cases, and you had your other hand on the dowser, and that's a shutter that separates the lamp house from the [film]. You start your motor when the first cue dot comes up on the screen and open up the dowser. Now, that doesn't let any light through yet because there's a secondary shutter. The film then is running – seven, six, five, four – and you're waiting on the [second cue] ... So it'll be running down: three, two, one, and you see the second cue in the top right hand corner and you hit the shutter button, which would close the shutter on the outgoing projector and open the shutter on the new projector. And if you'd done everything right the public wouldn't blink, they wouldn't see a thing, and the film would continue and you'd bring the sound across from one projector to the other. Your heart would be doing a hundred and twenty beats per minute, you'd be sweating because you might have gone [to the projector] a little bit early and you're getting tired because you thought it was two minutes to go, and 'Oh, I've been here too long now and my arm's hurting and will I see it? Where is the cue? What reel is this? Have I loaded up the right reel?' It all goes through your head at that time ... There was never a changeover when I didn't sweat, even though it never left you. Some people would say, 'Oh, a changeover, dah dah dah,' and slap it on, but for me it was life or death; it was brain surgery.

Having a team in the box aided the smoothness of the changeover greatly, and it was not uncommon during the nitrate era for two projectionists to work a changeover, one operating each machine, manually opening and closing dowsers and shutters in synchronisation. However, as Mike Williams says, this wasn't always possible, and, although the changeover was a complicated rhythm to learn, once up to speed 'It [could] be carried out by one man very easily.'

The cyclical routine of projection meant that as soon as the changeover was complete the process began all over again:

> When a reel ends you've got to put new carbons in [the arc lamp] because they've burnt away, and you rewind the reel that had just come off ready for the next show. Then go to the film bin and get the next reel out, put that on the projector which has got the new carbons, lace up the projector and check it to make sure everything's ready to go. You lace up, ideally on the gash film, so you're checking all your loops are correct, the sound loop is correct, everything's correct.[104]

104 Gash, or junk, film is the term given to the lengthy pieces of blank or damaged celluloid that would be attached to the front of a film reel to enable the projectionist to lace-up the projector without the start of

Throughout the nitrate era, the primary source of illumination came from the use of carbon arc lamps, which required their own particular maintenance routines. John Douglas describes the carbon arc as a 'lamp which burnt ... two carbon [rods], a negative and a positive, housed in a big metal housing with a huge mirror behind that' to reflect the light.[105] Those projectionists who used carbon arc lamps seem to have a genuine fondness for them, both for their aesthetic and technical qualities. Chandra Makwana describes the high-intensity light which they emitted as 'beautiful' and Neil Thompson recalls the carbon arc lamp as being 'what fascinated [him]' when he first got the chance to visit a projection box as a boy, and finding out that the light didn't emanate from a bulb but 'an empty lamphouse with two rods in and a reflector at the back.'[106]

Working with carbon arc projectors was not a particularly pleasant activity; Sam Lavington recalls that upon entering a projection box using carbon arcs, 'the first thing that hit me was the smell ... and then you combine that with the heat from the projectors and the carbon arcs – it just overwhelms you really'.[107] Neil Thompson adds that alongside the smell 'you had fumes as well' that 'weren't good for your health', and Paul Edmunds admits that 'with regards breathing' he 'often wondered about some of the old chaps, with the carbon dust' that was produced as the carbon rods burned away.[108]

The carbon arc's propensity for producing dust and ash naturally meant that a great deal of time was spent cleaning. Thompson's shift would often start about three hours before the first film began because of the quantity of cleaning that was required: 'When you went in you would open all the arc lamps from the back and you would clean them out because ... the mirror at the back used to get covered with carbon dust. We used to hoover them out every morning, get rid of all the dust and make them lovely and clean.' For Ray Reed, 'the arcs were labour intensive because they had to be cleaned out every morning and there was quite a lot of maintenance to do on them because parts wore, broke, burnt, so you were always having to maintain the arcs more than the projectors'.[109]

the film being missed. The closed shutter meant that the junk film passing through the projector would not be seen by the audience. The term 'gash film' seems most likely to derive from British Royal Navy slang for 'rubbish', but a more offensive and vulgar derivation, involving the word's use as a derogatory term for part of the female anatomy, is possible.

105 Mirror arcs were introduced in the 1920s and cut energy consumption by about two-thirds; see Cricks, *The Complete Projectionist*, 4th edn, p. 80.

106 Interview with Chandra Makwana, conducted by Richard Wallace, 16 March 2015.

107 Interview with Sam Lavington, conducted by Richard Wallace, 20 August 2015.

108 Interview with Paul Edmunds, conducted by Richard Wallace, 2 December 2014.

109 Interview with Ray Reed, conducted by Richard Wallace, 5 February 2015.

Simon Allen describes this job as being 'very unpleasant', and that, once the cleaning was finished, the next job would be 'getting the carbons ready for the day', and Frank Gibson adds that it was part of the projectionist's job to 'make sure you've got stocks otherwise you needed to see the manager and make sure that there was enough in to keep you going'.

Tending the arc during projection was particularly labour intensive, as John Douglas explains:

> when you put electricity through these two carbon rods and touched them together and then separated them a flame would appear between them [in the shape of an arc] ... To produce this light [the carbons] burn away ... [so] you had to make sure that ... the gap between the two carbons, where the flame was, stayed at the same distance. The trim ... it was called ... If the gap got too wide the carbons would burn away too quickly and ... the light would go out. If they jammed together the light would go wrong as well.

More specifically, Thompson recalls that 'if they went too far [apart] the picture would go blue, if they went too close the picture would go brown. They had to be about an inch apart. So, you had to keep going and checking them.'

This naturally required a great deal of attention throughout the film screening. Although the carbon feeds were motorised on some later models of projector, they were often unreliable and susceptible to external factors, such as fluctuations in the electrical supply as Mike Marshall recalls:

> Between 5:30 and 6:00 all the offices started closing down and you'd get a wee surge in the power. You'd already set your feed motor up for that day ... and all of a sudden your power would raise, your feed motor would start feeding and the carbons would jump together and drop your light out. You'd just see the light going duller and duller ... This would be every night except Saturday and Sunday ... because there was nobody in the offices. So, you were okay on a Saturday and a Sunday, but you'd to keep an eye on your carbons during the week.[110]

John Douglas suggests that this irregularity was 'why a projectionist always had to be on duty; sure as life, if you turned your back on the arc lamp for any length of time that's when it would go wrong'.

Another major challenge maintaining the carbon arc lamp was the need to replace the carbon rods – or 'carbon up' – at the end of each reel because, as Frank Gibson explains, 'After twenty minutes [the carbon had burned away] and it was burning plastic, so it wouldn't be a bright light and you would normally get a blank screen'. Phil Fawke gives a sense of the effort required to keep the arcs under control whilst preparing for an imminent changeover:

110 Interview with Mike Marshall, conducted by Richard Wallace, 22 June 2015.

> at the Regal, Foleshill Road at Coventry they had hand-feed arcs and if you can imagine trying to run a show on your own, which sometimes you had to do, trying to feed two arc lamps [on different sides of the box] ... it's a bit difficult ... You used to have to sort of feed the one up hoping that it didn't burn away while you're [getting the other projector ready to changeover] ... You did need to be a contortionist.

It's perhaps not surprising that mistakes did occasionally happen. Gibson recalls that 'sometimes you did forget [to carbon up] ... because you've got other jobs to do, rewinding the film and putting the next one on', and that this would only become apparent when the changeover took place and the screen was dark. More serious was the potential for electrocution during the change of the carbon rods. 'You've always got to remember to shut the power off before changing the short carbon', Gibson remarks, 'otherwise you get a shock. You open the light box to take it out and "Oh!", you realise you forgot to shut it off.'

Even though manufacturers progressively increased the length of time that a carbon rod could burn for, this imposed new demands upon the projectionist, as John Douglas explains: 'The longest carbon you could get in those days was up to one hour and you had to make sure when you laced a reel up that you had enough carbon in the arc lamp to last the twenty minutes of that reel.' Judging how long a carbon rod would burn for became just as important a skill as being able to tell how much film was left on a spool. 'You didn't have to change the carbons all the time,' Simon Allen notes, 'but you had to be constantly checking to make sure that you put the new carbon rods in [at the right time], because if you start a reel and you haven't got enough carbon then you're buggered really because it's going to give out.'

There were, however, certain techniques that could be deployed if it looked like the carbon might be running short. 'If you really got in trouble you could [reduce the ampage running through the arc lamp],' Andrew MacLean notes. 'You could just knock out ten amps and so it would burn a lot slower, but it would be a lot less bright.' He suggests that navigating such difficulties 'was a real art and it was instinctive, to know how long a carbon would burn. It was kind of beautiful.'[111]

111 The imprecise correlation between the durations of the carbon rods and the film reel meant that there were usually small amounts of carbon left over that were neither long enough to last a full 2,000 feet reel, nor short enough to be discarded. These could be used to show trailers or joined together to form a composite carbon rod, though Simon Allen noted that 'the light would go a bit funny' as it burned across the join. There was another reason why it was in the projectionist's interests to use as much of the carbon as possible. The carbon rods were covered in copper, which would melt as the arc light burned, dripping into a tray under the arc lamp. It was common practice for the projectionist to gather up these copped pellets and sell them for scrap, something that Allen describes as being 'a perk' of the job.

A viable non-flammable replacement for 35mm nitrate film was finally brought to market by Kodak in 1948. However, it wasn't until 1950 that the firm ceased manufacturing nitrate film, ostensibly ending the nitrate era in the west.[112] Leo Enticknap notes that

> The relaxation of nitrate health and safety precautions was not as straightforward as some in the industry had hoped, and the exhibition sector in particular had to maintain fire safety equipment on [sic] cinemas long after nitrate film ceased being produced on account of back catalogue titles which remained in circulation.[113]

Indeed, projection became briefly more complicated as a result of an additional check having to be made, and accounts in the *Ideal Kinema* during the transition from nitrate to safety film note several instances of film prints arriving at cinemas on a mixture of different bases. Apart from causing practical problems – given that repairing films required the use of different film cements depending on the base – it also posed a major safety risk. One correspondent noted a particularly confusing example where a safety copy, complete with 'SAFETY FILM' markings, had been used to strike a new nitrate film print, resulting in the safety markings being duplicated on the flammable film.[114] Other projectionists highlighted examples of film prints containing a mixture of bases *within* single reels.[115] Although the publication suggested that 'there would probably be no great objection to this at the present moment', there was concern that 'if this practice persists at a time when regulations are being relaxed it will be a serious matter'.[116] Indeed, this crossover period led to some potentially hazardous behaviour on the part of projectionists. The *Ideal Kinema* observed in February 1952 that 'many projectionists have already accepted the principle of safety film stock to the extent of smoking in the box'.[117] The author reminded projectionists that this was still 'a serious breach of regulations', and in September of that year reiterated that 'safety precautions in the box must not be relaxed until nitrate film has become a thing of the past'.[118]

112 Leo Enticknap, *Moving Image Technology: From Zoetrope to Digital* (London; New York: Wallflower Press, 2005), p. 22. After this period nitrate film became less prominent, although it remains an infrequent exhibition format to this day in specially licensed premises such as BFI Southbank (formerly the National Film Theatre).

113 *Ibid.*

114 'When "Safety Film" is not Safety Film', *Ideal Kinema*, 7 December 1950, p. 15

115 'Safety Last?', *ibid.*, 17 May 1951, p. 19; 'Breaking Regulations', *ibid.*, 13 March 1952, p. 13. For other accounts of films arriving in a mixture of bases, or with confusing identification markings, see: 'Missing Nitrate and Safety Base', *ibid.*, 10 Apr 1952, p. 13; 'Half and Half', *ibid.*, 12 June 1952, p. 17; 'Confusing Markings', *ibid.*, 4 Dec 1952, p. 11.

116 'Breaking Regulations', *ibid.*, 13 March 1952, p. 13

117 'Smoking', *ibid.*, 14 February 1952, p. 15

118 *Ibid.*, 11 September 1952, p. 17

Following the eventual wholesale replacement of nitrate film with triacetate safety film there was no longer a legal limit on the quantity of film that could be placed on a single reel, though many cinemas retained projectors with enclosed 2,000-foot spool boxes well into the acetate era. Although the carbon arc lamp had been a perfectly practical light source during the nitrate period, where both the film reels and the carbon rods had to be changed over every twenty minutes, in the era of safety film, the limited burning time of carbon rods became a 'reverse salient'. As Peter Howden notes, 'the long play stuff was impossible ... 60 minutes was about as much as you could get out of one carbon rod'.[119] One intermediate solution was to continue operating the changeover system, with projectionists taking advantage of the longer carbon burning times to limit themselves to one reel change per hour, rather than every twenty minutes. However, a replacement illumination technology that ultimately emerged – the xenon lamp – was not limited in this way, and, together with triacetate safety film, it resulted in a reconfiguration of the standard constellation of projection apparatus, which we are calling the 'xenon array'.

The Xenon Array

The arrival of sound constituted something of an anomaly in relation to the impact that technological changes within the cinema building have had upon the work undertaken by projectionists. Whereas sound dramatically increased projectionists' workloads, the majority of subsequent technological changes had the opposite effect, and the number of jobs for the projection team to do tended to reduce with each innovation (though, as we will see, this did not necessarily mean that *individual* projectionists had less work to do).[120] In this respect, the projectionist's obsolescence in the digital

119 Interview with Peter Howden, conducted by Richard Wallace, 13 November 2014.

120 Other exceptions include the brief fad of 3-D films in the mid-1950s, which required the use of carefully-synched machines projecting two images simultaneously; not only was this process far more complex, the overlayed images were said to cause eye-strain in the projectionists who had to monitor the screen for hours on end. See, for example: 'Research Needed on Projection: Causes of Eyestrain', *Kinematograph Weekly*, 23 Apr 1953, p. 9; 'Headache for Projectionists', *ibid.*, 30 Apr 1953, p. 1. The introduction of widescreen in the early 1950s also posed some practical issues for the projectionist, though the most drastic changes were to venues that required structural work to accommodate the new screens. (Kupper, 'The *Scope* Behind Cinemascope', *ibid.*, 26 March 1953, p. 7; 'Widescreen for Small Cinemas, *Ideal Kinema*, 13 August 1953, p. 7). Nevertheless, racking, focus and light issues were initially very common. The new ratios required more sustained attention than the standard 4:3 image, and more careful handling as well, given that 'the bigger the picture the more projector unsteadiness shows up'. ('A Wide Picture Needs Better Showmanship', *ibid.*, 8 October 1953, p. 15.) One projectionist highlighted that no fewer than seven additional processes had to be completed when switching between a standard image and a CinemaScope presentation, including changing the lenses and altering the masking (David M. Robson, 'How to Operate CinemaScope', *ibid.*, 14 January 1954, p. 9). However, the counter view was that once these processes has been amalgamated into the projectionist's daily routine 'there should be no more difficulty in handling an anamorphic picture than in dealing with any standard product' (Charles E. Talley, 'CinemaScope Through the Eyes of a Projectionist', *ibid.*, 5 November 1953, p. 3).

age can be seen as the latest point on a timeline of incremental technological rationalisation that stretches back to the introduction of motorised projectors in the 1910s.

Predictions concerning the possible impact of future technological developments upon the work of projection are a relatively common sight in the trade press at any given moment. These often anticipated the luxury of a more relaxing environment in the projection box once the next hypothetical innovation arrived. One instance of this is a cartoon published in 1944 in the *Ideal Kinema* (Fig. 1.4) in which two operators recline in easy chairs smoking their pipes and listening to the radio, supremely comfortable working conditions that the cartoon humorously envisions as a consequence of the future supersedure of the flammable films, 2,000 foot reels and carbon arc lamps associated with the nitrate projection array.

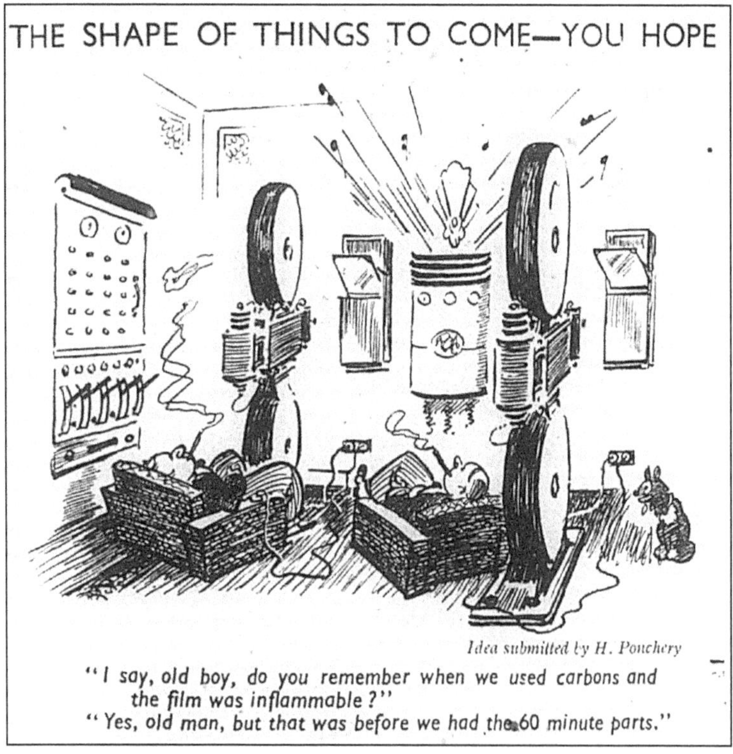

Fig. 1.4: An attempt to predict the changes which the supersedure of nitrate film, short reels and carbon arc lamps would bring.[121]

Although obviously tongue-in-cheek, this prediction is not entirely fanciful. As we shall see, the arrival of triacetate safety film

121 'The Shape of Things to Come – You Hope', *ibid.*, 6 January 1944, p. xv.

and the replacement of carbon arcs with xenon lamps did reduce the hands-on nature of film projection, and even more drastically than the cartoon imagines. This did not, of course, result in the kind of relaxed working conditions enjoyed by these fictional operators, and in fact it is quite possible that for any individual projectionists, work in the post-nitrate box was actually *more* laborious, even if the overall projection-specific duties were reduced, in part because these technological transitions facilitated a reduction in the number of on-duty projection staff that cinemas needed to employ.

The kind of set-up visible in the cartoon – two projectionists operating changeovers between projectors running 6,000 ft 60-minute spools – became very common once safety film became the dominant mainstream projection format. The amount of work needed to screen a movie was significantly reduced, and with minimal technological modification: carbon arc projectors were adapted to the new system simply by removing or enlarging the spool boxes. In so doing, the number of changeovers was reduced to a single instance per film. This streamlining was further accelerated with the incorporation of the xenon arc lamp, which removed the reverse salient of the carbon rod's 60-minute limit and made it possible for entire features to be spooled onto a single reel. First exhibited by the Zeiss Ikon Company at the 1954 Berlin Photokina trade show in Berlin,[122] the *Ideal Kinema* was quick to argue that 'there is little doubt that sooner or later the xenon lamp will supplant the carbon arc'.[123] By the start of the 1960s, British Thomson-Houston (BTH) were claiming that their own xenon lamp had been installed in more than 250 UK cinemas,[124] and a demonstration at the 1963 annual conference of the Cinematograph Exhibitors' Association (CEA) – a trade body which represented the collective interests of British cinema owners – showed that xenon running costs were finally below those of a carbon arc of similar light intensity.[125] Although the xenon lamp removed the need for changeovers entirely, the labour saved was not enjoyed by the projectionists, because when the second projector became obsolete, this allowed for a significant reduction of staffing levels in the box.

A number of the veteran projectionists interviewed for this book have suggested that the transition from carbon arcs to xenon lamps

122 Enticknap, *Moving Image Technology*, p. 152.

123 'Light Source of the Future?', *Ideal Kinema*, 1 December 1955, p. 12.

124 'A New Lamp for Old', *ibid.*, 11 May 1961, p. 117. This was in addition to lamps manufactured by Zeiss Ikon, Rank Kalee and others.

125 'The Advantages of Xenon Lamps', *ibid.*, 11 July 1963, pp. 22-23.

represented a point of disjuncture that is in some ways analogous to the later transition from celluloid to digital projection, in terms of the overall effect on the work undertaken by the projectionist, and the technological and social context in which that work took place. Peter Howden notes that when upgrading the projectors at the Electric cinema in Notting Hill, London to accommodate the larger reels, 'the big debate was do we keep the carbon arc or do we switch to xenon', and that 'by that stage this was the equivalent of the film and digital now'. Hinting at the impact that the xenon lamp had on the overall work of projection, John Douglas notes that the xenon lamp was 'more like your ordinary bulbs that you plug in', in that it lasted 'two or three thousand hours' and 'made the projectionist's life a great deal easier; you hadn't to tend an arc lamp all the time'. Phil Fawke describes the arrival of xenon lamps as 'a blessing' because they removed the fumes and carbon dust from the projection room, and Simon Allen argues that 'from the projectionist's point of view they were much less trouble because you didn't have to do the cleaning all the time, you didn't have to change the carbons all the time'.

However, Alan Foster takes a slightly more cynical view of the industry-wide conversion to xenon, arguing that it was 'a way of getting rid of the projectionists',[126] and Enticknap notes that it was clear that 'one of the key advantages of this new technology would be that the cinema industry could potentially use it to cut staff overheads'. In support of this assertion he quotes the chief engineer of a British manufacturing firm, who argued in 1957 that the xenon lamp 'will make the light on the screen independent of the operator'.[127] Xenon lamps 'did not require two people to be in the projection room,' Foster points out, 'ergo we only needed one projectionist ... that was the by-product; that it reduced the number of projectionists. It certainly didn't give a better light.'

Much as the aesthetic discussion of film versus digital has often turned to the question of the inherent qualities of the image produced by each medium – for example the idea that film is 'warmer', or that it produces richer black tones (see Chapter Four) – the debate around carbon arcs versus xenon lamps was similarly defined by questions of colour and brightness. Foster recalls that

> there was only one make of xenon lamp to start with, and one make of housing for it to go in, which was made by BTH ... and there was only one size of lamp, which was a two-thousand watt lamp. It didn't matter how big the screen was, and how long the throw was, that was the lamp.

126 Interview with Allan Foster conducted by Richard Wallace, 16 September 2015.

127 Enticknap, *Moving Image Technology*, p. 152.

This often resulted in 'a very inferior light' when compared with carbon. 'When you had carbon arcs you were getting a punchy light', Foster continues, whereas the first xenon lamps gave 'a blue tinge to everything', particularly those films produced in black and white.

Although they removed the fumes and dust that attended the carbon arc lamp, xenon bulbs were not without their own challenges and dangers, and Enticknap notes that protective clothing was required when changing bulbs because 'the pressure of the xenon gas inside the bulb creates a small risk of explosion'.[128] Simon Allen elaborates: 'when they go it's like a bomb going off. It makes an almighty bang and it would often completely smash the mirror as well. So that was then twenty minutes at the fastest ... to get a new mirror in'.

Apart from this quirk, the maintenance of the xenon lamp was relatively straightforward. Chris Blower recalls that 'all we had to do was basically log the xenon lamp hours and clean air filters, that was it'.[129] Thompson notes that it was still important to monitor the quality of the light from a xenon lamp because they did have a limited lifespan and 'if you overused it you'd ... have striking problems or the light would be terrible because ... you used to get blackening on the top [of the bulb]'. Despite the cost – Thompson suggests that xenon bulbs cost around £950 each by the early 2010s – it is clear that xenon illumination had a major impact on the projectionist's work, not least because, as Peter Douglas puts it, it 'allowed as much film as you wanted to show to be shown without any changeover', and this in turn enabled long-playing projection systems to be introduced.

There were two main forms of long-running projection apparatus. The platter, or cakestand, became the standard form of projection in the multiplex and will be discussed in the next section. The other long-playing system was the 'tower', which more-or-less amounted to a progression of the increased spools enabled by the relaxation of fire regulations at the beginning of the safety film era. Early long-playing systems of this kind were brought to market in the UK by Westrex in 1962 (10,000 foot capacity) and Phillips in 1963 (13,500 foot capacity) before becoming more common towards the end of the decade.[130] Enticknap describes the tower as

> [consisting] mainly of high capacity spools of up to 12,000 feet, which were mounted on heavy-duty spindles. These were either

128 *Ibid.*

129 Interview with Chris Blower, conducted by Richard Wallace, 11 August 2015.

130 '10,000ft on a Single Reel', *Kinematograph Weekly*, 31 May 1962, p. 105; 'Talking Technically', *Ideal Kinema*, 14 June 1962, p. 26; 'Productivity for Production Display at Photokina', *Kinematograph Weekly*, 11 April 1963, p. 18; 'Talking Technically', *Ideal Kinema*, 11 April 1963, p. 24.

> built into an enlarged pedestal underneath the projector mechanism and lamphouse, or positioned vertically on a separate structure known as a tower, situated behind or to one side of the projector.[131]

These spools could hold around two hours of film, allowing the uninterrupted projection of an entire feature for the first time: the film would be loaded onto the top of the tower and, after passing through the projector, would then wind on to the bottom spool. This would subsequently be removed, rewound and then re-mounted on the top of the tower in preparation for the next show.

There were some obvious issues caused by the size of the reels used on the tower. Loading and unloading required the projectionist to lift an entire feature from the tower to the rewinder and back again between every show. This was a significant amount of weight to bear. Neil Thompson recalls that there was a knack to heaving the film onto the top spindle that required considerable physical effort, and Frank Gibson notes that he got a hernia from the repetitive strain of the manoeuvre. Thompson also states that the different weights of the two spools meant that they didn't always rotate at the same speed. The result was that when the machine started up '[the bottom spool] had a tendency to ... snatch, and of course ... [the film] would just snap. ... [Y]ou had to learn how to hold the film steady until it took up properly'. Having the whole film on one reel also meant that it had to be rewound in one go between screenings, which took a significant amount of time, and if using a hand-powered rewinder also required substantial physical exertion which Chris Tweddell recalls 'was time consuming and not very practical'.[132]

Until the mid-1940s, the standard spool length as it was received by the projectionist, was 1,000 feet.[133] These were joined together to create 2,000-ft spools that were used throughout the 'nitrate array' period. One major change initiated by long-playing projection systems was the need to make up entire features, by turning the 2,000-foot spools that arrived at the cinema – which became the standard after the Second World War – into the 12,000-foot feature film that would be hoisted onto the projector. 'When a film comes in [to the cinema] it may be [in] six or seven or eight parts, or even longer if it's a long film', Neil Thompson recalls. 'And when you open the tins, the film's actually on a bobbin', a small metal or plastic core around which the celluloid was wrapped. To get the film ready for screening on a tower required these shorter reels to be joined together and then run onto a large metal spool

131 Enticknap, *Moving Image Technology*, p. 153.

132 Interview with Chris Tweddell, conducted by Richard Wallace, 12 November 2014.

133 Cricks, *The Complete Projectionist*, 4th edn, p . 211.

which could be loaded onto the projector. The film would then stay as one entity until the end of its run, when it would be broken back down into its constituent parts and returned to the distributor or sent on to another cinema. 'Making-up' the film print, as it was known, was thus a key part of the projectionist's weekly routine and standard practice from the deregulation of spool-box sizes in the 1950s until the final years of celluloid projection.

The making-up process was rendered particularly laborious by the frequent absence of clear labelling of the order that the reels needed to be assembled in, and by the need to carefully check the condition of the print and repair weak joins. Although each part was supposed to arrive with an identifying leader attached to confirm the title of the film, the part number and the orientation of the print (i.e. whether a particular end was the start or the conclusion of the part) this was removed during the making-up process, and so after the first screening its accuracy could not be guaranteed, especially if the print had passed through a cinema with poor projection standards. Good practice, then, was to create a system of 'reference frames' to help identify the parts, as John Neal, of the Curzon Cinema, Clevedon, elaborates: 'when you're making up a film for the very first time ... the first frame or two frames of a reel are left on the leader'. This made identifying part numbers simpler when prints were broken down again, by allowing the projectionist to compare images, rather than recalling part-beginnings from memory. 'You can match the frames on the [film reel] with those [on the leader]', Neal suggests, 'and that then reassured you that that is the [correct] reel'.

The separate parts were then joined together in sequential order, and checked as they were wound onto the reel in meticulous fashion. As well as being examined by eye, this involved physically handling every inch of film. 'It must run through your finger and thumb,' Mike Williams notes, suggesting that 'if you're a ... half-way qualified projectionist you will feel every imperfection on the film as it goes through', and badly damaged sections could be repaired. This process left a lasting physical mark on the body of the projectionists, and Williams recalls that 'after about six months of being a rewind boy you get a ... quite noticeable groove [in your fingers], and that's the groove you fit the film in'. (Such 'scarring' would no doubt have been experienced by projectionists working at every stage in the history of analogue film projection.)

This process only had to be done once – barring projection accidents – at the start of each film's run. The print would be made up before the first showing, broken down after the final showing and left on the projector between houses. This represented a radical reduction in the amount of film-handling when compared with the changeover system. These single instances of assembling and disassembling replaced the many man-hours taken up conducting changeovers, and although the film still had to be rewound between each house, the disruption (and physical effort) was minimal compared to the five or six occasions that reels would be loaded, unloaded and rewound *per show* in the changeover system. The second projector was no longer necessary and once the show was in progress the projectionist was not required to return to the machine every twenty minutes for the changeover as before. Where single-screen cinemas had once required a team of projectionists for safety and professional operation, and a rewind boy to pick up the slack, the entire operation could now be conducted successfully and without risk by a single individual.

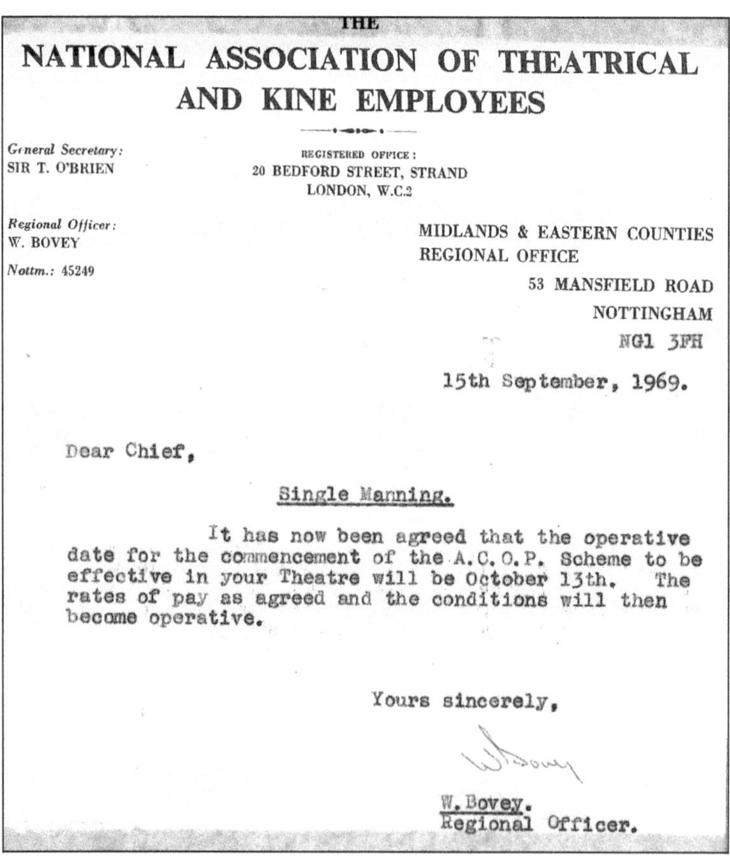

THE
NATIONAL ASSOCIATION OF THEATRICAL AND KINE EMPLOYEES

General Secretary:
SIR T. O'BRIEN

REGISTERED OFFICE:
20 BEDFORD STREET, STRAND
LONDON, W.C.2

Regional Officer:
W. BOVEY

Nottm.: 45249

MIDLANDS & EASTERN COUNTIES
REGIONAL OFFICE
53 MANSFIELD ROAD
NOTTINGHAM
NG1 3FH

15th September, 1969.

Dear Chief,

Single Manning.

It has now been agreed that the operative date for the commencement of the A.C.O.P. Scheme to be effective in your Theatre will be October 13th. The rates of pay as agreed and the conditions will then become operative.

Yours sincerely,

W. Bovey.
Regional Officer.

Fig. 1.5: A notice from the trade union responsible for cinema projectionists notifying chief projectionists in the ABC chain of the introduction of single-manning.[134]

134 Taken from the scrap books of Joan and Bill Pearson and used with permission.

These changes enabled a reduction of staffing costs through the elimination of much of the projection team structure at a time when annual cinema attendances were plummeting. Chapter Three will show that there was an industry-wide shortage of skilled projectionists in the 1960s, and the streamlining of labour needs documented here, which was known as 'single-manning' and occurred across the UK's cinema chains from the late 1960s (Fig. 1.5), can be seen in part as an attempt to address this problem as well as a cost-saving measure. This reduction of manpower is recalled vividly by those who worked through it, including Neil Thompson who notes that 'when I started, we had four people. Then things started to change into single-manning and ... that was a bit more stressful, having to see to things on your own'. Simon Allen observes that the move from a four-man team to a single-manned operation meant that 'as soon as the film started you were just chained to the projection room', and that it was 'a bit of a treadmill ... and nobody to talk to'. Loneliness became a defining feature of the profession in the multiplex era, which was the logical extension of a working context characterised by increasing use of labour-saving technologies.

The Multi-Screen Array

Although the tower system allowed some cinemas to operate as single-manned operations, they worked by straightforwardly continuing the expansion of spool capacities that had been enabled by the arrival of safety film; the fundamental film-handling processes and spatial organisation of the film print in relation to the projector were the same. However, the age of the multiplex cinema, which commenced in Britain with the opening of a ten-screen venue called The Point in Milton Keynes in 1985, required long-playing projection apparatus of an entirely different order. Although the tower removed the need for mid-film changeovers, the entire film still needed to be removed from the projector, rewound, remounted, relaced and restarted between each and every performance. This could be done by a lone projectionist tending one screen, but replicating this economy of labour across multiple screens within a single venue was more difficult.

Often referred to as a 'cake stand' in the UK, because of its aesthetic similarities to the 'three layered plate ... piled on a centre spindle' that – as Peter Douglas puts it – was a staple feature 'when you went to your granny for afternoon tea', the platter system revolutionised cinema projection. Designed by 'the world famous Philips organisation', the 'Projectawind' system, as the platter was initially known, made an early public appearance in the UK in an addendum to an advertisement for the ABC chain's upcoming display of new technological innovations, as part of the British Kinematograph Society's 'Film '69' technology conference. The ad describes

> A revolutionary new film device which allows the projection of films up to 7,000 metres ... without changeover, using only one projector and without the need to rewind for the next performance ... The basic system consists of a stand with three horizontal film discs, a control unit, a make-up table and a conveyor roller to the projector.[135]

A report on the conference published the following week does not feature any discussion of the new machine. (The Projectawind can be seen in a photograph of the demonstration area in the projection booth of the ABC, Edgware Road, but the delegates in the photograph are clearly more interested in the Cinetronic automation machine that dominates the picture (Fig. 1.6).)[136]

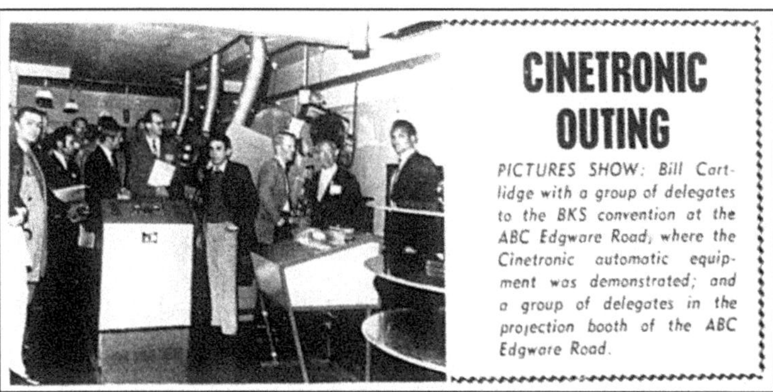

Fig. 1.6: An inauspicious debut for the cake-stand, visible at the right-hand edge of this image of a demonstration of Pathe's Cinetronic automation system.[137]

The system received more sustained attention in a lengthy article in the 9 August *Ideal Kinema* supplement, where R. H. Bomback reviewed the apparatus and gave an overview of its operation. It made 'use of large diameter horizontally positioned film reel discs each of which is large enough to accommodate the entire programme as a single reel on one disc', and the Projectawind system comprised three separate discs. The logic behind the making-up process was similar to that for the tower, except that the film was wound onto the platter leader-first, with the start fastened to 'a push-in ring ... placed centrally on the disc'.[138] There were three

135 'Cinetronic: The newest development in cinema automation by Pathe Equipment', *Kinematograph Weekly*, 21 June 1969, p. 17.

136 'ABPC Puts on four-in-one show at Film '69', *ibid.*, 28 June 1969, p. 7.

137 *Ibid.*

138 R.H. Bomback, 'Philips "no rewind" system for projection', *Ideal Kinema*, 9 August 1969, pp. 24-25.

significant features of the platter that made it suitable for widespread adoption within a multi-screen environment. Firstly, platters could accommodate a greater length of film than even the tower projectors, and a far greater length than the standard spools that were still in operation in many cinemas. Secondly, because they comprised three tiered plates (and up to five in some models), two films could be held simultaneously on separate plates, with the third plate left empty for the film to run onto after it had passed through the projector, becoming the equivalent of the take-up reel on a standard projector. Both films lay ready to be laced up at the appropriate times, enabling each cinema screen to show two different films across a day without any additional labour.[139]

The third, and perhaps most significant feature, was the platter's status as a 'non-rewind' system. Rather than feeding from the outside of the starting reel and returning to the centre of the take-up reel (as with all forms of spool-based projection), the platter system took the film from the centre of one plate and returned it to the ring at the centre of the take-up plate, meaning that it did not have to be rewound and was ready to be re-laced without any further effort from the projectionist.[140] Peter Douglas explains the impact that this had on the work of the projectionist:

> the whole programme lay on its side on one of these plates. And when the film was ready to start ... the projectionist would take this film from the centre of the platter, lace it through rollers around the projection room to ... the ... projector ... through the projector mechanism ... and then back ... onto one of the ... empty platters ... so you ended up at the end of a show with exactly the same as you started ... So, the projectionist's job really then was only to be there at the end of a film to re-lace it through, ready for the next run ... and then to be there to start the appropriate film at the appropriate time.

The fact that the film did not have to be continuously rewound was credited with a significant presentational advantage – identified at its earliest demonstrations – that because the film 'is at no time subjected to any undue strain ... it suffers less wear and tear than it would in the normal course of rewinding in the box'.[141]

This fundamental shift in projection technology was augmented by the widespread adoption of devices designed to automate other parts of the projectionist's workflow, and which had been in

139 This process required a certain level of concentration to 'make sure [that] you got the right one', as Rachel Dukes puts it and Adrian Pearce suggests that the greatest potential danger came when alternating between daytime matinee programmes for children and the evening programme of adult-oriented films. Interview with Rachel Dukes, conducted by Richard Wallace, 19 December 2014. Interview with Adrian Pearce, conducted by Richard Wallace, 20 October 2014.

140 A primitive non-rewind system can be found as early as 1924 as part of L. Kamm's "Wembley" projector, however, this appears to have developed no further that this one example. 'Kamm's Fireproof Super Projector', *Kinematograph Weekly*, 3 July 1924, pp. 56-57.

141 Bomback, 'Philips "no rewind' system', p. 25.

development since the mid-1940s. The Essoldo chain had begun to develop complex automated systems in 1946, and by July 1952, R. Howard Cricks could claim to have 'stood in the projection room of a London kinema [the Empire, Kilburn] and watched a robot device run the show'.[142] Cricks noted that

> The device makes the whole programme completely automatic, performing the whole sequence of operations normally done by hand, from the opening of the tabs, controlling the footlights between features, bringing in the non-sync., closing down the projectors and bringing up the houselights for the interval ... It is extraordinary to watch, as I did, the arc of the No. 2 projector strike, the motor start, and the changeover shutters operate and No. 1 projector shut down, all without anyone approaching the equipment.

Cricks's report includes the retrospectively portentous view that the success of the demonstration prototype meant that 'it might be assumed that all Essoldo kinemas will be equipped with it in due course' and that 'in time, automatic control will become universal, just as have motor-driven projectors and motor-fed arcs'.[143]

The roll-out of the Essoldo device (officially named the Essoldomatic) began in earnest in January 1953, when members of the main trade union for projectionists were able to inspect a working device in Newcastle, and it was being operated in fourteen cinemas by January 1954.[144] The take-up was further accelerated by the co-operation of Essoldo, Rank and GB-Kalee, a leading projector manufacturer, who furthered the development and market visibility of the Essoldomatic device, which was subsequently given the less proprietorial name 'Projectomatic'.[145] The next major turning point came in September 1958, when the Home Office incorporated the Projectomatic 'and similar systems of automatic projection' into amended safety regulations, noting that 'the operator in charge of a projection room may, from time to time, leave the projection room for a period not exceeding 15 minutes and without leaving an assistant in charge', providing that the projectors be automatically controlled.[146] By March 1960, Projectomatic equipment could be found in over 200 UK cinemas.[147]

The basic automation mechanism remained fundamentally the same from its introduction in the 1950s until the digitalisation of

142 'Projecting Without a Projectionist', *Kinematograph Weekly*, 28 January 1954, p. 7; R. Howard Cricks, 'I Watch a Robot Devise Run a London Show', *Ideal Kinema*, 12 June 1952, p. 17.

143 R. Howard Cricks, 'I Watch a Robot Devise Run a London Show', *ibid.*, 12 June 1952, p. 17.

144 'Projectionists Inspect Essoldomatic', *Kinematograph Weekly*, 15 January 1953, p. 8; 'Home Office Reviewing Projectomatic', *ibid.*, 25 July 1957, p. 1.

145 'Long Shots', *ibid.*, 8 December 1955, p. 4.

146 'Projectomatic Approved by Home Office', *ibid.*, 2 October 1958, p. 7.

147 'The Press-button Age in Projection', *Ideal Kinema*, 10 March 1960, p. 27.

projection boxes in the 21st century. A series of circuits were installed in the automation unit, each of which operated one aspect of the cinematic apparatus, such as striking the lamp, starting the motor on the projector, dimming the house lights or opening the tabs (Fig. 1.7). These circuits were activated by an electronic pulse sent from a proximity detector located on the projector, which responded to small pieces of metallic tape, added by the projectionist to the film strip at the appropriate points. Because the specific programme routines and the projection apparatus differed at each cinema (for example, the curtains in one cinema might take a few seconds longer to open than in another), it became part of the projectionist's routine to add or alter the metallic strips in accordance with the particularities of their cinema whilst making-up the film, and then removing them when breaking down the film. With the arrival of long-running projection systems and basic computers, automation units could be placed on a computer-controlled timer that allowed a fortnight's worth of films to be pre-scheduled. As Chris Blower notes, 'we could programme two weeks in advance, but we used to do a week because we used to get the timesheets week-by-week'. This greatly simplified the projection process. 'You could build a playlist up and keep it in there forever, basically', Blower recalls, noting that only the timings required alteration on a weekly basis to accommodate the new schedule of films.

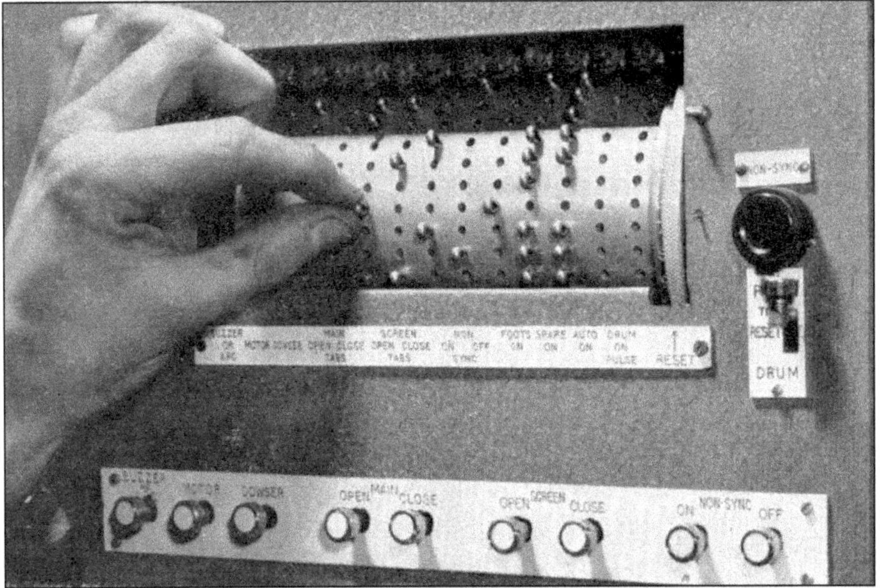

Fig. 1.7: The programming mechanism for the Essoldomatic automation system.[148]

148 R. Howard Cricks, 'A Device that Runs the Show', *ibid.*, 15 January 1953, p. 8.

Although greatly simplifying the projection process, Brad Atwill remembers that this computerised equipment was not particularly advanced:

> all your 35mm shows would be programmed into a really old computer that was actually running Windows 3.1 with a '95 emulator as if that made it better, and some really old Kinoton software in broken English. The warning message did actually say 'Achtung!' when it came up. ... Everything was scheduled up on the Thursday, then you check your daily film times just to make sure that no one made a mistake. ... [I]t was very rudimentary, but it did the job perfectly fine which is why the computer never had a big change. It was a nice blend of raw machinery with a little bit of digital and computerised ingenuity in the background.[149]

Blower recognises this technological aid as a step on the road to digitalisation, arguing that using the computerised timer system 'was like looking into the future because it's what we ... do with the digital playlist pretty much, just a really basic version of it'. The combination of the automatic projection system with the non-rewind platter provided a context in which the projectionist merely had to re-lace the projectors between screenings and the automation unit would take care of the rest. This potential had been recognised by some commentators when the cake stand had its first demonstration at Film '69; one reporter observed that 'I see no reason why [automated circuits and the platter system] should not be used in conjunction to provide between them a fully automated programme, using a single projector.'[150] This, the *Ideal Kinema* noted later in the year, meant that the system was 'of especial interest in those cases where there are two or more theatres in the same building and which can be operated through semi-automation systems by a reduced staff'.[151]

The possibility of single-manning a projection box that fed several screens drastically transformed the type and quality of labour undertaken by the projectionist. Rather than having to pay detailed attention to one screen, their responsibilities could be spread far more thinly in the service of multiple auditoria, and projection boxes were subsequently designed to facilitate this process. Prior to the purpose-built multiplex, many multi-screen cinemas had been created by re-configuring existing single-screen super cinemas. Generally referred to as 'twinning', this usually involved converting the circle seating into a separate screen of its own and appears to have been first introduced by Rank at the Odeon

149 Interview with Brad Atwill, conducted by Richard Wallace, 10 November 2014.

150 'Film '69 Report', *Kinematograph Weekly*, 5 July 1969, p. 20.

151 R.H. Bomback, 'Philips "no rewind" system for projection', *Ideal Kinema*, 9 August 1969, p. 25.

Nottingham in 1964.[152] Further modification could be achieved by dividing the lower stalls into two smaller screens, 'tripling' the original one-screen cinema into a three-screen venue.[153] This often required two small projection boxes – one on each level – to service these three screens, and therefore also required more than one projectionist to adequately and safely run the three simultaneous shows occurring across multiple levels. Simon Allen recalls the arrival of single-manning within the Odeon chain in the early 1970s by noting that 'the places that were a single screen, that's when you got single manning coming in'; however, if the larger cinemas had been 'tripled', as they often were during the 1960s, the management 'sort of reluctantly conceded that you probably did need more than one person to be on there'. The combination of automation and cake-stands meant that this was increasingly not always the case, and Chandra Makwana recalls single-manning being implemented in a split-level cinema by installing platters in all three screens and an automation system on the upper level, meaning that the projectionist only needed to find time to re-lace the pre-timed projector between shows; otherwise, they were left to oversee the two platters in the lower box.

The purpose-built multiplex projection box, however, was designed with an eye towards single-manning, and although the screens themselves operated as discrete units, the projection boxes tended to take the form of 'one long continuous room', running down the middle of the building.[154] Brad Atwill describes the projection box at the Cineworld (formerly Virgin Cinema), Boldon Colliery as 'just one long corridor with eleven screens running off either side of it. And in the middle we had our working area and a door into our own sort of kitchen and bathroom area, so we didn't ever have to go downstairs really.'

Adrian Pearce, who began working as a projectionist at Coventry's 14-screen Showcase cinema in 2000, gives an impression of how his day began in a multiplex box:

> they used to show films from 10:00am all the way through until 1:00am ... if it was a weekend it would be a 3:00am finish ... Usually you get in an hour before the first film's due to start ... and then usually you finish about half an hour after the last film finishes ... and you could quite often do the whole shift from 9:00am straight through. The first job of the day would be to have a quick once-over of the projectors, clean any dust off the rollers, lenses and so forth,

152 Allen Eyles, *Odeon Cinemas 2: From J. Arthur Rank to the Multiplex* (London: Cinema Theatre Association, 2005), p. 104.

153 For an overview of twinning and tripling, see *ibid.*, pp. 103-113.

154 Bill Chew, 'Projection Room Design in Multiplexes', *Cinema Technology*, 15:4 (2002), p. 18.

> and then it'd be a case of pre-lacing each show so then it'd be ready to start. They were automated, so you could put it on a timer.[155]

The early part of the day, therefore, comprised a process of preparing all of the screens for action and ensuring that the automated timers were set correctly. 'Although they'd be started automatically, you still are best to check that they have actually started properly', Pearce recalls. 'You would make sure everything's working correctly,' he continues, noting that although 'you'd have to do that for every screening anyway, the first showing is always the one that you'd have to check more than the others, just to check that the picture is as it should be and the sound is as it should be'. However, Atwill acknowledges that 'You try to be at each one as it's starting up just to make sure,' but that 'When you're plate-spinning so many screens it's tough.' In a situation where multiple screens were starting at the same time, 'you'd kind of position yourself between [them]' and then 'every sort of ten minutes or so you're doing a lap of [the box] just to check what's on the screen, make sure everything's okay ... so you would catch a lot of them as they're starting up anyway'.

Once all of the screens were up and running, the time was then split between daily maintenance tasks and a rigorous checking routine. Rachel Dukes notes that

> it was quite a hard environment to work in because you were always chasing time, so this is why you would put in place a series of checks to make sure that you've got things as correct as you can be. ... [I]n the big multiplexes you could be doing anything up to 72 shows in a day and it was quite a challenge really to be able to run that.

Pearce agrees, noting that

> Because [there were] fourteen [screens] ... an hour ... would be the maximum time where everything's running and you've not got to lace a film. Then, once that hour's up, they gradually all start coming off, and then they've got to go back on again. Usually there were five to six screenings a day [per screen], sometimes seven if it was a short film, so it was pretty constant. And even in that hour when everything's on, usually you're making a film up or you're sorting trailers out, adverts, breaking another film down or just basic maintenance cleaning ... There was something to do all the time, and quite often you wouldn't sit down, you were just attending to something constantly.

155 Atwill's account of his morning routine speaks to the minor differences that can be observed between individual cinemas. After 'a quick cuppa', he notes that the first job was to 'wander along, check [that] whoever was on the night before has laced up the first film for the next day'. This suggests a different protocol to Pearce. Rather than lacing up first thing in the morning – as was Showcase policy – at Cineworld, after 'your last show of a night you'd lace up the one for the next morning and then switch the projector off' so that 'the next morning when you came in it's all ready to go'. Atwill also recalls that his team kept 'a sort of diary' to enable each shift worker to signal any significant issues that their successor would need to pick up, 'so the first hour is just familiarising yourself with what's gone on since the last time you were in and getting your first shows all set and ready to go.'

This compact schedule meant that if something did go wrong with one of the projectors, it was unlikely that the projectionist would be standing beside it at the time. A dual system of acute sensory perception and technological fail-safes were employed to alert those in the box to faults as they developed. Andrew MacLean suggests that good projectionists have historically been 'very attuned to the machines' and that they can 'hear a bad join from a long, long way away; it's something that you just instinctively know'. This sentiment is echoed by John Neal of the Curzon cinema in Clevedon, who compares the sensory relationship between the projectionist and their machine with that of a driver and their car:

> you get to know the vagaries of the equipment and you're comfortable with it. It's uncanny how you get used to a sound. It's like driving your car. You get to know if something's wrong with the car; it doesn't feel right; it doesn't sound right. It's the same with a projector and you think 'Why's it making that noise?' ... [T]here's a little click, or the tone isn't quite right, and sure enough if you investigate it more closely you find that you've lost a bit of your loop or there's a bearing that's wearing. There's a whole range of things that you become sensitive to.

Although this instinct was a key skill during earlier periods, it became particularly important in the multiplex context, where projectionists were no longer wedded to the projectors. Atwill recalls that 'With that many projectors, you can work off sound quite a lot', reiterating MacLean's and Neal's observations that 'you can hear if something doesn't sound quite right. You can hear if a platter is struggling to keep up, or if a lens has just clunked rather than nicely slid into place, or lamps ticking and struggling to strike. So, that's probably what would alert you first.'

The projectionist was aided in the diagnostic process by a computerised system of alarms that would monitor the progress of each projector and alert the projectionist should anything appear amiss. Pearce notes that there were 'fail safes' located in various parts of the projector mechanism. 'There used to be one if the xenon lamp would go out,' he recalls, and there was a 'drop roller' below the gate which would 'signify a film snap, because they stay tight when the film's going through and then if there's no film they drop and then the alarms would go off'. These sensors would feed information to a central computer, with status displays strategically placed around the box. 'We had monitors placed in [various] areas', Atwill recalls. 'We had one in the kitchen and a few throughout the corridors, so that you can see every screen and you know what is programmed to show next and what position it's at ... you can kind of see at a glance, wherever you are, what every screen is doing.'

Although the platters were much safer and generally more reliable than older models of projector, the projectionist's inability to attend closely to each and every screen at all times meant that things did go wrong that may well have been avoided if a larger team of projectionists had been employed to take greater care of the show. It also meant that if something did go awry the results could be more serious and more difficult to rectify. Atwill recalls one incident in which the projector was working, but 'the take up platter had stopped spinning'. He stresses that

> Nobody in the screening would have been any the wiser because their film was still playing beautifully on screen. Yet, in the projection booth! It's another one of those where you can hear ... [something's] not right [and you] go up to the horror of film piling up underneath the projector.

This resulted in a frantic process of winding the film onto regular spools until the end of the screening to avoid further disruption: 'Then it was just spending hours winding on all the film that had dropped and ... making a couple of repairs here and there'.

More common are stories of the projectionist arriving in the box just in time to see 'the film disappear off the side of the platter onto the floor', as Ken Bagnall puts it.[156] Peter Douglas recalls an incident where a power surge had caused the platter to speed up suddenly 'and sort of flung the film off', but such incidents were usually the result of the take-up platter running unusually fast or slow. Such problems were exacerbated by the arrival of polyester film, which was much stronger than the acetate safety film, and less prone to tearing and snapping. Although generally a positive development so far as visible film damage was concerned, this property of polyester prints had some unintended consequences in that it could stop the film from breaking when placed under unusual strain. Alan Foster recalled that if the projector did not shut off when the film jammed then '[it] was so strong that it actually physically moved the projector' and Neil Thompson recalls that if the projectionist didn't attend to a rapid build-up in tension quickly 'it would pull all your rollers off and cause a lot of damage'. This led to the addition of sensors to the apparatus that would shut the projector down in the event of excessive strain being detected.

156 Interview with Ken Bagnall, conducted by Richard Wallace, 17 September 2015.

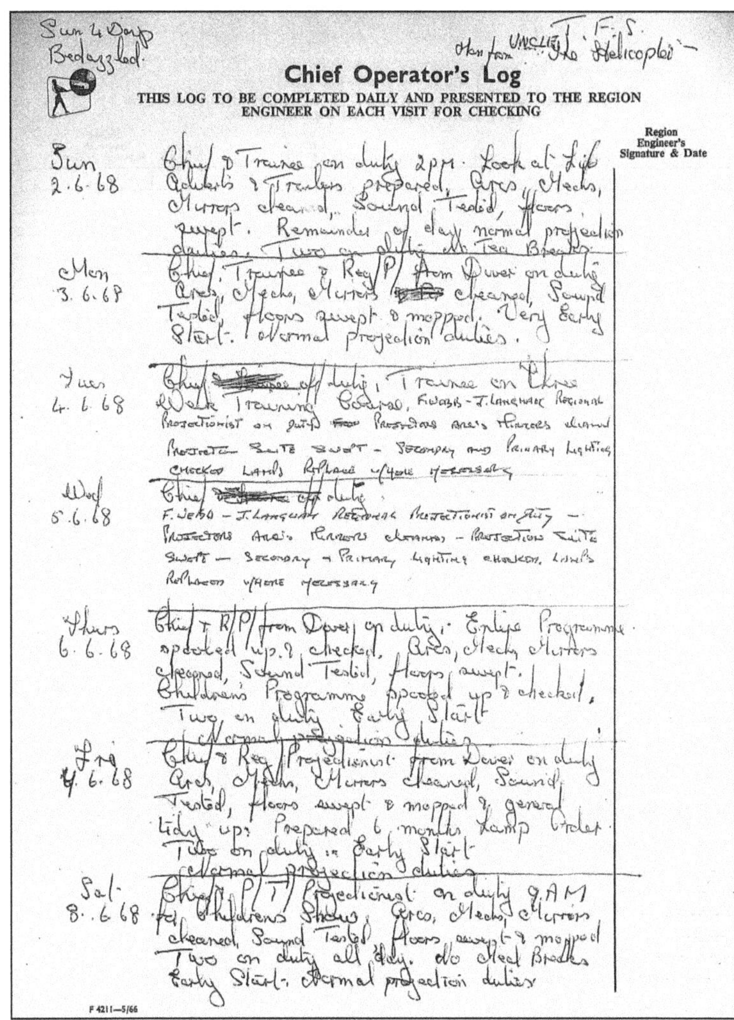

Chief Operator's Log

THIS LOG TO BE COMPLETED DAILY AND PRESENTED TO THE REGION ENGINEER ON EACH VISIT FOR CHECKING

Region Engineer's Signature & Date

F 4211—5/66

Fig. 1.8: The weekly schedule for the Odeon, Sevenoaks for the week beginning Sunday 2 June 1968, with Bedazzled screening from Sunday to Wednesday and The Helicopter Spies (a compilation of Man from U.N.C.L.E. television episodes) screening from Thursday to Saturday, with a children's matinee on the Saturday morning.[157]

Another area where the labour process was intensified was in the making-up and breaking down of prints. A typical one-screen cinema prior to 1970 would usually show around three separate programmes in a single calendar week (usually including a Saturday morning children's matinee) (Fig. 1.8). This would result in a total of between three and five feature-length film prints, plus an accompanying short and single reel of adverts and trailers, having

157 'Chief Operator's log book, Gaumont Cinema (Odeon Cinema), Jordan Well, Coventry', PA118/1-1-4, Coventry History Centre.

to be prepared for screening and then packed away by the projection team each week. In contrast, each platter of a fourteen-screen multiplex could contain two films, each with their own programme of adverts and trailers, making a potential total of 28 film prints, and a similar number of ad reels, that would need to be made-up and broken down each week. Depending on the weekly schedule and how far in advance the films for the following week arrived in the cinema, much of this process would take place across one day. Although the first day of the cinema week has changed over time, for much of the multiplex era it has been Friday, meaning that Thursday was usually the projection room's busiest day and one of the few days where more than one projectionist would be on shift at the same time.

Newly arrived films would be made up at some point between their arrival at the cinema (which could be anything between a week and a matter of minutes in advance of their first screening) and spooled onto the platter once there was sufficient space. However, a logistical problem unique to the multiplex was created by the expansion both of the number of films any one cinema could show at a time *and* the increased window of time in which each film might be shown. Individual film prints would often remain within the venue for multiple weeks, moving between different sized screens as determined by demand, or, as a 2002 article on multiplex design stated, 'newly released films are shown in the "main auditoria" and are then relegated to the smaller screens over time to make way for new releases'.[158] Pearce recalls that the decision on which films were to move 'came from head office so we'd have no clue' in advance, and that, because these decisions were made remotely, they didn't always make logical sense when applied to the specifics of the individual cinema. 'Quite often you'd have screens that are the same size but ... they used to flip the films round', Pearce notes, whilst Brad Atwill points out that in some circumstances 'you would get [a film] that will play on one screen during the day and switch to a different one on the night', necessitating the film having to be carried between platters in the middle of the day.

Perhaps the most notable aspect of the Thursday evening routine is that it was one of the few points during the week when the projectionist would not be working alone in the box. This loneliness is an aspect of single-manned projection routines that a number of projectionists have commented upon. Peter Douglas suggests that

> you had to have an attitude of mind where I suppose you could cope with [being on your own], where you didn't have someone else to

158 Bill Chew, 'Projection Room Design in Multiplexes', *Cinema Technology*, 15(4) (December 2002), p. 18.

> depend on, or someone else to talk to even. You spent your time running around making sure you were in the right place at the right time and doing the right thing.

Chris Tweddell notes that 'as a projectionist, it's very, very easy to slip into that lonely, "never see anybody" [mindset], and you'll meet these people who didn't want to interact with anybody'. Thursday evenings were embraced by projectionists like Atwill, who recalls that 'Even though it was the busiest night of the week, it was the one you looked forward to because you were on shift with somebody for a change'.

What is clear about the arrangement of the technology and the working practices is that the multi-screen array represents a clear step towards the style of projection found within a modern digital projection room, where, with very few exceptions, there are no longer dedicated projectionists. The development of labour-saving projection equipment was a response to personnel shortages and economic pressures within the industry, and removed many of the safety issues found within the technologies of earlier periods, whilst offering a lower potential for errors to be introduced into the projection process because the film itself was handled far less frequently. As the director of the Star Cinemas circuit argued as early as 1960, 'The combination of Projectomatic and the Xenon lamp represents the finest development in the industry for ensuring faultless presentation.'[159] However, the combination of the non-rewind platter, automation and single-manning employment policies meant that the erosion of human agency, first seen in the industry with the introduction of motor-driven projectors in the 1910s, accelerated dramatically during the multiplex era. No longer would a team of projectionists be able to give their full attention to the quality of projection at an individual screen across the duration of the screening, and this extended to their capacity to spot and rectify problems as they developed. The more intricate projection and automation equipment, combined with a lower level of technical proficiency from the multiplex projectionist, meant that an issue that could once have been fixed by the projection team was either delegated to an engineer or else could no longer be fixed in a timely manner. Recalling a jammed intermittent sprocket, Adrian Pearce adds that

> that was a job that I couldn't fix because (a), we didn't have any spare intermittent units, and (b), I wasn't trained. That was a big job; you had to take out every gear unit and change it. So, that would be a case of phoning up our head office technical team, and someone would usually come down from Leeds or somewhere like that; so, that

159 'The Press-button Age in Projection', *Ideal Kinema*, 10 March 1960, p. 28.

> screen then would be off for a number of hours until they could fix it.

Peter Douglas, who worked with the majority of the projection arrays discussed in this chapter, argues in relation to the changes introduced to the industry by the platter that

> if for some reason you got a break, [because the film is] going round all these rollers and everything, it was a good twenty to thirty minutes to get that all sorted out and back on the screen. The old methods we used to use at least got the shows on quickly, but with some of the new equipment there was a bigger delay and sometimes even shows have to be cancelled.

This removal of agency is characterised by the reduction in the size of projection teams from the five-person (or more), single-screen teams of the 1930s, '40s and '50s to the single-manned multiplex of the 1990s and 2000s. Phil Fawke highlights the stark transformation in the industry between his first position in 1940, as a fifth projectionist at the Regal Cinema, Leamington Spa, and his retirement in 2008 by observing that 'when I started there were five projectionists for one [single-screen] theatre, then there used to be three projectionists for a multiplex of about 12 screens, and now it's one technician for a multiplex'. This is a trend that found its ultimate expression in the digital boxes of the 21st century, where in most cases the projectionist was removed altogether from the projection process - a development that will be explored in detail in Chapter Four.

A 'Jack-of-All-Trades'

So far, the activities outlined in the chapter have been limited to an exploration of the labour required simply to get a celluloid film print onto the cinema screen at various points in the evolving landscape of cinema projection. However, as we suggested at the start of this chapter, this represents only a portion of the work undertaken by members of the projection team. Much of the rest of this work was of a manual character, that was both mundane and time-consuming.[160] The volume of this non-projection work was, to some extent, array-dependent (with more of the job being taken up in this manner with the 'xenon array' than the 'multi-screen array', for example). However, some non-projection elements persisted across all time periods, and so the activities

160 Another strand of work that is worthy of mention stemmed from the use of large cinemas as venues for 'one night two-performance stands by touring pop groups' throughout the 1960s, a situation that Allen Eyles puts down to the fall in cinema attendance (*Odeon Cinemas 2*, p. 86). The projectionist would be involved in various aspects of a show's staging, from setting up the stage (Douglases), checking the safety curtain and being a general 'gofer' (both Allen) to lighting the performance (Allen) and even mixing the sound (Douglases). Indeed, John Douglas admits that he 'did make some illicit recordings' of certain acts.

documented here are not so strictly regimented by array as the labour described previously in this chapter.

Logbooks compiled by Florence Barton, the chief projectionist at the Odeon, Sevenoaks, between 1967 and 1972, still exist and provide an itemised account of the daily work undertaken by the projection team (Fig. 1.8). Of particular note is the repeated use of the phrase 'Normal projection duties', which serves as shorthand to cover most of the routine work involved in actually screening films. Below are two fairly typical examples of daily summaries:

> Monday 2 October 1967
>
> Chief & 3rd on duty. Arcs, mechs and mirrors cleaned. Sound Tested, floor swept and mopped. Circle Extractor fan thoroughly washed with Paraffin & greased & oiled. Royal Ballet spooled up & checked. Remainder of day normal projection duties.
>
> Friday 26 July 1968
>
> Westrex Engineer Service Day. 2nd off duty, Chief & Trainee on duty. Arcs, Mechs, Mirrors cleaned, Sound Tested, floors swept. Café & lounge & Stalls Entrance taken down & washed. Top of canopy swept. Continued painting walls Resistance Room. Normal projection duties.[161]

The concluding phrase is used almost every day on which Barton completed the entry and, in occluding much of the work done actually projecting film, it gives space to the rest of the projectionist's labour, which comes to dominate the logbooks.

A number of other sources published in the first half of the last century give a good general overview of the kinds of non-projection work required of projectionists. The first of these is a letter, published in *Kinematograph Weekly* in 1926 under the title 'The Jack of All Trades' and signed 'for obvious reasons' by 'Early Bird'. 'Early Bird' complains that in enquiring about a job advert for an operator-electrician to work a once-nightly show – described by the employer as 'an easy job, with nothing much to do' – it became clear that the job actually entailed the following:

- Operator must be an electrician and understand the gas engine and be able to carry out his own repairs.
- Clean the hall daily; twice on Saturdays.
- Whiten the borders in the entrance and balcony stairs once weekly, and the screen once a month.
- Keep the seating in good repair.

161 'Chief Operator's log book, Gaumont Cinema (Odeon Cinema), Jordan Well, Coventry', PA118/1-1-4, Coventry History Centre. Although this artefact has been catalogued as showing the daily routines at the above listed cinema, it is clear from the details within the logbooks that they in fact pertain to the Odeon, Sevenoaks, another cinema at which the chief projectionist, Florence Barton, is known to have worked.

- Post the front of Hall and do the billing round the town ...
- Operate and keep in running repair the projector, with no assistant.
- Take films to station.
- Act as stage manager when Companies are engaged, and fit up their scenery, etc.
- Look after gas engine and generator, keeping them spotlessly clean, all brass and steelwork polished and the concrete beds kept whitened.
- Write slides and assemble programme board; clean windows, wash and scrub floors when necessary.
- Keep lavatories clean and lime-washed once a month.
- Expect to work Sunday when required without remuneration.
- Keep the show free from dust on ledges, door frames, etc., and generally look after the place single-handed.
- See that the night staff of attendants and cashiers are at their posts in time for opening and then open the doors and start at the right time.
- No help in the daytime from any source.
- Must be married and a total abstainer.
- Should the feature film not turn up by 1 p.m., to go to the managing partner's house and inform him, and then proceed to the office of the other partner to 'phone as per instructions.
- **All this was required for the magnificent sum of three pounds per week.**

The letter concludes with the assertion that 'it will be agreed that it is most unfair to expect an operator to carry out all these duties and do justice to them' and that 'the proprietors and managers should be made to realise that hours and conditions of labour must be within reason, instead of expecting the most important members of their staff being jack of all trades'.[162] Things had scarcely improved fourteen years later when, in March 1940, the CEA attempted to quantify and classify the duties of the projectionist in a document submitted to the Ministry of Labour. It began by observing that the job title of 'projectionist' was 'a misnomer, in so far as it indicates that the sole duty of such men is to operate projection apparatus', when in fact their responsibilities covered:

162 'Early Bird', 'The Jack of All Trades', *Kinematograph Weekly*, 29 July 1926, p. 57.

(a)The picture projection apparatus.

(b)The optical and light producing apparatus.

(c)The rotary or static electric conversion apparatus for the supply of the light-producing apparatus.

(d)The similar equipment for the supply of electric current to secondary batteries (where installed) used for emergency lighting, and including maintenance of such batteries.

(e)Electric motors and apparatus used for heating and ventilation purposes, including oil-burning and mechanically-fed heating boilers where no stoker is employed.

(f)The sound-producing and amplifying apparatus.

(g)The stage electrical and mechanical equipment, where installed, and where short variety turns are staged.

(h)The general electrical installation, apart from the foregoing items.[163]

This submission was part of an attempt to convince the wartime government that projectionists over the age of 25 should be placed on the list of reserved occupations protected from military conscription, arguing that cinemas could not adequately replace them and would not be able to stay open without them. One might, therefore, be tempted to suspect the CEA of embellishing their case. However, this was actually a rather modest summary of the work that projectionists did, whether this be visible or invisible to cinema patrons, and in 1952 *Ideal Kinema* printed an article that itemised '60 separate pieces of electrical and technical equipment which the chief projectionist must watch and either keep in good order himself or, where items are highly specialised, call in the district engineer or the manufacturer's service engineer.'[164] An advert in the *Kinematograph Weekly*'s 'Situations Vacant' column from June 1969 – which indicates, without apparent irony, that the Aviemore Centre in Inverness-shire required a second projectionist 'Who is prepared to work a 26 hour day on a variety of duties i.e. Cinema, Conferences, P.A. Systems, Live Shows, Etc.' – suggests that these working conditions continued to develop and diversify right up to the multiplex era.[165] Indeed, the interviews we have conducted with projectionists describe in great detail many tasks that might appear to be ancillary to the work of projection, but which did, in fact, make up a much of the day-to-day work in the pre-multiplex era.

163 'New C.E.A. Appeal for Reservation of Operators', *ibid.*, 7 March 1940, p. 3.

164 G.E. Fielding, 'The Essential Knowledge to Put Prevention Before Cure', *Ideal Kinema*, 13 March 1952, pp. 6-7.

165 'Situations Vacant', *Kinematograph Weekly*, 28 June 1969, p. 26. This publication's 'situations vacant' column provides a wealth of information as to the number and kinds of projection roles available at any given point between 1907 and 1970; for our purposes here, it is worth noting that positions were often advertised for an 'operator-electrician', demonstrating the multiple requirements of the role.

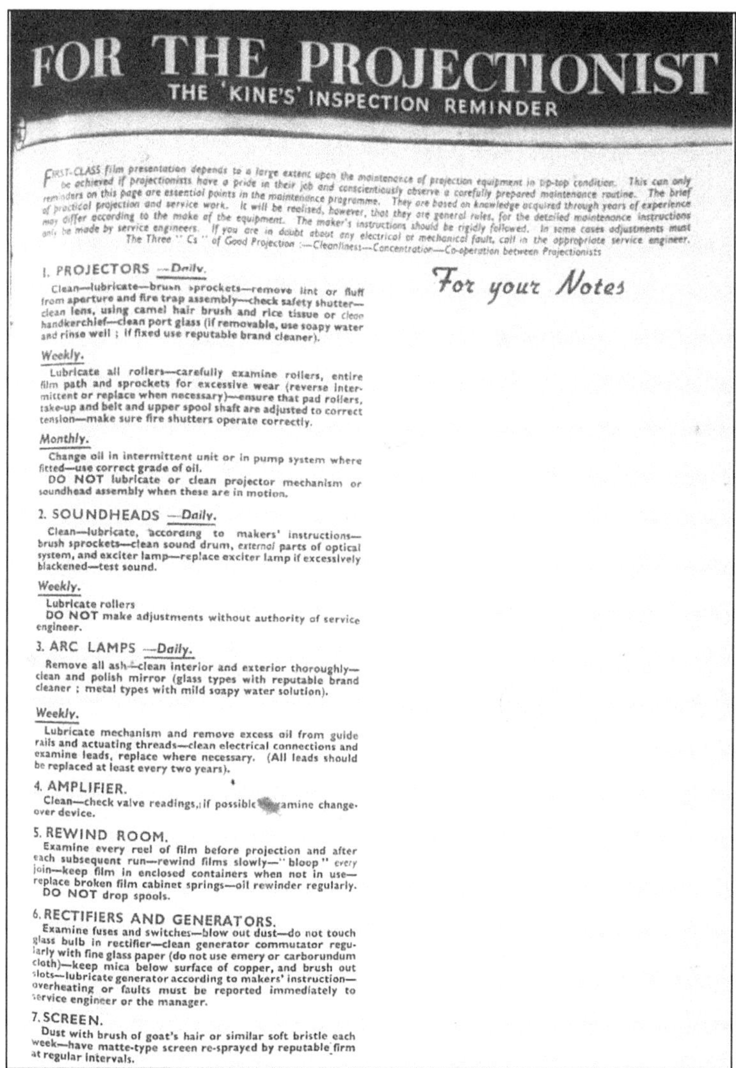

FOR THE PROJECTIONIST

THE 'KINE'S' INSPECTION REMINDER

FIRST-CLASS film presentation depends to a large extent upon the maintenance of projection equipment in tip-top condition. This can only be achieved if projectionists have a pride in their job and conscientiously observe a carefully prepared maintenance routine. The brief reminders on this page are essential points in the maintenance programme. They are based on knowledge acquired through years of experience of practical projection and service work. It will be realised, however, that they are general rules, for the detailed maintenance instructions may differ according to the make of the equipment. The maker's instructions should be rigidly followed. In some cases adjustments must only be made by service engineers. If you are in doubt about any electrical or mechanical fault, call in the appropriate service engineer.

The Three "Cs" of Good Projection :—Cleanliness—Concentration—Co-operation between Projectionists

1. PROJECTORS —*Daily.*

Clean—lubricate—brush sprockets—remove lint or fluff from aperture and fire trap assembly—check safety shutter—clean lens, using camel hair brush and rice tissue or clean handkerchief—clean port glass (if removable, use soapy water and rinse well ; if fixed use reputable brand cleaner).

Weekly.

Lubricate all rollers—carefully examine rollers, entire film path and sprockets for excessive wear (reverse intermittent or replace when necessary)—ensure that pad rollers, take-up and belt and upper spool shaft are adjusted to correct tension—make sure fire shutters operate correctly.

Monthly.

Change oil in intermittent unit or in pump system where fitted—use correct grade of oil.

DO NOT lubricate or clean projector mechanism or soundhead assembly when these are in motion.

2. SOUNDHEADS —*Daily.*

Clean—lubricate, according to makers' instructions—brush sprockets—clean sound drum, *external* parts of optical system, and exciter lamp—replace exciter lamp if excessively blackened—test sound.

Weekly.

Lubricate rollers

DO NOT make adjustments without authority of service engineer.

3. ARC LAMPS —*Daily.*

Remove all ash—clean interior and exterior thoroughly—clean and polish mirror (glass types with reputable brand cleaner ; metal types with mild soapy water solution).

Weekly.

Lubricate mechanism and remove excess oil from guide rails and actuating threads—clean electrical connections and examine leads, replace where necessary. (All leads should be replaced at least every two years).

4. AMPLIFIER.

Clean—check valve readings, if possible examine change-over device.

5. REWIND ROOM.

Examine every reel of film before projection and after each subsequent run—rewind films slowly—"bloop" every join—keep film in enclosed containers when not in use—replace broken film cabinet springs—oil rewinder regularly.

DO NOT drop spools.

6. RECTIFIERS AND GENERATORS.

Examine fuses and switches—blow out dust—do not touch glass bulb in rectifier—clean generator commutator regularly with fine glass paper (do not use emery or carborundum cloth)—keep mica below surface of copper, and brush out slots—lubricate generator according to makers' instruction—overheating or faults must be reported immediately to service engineer or the manager.

7. SCREEN.

Dust with brush of goat's hair or similar soft bristle each week—have matte-type screen re-sprayed by reputable firm at regular intervals.

For your Notes

Fig. 1.9: A suggested maintenance routine for projection equipment.[166]

Cleaning projectors

A key part of the projectionist's work was what Michael Marder has characterised as 'a doomed fight against dispersed dry matter' – dust – which has the potential to degrade.[167] Adrian Pearce reiterates the importance of cleaning as part of this fight, noting the labour intensive effect of this in a multiplex environment:

166 'For Your Projectionist', *ibid.*, 14 Dec 1950, p. 155

167 Michael Marder, *Dust* (London: Bloomsbury, 2016), p. 3.

> the biggest enemy of the 35mm film was dust and dirt because it could degrade the film quite dramatically. Even if you left it just a couple of days not cleaning the projector, it would cause a lot of damage to a print. So ... you would have to clean almost every roller on the projector ... at least twice a week.

Controlling the dust – which the *Ideal Kinema* once characterised as 'The cause of ALL the Trouble' – naturally extended beyond the projector itself and into the box as a whole.[168] Sam Lavington recalls that 'Projection rooms were kept very, very clean', and Peter Douglas's account of his morning routine includes the fact that 'We had to make sure the projectors were always clean and the rewinding benches were spotless and the projection room itself was clean. Because film attracts dust, of course, so you'd keep everything as clean as possible.' Comments on the clinical cleanliness of projection rooms are a common trope in our interviews. This is epitomised in Mike Williams's account of entering the projection box at the Olympia Cinema, Cardiff for the first time in 1956:

> everything was highly polished. I've never seen anything like it in my life. Even though they were only painted cement floors they were polished so highly you could see your face in the damned things. Everywhere was gleaming and my first impression was operating theatre status here, you know, it was so clean.

Once the projectors were cleaned and ready to be laced up, and the projection room was ready for the show, attention spread to other areas of the cinema building. Cinemas developed routines for when and how often equipment needed testing and maintaining, as is indicated in a 1950 'inspection schedule' for projectionists (Fig. 1.9). Chris Blower notes that 'depending what day of the week it was, we'd go round and do screen checks. Check the screen condition, check the light on the screen, check all the speakers were working, things like that.' The condition of the screen was obviously an important factor, and Brad Atwill notes that the screen would be brushed down on a weekly basis. The Sevenoaks logbooks also suggest that, in tandem with the screen checks, there would be an assessment of the sonic conditions within the theatre, and 'Sound Tested' is a phrase used on a daily basis.

Other maintenance would also take place in the auditorium. Frank Gibson recalls that the projectionist would attend to 'any loose seating, you'd check them out and make sure that's alright' and that, although in more recent times a cinema might get a contractor to carry out this sort of job, 'while you're waiting for them to come in you might as well do the job yourself because you know you're

168 G.E. Fielding, 'The Essential Knowledge to Put Prevention Before Cure', *Ideal Kinema*, 13 March 1952, p. 7.

going to do a better job than they do, because they want to be in and out, and be somewhere else'. The curtains in the theatre also needed attention, and Thompson notes that 'now and again you had to go down onto the stage to make sure that the masking was okay. You had to keep an eye on the masking cables to make sure they were taut or if they were frayed you had to get them replaced and you had to make sure the curtain motors were okay'.

Phil Fawke recalls that another key job undertaken by projectionists 'was to clean all the light fittings in the auditorium and replace all the bulbs'; the scale of this task is emphasised by Peter Douglas's observation that 'you'd be amazed how many lightbulbs are in a cinema, and it was our job every day to go round and check every one of those lightbulbs to make sure they were on'. This included the auditorium but also the lamps in the toilets, the exit signs and other public areas. Although working in a multiplex some decades after Fawke and Douglas began their careers, Adrian Pearce recalls that the projection team 'had to make sure every light bulb in the building was lit' and that 'we used to have spot checks every month. Head Office used to come in and even one light bulb out used to go down as a bad mark, so to speak.'

Given the ornate design of many cinema buildings of the pre-multiplex era, and the size of many individual screens within these buildings, it is not surprising that replacing lamps was not always an easy, clean, or particularly safe job. Frank Gibson recalls that because audience members were permitted to smoke, cleaning the lamp fittings in the auditorium 'was quite a big job because ... they were always thick with gunge'. Mike Williams seconds Gibson's assessment, noting that his 'favourite hate job was cleaning house lights' and that he would 'go up into the ceiling void ... with buckets of hot water and wash the nicotine, such a filthy job ... You'd go in early ... get up there and start scrubbing house light fittings and hope you'd be finished by the time the show started.'[169]

Maintenance

Alongside the cleaning there was a great deal of electrical and other laborious work to do around the cinema, including the weekly examination of electrical fuses,[170] and the re-greasing of extractor fans.[171] Williams notes that

> there were so many other jobs that a projectionist used to do beside projecting film ... [A]ll the signage in the cinema would be cleaned by the projectionists; some degree of painting would be done by

169 John Young recalls changing lights *during* screenings, noting that 'The only danger was that you had to make sure you didn't drop any bulbs down through the hole or they just land on the audience.'

170 'Rules for Projectionists', *Kinematograph Weekly*, 31 October 1935, p. 62.

171 J. Whitnall, 'Running the Show – II', *Ideal Kinema*, 6 November 1941, p. xii.

> projectionists; rewiring would be done by projectionists. So, it was quite a complex job beside showing film.

Neil Thompson suggests that much of this non-projection work was a product of the projectionist's unique position as 'the sole technical guy in the cinema', and Simon Allen suggests that, because of this, 'you ended up getting all the jobs like repairing the usherette's ice cream trays, making sure the light worked and the batteries were in it'. Much of the day-to-day work involved similar minor electrical fixes and small maintenance jobs. Thompson recalls fixing kettles and mending vacuum cleaners, and Ray Reed remembers with some distaste that once long-playing projection systems came into circulation, greater demand was made on projectionists working in small cinemas, who found themselves with time to spare during the screening: 'you'd get more building maintenance jobs to do when they were running. And it was stupid little jobs like a blocked toilet, or the hot dog machine had gone off; silly little things like that. It was quite mind bending.'

John Young recalls arriving at work one morning to find his colleague dealing with a blocked toilet, standing 'in about half a foot of sewage with a rod poking down the toilet to get it away'. As he notes, 'nobody had thought about getting a plumber'; instead, it was simply a case of 'call the projectionist, he'll clear it up'. Although working in different cities and in roughly different time periods (though with a twenty-year overlap) this is a sentiment that is almost directly replicated by Peter Douglas when he notes that 'anything that went wrong in the cinema ... first person they call is the projectionist, you know; "He'll sort it out."' It is no wonder that the phrase 'jack of all trades' appears a number of times in the interviews we conducted, and in the projection columns of the trade press, and Frank Gibson acknowledges that to be a competent projectionist 'I tell you, you've got to be an all-rounder'.[172]

In modern cinemas, particularly smaller independent cinemas and arts venues that still employ technical staff, this work has continued, and, with the digitalisation of film projection, it has perhaps even come to dominate the 'technician's' daily routine. As Brad Atwill, Technical Manager at The Tyneside Cinema, Newcastle, notes, his team are responsible for

> the building maintenance, the IT for the whole building and any live events as well. It's pretty much at the point where if it plugs in we fix it; it's our responsibility. Often, if it doesn't plug in, that's also our responsibility ... [A] lot of maintenance-y things get passed down to you ... I spend probably about 70% of the day out of the projection booth doing other things. ... [A] general technician here will be in and out the booths and unfortunately, and through no fault of their

172 The phrase is specifically used by Peter Douglas and John Young.

> own, for no lack of caring, won't have a great deal of time just to look at the film side of things. ... [Y]ou spend your day firefighting more than anything else.

More complicated jobs were also within the purview of the projection staff. Simon Allen notes that as well as these minor maintenance fixes, the projectionist was considered responsible for 'all the heating, making sure you knew how to operate the boiler and check how much fuel was in there'. Although Allen recalls that 'you had an engineer that you could call out if there was a problem', because 'there were some things that you just couldn't do', in many cases the knowledge gained from watching the regional engineer in action meant that even some of these overly-technical jobs were picked up over time. 'Over the years you'd had lots of experience,' Allen recalls, and you'd 'know how to fix this, so you could do lots of first-line maintenance'. The extent to which this kind of work was an expected duty of the projectionist is made clear in Ray Reed's account of attending training sessions in the mid-1960s: 'when I started for Rank, when you went on a course down to London, it wouldn't be so much projection; it was like oil-fired burner maintenance, things like that, because that was part of your job'.

Publicity

From the 1910s through to the 1940s, projectionists were tasked with producing lantern slides to announce forthcoming attractions, communicate messages from cinema management or to advertise local businesses.[173] 'The genuine projectionist takes every interest in the success of his house', the chief at the Forum, Nottingham argued in 1941, suggesting that it was also part of their job to come up with ideas for front-of-house promotional displays.[174] Mike Williams recalls that he 'would do publicity for [the cinema], taking publicity around Cardiff and putting show cards everywhere around the City', and that he 'organised a few publicity schemes' when he was a rewind boy. Most memorable in this regard was the time he borrowed an elephant to publicise the release of the circus musical *Billy Rose's Jumbo* (USA, Charles Walters, 1962):

> Chipperfield's circus was in Cardiff, so I thought, on my way home, on my bicycle one day, I popped in and said 'could we borrow an elephant to go to the cinema?' and they thought it was great. They marched this damned elephant down through Cardiff into the cinema on the Sunday night. ... I thought it was a good thing to do. And the cinema thought it was wonderful, you know, they hadn't had

173 See, for example, 'Artistic Slides', *Kinematograph Weekly*, 31 May 1928, p. 63; 'An Artist in Slide Design', *Ideal Kinema*, 10 March 1949, p. 21.

174 J. Whitnall, 'Running the Show – III', *ibid.*, 4 December 1941, p. ix.

> many elephants go to the cinema. ... Wonderful publicity. And, of course, kudos for me, you know.

Most of the promotional work that extended beyond the projection box was not so creative, however. Projectionists were responsible for the upkeep of neon signage and other external publicity displays,[175] and Frank Gibson notes that 'putting the pictures in the quad frames outside, that job was ours as well'. These duties could occasionally lead to some hair-raising aerial acrobatics. Peter and John Douglas, for example, recall the process of changing the 'readergraph' at the Odeon cinema in Renfield Street, Glasgow. The former recalls the sign stretching 'the whole height of the front of the Odeon' and listing the films showing in each of the cinema's three screens. John explains that, because of its height, 'to change the film titles ... became the projectionist's job'. This was usually done on a Sunday morning because it required the use of a platform crane. He continues:

> We had a letter store where we kept all these letters, and during the week we had to sort out what the management wanted the writing to be. And then the Sunday morning would come, and we'd have to transport all these [letters] along to the front of the Odeon. We had to put a rope all round the pavements, and we got this crane, and two or three of us would get in this platform crane box and go up and down and up and down, backward and forward, taking off all the old letters and putting up all the new ones. And that used to take us a couple of hours on a Sunday morning.

Peter Douglas adds that the change of release day to Thursday meant the end of the readergraph because 'They wouldn't get permission on the busy weekday to have people out there going up and down halfway out in the road'.

To some extent, these accounts are imbued with the semi-humorous tinge of nostalgia for a bygone era. For the Douglases, the danger and, presumably, discomfort of re-lettering the readergraph (the Glasgow weather was surely not always obliging for two hours every Sunday morning) becomes a cosy anecdote, and Williams's colourful account of the elephant in some senses overwrites what may have been a resented bloat of the projectionist's duties. Indeed, the various extra responsibilities that were imposed upon projection staff were extremely contentious. Angry debates persisted over several decades as to whether it was fair that projectionists should be required to undertake bill-posting.[176] A disillusioned operator complained in 1926 that his duties at a small cinema in Devon he had just resigned from extended to

175 'Rules for Projectionists', *Kinematograph Weekly*, 31 October 1935, p. 62.

176 See, for example, '*Ich Dien*. – The Operator's Charter', *The Bioscope*, 6 February 1913, p. 399; 'Operator's Conditions', *Kinematograph Weekly*, 27 November 1930, p. 65; 'Chief Inquisitor T. O'Brien', *Ideal Kinema*, 8 June 1944, p. ix.

> billposting, house to house bill delivery, occasional seat mending, the care of a motor-bike and sidecar, sweeping the yard out and, once, digging it up with a pickaxe. Whilst I was there a pushcart was being constructed which was to be covered with posters and which it was *my* job to push this round the streets.[177]

This does not by any means represent an exhaustive list of the tasks undertaken by projectionists in order to ensure the safe, orderly and successful operation of their cinemas, and in the next chapter we will consider how the processes of film projection had a direct impact upon the form and quality of the viewing experience. Nevertheless, it is clear from this overview that, for the vast majority of cinema's history, the projectionist was one of the most important – if not *the* most important – member of staff in the cinema building. As well as maintaining the projection apparatus and ensuring that the film went on the screen when it was supposed to, they were also responsible for keeping the building in good working order across each of the different 'arrays' of cinema projection. For a final word on these considerable burdens, we turn to the particularly candid accounts left by Florence Barton.[178] In an archival interview conducted in the 1980s, she describes the projectionist as 'head cook and bottle-washer of the whole blithering place', and in the Odeon Sevenoaks logbooks her frustrations with the quantity and quality of the work is clear to see. Regularly exasperated by the unreliability of her junior colleagues, she frequently documents long days with little support, and few tea and meal breaks. On 27 December 1969, Barton notes that the combination of an early start, 'only ½ hr for lunch' and 'No tea break', meant that she was 'thoroughly cheesed off'. However, most pointedly, the net impact of single-manning of the cinema led to the following record of 1 February 1970: 'Chief on duty 11-AM to check arrival of programme. Entire programme spooled up & checked. Arcs, Mechs, Mirrors cleaned. Sound Tested. Lamp Check. Screening 5.41. Alone again. Talk about slave to the lamp.'

It is a stark reminder that although the interview material often recalls the laborious tasks undertaken by the projectionist in somewhat fond, nostalgic tones, in reality the work was frequently unpleasant. As such, the view of the projectionist as the 'head cook and bottle washer' and as a 'slave to the lamp' evocatively characterises the quantity and variety of work that the cinema projectionist was expected to undertake in cinema buildings throughout the 20th century, in order that the show continued to 'go on'.

177 'The Small Hall Operator', *Kinematograph Weekly*, 8 April 1926, p. 55.

178 For a more in-depth portrait of Barton, see Richard Wallace, Rebecca Harrison and Charlotte Brunsdon, 'Women in the Box: Female Projectionists in Post-war British Cinema', *Journal of British Cinema and Television*, 15:1 (January 2018), pp. 46-65.

Chapter Two

The Art of Cinema Projection

What did it mean to be a good projectionist? The Guild of British Kinema Projectionists and Engineers – a trade organisation operating between 1929 and 1943 – sought to encourage a perception of projectionists as '*craftsmen* and not *machine minders*'.[179] But can we meaningfully talk about an 'art' of projection? Did projectionists contribute to the development and consolidation of key aesthetic characteristics of the cinema? One of the relatively small number of journalists who commented upon the impending extinction of cinema projectionists, during the transition to digital projection, described the process as 'A quiet revolution ... going on behind your back', and posed the question: 'is this a good or a bad thing?'[180] The implication here is that the replacement of human projectionists with automated digital systems did not represent a form of change that audiences could actually be expected to notice upon the screen in front of them. We will argue that the agency of human projectionists did make a very significant impact upon the defining contours of the mainstream cinematic experience. Although there has previously been very little acknowledgement of the place of the projectionist within film theory, we will document a 'vernacular' set of important aesthetic precepts that were embellished, and carefully observed, by generations of projectionists.[181] We will also suggest that these tenets and their impact were historically both mutable and circumscribed. If the methods of film presentation typically found in the digitalised cinemas of today had been introduced to a large circuit cinema in the 1970s, we could expect audiences of that time to be highly conscious of a significant transformation, in a way that the audiences of the early 2010s apparently were not.

179 '"Rear Shutter" Replies to "Jack a Dull Boy"', *Ideal Kinema*, 12 July 1934, p. 43.

180 David Jenkins, 'Where Did All the Projectionists Go?', *Time Out London*, 14 April 2011.

181 The concept of vernacular cultural theory has been influentially developed in Thomas McLaughlin, *Street Smarts and Critical Theory: Listening to the Vernacular* (Madison, WI: University of Wisconsin Press, 1996).

Projection as an Element of Film Production

It was repeatedly suggested during the first half of the 20th century that the work of the projectionist should be thought of as an extension and continuation of the processes of film production. '[M]otion pictures are not manufactured like an automobile in a single factory', argued one commentator, 'but are an assembled product passing from place to place and finally delivered to the public through those little factories – the projection rooms – away up the top and at the back of the house'.[182] The head Projection Engineer for the Granada circuit made a similar analogy in describing the projectionist as 'the final medium between the producer and the patron; he it is that last of all handles the product which is the culmination of the efforts of wealth, scientists and experts'.[183] R. Howard Cricks began the fourth edition of his manual for projectionists by suggesting that they were 'the last link' in a 'lengthy chain' made up of actors, cameramen, sound recordists, musicians, editors and laboratory workers.[184] Neil Thompson provides a particularly evocative account of how he perceived his role as a projectionist of 70mm film prints at the Queen's Cinerama Theatre, Newcastle:

> When you had hold of this massive film ... and you're showing it on a massive screen and you had a full audience, that's what drives you on, that's what the adrenalin is all about. You think ... 'This film's cost so many millions to make and it's me that's in charge showing it, I'm the last link in the chain.' Which is what I always think a projectionist is. You are the last link in the chain from a story to a screen play, then a crew's got ready, and then they get the actors and it's filmed, it's processed, then it's sent to cinemas for people to see. You're the last link in the chain so it's up to you to present it properly.[185]

This view persisted into the multiplex era, and Ken Bagnall makes a direct link between his work and that of the filmmaker when he notes that 'there's millions being spent on these films, and you're in charge. ... [Y]ou've got to make sure that this person's vision is on that screen'.[186] From the opposite perspective, the American film director David Lynch has stated that the 'process of making

182 P.A. McGuire, 'Let's Have Co-ordination', *Projectionists' Journal*, April 1933, p. 1.

183 Percy Pilgrim, 'The Projectionist is Still the "Life" of the Show', *Kinematograph Weekly*, 15 December 1949, p. 203.

184 R. Howard Cricks, *The Complete Projectionist: A Textbook for all who Handle Sound and Pictures in the Kinema*, 4th edn (London: Odhams Press, 1949), p. 1.

185 Interview with Neil Thompson, conducted by Richard Wallace, 11 November 2014.

186 Interview with Ken Bagnall, conducted by Richard Wallace, 17 September 2015.

the film doesn't stop until someone sits down in the theatre. Like they say, the projectionist has final cut.'[187]

In the only sustained attempt – that we are aware of – to theorise the projectionist's contribution to the filmic signification of meaning, Timothy Barnard has developed a similar argument. Concentrating upon the period in which a basic grammar of narrative film style was being established within American cinema (in the early 1910s, when most screening venues were small converted shopfronts), Barnard claims that we should

> understand production as extending across a continuum that reaches right into the storefront cinema at the moment of consumption, in an act of intervention which ... visibly inscribes the operator's labour onto the film – even as all the other labour that went into its production has been successfully effaced ...[188]

Barnard urges a revision of our 'view of the film as commodity during this period', on the basis that it was not understood to be a 'fixed' text when it left the studio or arrived at the cinema.[189] He draws upon the authority here of a number of French and American commentators upon projection issues in the 1910s, particularly F.H. Richardson, author of the leading silent era handbook for American operators. Richardson argued that the opportunity, and necessity, for the operator to vary the projection speed of a film from scene to scene for maximum dramatic impact 'lifts the real operator out of the class of the ordinary mechanic and makes him something of an artist'.[190] Because camera filming speeds could vary from shot to shot in the silent period, and because certain kinds of action were perceived to be more effective when respectively projected with an increase or reduction in pace, it is suggested that the operator played a vital role in both revising and completing the production of each filmic text during the act of its exhibition. Barnard concludes, however, that the system of projection through which audiences were 'constantly aware of [the operator's] presence through the visible signs of his labour on the

187 David Breskin, 'Interview With David Lynch', in Richard A. Barney (ed.), *David Lynch: Interviews* (Jackson: University Press of Mississippi, 2009), p. 82. Lynch is not the only filmmaker to state such a view. Others include Paul Thomas Anderson, William Friedkin and Walter Murch. See: Ambrose Heron, 'Letters to Projectionists', http://www.filmdetail.com/2011/06/26/letters-to-projectionists-kubrick-lynch-malick-bay/; Ryan Lamble, 'John Landis Interview: Monsters in the Movies, Genre Cinema, Political Zombies, Aliens, and More', https://www.denofgeek.com/movies/alien/18272/john-landis-interview- monsters-in -the-movies-genre-cinema-political-zombies-aliens-and-more; Walter Murch, 'Who Has Final Cut on the Film? The Projectionist!', https://www.webofstories.com/play/walter.murch/108;jsessionid=5D6DCEB9CF9A7FEF5975A1F7B 1F9EFAC (all accessed 10 July 2019).

188 Timothy Barnard, 'The "Machine Operator": *Deus Ex Machina* of the Storefront Cinema', *Framework*, 43:1 (Spring 2002), p. 68.

189 *Ibid.*, p. 69.

190 F.H. Richardson, *Motion Picture Handbook: A Guide for Managers and Operators of Motion Picture Theaters*, 2nd edn (New York: Moving Picture World, 1912), p. 319 – quoted in *ibid.*, pp. 59-60.

film' was exclusively confined to the silent period.[191] The increasing consolidation of filmmaking conventions at the point of production, and the imposition of a fixed projection speed following the introduction of synchronised sound, meant that films subsequently entered distribution as a finished product; projectionists thereby became 'completely invisible, and the screen bears no trace of their labour'.[192]

Barnard confidently suggests that the idea of operators improving and 'redirecting' silent films by making constant adjustments in projection speed was advocated and practised with equal enthusiasm in Britain,[193] but we have found a greater volume of evidence to the contrary. The most elaborate case made in the early 1910s in favour of the view that 'The subject, in a great measure, should govern the rate of running', was accompanied by its author's complaint that, at the majority of cinemas, films were screened at a constant speed that was much too fast.[194]

Protests concerning excessive projection speeds were repeatedly voiced throughout the decade.[195] A film reviewer in the *Manchester Guardian* argued in 1918 that the projection of an art of movement as complex as Charlie Chaplin's 'needs to be regulated with an instinct for *tempo* not less than that demanded in the performance of a piece of music', whilst suggesting that the prevailing tendency in screening his films was to adopt 'a certain pace – usually too fast – and to keep them unchanged at that pace throughout'.[196]

Kevin Brownlow has shown that camera cranking speeds used in the production of Hollywood films were significantly increased in the 1920s.[197] This shift was also observed by British trade commentators, who firmly suspected that the new style was specifically intended as an act of 'self-defence' against the standard practice of films being hurtled through the projector at unnatural rates.[198] We must assume that operators simply made an equivalent adjustment to their frame rates in response, because there was no diminution of complaints about exaggerated projection speeds across the remainder of the decade, within both trade papers and the national

191 Barnard, 'The "Machine Operator"', p. 63.

192 *Ibid*., p. 70.

193 *Ibid*., pp. 57, 58.

194 A.C. Tolputt, 'Observations on Operating', *Kinematograph and Lantern Weekly*, 11 May 1911, p. 57.

195 See, for example, James W. Barber, 'The Projector and the Film', *The Bioscope*, 30 April 1914, p. 523.

196 'Charlie Chaplin as Recruit', *Manchester Guardian*, 10 December 1918, p. 4.

197 Kevin Brownlow, 'Silent Films – What Was the Right Speed?', in Thomas Elsaesser with Adam Barker (eds), *Early Cinema: Space, Frame Narrative* (London: BFI, 1990), pp. 286-287.

198 Colin N. Bennett, 'The Photographer's Speed', *Kinematograph Weekly*, 11 May 1922, p. iv.

press.[199] A cartoon published in the *Kinematograph Weekly* in 1922 shows a policeman, with a 'KRS' (Kinematograph Renters' Society) badge on his helmet, confronting a projectionist for 'Exceeding the Speed Limit' (see Fig. 2.1).

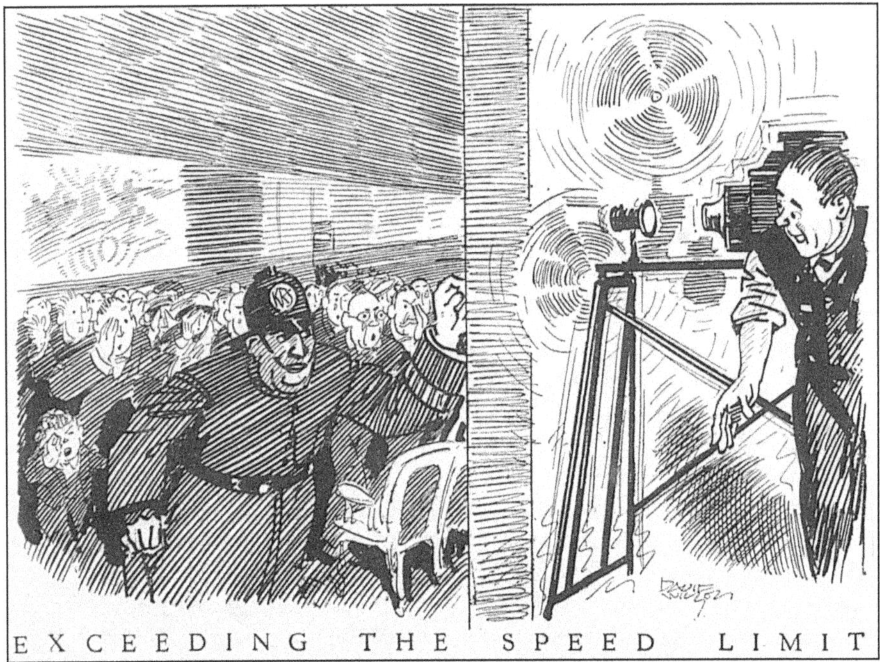

Fig. 2.1: Cartoon satirising 'criminal' projection speeds.[200]

Projectionists themselves were not generally considered to be directly culpable for this trend. In response to a marked national slump in audience attendance experienced in 1921 (see Chapter Three), the practice of programming double-features became firmly established for the duration of the silent era, and projection staff accused cinema managers of forcing them to maintain a fast pace of projection in order to accommodate two long films in a tight performance slot.[201]

It is reported that variable projection speeds were carefully employed at some super-cinemas, but all such adjustments in these cases seem to have been dictated by the resident musical director.

199 See, for example, F. Hill, 'Running Speeds', *ibid.*, 14 December 1922, p. 37; F. Morris, 'The Real Speeding Evil', *ibid.*, 18 January 1923, p. v; 'First National's Convention', *ibid.*, 14 August 1924, p. 42; 'The Observation Window', *ibid.*, 29 April 1926, p. 71; Walter Smyth, 'Badly Shown Films', *Daily Mail*, 26 October 1927, p. 10.

200 'Exceeding the Speed Limit', *Kinematograph Weekly*, 21 December 1922, p. 34.

201 Colin N. Bennett, 'Mind Your Own Business', *ibid.*, 26 May 1921, p. vi; 'Operators and Film Damage', *ibid.*, 22 June 1922, p. vii.

The latter would seek to ascertain in rehearsal screenings whether any of their preferred musical cues exceeded the duration of particular scenes when the film was shown at the operator's default speed, and thus required a slower pace of projection.[202] Colin N. Bennett, the editor of the *Kinematograph Weekly*'s projection-related columns throughout the silent era, actually went so far as to openly mock F.H. Richardson's supposition that speed variation constituted a basis for classifying film projection as an artistic practice: 'Motion picture projection is not a creative art at all, and ought not to be thought to be so', he chided.[203]

If the modulation of frame rates to enhance narrative impact was not a common procedure amongst projectionists, then it cannot serve as a strong justification for categorising projection as an extension of film production. There is, however, a core element of projection practice within both the silent and sound eras that effectively reshaped the material characteristics of the film text, as configured prior to exhibition, and often graphically inscribed the projectionist's labour upon the screen. We are thinking here about instantaneous reel changeovers achieved through the use of visual cue marks added to several frames near the end of each separate segment of a print (the mechanics of which are described in Chapter One) – a technique that seems to have been originally designed by projectionists rather than being mandated by producers and distributors. In implementing and refining this innovation, projectionists acted as a key mediator between filmmakers and audiences in helping to manage an institutional transformation that has been characterised by scholars as 'one of the most significant in film history, on the order of the shift from attraction-based to narrative cinema': i.e., the transition from an entertainment model based upon the provision of a large variety of short films to a new form of programming dominated by multiple-reel feature films.[204] Projectionists' handling of instantaneous reel changeovers also attracted considerable controversy, both at the inception of the practice and over the course of much of the 20th century.

In a penetrating analysis of the narrative structure of the earliest multi-reel feature films, Ben Brewster has argued that before the First World War, the producers of feature-length films predominantly treated each individual 1,000-foot reel as a discrete segment. The end of every intermediate reel resembled the end of an act in a theatrical play; that is to say, some form of mini-resolution or

202 D.A. Whiston, 'A Word on Operators', *ibid.*, 27 November 1924, p. 78; A.W. Owen, 'Operator and M.D.', *ibid.*, 23 August 1928, p. 69.

203 Colin N. Bennett, 'For the Operator's Protection', *ibid.*, 17 January 1924, p. 74.

204 Michael Quinn, 'Distribution, the Transient Audience, and the Transition to the Feature Film', *Cinema Journal*, 40:2 (Winter 2001), p. 36.

element of suspense signalled a moment of pause in the narrative when each reel finished.[205] Brewster identifies the emergence of a radically different narrative paradigm with the production in 1913 of the Imp Company's six-reel *Traffic in Souls* (USA, George Loane Tucker, 1913). In this film there are no narrative hiatuses between the end of some reels and the beginning of their successors; action continues across these reel breaks without interruption.[206] This is the model of narrative construction that would in due course become the universal norm, but Brewster suggests that it is highly unlikely that the direct continuity of action across reels in *Traffic in Souls* would have been replicated at the point of projection when the film was originally released. Having consulted numerous manuals for cinema operators published in both Britain and America in the 1920s, and found no references whatsoever to the use of cue marks to implement quick transitions between reels, he concludes that precise, instantaneous changeovers from the end of one reel mounted on one projector to the next reel laced up on a second projector were probably not seen in cinemas until the sound era.[207]

In actual fact, it can be clearly established that visual cue marks designed to help facilitate rapid changeovers from one projector to another began to be used in Britain at some point during the First World War. However, this practice remained extremely contentious for the remainder of the silent period – which explains why it was not encouraged in manuals and handbooks. It was common practice to install two projectors in a cinema for some time before the advent of multi-reel features, but the principal reasons for this had nothing to do with feature film reel changes: having two machines allowed for the screening of successive short films without the delays that would be involved in lacing up each separate reel on a single projector, and also prevented disruption if one machine succumbed to mechanical failure.[208] Despite the prevalence of multiple projector set ups, the standard procedure initially adopted for the screening of long feature films seems to have been a deliberate accentuation of the pauses between the separate parts. For example, when Pathé's ten-reel adaptation of *Les Miserables*

205 Ben Brewster, '*Traffic in Souls*: An Experiment in Feature-Length Narrative Construction', *Cinema Journal*, 31:1 (Autumn 1991), pp. 40-42.

206 *Ibid*., pp. 43-44, 47-48.

207 *Ibid*., pp. 51-52. Jan Olsson has more recently drawn attention to various U.S. trade paper reports suggesting that it was becoming relatively common by 1914 for large metropolitan American cinemas to present multi-reel films in a seamlessly continuous fashion, but does not acknowledge any discussion of the changes in projection technique that would have been necessary to facilitate this: Jan Olsson, 'Exhibition Practices in Transition: Spectators, Audiences and Projectors', in Santiago Hidalgo (ed.), *Technology and Film Scholarship: Experience, Study, Theory* (Amsterdam: University of Amsterdam Press, 2018), pp. 59-60, 68-69, 70.

208 Frederick A. Talbot, *Moving Pictures: How They are Made and Worked* (London: William Heinemann, 1912), p. 135.

(France, Albert Capellani, 1912) was screened at the Alhambra Theatre in London's Leicester Square in December 1912, intermission slides were apparently shown between each reel change.[209] Various sources suggest that similar approaches remained in use at some cinemas through to the early 1920s. One experienced projectionist, who dubbed himself 'One of the Old Hands', argued in 1918 that a pause between the presentation of each reel of a long film provided 'an opportunity for beneficial discussion of the past acts, avoid [sic] the appearance of rush and hustle, and give [sic] the audience a better grasp of the story'.[210] Another suggested that 'It makes a picture seem more finished' for the audience if they were shown the 'End of Part I', 'End of Part II' titles, etc., attached to the conclusion of each reel.[211]

In the spring of 1917, various concerned and bemused operators began to report to the trade papers that they were finding circle- and diamond-shaped holes punched in frames near the end of feature film reels, and the 'Disgrace of Film Punching' henceforth became a subject of sustained debate.[212] One outraged correspondent suggested that 'the operator who persists in cutting diamonds and holes to denote the end of a reel is like the Hun who laid beautiful Belgium waste for no reason whatever'.[213] As the latter part of this comment suggests, despite the rush to condemn these markings, there was initially very little understanding as to why they were being made. The general assumption amongst those offended was that lazy operators were giving themselves a visual warning that the end of the reel was nearing so that they didn't make the mistake of casting a bright flash of arc light on a blank screen.[214] The struggle to comprehend the purpose behind the holes clearly suggests that the practice was not initiated and coordinated at the behest of distributors, but was rather developed by other operators acting upon their own initiative. Eventually, a few of the latter came forward to clarify and defend their actions. One operator from Altrincham explained that he had decided to adopt a new method when screening multi-reel films:

209 As recounted in Frank Fowell, 'Then Nobody Was Called "Chief"', *Ideal Kinema*, 11 August 1955, p. 22.

210 'Thoughts on Films', *Kinematograph and Lantern Weekly*, 28 February 1918, p. 84.

211 W.J. Tomkins, 'A Matter of Opinion', *ibid.*, 5 June 1919, p. 78. See also P.H. Berridge, 'A Changing-over Signal', *Kinematograph Weekly*, 19 July 1923, p. v.

212 G.H. Smith, 'The Disgrace of Film Punching', *Kinematograph and Lantern Weekly*, 9 August 1917, p. 102. See also H.E. Scriven, 'Operators and Films', *ibid.*, 31 May 1917, p. 48; Jack H. Ross, 'The Renters Must Act', *ibid.*, 23 August 1917, p. 116.

213 Jack H. Ross, 'Operators and Renters Too', *ibid.*, 18 October 1917, p. 75.

214 F. Petherick, 'An Operator on Service', *ibid.*, 16 August 1917, p. 103; Colin N. Bennett, 'To Stop Film Punching', *ibid.*, 13 September 1917, p. 109. Some pre-war operators did insert small diamond-shaped cue marks to help them avoid 'a white sheet and a jarred audience' when showing old prints that had lost their concluding frames: see 'Weekly Notes', *ibid.*, 27 November 1913, p. 6.

> instead of waiting to screen 'End of Part – Next part follows immediately,' I change over on to the other machine; and instead of showing the title again and the number of part, I start off with the sub-title. The idea not only saves time, but also improves the sequence of the film story.[215]

Some devised their cue marking system in response to the demands of their employers:

> My manager intimates to me that he requires the eight parts of a film run off as a single picture. I must show the title of the first part, and from then onward there is to be no break, no beginnings or leads of the subsequent parts right through till *the end* appears. No blank screen must occur during the whole run, nor must I show white spacing, nor anything but picture. There is the proposition my manager sets before me, and there, in the solution of it you have the reason for the disfiguring punch holes.[216]

Rendering the separations between the reels invisible and creating the illusion of a single seamless text required precision timing to switch from one projector to the other without any stoppage. An operator from Greenock asked how else he could judge 'when to start his other machine without missing too much of the picture, and still keep the screen from being blank between parts? I cannot see what harm a small hole in the end of a film can do'.[217]

Building upon the pioneering example set by *Traffic in Souls*, filmmakers in the later years of the First World War increasingly conceived multi-reel features as a continuous blend of action and narration. But it would appear that they did not take any steps to convey instructions about how cinemas might replicate this ideal conception of the feature as a singular uninterrupted text during screenings. Cinema managers and their projectionists obviously started to recognise this stylistic shift without overt prompting, and the latter improvised a very effective method of achieving instantaneous changeovers in order to maximise its impact. (Managers of cinemas running continuous performances of films would have had a secondary motive for welcoming a faster method of showing multiple-reel films, if it freed up sufficient time for an extra screening to be squeezed in.) The ingenuity, skill and additional effort of projectionists thus facilitated a supplementary form of 'live' editing that was not possible in the studio, and made a considerable impression upon the viewing experience.

The emergence of a definitive explanation for the hole punching did very little to assuage the hostility of the trade's leading technical

215 Edward J. Horley, 'Quick Change-Over', *ibid.*, 11 October 1917, p. 124.

216 D.S. Hunt, 'The Problem Stated', *ibid.*

217 Duncan Mailer, 'The Proposed Good Condition League', *ibid.*, 13 September 1917, p. 111.

experts and many other projectionists towards the practice, however. Colin N. Bennett declared that 'The main reason against permitting "one small hole" in the film end is the same as the main reason against permitting one small person to slip into the show without paying. It undermines the whole essential principle for which we are contending.'[218] This cryptic comment begs the question of what 'essential principle' was seen to be threatened here and why. A projectionist writing in 1924 condemned cue marks because they compromised the representational integrity of the projected image:

> The endeavour of all concerned with the production and exhibition of films is to create an illusion of realism, which means absolute perfection. ... From the projection point of view film breaks and mis-racks are well-known factors in destroying the illusion of realism, but we should not lose sight of the fact that screen signals ... have the effect of diverting the spectators' attention from the screen to the operating-room.[219]

By this logic, the device that had been adopted to minimise interruption of the image was problematic because it raised awareness of activities in the projection box. This author's preferred solution was for the individual components of a feature film to be partially re-segmented once again, so that each reel ended with 'a moderately slow fade-out', giving the operator more time to make the changeover. Over the course of the 1920s, the goal of immediate transitions between reels gained wider acceptance as an ideal to be strived for, but cue marks were continually lambasted as an inappropriate means to that end. They were an 'abomination' and incompatible with 'artistic presentation', according to a commentator writing in 1929.[220]

In order to understand this bellicosity concerning the use of cue marks, it is important to be aware that generations of projectionists have been encouraged to consider the concealment of their own labour as a primary form of proof of their competence. Barnard correctly points out that the introduction of cinema projection boxes in the 1900s and 1910s 'was the first step in effacing the presence of the operator in the hall and his visibility in the film itself'.[221] This would lead to a popular characterisation of the projectionist as a troglodytic figure, with David Rosenbaum going so far as to compare the projectionist (along with other 'slaves to the ... celluloid' such as those who 'toil in the labs, in the shipping

218 Colin N. Bennett, 'The Proposed Good Condition League', *ibid.*

219 Sidney J. Ottaway, 'Part-End Signals', *Kinematograph Weekly*, 11 December 1924, p. 77.

220 'Film Mutilation', *ibid.*, 28 February 1929, p. 88.

221 Barnard, 'The "Machine Operator"', p. 70.

rooms and in the projection booths') to the 'fat, ugly and squat' Morlocks from H.G. Wells's novel *The Time Machine*.[222]

For many of the projectionists that we interviewed, however, invisibility was not simply viewed as a regrettable consequence of their physical marginalisation; it was a key objective, a measure of their skill, and an inverse sign of their agency. Neil Thompson suggests that when changeovers between reels were done well 'people weren't aware it was happening', and that 'if you haven't seen it, well I've done my job right'. Simon Allen uses the metaphor of 'a swan serenely going along the water but the feet frantically flapping underneath', and suggests that 'when it goes perfectly [the audience is] oblivious'.[223] Peter Howden argues that 'the projectionists should, indeed, be invisible',[224] and both Chris Tweddell and Ken Bagnall frame invisibility as a key criterion of a 'good show'. For Tweddell, 'the best show in terms of the public is they don't even know you're there', and for Bagnall 'the projectionist's job was to be invisible. They shouldn't even think about whoever's up there behind that screen. ... [A]s long as they don't know you're there then that's a good show, for me'.

As Mike Williams puts it:

> In the perfect show, in the perfect cinema, they shouldn't be aware that there's a projectionist showing the film. It's a magic window on the world and that's where the picture is ... down there in front of them. So that makes them forget what's going on behind them. One of the greatest things, as far as I'm concerned, is the stopping of smoking in the cinemas, because with that beam ... you knew the picture was coming from behind you. Get rid of the smoke, that window on the world is clearer. That's what it's all about, feeding people's imagination; not letting them know that you're feeding them ...[225]

This professional obligation on the part of projectionists to stay hidden initially became lore around the same time that the classical filmmaking paradigm was being codified, and mirrors the latter's complementary privileging of 'covert, diegetically motivated' and generally non-visible forms of narration.[226] On the face of it, this drive for invisibility poses a problem for this chapter – and to some extent the book as a whole – in its aim of showing that projection-

222 David Rosenbaum, 'Trysting With Trolls', *Film Comment*, 11:3, (May–June 1975), pp. 36. One projectionist we interviewed recalls being able to identify a group of projectionists gathering to help fit out a new cinema by their physical characteristics alone, because they were 'pasty vampire-looking dudes'. Interview with Chris Tweddell, conducted by Richard Wallace, 12 November 2014.

223 Interview with Simon Allen, conducted by Richard Wallace, 8 March 2016.

224 Interview with Peter Howden, conducted by Richard Wallace, 13 November 2014.

225 Interview with Mike Williams, conducted by Richard Wallace, 24 August 2015.

226 David Bordwell, Janet Staiger and Kristin Thompson, *The Classical Hollywood Cinema: Film Style & Mode of Production to 1960* (London: Routledge, 1985), p.83.

ists had a meaningful and material impact on the film-going experience. How can a core goal of invisibility be squared with the idea that the presence of projectionists made a substantial difference to the process of film viewing? From the 1910s onwards, the projectionist's invisibility was posited as a constituent feature of the standard cinema experience and internalised as a key component of the aesthetics of good projection. We would argue, however, that it sits alongside, and in tension with, a variety of practices and aesthetic values that simultaneously position the projectionist as a very tangible part of the cinema experience.

This tension comes directly to the fore in the controversy over cue marks. In order to better support the ideal of invisible projection, some commentators advocated an alternative method of achieving smooth changeovers via the use of cue sheets. This involved projectionists familiarising themselves with the film in rehearsal, and writing descriptions of the action that occurred at each moment when the changeover needed to commence. Various devices for mounting the compiled cue sheets upon the projector in the manner of a sheet music stand, for the operator to somehow follow whilst simultaneously paying attention to the screen, were devised and marketed.[227] Operators gifted with excellent memories were advised to try 'assimilating the continuity of the film story, just as an actor would study his part'.[228]

It seems very likely that the cue sheet system, which relied upon approximate descriptions of image content, did not generally match the tight precision of reel changes achieved when responding to cue marks stamped upon the print. We are led to this conclusion by developments in the early sound era. Films with optical soundtracks demanded particular exactitude in the changeovers, because the combination of discontinuous sound with the sight of blank spacing or an unintended jump cut was more emphatically jarring and abrupt, and any loss of dialogue potentially compromised narrative clarity. As R. Howard Cricks put it, 'Change-overs cannot now be right to the nearest hundred feet, but must be perfectly timed to suit both picture and sound.'[229] In July 1930 the American Society of Motion Picture Engineers (SMPE) took steps to address the increased challenge by designing the Standard Release Print. Film distributors adopting this format abided by a set of conventions, which included the optical printing of two sets of 'circular opaque marks', each running across four

227 E.g., 'Change-over Card Holder', *Kinematograph Weekly*, 9 July 1925, p. 103; 'Film History Sheet', *ibid.*, 11 March 1926, p. 77; 'The Change-Over', *ibid.*, 23 June 1927, p. 73.

228 Colin N. Bennett, 'Better Technique', *ibid.*, 1 January 1925, p. 106.

229 R. Howard Cricks, 'Staffing the Projection Room', *ibid.*, 5 November 1931, p. 61.

frames at the ends of intermediate reels: the motor cue and the changeover cue.[230] The motor cue told the operator when to start the second projector in readiness for the transition, and the changeover cue signalled the precise moment when the switch should be made.

There was initially strong criticism in Britain of the Standard Release Print as a 'retrograde step', because it sanctioned and indelibly perpetuated the on-screen signalling procedure.[231] Nonetheless, the principles of this system were widely adopted for most of the remainder of the analogue projection era. We might view the fact that this method was chosen, rather than the alternative option of having distributors prepare official changeover cue sheets, as the ultimate institutional recognition of the fact that the punch-hole system devised by projectionists was the most efficient and effective technique for preserving narrative continuity – even as the SMPE sought to pre-empt them from imprinting their own marks upon the image.[232] It was, in this sense, an indirect form of tribute to the contribution that had been made by projectionists to the development of screen presentation conventions when the industry shifted its focus from shorts to features.

Although the Standard Release Print was supposed to obviate the need for projectionists to draw upon, scratch or pierce frames themselves, it is a curious fact that no significant abatement of these practices seems to have taken place. Fifteen years after its introduction, a Birmingham projectionist observed that 'the number of projectionists who mark films outnumber by far those who are content to use the standard dots'.[233] Throughout the sound era, British trade papers and technical journals encouraged readers who worked for cinemas and film distribution companies to provide examples of the personalised cue marks added by 'mutilation fiends' by sending in cut-out frames, and specimens were regularly published over a period of several decades in an attempt to fan outrage and shame the perpetrators.[234] These handmade cue marks were variously attributed to projectionists' myopia, laziness,

230 'Academy Specifications for 35mm Motion Picture Release Prints', *Journal of the Society of Motion Picture Engineers*, December 1930, p. 820.

231 R. Howard Cricks, 'The Standard Release Print', *Kinematograph Weekly*, 30 April 1931, p. 73.

232 Matthew Soar, 'The Beginnings and Ends of Film: Leader Standardization in the United States and Canada (1930-1999)', *The Moving Image*, 16:2 (Fall 2016), pp. 27, 29. Some distributors had taken the step of adding their own cue marks when preparing their prints for release earlier in the 1920s. Universal's British agency started doing this in 1924 (Colin N. Bennett, 'European Method', *Kinematograph Weekly*, 7 August 1924, p. 62), and First National followed suit a few months later ('Part End Warnings', *ibid.*, 22 January 1925, p. 82). Both were heavily criticised for their 'horribly perfect' reproductions of the projectionists' punch holes: Colin N. Bennett, 'The Observation Window', *ibid.*, 16 July 1925, p. 71.

233 S. Reith, 'Kindness to Mutilators', *Ideal Kinema*, 10 January 1946, p. xxxiii.

234 R. Howard Cricks, 'Mutilation Continues', *ibid.*, 12 October 1939, p. vii.

illiteracy, viciousness and even their 'disordered brains'.[235] Such marks were also frequently described – sarcastically – as projectionists' trade marks,[236] or even as their 'works of art'.[237] The latter joke was expanded upon in a 1947 cartoon imagining the exhibition of reel end frames in an art gallery (see Fig. 2.2).

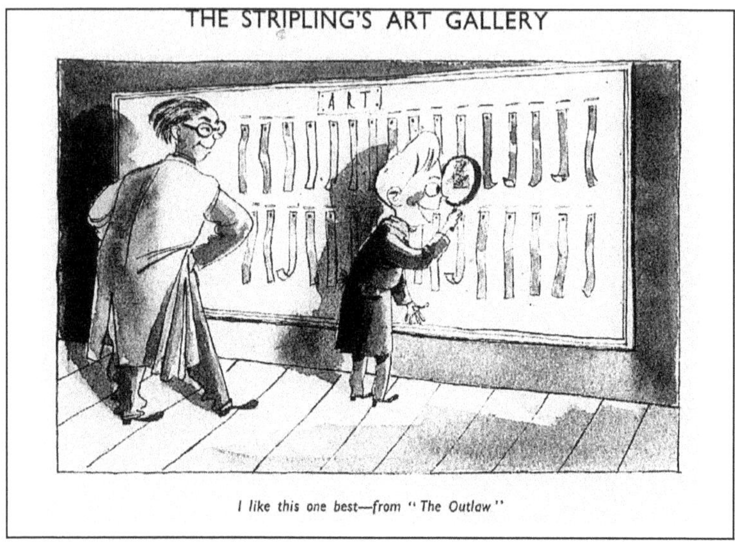

Fig. 2.2: The cue mark ironically imagined as an art gallery exhibit.[238]

Such jokes touched upon the fact that some of the cue markings were quite elaborately and/or imaginatively produced (using techniques, it might be noted, that we now more readily associate with avant-garde film artists such as Len Lye and Stan Brakhage). In 1944 a cinema manager from Dartmouth, Devon, forwarded a cutting that had been designed to produce an animated effect when projected:

> Note the care with which the ¼-in. holes have been punched, each slightly lower on each successive frame. Whoever is responsible for this damage evidently requires a white hole roughly 3 ft. diameter on the screen, and travelling from top to bottom of the screen in addition, as change-over warning! Each change-over was marked in this way.[239]

In the cutting on the left in Fig. 2.3 we see a character momentarily given spectral form through careful scratching of the emulsion

235 J. Whitnall, 'Running the Show – I', *ibid.*, 9 October 1941, p. ix; J. Whitnall, 'Stop Film Print Ruin', *ibid.*, 8 July 1943, p. xvi; R. Howard Cricks, 'Appalling Ignorance', *ibid.*, 8 July 1943, p. xiv; Cricks, 'Mutilation Continues'; R. Howard Cricks, 'The Guild Apprenticeship Scheme', *ibid.*, 13 December 1934, p. 36.

236 'Film Mutilation', *Kinematograph Weekly*, 31 January 1929, p. 73.

237 Charles Ablett, 'Who is to Blame for Film Mutilation?', *Ideal Kinema*, 5 December 1946, p. xx.

238 'The Stripling's Art Gallery', *ibid.*, 9 January 1947, p. 23.

239 R. Howard Cricks, 'A Renter's Cue Mark?', *ibid.*, 13 July 1944, p. ix.

within his silhouette, and the frame reproduction on the right shows how one projectionist contrived to present the changeover signal by flashing the arc light through Merle Oberon's scratched-out eyes and mouth.[240]

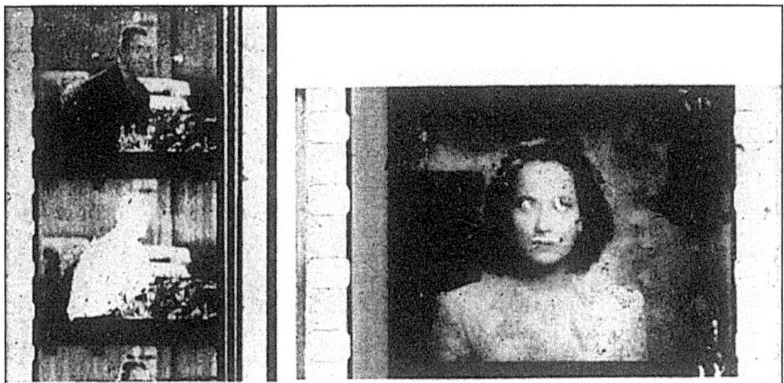

Fig. 2.3: The real art of the cue marker.[241]

We clearly need to ask why projectionists continued to add their own customised, and sometimes quite eye-catching, markings, despite the introduction of an official system of changeover dots. Some suggested that private marks existed because many projectionists were 'too unobservant to notice the [existing] cues'.[242] There were a number of practical considerations that should be taken into account. Some distributors/laboratories outside North America were either very slow to embrace the Standard Release Print specifications, or simply never adopted them.[243] R. Howard Cricks noted in 1951 that 'there are still far too many copies in circulation without standard cue-dots', a situation that was tacitly acknowledged by the arrival on the market of a device specifically designed to punch cue-dots in film prints that lacked them.[244] If the dots were printed against dark backgrounds they could be very difficult to see, and would sometimes require augmentation.[245] A projectionist from East Anglia observed that the motors on older projectors could become so sluggish that they needed more time

240 One submission included the more straightforward messages 'IT'S COMING' and 'STRIKE UP' scratched into a print of *Loser Take All* (USA, William Asher and Richard Quine, 1948): P.J. Ashley, 'Unconventional Cues', *ibid.*, 15 January 1953, p. 29.

241 Images reproduced in R. Howard Cricks 'Leisure Moments', *ibid.*, 12 July 1945, p. xiii; R. Howard Cricks, 'Punch Drunk', *ibid.*, 19 June 1947, p. 15.

242 R. Howard Cricks, *The Complete Projectionist: A Textbook for all who Handle Sound and Pictures in the Kinema* (London: Kinematograph Publications, 1933), p. 157.

243 The production of 35mm prints without cue dots continued into the 21st century. See discussions amongst projectionists on this topic on the Film-Tech Cinema Systems forums: http://www.film-tech.com/ubb/f1/t006863.html, accessed 1 December 2017.

244 R. Howard Cricks, 'Absent Cue-Dots', *Ideal Kinema*, 14 Jun 1951, p. 13.

245 R. Howard Cricks, 'Is it the Renters' Fault?', *ibid.*, 15 June 1933, p. 77.

to gain speed than the standard motor cues allowed for, necessitating the addition of cues that compensated for contingent machine quirks.[246]

It is probable, though, that these factors alone do not fully explain the scale of unofficial cue marking that seems to have taken place. R. Howard Cricks described the typical perpetrator of scratch marks and punch holes as a 'projectionist who likes to let his audience into the secret'.[247] As sarcastic as this characterisation is, it may provide a useful insight. Chapter Three will document how this profession was blighted by decades of low pay and poor working conditions. It is possible that many projectionists, in protest against their exploitation and general occlusion, deliberately added their own signature forms of 'graffiti' to subtly subvert the ideal of invisibility and ensure that a sign of their labour was directly inscribed upon the projected image for a fraction of a second.

Was this a straightforwardly reprehensible practice, as so many commentators suggested? One of the objections made was that it hastened print deterioration, adding so much visual noise to the reel end frames that they would invariably get removed by another projectionist further along the distribution chain, before the process began again when the adjacent set of frames would need to be marked up. These consequences are no doubt beyond dispute, but was it otherwise injurious to the cinemagoing experience? The chief projectionist of a city centre super cinema in Nottingham opined in 1941 that 'I have always found it a good plan to place myself, so to speak, in the position of the person paying for admission, and thinking to myself how I would enjoy seeing crosses, circles and all manner of marks spoiling my entertainment.'[248] We should view this kind of claim with more caution. The general impact upon audiences of subliminal signals that lasted for considerably less than a second on screen must remain a matter for speculation. 'Nobody knows they saw them, but they did', suggests the narrator in *Fight Club* (USA, David Fincher, 1999), during a sequence set in a projection box.[249] It was reported in 1935 that at one cinema in London, the manager instructed his projectionists to embellish the cue marks because he enjoyed watching the reel changes.[250] Both of the authors of this book have

246 'Individual Change-Over Cues – II', *Kinematograph Weekly*, 23 September 1943, p. 29.

247 R. Howard Cricks, 'More About Mutilation', *Ideal Kinema*, 10 May 1934, p. 41.

248 J. Whitnall, 'Running the Show – I', *ibid.*, 9 October 1941, p. ix.

249 Technically, this comment is made concerning frames of pornography interpolated by the projectionist into a screening, but the film metaphorically equates this practice with changeover cues (which it – fancifully – claims are known as 'cigarette burns' within the industry).

250 'London Projectionists Discuss Change-Cues', *Kinematograph Weekly*, 6 June 1935, p. 41.

clear memories of learning about the cue marks as children and being encouraged to look out for them at the cinema, and doubt they are alone in having acquired this knowledge as part of a pleasurable rite of initiation into the systems of smoke and mirrors that underpin screen entertainment.[251]

Presentation and Showmanship

It was sometimes argued that good projection was not simply the final stage in the production of a film, but was also a craft that could materially enhance the quality of the screened material. The secretary of the Guild of British Kinema Projectionists and Technicians delivered a speech at the annual Cinematograph Exhibitors' Association conference in 1939, arguing that 'an efficient projectionist with good judgement and showmanship may possibly be able to improve a picture with uneven photography or bad sound by using his artistic sense in manipulation of his controls'.[252] What might this mean in practice?

As we explained in Chapter One, when sound was first introduced, projection boxes were fitted with fader (or volume) dials, and adjustment of the volume controls – both preparatory and on the fly – became a significant part of the job. Films were often rehearsed prior to their first screening, and, although this process was partly intended to check the quality of the print and ensure that it had been made-up correctly, Mike Williams notes that 'the chief or the senior second would sit in the auditorium and cue them so the sound was all right all the way through. And you'd run by that cue sheet then all through the week. [The chief] used to consider that a necessity'. These cue sheets would highlight any imperfections in the soundtrack, such as the loud pops and cracks associated with cement or tape joins. Chris Tweddell recalls that these joins could be muted manually by the projectionist, 'so that the public never perceived [them] going through [the projector]'.

In many cinemas, cue sheets were used to facilitate the manipulation of volume controls in order to achieve particular dramatic effects. The first edition of R. Howard Cricks's *The Complete Projectionist* suggests that 'A tense dramatic film needs but low volume; a humorous film needs considerable volume to overcome the laughter ... while a boring film will create a bored, fidgeting

251 André Habib, reflecting upon the obsolescence in the digital projection era of this foundational element of the cinema experience, has similarly acknowledged the 'private pleasure tied to these cue marks, a pleasure partly due to the fact that they are not meant to be seen by the viewer': André Habib, 'Reel Changes: Post-mortem Cinephilia or the Resistance of Melancholia', in Santiago Hidalgo (ed.), *Technology and Film Scholarship: Experience, Study, Theory* (Amsterdam: University of Amsterdam Press, 2018), p. 87.

252 F.H. Woods, 'Education', *Projectionists' Journal*, August-September 1939, p. 8.

audience, needing rather more volume.'[253] Some saw this as an opportunity to exercise a more methodical level of corrective artistic judgement. A 1933 manual for projectionists took the view that

> In the matter of volume control, a good operator will get more out of a film than an indifferent one. Of course, anyone can push the fader right up for a train smash, but there are far more subtle shades of volume control than just that, difficult to describe but easy to appreciate when listening to the result. For example, in one film there may be a stealthy scene in which no noise is to be heard for quite a long while. Here, then, bring the fader down to zero, thus making a complete silence without even any background or surface noise. Similarly, a reiterated cry for help can be given one extra fader step every time it is heard, thus heightening the dramatic effect.[254]

Sam Lavington recalls achieving a similar effect when screening horror films, noting that 'there are certain parts in the film where you'd just up the sound a bit, just to give them a bit of shock. You know, if it's a horror film: ⋆WALLOP⋆ ⋆BANG⋆, you know. "Gotcha!"'[255]

There is no shortage of anecdotal evidence to suggest that the judgements of projectionists and filmmakers concerning the most important and effective qualities of a soundtrack could differ considerably. In an introduction to a screening of *Bonnie and Clyde* (USA, Arthur Penn, 1967) at the American Film Institute, Warren Beatty recalled how the projectionist at a London press show claimed to have 'saved' the film by levelling out the abrasive gunshot sound effects, which had, of course, been carefully mixed with this extreme loudness in mind.[256] Projectionists who took it upon themselves to try and compensate for, and improve upon, the quality of photography in particular films would also sometimes misunderstand the intentions of filmmakers, and produce a clash of sensibilities on screen. In the 1920s, there was a pronounced trend, initiated by Hollywood cameramen, for a softened style of cinematography that avoided sharp focus for aesthetic effect, utilising particular combinations of filters, gauzes, lenses, and lighting arrangements.[257] One source suggests that numerous British projectionists struggled to understand this look at first, and

253 Cricks, *The Complete Projectionist*, 1st edn, p. 129.

254 R. Pitchford and F. Coombs, *The Projectionists' Handbook: A Complete Guide to Cinema Operating* (London: Watkins-Pitchford, 1933), p. 61. Later editions of Cricks's manual advised that 'a good showman will ... boost the sound momentarily to enhance the effect of gunfire, the zooming of an aeroplane, or a storm scene': R. Howard Cricks, *The Complete Projectionist: A Textbook for all who Handle Sound and Pictures in the Kinema*, 3rd edn (London: Kinematograph Publications, 1943), p. 172.

255 Interview with Sam Lavington, conducted by Richard Wallace, 20 August 2015.

256 American Film Institute, 'Warren Beatty Introduces BONNIE AND CLYDE', https://www.youtube.com/watch?v=v3_i7w2XPIE, accessed 6 Mar 2020.

257 Bordwell, Staiger and Thompson, *The Classical Hollywood Cinema*, pp. 287-293.

erroneously tried to compensate for it: 'the new idea of introducing diffusion of focus into certain scenes of a dramatic film has already introduced to the mind of many a conscientious operator doubts which have caused him to rack the lens when it should have been left alone'.[258] Similarly, projectionists seem to have mounted a degree of professional resistance to the 1940s fashion for high-contrast cinematography, with its intensely dark shadows, as popularised by films like *Citizen Kane* (USA, Orson Welles, 1941) and the film noir genre. A projectionist from Birtley, in the north-east, complained that 'Neither "bloomed" lenses nor High Intensity light will make them clear to the audience. They show nothing but a sequence of dark shadowy figures floating on the screen.'[259] As this protest reveals, the aesthetic judgements made by projection staff could be unhelpfully driven by a singular preoccupation with clarity of visual information.

Although this chapter argues that film screenings could be greatly enhanced by the careful attention of a projectionist, there is a logical corollary to this, which is that an inattentive or unsympathetic projectionist could become a liability. As Phil Fawke argues, 'they spend thousands of pounds on a film ... but projectionists can ruin that film. It doesn't matter how much money they've spent on it, he can ruin it if he's not putting his full attention to it.'[260] Viewed in this light, the projectionist as 'last link in the chain' becomes a potential problem to be overcome. Right through to the end of the analogue projection era, it was not uncommon for filmmakers to issue specific directives to projectionists as to how a film should look and sound. Guidance sent out by David Lynch to cinemas with prints of *Mulholland Dr.* (USA-France, 2001) asked that the projectionist 'PLEASE RAISE VOLUME 3db HOTTER THAN NORMAL'. For the release of *Indiana Jones and the Last Crusade* (USA, 1989), George Lucas and Steven Spielberg asked projectionists using a platter to 'please use clear tape rather than opaque tape to join the reels of your print when you are building it up'. And in a letter addressed to 'the last remaining artisans of movie exhibition', accompanying the release of *The Tree of Life* (USA, 2011), Terrence Malick wrote that 'With a friendly salute, we urge you to ... keep the faders at a minimum of 7.5, though we hope to set as high as 7.7 if the sound system permits'. Such directives are often at pains to position the projectionist within the creative flow of the production process. In a similar spirit to Malick's appeal, David Yates's note accompanying *Harry Potter and*

258 Colin N. Bennett, 'Projection Points', *Kinematograph Weekly*, 9 December 1920, p. x.

259 E. Richard Eadie, 'Brighter Scenes, Please', *Ideal Kinema*, 14 February 1946, p. xvii.

260 Interview with Phil Fawke, conducted by Richard Wallace, 4 December 2014.

the Deathly Hallows Part 2 (UK-USA, 2011) argued that 'In my mind you are the extra member of our crew', and Michael Bay told prospective projectionists of *Transformers: Dark of the Moon* (USA, 2011) that 'we are all in this together'. Perhaps most impassioned is Stanley Kubrick's address to projectionists handling the presentation of *Barry Lyndon* (UK-USA, 1975) as key collaborators:

> An infinite amount of care was given to the look of "Barry Lyndon"; the photography, the sets, the costumes; and in the careful grading and overall lab quality of the prints, and the soundtrack – all of this work is now in your hands, and your attention to sharp focus, good sound, and the careful handling of the film will make this effort worthwhile.

However, the ultimate intent is clearly to wrestle creative control over the final performance back from the rogue (or inattentive) projectionist through the prescription of specific aesthetic standards.[261]

Irrespective of the views of filmmakers, there were certain techniques practised regularly by projectionists, with the aim of enhancing and embellishing the cinemagoing experience, that were strongly encouraged and approved by their peers throughout most of the 20th century. They involved careful manipulation of the screen curtains, lighting, and non-synchronous music, which were all typically the responsibility of the chief projectionist. In order to explain the significance of these apparatus, it is helpful to consider a recent scholarly attempt to rethink the history of film exhibition. William Paul has argued that from the mid-1910s through to the 1970s, cinema was predominantly conceptualised and experienced as a form of theatre. By this he means that 'seeing a movie always meant something more than just seeing the film itself'.[262] That 'something more' was a particular experience of the grand architectural space of the venue. Film screenings were organised as theatrical events in part, Paul suggests, as a means of offsetting the potentially uncanny experience of watching projected images. Although photographic moving pictures have always had the capacity to directly record and replicate reality in a way that the theatre cannot, they lack the latter's vivid sense of corporeal embodiment: 'In theatre, every object on the stage was present and existed in a space it shared with the audience. In film, the image presented a seeming physical reality contrived from a mere play of light-and-shadow.'[263] Throughout the silent era, substantial theatrical accou-

261 A collection of filmmakers' letters to projectionists (including those of Bay, Kubrick, Lucas/Spielberg, Lynch, Malik and Yates) can be found at Paul Bradshaw, 'The Best Letters Film Directors Sent to Projectionists', *Den of Geek*, 16 August 2018, https://www.denofgeek.com/movies/the-best-letters-film-directors-sent-to-projectionists/, accessed 25 January 2021.

262 William Paul, *When Movies were Theater: Architecture, Exhibition and the Evolution of American Film* (New York: Columbia University Press, 2016), p. 1.

263 *Ibid.*, p. 193.

trements, such as pictorial stage settings and live action prologues, were employed 'as a bridge from the physical world we shared with the space of the stage to the incorporeal reality of the film, as if something were needed to ease the transition from the familiar to the strange'.[264]

The additional representational capacity that synchronised sound brought to the screen seems to explain the rapid extinction of picture settings and prologues in cinemas in the early 1930s, but certain theatrical paraphernalia – particularly motorised curtains and stage lights – persisted for another fifty years. There is not a single mention of projectionists in Paul's book, but we would argue that they assumed primary responsibility for the orchestration of cinema as a theatrical experience throughout the first half century of the sound era. In many cinemas, their labour constituted the last element of live performance that remained once actors and musicians were no longer employed, and, just as crucially, they were tasked with responsibilities akin to those of a stage manager. Throughout the era in which cinema was imbued with the contours of a theatrical experience, it was repeatedly argued that 'showmanship' – also known as 'presentation' – was an essential component of the job of film projection; indeed, it was suggested that 'a projectionist who is not a showman is not a first-class projectionist, although he may be perfectly capable technically'.[265] John H. Graham, the chief projectionist at the Regal cinema in St. Leonards, Sussex, defined showmanship in the domain of projection as 'the exploitation of all dramatic qualities as they occur in the programme in such a way as to enhance and emphasise effects already in being, and to bring out latent effects that would otherwise be lost'.[266]

How exactly were dramatic qualities exploited and effects emphasised by projectionists? Skilful handling of the screen curtains was particularly crucial here. R. Howard Cricks argued that 'The first aim of showmanship, as far as it concerns the projectionist, is to make his patrons forget that they are watching an optical illusion whose origin is a bit of celluloid enlarged upon a flat screen.'[267] This obviously supports Paul's supposition that a primary motivation behind the emulation of theatrical presentation in cinemas was to cloud awareness of the fact that the entertainment was a physically insubstantial visual trick. To this end, there is a fundamental principle of good projection that has been emphatically articulated

264 *Ibid.*, p. 224.

265 R. Howard Cricks, 'Psychology and the Projectionist', *Ideal Kinema*, 3 December 1942, p. xiii.

266 John H. Graham, 'Dramatic Presentation of Feature Films', *ibid.*, 9 September 1948, p. 23.

267 R. Howard Cricks, 'Mr. Projectionist – Showman', *ibid.*, 15 August 1935, p. 37.

throughout the history of the cinema. It can be found in the first British manual for projectionists, published in early 1910: 'Above all things avoid showing a white screen.'[268] Screen curtains were not a standard fixture in cinemas of the 1910s, and the injunction here is a warning against keeping the arc light on past the point when each reel has unspooled. By the 1920s it was consistently argued that no form of blank screen, whether illuminated or not, should ever be displayed to the audience, and the installation of motorised curtains was encouraged specifically for this reason.

A 'blank white screen expanse' without moving images was considered unsettling in its lifelessness and 'coldness'.[269] Patrons could not be allowed to 'know how bad a blank screen really looks'.[270] Paul Edmunds describes letting 'the screen go blank' as 'taboo',[271] and Mike Williams recalls that this aspect of showmanship was 'one of the first things [the chief] drummed into me' upon taking up his position as a rewind boy:

> I think maybe the second day, we stood at the back of the auditorium in the morning and the screen was open. The tabs were open, the skirtings were open. And [the chief] said, 'Mike ... you see that down there? It's the screen ... and I never want to see that again'. And I sort of looked at him and I said, 'What do you mean?' He said, 'That screen there ... when the tabs open it's the punters' window on the world. They don't want to see a screen, they want to see a picture on the screen and lose themselves in their imagination. ... That's the job that we do. If you show them the screen, they lose the imagination, it becomes a picture on a screen instead of a picture in its own right. ... I never, ever want to see you open those curtains on a blank screen.' And I only ever did it once and he sent me home. Literally, I thought I'd had the sack. He said, 'You don't do that in my theatre, you go home now and think about it.'

Projectionists were the gatekeepers in charge of ensuring that this illusory 'window on the world' was not compromised, and by making sure that the curtains 'were always closed except when projection is taking place the impression is created that there is a greater depth, or, in fact, a stage'.[272]

Paul has noted that projection did sometimes occur in the 1920s whilst the screen remained draped in fabric. He suggests that this technique was adopted as a means of conveying an impression that the film had tangible substance and solidity when it appeared on

268 Anon. [Arthur S. Newman], *The Modern Bioscope Operator* (London: Ganes, 1910), p. 110.

269 Colin N. Bennett, 'The Furse Curtain Control', *Kinematograph Weekly*, 14 December 1922, p. v; 'Why Not Screen Curtains?', *ibid.*, 6 September 1928, p. 83.

270 'Discipline in the Projection Room', *ibid.*, 30 September 1943, p. 24.

271 Interview with Paul Edmunds, conducted by Richard Wallace, 2 December 2014.

272 'Why Not Screen Curtains?'

the screen, in comparison to its initial manifestation on an undulating surface:

> Presenting the film image on the curtain at the beginning and end of the show was a way of temporarily granting the image its uncanny due: from the strange spectral image that billowed with the folds of the opening curtain we could move further in ... to a space where the image asserted, by contrast, a seemingly concrete reality.[273]

This practice seems to have continued to some degree in the 1930s and '40s, but the evidence for this is the fact that it was occasionally discussed as an example of inappropriate and counterproductive showmanship.[274] More than one projectionist that we interviewed argued that 'you should never see light on a still curtain',[275] and one objection published in the trade press suggested that it was evident 'from actual conversations with patrons that they think the tabs have "stuck" on these occasions'.[276]

There was a much stronger accord in favour of carefully timing the movement of the curtains so that they opened at the exact moment when the credits started, and closed right upon cue at 'The End'. 'There is something very satisfactory in the effect of curtains slowly closing at the end of a drama', one commentator explained.[277] Another suggested that

> the height of dramatic effect is best achieved by the smooth and rapid change from one picture to another in *synchronisation* with curtain movement, the curtains meeting precisely on the last note of the playout on one picture to open immediately to disclose the censor's certificate on the next.[278]

This consensus lasted right up to the arrival of the multi-screen projection array (see Chapter One), when the labour required to tend to and maintain the curtains across several screens in a single venue became too costly. Prior to this moment, however, the start of the show was a very carefully planned part of the projectionist's routine. It involved not only the careful timing of curtains, but also the choreographing of additional elements such as the auditorium lighting and ambient music. In presentation-conscious cinemas, great attention would be paid towards selecting music and lighting schemes that complemented the film to be screened.

Between shows and during intermissions, projectionists would be responsible for selecting and timing the atmospheric 'non-sync'

273 Paul, *When Movies were Theater*, p. 228.

274 See, for example, R. Howard Cricks, 'Mr. Projectionist – Showman', *Ideal Kinema*, 15 August 1935, p. 37; James Benson, 'Flooding the Screen', *Kinematograph Weekly*, 25 June 1942, p. 51.

275 Interview with Andrew MacLean, conducted by Richard Wallace, 25 August 2015.

276 Graham, 'Dramatic Presentation of Feature Films'.

277 E. Fletcher Clayton, 'The Screen and its Surroundings', *Kinematograph Weekly*, 5 February 1920, p. xiii.

278 Graham, 'Dramatic Presentation of Feature Films'.

music.[279] Williams notes that 'we couldn't use any records that weren't sympathetic towards the film we were showing', though he goes on to recount an incident that suggests that the other major music policy – that the music be 'non-vocal' instrumental music – trumped the question of sympathetic aesthetic augmentation:

> I brought a rock 'n' roll record in one day because we were showing *The Tommy Steele Story* [UK, Gerard Bryant, 1957] and I suggested that we play this record and [the chief] went absolutely bananas. 'We don't play music like that in cinemas! We don't play vocals in the intermission. Vocals are not on.'

As well as facilitating the close monitoring of the film's soundtrack and the creation of cue sheets, the rehearsal process was also used to carefully time the play-in music for dramatic effect. 'We'd have forty minutes of music,' Butler recalls. 'We would start it, you know, "Okay, start now," and that last note on the soundtrack would coincide with the first frame of the screen ... and the tabs would open'.

One of the most flamboyant forms of showmanship that projectionists were encouraged to practice in the era of 'theatrical' presentation was the flooding of the screen area with coloured beams of light. In the late 1920s and 1930s, a standard component of any new projection box installation was a Master Brenograph, a light projection apparatus manufactured by the Brenket company of Detroit. This device consisted of two large magic lantern projectors mounted one above the other on a stand. As well as projecting slides, different gels and filters could be added to the lamps, which permitted combinations of coloured spot, strobe and patterned lighting effects. Directional mirrors attached to each lamp allowed the light beams to be freely moved whilst the stand remained stationary.[280] (British equivalents, such as the Ross Sceneograph, were subsequently manufactured.) Fig. 2.4 shows that in the projection box at the Regal cinema, Edmonton, in 1934, there were two Brenographs fitted either side of three film projectors. Patterns of coloured light could thus be cast upon the screen curtains.[281] Mike Marshall recalls creating changeable colour schemes that rotated on a seasonal basis, and that 'in the winter you used a red [filter] because it made it much warmer. In the summer you use a lighter colour'.[282] In each case, the colour effects would end with 'a green change' to match the green triangle logo that fronted the

279 'Non-sync' was an enduring, though swiftly outdated, term originally employed to differentiate the ambient music/music player from the sound-on-disc system of early film sound, which *did* have to be synchronised to the image.

280 'The Projection Box', *Kinematograph Weekly*, 29 November 1928, p. xx.

281 Cricks, *The Complete Projectionist*, 3rd edn, p. 215.

282 Interview with Mike Marshall, conducted by Richard Wallace, 22 June 2015.

Odeon adverts at the time, and 'people got used to that; they'd know it was just about time to start when you change them to green'. Phil Fawke recalls using a similar device to the Brenograph to project animated images and shadows onto the curtain. As he explains, 'you could make models of planes and you could have them going over the curtains before the thing started, you know, and make it an experience to be in there'.

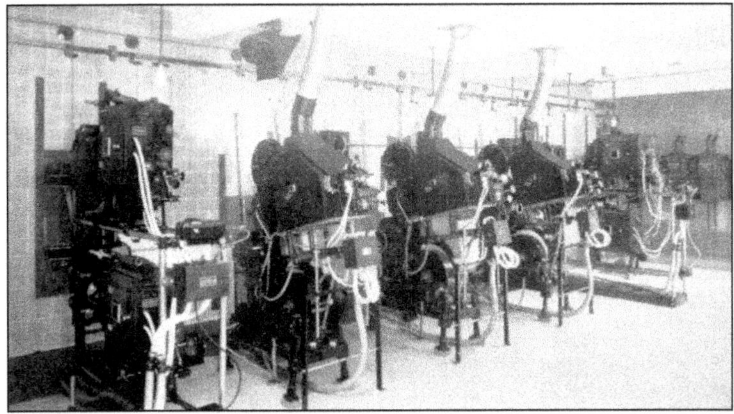

Fig. 2.4: The Master Brenograph.[283]

Although the lighting of curtains prior to the screen was a standard feature of the cinemagoing experience, it may come as more of a surprise – for anyone not old enough to have visited cinemas when black-and-white films predominated – to learn that projectionists were also strongly encouraged to use gelatine slides to throw coloured lights upon a film's credit sequence.[284] This practice appears to have been widespread, and lasted for several decades. '[T]he projectionist can display really good showmanship in the use of colour floats', the chief at the Forum cinema, Nottingham, emphasised in an article aimed at wartime newcomers to the box.[285] For the most effective deployment of this technique, it was considered essential that 'the colour should be appropriate to the subject'.[286] An eerie blue colour was recommended when screening the titles of *The Ghost of St. Michael's* (UK, Marcel Varnel,1941), for example, and John Douglas recalled shining green lights over the opening of *The Cruel Sea* (UK, Charles Frend, 1953), which 'looked very good just as the title came up'.[287] It was advised that

283 *Motion Picture News*, 14 July 1928, p. 119; 'This Week's Projection Room', *Kinematograph Weekly*, 15 March 1934, p. 45.

284 R. Howard Cricks, 'The Screen Setting', *ibid.*, 2 August 1928, p. 59. Stage lights – at cine-variety venues – or simply a removeable slide attachment on the second projector were also used for this purpose.

285 J. Whitnall, 'Running the Show – I', *Ideal Kinema*, 9 October 1941, p. x.

286 'Problems of Picture Presentation', *Kinematograph Weekly*, 22 March 1945, p. 54.

287 Interview with John and Peter Douglas conducted by Richard Wallace, 24 June 2015.

newsreels should generally begin with a single bright colour, but red light was best if there was an item about Russia.[288] It was generally recommended, though, that colour flooding should not be utilised if the title cards were 'very artistic' and had been carefully designed 'to provide an atmospheric introduction of the film', because 'the introduction of additional colour effects only succeeds in killing detail and swamping the background'.[289] There was also broad agreement that it was unnecessary for films shot in colour to be embellished,[290] although one chief suggested that there could be a case for the use of projected colour lighting 'as a contrast to the screen colour, which might give rise to a new and more complicated technique'.[291] Coloured lighting was a particularly overt means by which projectionists sought to 'improve' a film. Commentators on the subject do not provide us with a deeper rationale for this form of enhancement, though it was suggested that 'the practice is one which induces an "atmosphere" favourable beforehand to the picture's story'.[292] We might thus explain it as a supplementary means of helping audiences to negotiate the transition from a corporeal space to an illusory realm – a perceptual journey that the film exhibition industry obviously saw as particularly important, and requiring special care and attention.

It was generally suggested that the transition from the 'non-filmic' space of the auditorium, to the cinematic space of the film experience should be a gradual one, with the projectionists managing the shift by acclimatising the audience through the various presentation techniques at their disposal. This process began well before the film started, and John Neal suggests that 'prior to the film going on you had to create the right mood and atmosphere', whilst Brad Atwill argues that as well as the music choices and lighting effects already discussed, the close monitoring of the temperature was also key to the creation of a pleasant viewing atmosphere.[293] More fundamental, however, was the orchestration of the house lights, which John Young suggests 'put people in the mood'.[294] Simon Allen suggests that prior to the film beginning 'you'd take [the lights] down to half-mast so that people could settle and know that

288 J. Whitnall, 'Running the Show - I', p. x.

289 'The Voice of the Projectionist', *Kinematograph Weekly*, 11 December 1947, p. 29.

290 E.S. Tompkins, 'The Colour Enthusiast at the Cinema', *British Journal of Photography*, 19 June 1942, p. 226; R. Howard Cricks, 'Showmanship as the Projectionist's Responsibility', *Ideal Kinema*, 14 February 1946, p. xvii.

291 John M. Graham, 'Dramatic Presentation of Feature Films', *ibid.*, 9 September 1948, p. 23.

292 James Benson, 'Flooding the Screen', *Kinematograph Weekly*, 25 June 1942, p. 51.

293 Interview with John Neal, conducted by Richard Wallace, 15 January 2015; interview with Brad Atwill, conducted by Richard Wallace, 10 November 2014.

294 Interview with John Young, conducted by Richard Wallace, 5 February 2015.

it was about to start', an aesthetic manoeuvre that taps into film-viewing as what Philip Auslander calls 'a highly ritualized and convention-bound event', and through which the projectionist orchestrated key audience behaviours, preparing them for the experience of watching a movie in a cinema space.[295] As Sam Lavington argues, this initial reduction in light 'was telling the people, "please be quiet now, we're starting the show"'. This is the kind of traditionally overlooked labour that Ben Highmore has categorised as 'mood work', and was a key responsibility of the cinema projectionist.[296]

Although there was general agreement as to the overall principles of how the show should begin and end, projectionists reveal some striking disagreements as to how this perfect transition should be achieved in practice. To return to the specific example of choreographing the opening of curtains, Young suggests that 'everybody had their different ways' and specifies that 'I would want the [certificate] on the curtains and then have the curtains opening up. And the same with the masking, when you change to widescreen ... I always liked the picture to hit the [screen] as the masking opened, so people got the illusion that it was opening out.'

However, Neil Thompson holds some strong views about this routine: 'one cinema I used to go to which will remain nameless ... when the feature started ... the curtains were still closed on the censor ... And I used to think, "well why do they do that?", because you can't read it. Then they would open. Now that to me is bad presentation.' In contrast, Thompson suggests that the 'proper presentation' that he was taught at the Queen's Cinerama Theatre, Newcastle was as follows:

> what we used to do was to start the machine and then take the lights down and then open the curtains because it took a long time for the curtains to open because they were very slow. And by the time they'd got to the start of the picture ... the curtains would be, say, two thirds of the way open, so your picture went on the screen and not on top of them.

Both of these viewpoints emerge elsewhere in the interviews. Mike Williams suggests that he would 'show the certificate on the curtains', whereas Mike Marshall 'didn't like that at all', and Simon Allen's instinct was that 'as the curtains were halfway opening, the film would hit the screen'. However, in both Young's and Thompson's accounts, the projectionists articulate a strong rationale for their preferred method: Young avoids the blank screen and engineers a perceptual experience where it is suggested that the

295 Philip Auslander, 'Musical Personae', *TDR*, 50:1 (Spring 2006), pp. 100-119.

296 Ben Highmore, *Cultural Feelings: Mood, Mediation and Cultural Politics* (London; New York: Routledge, 2017), pp. 2-3.

projected image itself is responsible for the transformation in staging; Thompson strives for clarity, arguing that in Young's method the portions of the image that are projected over the curtains are illegible. In each case we can see the projectionist making – and rationalising – different aesthetic choices that affected the experience of the audience.

The notion that each projectionist had their own way of starting the show positions these small, but perceptible, decisions as a kind of signature that could be unique to each individual operator. As with the DIY changeover cues, projectionists inscribed themselves into the spectator's experience through these minute differences in projection style. We perhaps see here the clearest sign of tension between the projectionist's professional obligation to remain invisible and the overt role that they were simultaneously encouraged to play as a silent 'master of ceremonies'. It is telling that in the early 1960s, the British cinema equipment company J. Frank Brockliss Ltd introduced a console that could remotely control 'every function' of compatible projection equipment from within the auditorium, including presentational accoutrements like the curtains, lighting and music (Fig. 2.5), thus making the projectionist a significantly more visible part of the show.[297] It is equally telling that the console was never widely adopted.[298]

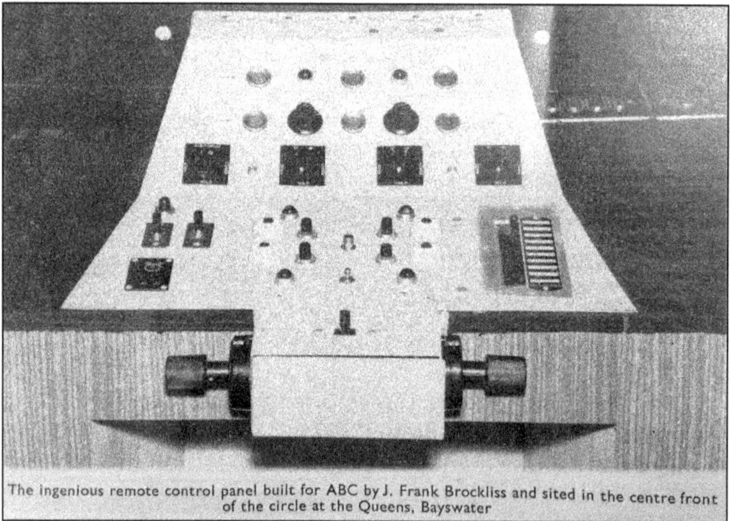

Fig 2.5: The control panel installed within the auditorium of the Queen's Cinema, Bayswater in 1960, from which the chief could control the presentation of the film.[299]

297 R. Howard Cricks, 'These are the Years of Progress', *Ideal Kinema*, 11 May 1961, p. 115.

298 Allen Eyes recalls seeing a console like this installed on the balcony to the left of the screen at the Classic Baker Street in the early 1960s, but notes that it constituted 'a bit of a distraction [for spectators] with its flashing lights' (Allen Eyles, 'Classic Repertory Cinemas' *Picture House*, 45 (2020), p. 36).

Peter Howden suggests that, at least within the industry, there should have been more recognition of the work projectionists did, and it is perhaps for this reason that despite aiming for invisibility more broadly, projectionists can be said to have 'signed' their work through their varied presentation styles, by the personalisation of end-of-reel cue markers and through the live 'remixing' of sound. These are all ways in which a 'good show' took corporeal form for the audience, and could be judged by employers, and those negotiating wage increases, as the visible products of concerted labour.

This also harkens back to the earliest days of cinema projection, and although we have been suggesting that in some respects the institutionalised projectionist eschewed the visibility of the travelling showman, a common thread of visibility remains through responsive and personalised presentation. John and Peter Douglas make this connection directly, with Peter suggesting that showmanship and presentation are 'in the ethos of cinema from those very early days' and John noting that the nature of the 'show' suggests an element of 'live theatre'. This sense of each film screening being a form of performance is powerful and finds perhaps its most direct articulation in Howden's idea that presentation is 'part of the magic of going to the cinema; of putting on a show rather than just showing a film'. This speaks to a much broader question of what cinema itself actually is, was, and will be in the future, and it can be coherently argued that, at least during a certain period of the 20th century, the cinema experience was synonymous with presentation.

The digital era threatens some of these long-held conceptualisations of what cinema is. It is repeatedly suggested by our projectionist interviewees that going to see a digitally projected movie in a multiplex is like watching a big television, with the process of projecting 'like putting an ordinary DVD on'.[300] This sense of cinema becoming something 'other' than cinema is not just about the change in format and the loss of the materiality of film, but is also about the attendant loss of manpower, which in turn has resulted in a decline in presentation standards. For Fawke, the screen shouldn't look like a blank television when you walk in, and should 'retain the atmosphere of a cinema' as opposed to the multiplex, which he characterises as 'a popcorn selling place and a supermarket for showing films'. For Frank Gibson, cinema means the projectionist doing more than just pressing play.

This returns us to the question of what all of these aspects actually contribute to the experience of cinemagoing. Although we have

299 'Talking Technically', *Ideal Kinema*, 14 Apr 1960, p. 30

300 Interview with Frank Gibson, conducted by Richard Wallace, 14 October 2014.

demonstrated a range of tangible, physical processes through which the aesthetics of cinema presentation are managed, the ultimate aim was something more metaphorical, intangible, and poetic. Ken Bagnall addresses what he calls the 'Freudian' aspects of cinema presentation, when he suggests that

> when everything runs through as it should, the film is presented as it should ... you are in that dark cinema, and ... it's that dream-like state. And if you've got your audience staggering out, blinking into the light because they've been in that dream-like state, because they've been totally absorbed in that film, then we've done a good job.

These aesthetic goals were not shared by all projectionists. Peter Douglas is blunt that 'some of the projectionists we worked with even in the earlier days couldn't care less about showmanship. They would just get the film on and that's it', and Mike Williams remembers that 'you had no showmanship in a lot of the suburban cinemas'. However, for those who subscribed to the view that their job was to make the screening of a film into a special event, it is clear that they viewed this job with considerable pride. Williams addresses the personal elements of presentation by arguing that cinema projection wasn't about being skilled but about 'loving what you do', that it was 'something embedded in you, and I think you either have it or you don't'. There is a suggestion here that although the practicalities of presentation could be taught, the instinctive nature of the job could not. This sense of gaining meaning from the job through the satisfaction of others is striking, and Williams suggests that the 'it' that the projectionist must have is 'a deep love of providing a competent showing for the public. It doesn't matter what the show is, if the public like it and it's presented properly, that's the projectionist's job'. Like Williams, Rachel Dukes addresses the emotive satisfaction of a job well done, arguing that 'it was lovely when the film was on and everyone was happy, and they're all absolutely glued to it. It's just a really amazing feeling'.[301]

Brad Atwill suggests that 'it's the little nuances' of presentation that are 'the whole point of cinema', and what gives people a reason to leave the house. In so doing, he makes a convincing argument that what's going to kill cinema 'is people not caring'. Throughout this and the previous chapter we have seen clear and detailed descriptions of the minutiae of the job of the projectionist that cumulatively place the feelings of others at its centre. Whether we look to the careful checking of film prints frame-by-frame, the constant

301 Interview with Rachel Dukes, conducted by Richard Wallace, 19 December 2014.

cleaning of apparatus, the re-lamping of cinema auditoria or more aesthetic considerations of film presentation, the question of 'caring' is always at the centre of the competent projectionist's work, as it is articulated by those we interviewed; the care taken in creating an intangibly satisfying experience through the tangible labour of projection work. Andrew MacLean likens it to the circus: 'you've sort of sold them the circus bit for the night' and as a projectionist 'you're sort of in charge of the trick'. The notion of cinema as a magical event is also present in Williams's comprehensive overview of the cinemagoing experience:

> Remember in those days visiting the cinema was a night out. So, if you could extend the night out for the enjoyment of the audience, that's what showmanship is all about. If people can come out and they've been to Brazil and they've been to London and they've been to Rome and they've enjoyed the experience you feel good. ... [Y]ou could tell that an audience had been entertained, you could feel it and it made you feel good, that you knew the performance had been a success. And it comes from the stage days, you know. You're only happy with a stage production if the whole production has gone right. We used to feel the same about the cinema. It had to run right, it had to give people entertainment. It had to feel as though they moved into a magic kingdom. That's what cinema was all about.

It is not ultimately difficult, then, to reconcile the apparently paradoxical relationship between invisibility and good presentation. John Belton has argued that rather than viewing cinema as a configuration of elements – specifically: projector/film; screen; spectator – that we should instead think of it as not 'just an apparatus' but more 'an *experience* of the apparatus'.[302] We have been arguing here that the projectionist is key to this idea of cinema because, in being at the centre of this configuration, they are responsible for mediating the experience. Lisa Cartwright suggests that by paying attention to the projector 'we can look for evidence of the invisible work of the technician's hands in certain in-between stages of the photographic and cinematic process, stages that anticipate the sharing of the image', and that the projectionist plays an 'intimate and discerning role in this perceptual experience'.[303] Evident in each of the cases we have examined in this chapter – whether the personalisation of cue markers, or the individualised routines for timing the opening of theatre curtains – are moments in which the aesthetic sensibilities of the projectionist are manifested as tangible aspects of the cinema experience, acting as personalising gestures – or signatures – that the nominally invisible operator attaches to their finished work.

302 John Belton, 'If Film is Dead, What is Cinema?', *Screen*, 55(4) (Winter 2014), pp. 468, 470.

303 Lisa Cartwright, 'The Hands of the Projectionist', *Science in Context*, 24(3) (2011), pp 447, 448.

Changing Standards

> I would say multi-screens really killed showmanship
> –Peter Douglas

We have suggested throughout this chapter that the projectionist has been a key figure in orchestrating a sense of performance in the cinema and elevating screenings. Or, as Peter Howden puts it, 'putting on a show rather than just showing a film'. We have also indicated that what this showmanship entailed has shifted over time, in line with the changing industrial landscape of cinema exhibition. To conclude this chapter, we wish to consider the more recent history of multiplex cinema projection, which is, to a great extent, characterised by the absence of presentation and showmanship, and which asks us to re-consider the question of 'invisibility'.

In the previous chapter we saw how the confluence of automated projection, multiplex venues and single-manning changed the day-to-day job of the projectionist. This inevitably had a profound knock-on effect on the experience of the audience. As we have seen, one of the key requirements for good presentation was the direct attention of the projectionist, who would ensure that everything looked as good as it possibly could. In the pre-multiplex, pre-automation era, where a single-screen cinema could not operate without a competent projectionist on duty – thus guaranteeing, at least in principle, that each screen would be carefully overseen – the basic cost involved in employing such individuals to operate the projectors was unavoidable. However, wider industrial changes meant that economies could be made by employing fewer and fewer projectionists for more and more screens. The role of presentation thus became subject to cost-benefit financial discussions.

Andrew MacLean argues that 'there's a lot of core presentational stuff which is hard and complicated and expensive and difficult to do', and that although presentation 'does end with the projectionist it also starts with the accounts department', and the question asked about each aspect of the cinemagoing experience becomes 'Well how much money do you want to spend on it? Do you want to have a guy working there permanently doing it?' This attitude extended to the equipment budget, and financial considerations played a direct role in the removal of curtains and masking from most cinema chains, and even compromised the performance of the projection light source. John Young recalls that to run xenon lamps effectively for the projection of 21st century 3-D films, the specifications suggested that the bulbs be run 'for no more than 500-600 hours'; he calculated that, if run to spec, this would cost his cinema around £35,000 per year in replacement bulbs. This led the management to ask: 'Can you run them a bit longer?' By the point of his redundancy, Young notes that the bulbs were being run for over a thousand hours, which, whilst more than halving the budget, also resulted in a much poorer quality of light on the screen.

The most significant impact of the cost-saving measures implemented within the multiplex system was the reduction of manpower in the projection room, as described in the previous chapter. Chandra Makwana argues that, regardless of the cinema, 'with single-manning, there is no presentation', because the time-pressures make it impossible to pay close attention to each and every machine.[304] Mike Marshall suggests that there is nothing to preclude automated or digital projection systems from providing a mechanised version of cinema presentation. What *is* missing is the will of exhibitors to spend money on the apparatus and on the labour of a projectionist with an aesthetic eye whose job it is to programme the systems. 'It's nothing to do with technology, it's all down to money', Marshall concludes.

Perhaps the most commented upon consequence of these transformations is the manner in which multiplex projectionists are alerted to any issues in the screening of a film. In the nitrate era of cinema projection, significant malfunctions would have been caught within seconds of them developing, due to the proximity of the projectionist to the projector. In the multiplex these were more likely to be signalled by an alarm board. Where they would once have been dealt with very quickly in a well-populated projection box, less catastrophic failures that have deleterious aesthetic consequences – the film going out of rack, losing focus or being screened in the wrong ratio, or the sound failing, for example – were unlikely to promptly catch the attention of the multiplex projectionist.

We have noted that projectionists have a tendency to define their invisibility in negative terms: that cinema projection is not noticed when it is done well, only when it goes wrong. A commonly used metaphor compares the cinema experience to the elegant swan whose laborious paddling occurs out of sight. A key result of the reformulation of the cinema projection box in the multiplex era is that, in reducing the human labour, the swan proceeds in a far less graceful manner. Rather than it being the projectionist who detects and corrects fundamental errors, more often than not this diagnostic task has become the purview of the audience. There is a repeated refrain from a number of those interviewed to this effect, summed up by Chris Tweddell:

304 Interview with Chandra Makwana, conducted by Richard Wallace, 16 March 2015.

> you're not going to know about it until somebody comes and tells you because there's nobody watching it. ... [Y]ou're relying on the public, the paying public, to come and tell you that there's something wrong, which is not ideal, but that's the way it is, because it's down to cost, and you can't be everywhere.

David Rosenbaum asks a key question of his metaphorical troglodytes in the projection box: 'does anyone ever give them a thought?' He answers thus:

> Well, yes and no. No, when everything goes well and the reels are rolling smoothly. Yes, when the screen goes dark, or the image goes out of focus, or the film is scratchy, or the sound crackly. It's only when things go wrong that the Morlocks materialize, squinting into the unaccustomed glare of attention.[305]

The opposition between success/invisibility and failure/visibility is implied in many of our interviews, and made explicit by Sam Lavington, who says that 'a good projectionist is never seen, never heard. In other words, you don't make mistakes.' Chris Blower suggests that 'the only time I actually dealt with the audience was when it was something bad' and that as a result he 'never got any positive feedback from them,'[306] and Peter Howden argues that as a result 'the projectionist is undervalued, largely because unless something happens then you don't know they're there'. This speaks to a fundamental issue within the profession: that good work frequently went unrecognised because of its relative intangibility. The next chapter will investigate the full implications of this fact, and its cynical exploitation by cinema owners, in documenting the history of British projectionists' pay, working conditions and unionisation.

305 Rosenbaum, 'Trysting with Trolls', p. 36

306 Interview with Chris Blower, conducted by Richard Wallace, 11 August 2015.

Chapter Three

Terms and Conditions

Figure 3.1, a photograph published in the British Communist Party newspaper, the *Daily Worker*, shows a section of over 300 striking workers gathered in 1938 for a demonstration in Hyde Park. They are part of the so-called 'Film Strike'; this was a more specialised affair than it sounds, having been specifically organised to champion the grievances of cinema projectionists in London, Manchester and Hull. Cinemas were picketed in the first two cities for six weeks, whilst projectionists in Hull remained on strike for over eight months. The long duration of this industrial action gives us a clear sense of the strength of feeling involved, and it is somewhat shocking to discover what the projectionists were fighting for. They were campaigning for the basic right to have their union recognised by their employers, for a working week no longer than 48 hours (something that had been granted to all British factory workers back in 1919), rather than the 60-70 hour weeks most projectionists were accustomed to, and for an improvement in pay that would address the fact that average weekly wages for projectionists were lower in the late 1930s than they had been at the start of the 1920s. One of the strikers' banners aptly suggests that 'Pleasure for the Patrons' was being delivered at the cost of 'Prison Conditions for the Projectionists'.

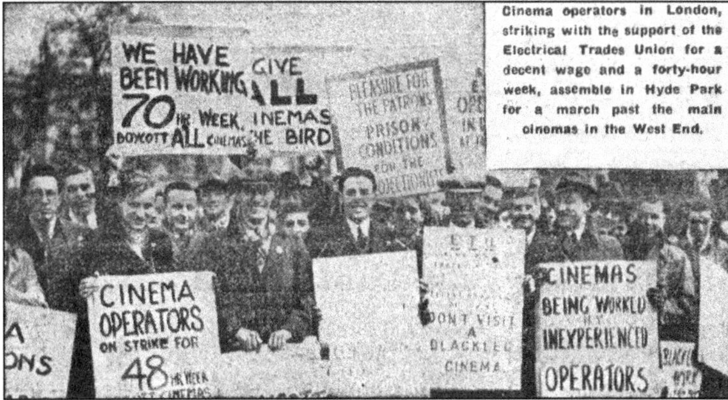
Cinema operators in London, striking with the support of the Electrical Trades Union for a decent wage and a forty-hour week, assemble in Hyde Park for a march past the main cinemas in the West End.

Fig. 3.1: Projectionists assembled in Hyde Park for the 1938 'Film Strike'.[307]

307 *Daily Worker*, 23 April 1938, p. 1.

It seems surprising that slogans and images like these have not previously been widely reprinted within British cinema scholarship. How can it be that canonical studies of mainstream British film culture in the 1930s and dedicated histories of film exhibition in this country fail to make even a passing mention of this militant workers' struggle unfolding beyond the screen?[308] Michael Chanan has argued that the film industry trade press deliberately trivialised the strike and flagrantly downplayed its scale, duration and public impact.[309] Given that film scholars often have to rely upon these sources as journals of record, their partisan reporting offers one explanation for this general oversight.

Another reason is conceivably the fact that this was a much messier conflict than we might prefer it to be. Some contemporary journalists were genuinely confused and ambivalent about how they should cover the dispute, given that they knew that the strike was not simply a conflict between workers and employers, but was also partly an attempt by one union to demonstrate that it could do a better job of representing cinema projectionists than a rival labour organisation.[310] In fact, the strike was dogged by accusations that projectionists affiliated to the rival union were crossing the picket line to help keep the affected cinemas open; the rally in Hyde Park itself was apparently disrupted by workers who belonged to the other side.[311] And, contrary to the impression given by the only two film scholars to have previously paid attention to these events,[312] the Film Strike achieved none of its campaigning or negotiating objectives, and ended miserably, with many striking projectionists unable to regain their jobs. As this chapter will repeatedly demonstrate, the history of cinema projectionists' pay, working conditions and industrial relations is partly a tale of their ruthless exploitation by cinema proprietors. But it is also a story that involves a frequent lack of solidarity amongst projectionists, and territorial disputes between, and flawed decisions taken by,

308 The strike is conspicuous by its absence from, for example, Jeffrey Richards, *The Age of the Dream Palace: Cinema and Society in 1930s Britain* (London: Routledge & Kegan Paul, 1984), and Stuart Hanson, *From Silent Screen to Multi-Screen: A History of Cinema Exhibition in Britain Since 1896* (Manchester and New York: Manchester University Press, 2007). Such omissions bear some responsibility for the fact that BECTU, the amalgamated union for all branches of the contemporary film and television industries, could wrongly claim in February 2017 that an industrial dispute involving around 50 employees of the Picturehouse cinema chain was the 'Largest cinema workers strike in UK history': https://web.archive.org/web/20181022025144/; https://bectu.org.uk/news/2676, accessed 26 August 2020.

309 Michael Chanan, *Labour Power in the British Film Industry* (London: BFI, 1976), p. 51.

310 As evidenced by an enquiry about the strike from W.W. Blair-Fish, editor of the *Rotary Wheel* (the magazine of the British branch of Rotary International), directed to the Trades Union Congress (TUC) secretariat, 5 August 1938, MSS.292/253/23/1, TUC Archive, Modern Records Centre, University of Warwick (hereafter MRC).

311 'E.T.U. Strike Fading Out', *Kinematograph Weekly*, 28 April 1938, p. 5.

312 Chanan, *Labour Power in the British Film Industry*, pp. 48-51; Rachael Low, *Filmmaking in 1930s Britain* (London: George Allen & Unwin, 1985), p. 21.

competing unions. One commentator suggested that it could never be easy 'to get any unanimity of action amongst members working in isolated units'.[313] The seclusion that was endemic to the job was exacerbated by the sheer variety of different cinema working environments, as well as divisions between chief projectionists and the lower ranks. But this did not stop North American projectionists from securing what film historians have adjudged to be extremely powerful and effective union representation.[314] We will show that bitter contention – stretching across many decades – about the kind of union considered appropriate for projectionists, fuelled by various forms of class-based snobbery and resentment, magnified the basic organisational challenges of providing effective labour organisation in Britain, and created a toxic legacy.

The British Film Industry's First Union

The developments that led to the provocative industrial action of 1938, and its ultimate abject failure, were many years in the making. To reach an adequate understanding of how things came to such a pass, we need to first begin with events surrounding the formation of the earliest union for projectionists – the National Association of Cinematograph Operators (NACO) – back in 1907.[315] Projectionists were the first film industry workers to become unionised, which would seem, on the face of it, to suggest that they recognised the need for organisation very quickly, and showed a pugnacious determination to resist their exploitation; this has certainly been the way in which some historians have chosen to interpret the fact of NACO's early formation.[316] We will argue in the first section of this chapter that NACO represented an unusual case of premature unionisation, the main consequence of which was to create and perpetuate a momentous split between different branches of the labour movement concerned with the cinema.

As we explained in Chapter One, the operator had been a more visible and publicised component of moving image entertainment before the advent of cinema buildings. Looking back in 1910, *The Bioscope*'s regular technical correspondent described a 'time, not long past, when an amount of mystery surrounded the working of

313 R. Howard Cricks, 'Varying Standards of Projection', *Ideal Kinema*, 11 February 1937, p. 35.

314 David Bordwell, *Pandora's Digital Box: Films, Files and the Future of Movies* (Madison, WI: Irvington Way Institute Press, 2012), p. 68.

315 For a fuller account of the history of NACO, see Jon Burrows, '"Certificated Operators" versus "Handle Turners": The British Film Industry's First Trade Union', *Journal of British Cinema and Television*, 15:1 (2018), pp. 73-93.

316 See, for example, Rachael Low, *The History of the British Film 1906-1914* (London: George Allen & Unwin, 1949), p. 70; Bert Hogenkamp, 'Labor Movement: Europe' in Richard Abel (ed.), *Encyclopedia of Early Cinema* (London and New York: Routledge, 2005), p. 367.

a projector, and when the wonderful man who could operate a picture machine was looked upon by his friends and acquaintances as being little short of a perfect genius'.[317] The job of a travelling operator required considerable mechanical knowledge and demanded high levels of flexibility and initiative, and it was consequently relatively lucrative work. Various sources suggest that a common rate of pay for an operator in the mid-to-late-1900s was 60 shillings (£3) a week.[318] To put this into context, the average weekly wage in Britain between 1905 and 1909 was around 36.5 shillings (£1-16-10).[319] A trade paper editorial piece in early 1908 confidently asserted that 'the man who is prepared to conscientiously apply his mind and energy to the work of operating a machine can reasonably expect to be well paid for his trouble', and went so far as to predict that the 'operator of the future will be a man of dignity, justifiably proud of holding a position sought after by many, but held by few; whilst the audience before whom he will have to appear will often be of a select and highly educated class'.[320]

This was not an accurate forecast of how the British film exhibition industry was imminently set to evolve. The following year, 1909, saw the emergence of the first significant numbers of fixed-site picture theatres and the beginnings of a transformation of the cinema into a mass medium offering cheap entertainment, primarily – at first – for the benefit of working-class audiences. Despite the fact that similar developments in continental Europe and the United States pre-dated the British cinema boom by several years, this outcome was not broadly anticipated by native trade commentators. Timothy Barnard has observed that the mass expansion of the film exhibition sector on both continents quickly resulted in a 'proletarianisation of the operator', with regards to both pay and working conditions.[321] It has been assumed that NACO was established in direct response to changes in operators' terms of employment once 'film exhibition took on a new shape',[322] but the key dates simply do not match up. NACO was formed on 5 April

317 Arthur S. Newman, 'Improvement and Room for More', *The Bioscope,* 24 November 1910, p. 21.

318 'A Candid Critic Candidly Criticised', *Kinematograph and Lantern Weekly*, 7 June 1907, p. 51; 'The Operators' Meeting', *The Bioscope*, 4 February 1909, p. 5; Edward H. Mason, 'The Case for the Operator's Charter', *Kinematograph and Lantern Weekly*, 30 November 1911, p. 219.

319 Charles Feinstein, 'New Estimates of Average Earnings in the United Kingdom, 1880-1913', *Economic History Review*, 43:4 (November 1990), p. 609.

320 'Spirit of the Times and its Effect on the Trade', *Kinematograph and Lantern Weekly*, 13 February 1908, p. 235.

321 Timothy Barnard, 'The "Machine Operator": *Deus Ex Machina* of the Storefront Cinema', *Framework*, 43:1 (Spring 2002), p. 50.

322 Michael Chanan, *The Dream That Kicks: The Prehistory and Early Years of Cinema in Britain* (London: Routledge & Kegan Paul, 1980), p. 258. See also Barnard, 'The Machine Operator', pp. 42, 49.

1907.[323] Early examples of permanent cinemas in converted shop fronts did exist by this juncture, but it can be ascertained that by the summer of 1907 there were no more than twelve storefront cinemas throughout the whole of London, and only a handful of limited liability companies involved in the field of film exhibition had been set up nationally before 1909.[324]

If the unionisation of projectionists was not a reaction to a cinema boom that had yet to properly commence in the UK, we obviously require a different explanation as to the circumstances that precipitated their organisation at this particular juncture. It is important to note here the contemporaneous activities of the Variety Artistes' Federation (VAF). The VAF was a new union representing music hall performers, which had called a highly publicised and well-supported two-week strike action at London's variety theatres in January 1907, and thereby successfully pressurised employers to sign agreements concerning minimum rates of pay and working hours. The centrality of the music hall industry to the aims and ambitions of NACO's founders is partly reflected in the fact that it was set up as a branch of the main union for backstage theatre workers, the National Association of Theatrical Employees (NATE), established in 1890. It was actually suggested by contemporary journalists that NACO had been specifically established by NATE to suit its own needs. Some music halls had managed to remain open for business during the first week of the VAF strike by replacing live acts with expanded cinematograph turns. Unionisation of projectionists was therefore a simple means by which VAF and NATE could ensure that all key theatre workers would respect any similar strike actions in the future.[325]

A summary of NACO's principal goals, published in late 1908, stated

> the Association aims at enrolling all qualified operators for their mutual benefit and protection, to assist them to keep in touch with improvement and new inventions connected with their business, and to protect them against the amateurs who unfairly compete with the operator dependent upon his skill for a living.[326]

The last of these aims was specifically framed in response to the fact that some music halls had begun to replace their specialist

323 'Important to Operators. Promising Trade Union Formed', *Optical Lantern and Cinematograph Journal*, April 1907, p. 151. For its first few months of existence NACO was known as the Bioscope Operators' Association (BOA); the name was subsequently changed to avoid confusion with the acronym for the British Optical Association (*Kinematograph and Lantern Weekly*, 27 June 1907, p. 97).

324 Jon Burrows, 'Penny Pleasures: Film Exhibition in London During the Nickelodeon Era, 1906-1914', *Film History*, 16:1 (2004), p. 79; Jon Burrows, *The British Cinema Boom: A Commercial History, 1909-1914* (Basingstoke: Palgrave Macmillan, 2017), p. 40.

325 'From the Editor's Pen', *Optical Lantern and Cinematograph Journal*, February 1907, p. 87; 'Important to Operators', p. 151.

326 'N.A.C.O.', *The Bioscope*, 6 November 1908, p. 18.

operators with existing theatre electricians, who were paid a modest weekly salary increase to combine both roles.[327] NACO prioritised this topic in its campaigning activities well into the era of permanent cinemas; diatribes against theatre electricians usurping projectionists were a dominant feature of the union's public pronouncements throughout its first five years of existence.[328] A focus upon issues that were of most concern to operators who had joined the trade back in its pioneer nomadic phase was enshrined in NACO's constitution. Anyone new to the business of film projection was prohibited from joining the union: membership was restricted to established operators over 21 years old who either had at least two years' experience of theatre/music hall projection, or who had been professionally exhibiting longer touring shows before the public for a minimum of eighteen months.[329]

NACO's determination to restrict its membership was ill-fitted to the challenges presented by the radical changes to the employment market for projectionists that followed the rapid spread of fixed-site cinemas from 1909 onwards. The passing into law of the Cinematograph Act (1909), in January 1910, stimulated the investment of large sums of capital in film exhibition,[330] but, prior to this moment, the first significant numbers of cinemas to be established in some of the major cities of England took the form of small converted shop fronts, typically accommodating between 50 and 300 spectators, and charging as little as one penny for admission. The entrepreneurs behind these ventures typically expected significantly longer working hours from their operators than music hall proprietors did. Generating profitable ticket sales at penny prices with a tiny auditorium was practically impossible if the standard live theatrical format of one or two performances per evening was adopted. Consequently, shop-front cinemas pioneered the concept of the continuous performance, maximising revenue by constantly admitting customers throughout the day. This would commonly require the projectionist to work continuously from lunchtime until very late at night.

The initial spread of fixed-site cinemas was responsible for a marked deterioration not only in working conditions, but also salaries. Throughout 1909, film industry trade papers received

327 'A Candid Criticism of the Operators' Association', *Kinematograph and Lantern Weekly*, 30 May 1907, p. 37; 'A Candid Critic Candidly Criticised', *ibid.*, 7 June 1907, p. 51.

328 See, for example, 'N.A.C.O. and Electricians', *The Bioscope*, 4 March 1909, p. 12; William Johnson, 'N.A.C.O.', *ibid.*, 13 May 1909, p. 23; 'N.A.C.O.', *ibid.*, 16 September 1909, p. 23; 'Licensing of Operators', *ibid.*, 26 October 1911, p. 289; 'Operators at Lunch', *Kinematograph and Lantern Weekly*, 8 April 1909, p. 1375; John Hutchins, 'Music Hall Operators', *ibid.*, 12 October 1911, p. 1305; 'Annual Meeting of the N.A.C.O.', *ibid.*, 25 January 1912, p. 679.

329 'National Association of Cinematograph Operators', *The Bioscope*, 9 September 1909, p. 45.

330 Burrows, *The British Cinema Boom*, p. 42.

numerous letters from disgruntled operators protesting about declining pay.[331] As one correspondent from London explained,

> I find that even if I refuse a salary very comfortably under £3, it means that I join the ranks of the unemployed, and I am an operator of many years, not a few weeks' standing, thoroughly competent and practical in operating, photography, optics and electricity, also building and repairing machines ... As an instance of the wonderful salaries we can command, I may mention that some time ago I took an outfit to a new concern up North to fit up and set it going. Having done so, the proprietor asked me to stay on with him. I did so, but he would not pay more than £2. For that I had to give shows from about mid-day until 11 or 12 p.m., and pay my own travelling expenses (we were doing one or two pitches per week). After the show had been running a couple of months or so, the boss was told by another in the business that he could get a man (I won't say operator) to operate, help build up and pull down, and be a general navvy for 25s. per week. He came to me in a shamefaced way and told me about it, saying that he had someone coming to take my place. He guessed it was no use asking me to accept the terms he offered.[332]

A 25 shilling pay packet was five shillings less than the average weekly wage for an unskilled labourer in London at this time.[333]

The period in which penny shop-front cinemas predominated was fairly short-lived, but the introduction of the Cinematograph Act stimulated an even more intensified phase of mushroom development for the industry between 1910 and 1914, with over 1,800 limited liability companies being formed in Britain for the purpose of running cinemas during these five years, representing a combined authorised capital in excess of £10 million – a figure roughly equivalent to over £900 million in today's money.[334] This investment produced significant improvements in cinema architecture, but the court case reports and correspondence pages of the trade press suggest that it did nothing to arrest the steep material decline in terms and conditions of employment that had been experienced by projectionists since 1909.[335] In response to one cinema owner's suggestion that projectionists could not reasonably expect to be

331 See, for example, F.A.H. Jameson, '"Five a Penny" Result', *The Bioscope*, 20 May 1909, p. 23.

332 'Operator or General Utility Man', *ibid.*, 28 October 1909, p. 15.

333 Edward H. Hunt, *Regional Wage Variations in Britain 1850-1914* (Oxford: Clarendon Press, 1973), p. 92.

334 Burrows, *The British Cinema Boom*, pp. 40, 42.

335 See, for example, 'The Status of the Operator', *The Bioscope*, 28 April 1910, p. 55; 'Unsuccessful Claim by an Operator', *ibid.*, 14 July 1910, p. 39; 'A Day from the Diary of an Operator', *ibid.*, 28 July 1910, p. 55; A. Hughes, 'Licensing of Operators', *ibid.*, 19 October 1911, p. 179; '*Ich Dien.* – The Operator's Charter', *ibid.*, 13 February 1913, p. 487; '"*Ich Dien,*" The Operator's Charter', *ibid.*, 27 March 1913, p. 987; 'Help in Trouble', *ibid.*, 16 April 1914, p. 310; 'Weekly Notes', *Kinematograph and Lantern Weekly*, 3 August 1911, p. 661; 'Stroller's Notes', *ibid.*, 15 February 1912, p. 839; 'The Bitter Cry of the "Small" Manager', *ibid.*, 25 December 1913, p. 48; 'Operator Sues for Wages', *The Cinema*, December 1912, p. 91; Lucas, 'The Operator's Page', *ibid.*, 5 March 1913, p. 41.

paid more than a basic mechanic's salary, an exasperated employee from Wolverhampton pointed out that

> an ordinary skilled mechanic is not working in the heated atmosphere of 90 to 100 degrees, with a 4,000 to 5,000 candle-power light under his eyes for ten hours per day (Saturdays, and, in numerous cases, Sundays included); that when a mechanic has finished his day's labour he is at liberty to seek a full night's enjoyment, whilst his more 'fortunate' brethren, the operators, are still perspiring, in some cases in a box not sufficiently large to turn around in comfort, projecting pictures he has seen a dozen or more times previously.[336]

The degradation of film projection into an occupation which bore several of the hallmarks of 'dirty work',[337] as influentially characterised by the sociologist Everett Hughes – such as low pay, exhausting labour and unpleasant working conditions – is most eloquently expressed in a poem of heartfelt desperation written in 1914 by an operator of unknown provenance called W.A. Williamson:

Never give the beggar best—
'E' s a low-born Operator.
Leave 'im no more chance of rest
Than a bloke on Etna's crater.
If a film be scratched or worn,
If a sprocket-hole be torn—
Well, It's no concern of your'n.
Kick the poor old Operator!

I'm here alone in a fireproof box that is hot as a stokehole floor,
And my head goes round to a clicking sound and a rickety motor's roar.
And my nose smells FILMS, and my tongue tastes FILMS,
And my eyes they can see FILMS too,
Till I'm sick unto death at the thought of F I L M S
(Convict-son-shot-by-his-father FILMS),
(Out-of-work-burgles-a-bunshop FILMS),
And—Oh, rattle that programme through!

I've spoiled my life, and I'm sorry now, but my sorrow has come too late;
And I'm only fit to be pulling films through the slits of a rusty gate.
And all for the sake of mother and home and twenty-five shillings a week.
I'm working here up to my neck in FILMS
(Outlaw-redeemed-by-a-baby FILMS)
(Thunder-and-blood-and-sensation FILMS),
nd—Oh, lor'! How that belt does creak!

I've broken films and I've mended films till my fingers are skin and bone;
But the crowds that go to each picture show never think how a film

336 '"Ich Dien," The Operator's Charter', *The Bioscope*, 27 March 1913, p. 987.

337 Everett C. Hughes, 'Good People and Dirty Work', *Social Problems*, 3:1 (1962), pp. 3-11.

> is shown.
> And when I'm asleep I shall dream of films—
> though it's little of sleep I take,
> Through nightmare that cumbers my bed with F I L M S
> (Redskins-attacking-the-white-folk FILMS)
> (Mother's-lost-ninepence-at-ludo FILMS),
> And—Confound it! Another break!
>
> I have to pay if a thing goes wrong, for the management dock my screw;
> It' s a penny a rack and a penny a break, though the programme is far from new.
> And never iron has entered a soul as the celluloid's entered mine.
> It's, Oh! to be shot of the sight of films
> (Comic-chase-over-the-housetops FILMS)
> (Ought-to-be-cut-by-the-Censor FILMS),
> And—A carbon's gone—Sixpence fine!
>
> I'm wet with oil and I'm choked with dirt till I haven't the heart to eat;
> It's a joy to know where the bad folks go that a film couldn't stand the heat.
> To be clear of films, to be rid of films, would be happiness grand and true.
> Sometimes I hardly can breathe for FILMS
> (Railway-and-Injun-and-Cowboy FILMS)
> Tragedy-Comedy-Scenic FILMS),
> And — Thank Heavens! The programme's Through!
>
> **Now rewind the films once more**
> **Like a careful Operator.**
> **Patch 'em nicely where they've tore**
> **Or they'll blame the Operator.**
> **Never mind your aching head,**
> **Think about your Films instead.**
> **Then they'll let you go to bed;**
> **Ain't you grateful, Operator?**[338]

The fourth president of NACO, Edward H. Mason, offered the following reflections on how the industry, and the operator's place within it, had been utterly transformed:

> With [the picture palace's] advent the whole condition of employment changed. ... The abnormally rapid growth of the continuous show left many small employers struggling for existence; they eagerly embraced the opportunity of employing the cheapest labour they could command, satisfied if a picture of some sort was put upon the screen, so long as they could manage to keep afloat. Some big syndicates did not scruple to subordinate everything to the desire to pay huge dividends, and the employee was sweated to that end. These are the causes which have been responsible for the gradual deterioration of the profession, and unless this downward tendency is

338 W.A. Williamson, 'The Operator', *The Bioscope*, 22 October 1914, p. 340 (emphasis in original).

> checked, it will not be long before the experienced man seeking a fair remuneration for his services will be driven out of the profession altogether. Six years ago the operator's average rate of pay was £3 per week, and that for a show lasting at the utmost limit two hours, and more often than not, not more than twenty minutes. Today the average rate of pay is £1 10s. for a continuous show of nine hours a day or more. ... There are dozens of cases brought to the notice of the N.A.C.O. by members who have been offered 25s. per week for a continuous show, and advertisements are continually appearing where even a lower wage is offered.[339]

In several respects this is a persuasive and no doubt accurate analysis of the downturn in pay and working conditions experienced by projectionists, but it is important to note that it took until November 1911 for a NACO official to make any public criticism of the culpability of cinema owners. It was an inescapable fact that the rapid expansion of the film exhibition sector demanded an enlarged workforce, and there is no question that the union did not responsibly face up to the challenge of how the escalation in recruitment should be managed and new operators fairly treated. Edwin S. Catlin, the founding president of NACO, had previously argued that

> An operator is a man who can work on any voltage or any machine from a Chrono to a Walturdaw, from an Edison to a Kineto, a man who, when his employer says, I want you to go to such a place and give 1 two-hours' show in the Corn Exchange, the voltage is 220 (either current), take what resistance you require and catch the 9.20 train in the morning, can pack up his entire outfit, proceed on his journey, and give an exhibition that is a credit to himself and the firm he represents: and then go on to another town the next day and give a show in a drawing-room, with limelight, with the same results. Let him do this night after night for a year or two and he can call himself an operator ...[340]

The reality was that many of the skills described here had limited relevance to the era of permanent projection installations, and the supply of men with this level of experience was totally insufficient to service the industry's growing needs. In 1911, Catlin was still protesting that 'good men [are] out of employment, whilst duds run the shows', and restated his sympathies for 'the competent operator, not the handle-turner.'[341] NACO officials repeatedly used the derogatory sobriquet of 'handle-turner' to describe neophyte operators, implying that they were capable of the menial labour of hand-cranking film through a projector, but nothing

339 Edward H. Mason, 'The Case for the Operator's Charter', *Kinematograph and Lantern Weekly*, 30 November 1911, p. 219.

340 Edwin S. Catlin, 'N.A.C.O.', *ibid.*, 29 April 1909, p. 13.

341 Edwin S. Caitlin, 'Thanks for the KINE's Help', *ibid.*, 19 October 1911, p. 1357.

more.[342] One might reasonably argue that, by denigrating the majority of people working as projectionists, this rhetoric ultimately played into the employers' hands. It effectively endorsed the idea that most operators were unskilled drudges, and unworthy of a better rate of pay.

NACO's failure to engage with the needs and concerns of the majority of projectionists is clearly demonstrated by its extremely modest enrolment figures. By the time of its third anniversary, the union had only managed to recruit 200 men. This was estimated to represent only 5-6% of the total number of people then working as projectionists in Britain.[343] NACO continued to steadily expand over the next few years, but hardly kept pace with the exponential growth of the industry. Total subscriptions had reached 350 by April 1911 and just under 550 a year later.[344] In early 1912 it was finally accepted that NACO's structural constitution was unfit for purpose in the era of fixed-site cinemas; a report proposing radical changes to the organisation noted that

> when the Association was founded less than five years ago, the continuous show of the present day was not in existence. A few shop shows had made an appearance, but that was the extent to which the modern picture palace had attained. In those days an operator had to be prepared to carry everything necessary for an exhibition with him, to fit up under any and every condition, and change from lime to electric illuminant as often as the circumstances required. This man was an operator in the true sense of the word. Modern conditions have modified the operator's existence. The picture palace of the present day is fitted with every appliance for giving a perfect show under ideal conditions, and has called into existence an operator who is qualified to meet the demand, but would be perfectly useless under the old ones. ... Under the old constitution of the Association, the fully qualified man, who was prepared to go anywhere and do anything bioscopic was alone recognised; under the new, all engaged in projection work will be recognised and graded into classes, so that the sometime complaint that was levelled against the Society of exclusiveness is swept away.[345]

Two additional classes of operator were recognised under the new rules: 'Assistants', who were at least eighteen years old, and had been working in cinemas for six-to-twelve months, and 'Juniors', in the same age bracket, who had just begun working in the

342 See, for example, J. Wood, 'National Association of Cinematograph Operators', *The Bioscope*, 30 September 1909, p. 51; John Hutchins, 'The Registration of Operators', *ibid.*, 9 February 1911, p. 3; W. Allan Waldie, 'Murdering New Subjects', *Kinematograph and Lantern Weekly*, 22 February 1912, p. 937.

343 'National Association of Kinematograph Operators. Successful Third Annual Luncheon', *Kinematograph and Lantern Weekly*, 21 April 1910, p. 1323.

344 'Kinematograph Operators at Lunch', *ibid.*, 27 April 1911, p. 1718; 'The N.A.C.O. Annual Luncheon', *ibid.*, 2 May 1912, p. 75.

345 'N.A.C.O. Notes', *ibid.*, 1 February 1912, p. 741.

projection box. The condition of eligibility for the original 'Class A' membership status was simultaneously reduced to twelve months' experience, rather than two years. These were all sensible moves, but they seem to have been implemented too late in the day to persuade non-unionised operators that NACO could effectively represent their interests. The growth rate of NACO actually started to decline in 1912: only 116 new members joined the union in the twelve months following this radical revision of the rules of admission, compared with nearly 200 new recruits in the preceding year.[346] The figures suggest that NACO had come to be regarded with mistrust or indifference by most operators by this stage.

The inevitable demise of NACO was as low-key as much of its operational activity had been. Throughout the duration of the First World War no public statements were issued and no meetings were held. In June 1919 the parent union NATE announced that it was comprehensively reorganising its cinema branch to represent all members of cinema staff – ticket sellers, ushers, doormen and cleaners – alongside projectionists. The concept of an autonomous union called NACO that exclusively served the needs of projectionists was henceforth dropped.[347]

Michael Chanan has argued that 'The real weakness of NACO ... was that it was the wrong type of union'; because it was constituted as a traditional craft union for skilled workers, he suggests, NACO failed to exploit the opportunity to effectively pressurise employers by mobilising all cinema workers within the framework of a modern industrial union.[348] We will show later in this chapter how NATE's decision to reconstitute itself as a union representing the entire film exhibition industry did deliver very significant gains to its strength and influence. However, we will also see that NATE's expansion resulted in a significant loss of support from projectionists, many of whom saw organisation on a craft basis as vital to the adequate representation of their interests. The failure of NACO was partly a problem of bad timing. Its founding aims and objects were swiftly rendered anachronistic by the rapid and radical transformation of the cinema industry after 1909. And, having grown accustomed to very different working conditions over the preceding decade-and-a-half, its executive appeared to be constitutionally incapable of accepting and adequately confronting the consequences of the downward social mobility of the profession. The

346 'The National Association of Cinematograph Operators', *ibid.*, 6 February 1913, p. 1529.

347 Curiously, the revival of a NACO correspondence exam paper inaugurated back in 1907 was announced in 1919 ('Half-Yearly Examination for Operators', *ibid.*, 19 June 1919, p. 117), and was issued again the following year ('N.A.C.O.'s Quarterly Examination', *ibid.*, 11 March 1920, p. xix), but the distinct branch name was otherwise hardly ever used by NATE again.

348 Chanan, *Labour Power in the British Film Industry*, pp. 15-16.

legacy of NACO was unfortunately enduring and predominantly negative. The divisions that it opened up and exacerbated between operators of differing ranks and experience levels would continue to present a serious obstacle to effective labour organisation amongst this group of workers for decades to come. Because it had been first in the field to represent operators, NATE steadfastly refused to surrender its claims upon them. But because the weaknesses and eventual collapse of NACO had seriously compromised NATE's credibility amongst many projectionists, competition was able to enter the fray, inaugurating a long period of damaging internecine conflict.

Short-lived Militancy

The Electrical Trades Union (ETU), the primary national union for electricians, founded in 1889, seems to have begun recruiting cinema operators in Manchester in 1915 or '16. This first move into the film industry proved to be something of a false start for the union: their projectionist membership peaked at fifty, before migration to the colours progressively reduced this to three, and its operators' branch was consequently closed down.[349] For the duration of the war, then, employment practices continued to be largely untroubled by any form of union regulation. Monumental labour shortages were created by military mobilisation: general conscription for all healthy men between the ages of eighteen and 41 came into force from the summer of 1916, and no exemptions were made for cinema workers. This led cinema owners to adopt hiring policies that generated so much resentment amongst operators returning from the armed services after the war that they helped to catalyse a new phase of ardent union recruitment, spearheaded by the ETU.

Ironically, the two best-documented developments affecting cinema projection boxes during the war – the employment of women and the training of disabled soldiers as operators – were not the most controversial. Female operators were a distinct rarity before the War, with only two cases of women undertaking the role known to the licensing authority for inner London between 1910 and 1914.[350] The very idea of a woman successfully handling a projector was predominantly treated as a subject for comic fantasy during the cinema boom period. A cartoon published in *The Bioscope* in 1909, accompanying a fictional report on the 'Grand Opening of the School for Lady Operators (We Don't Think)', depicts a scene of chaos, partly caused by nosy women pupils meddling dangerously with the electrical generator, their terrified

349 'Operators and Unions', *Kinematograph and Lantern Weekly*, 3 April 1919, p. 101.

350 Letter from the LCC to the Home Office, 10 May 1915, NA HO45/20876.

reactions to a mouse, and the male instructor being distracted by amorous desires for the prettiest member of the class (see Fig. 3.2).

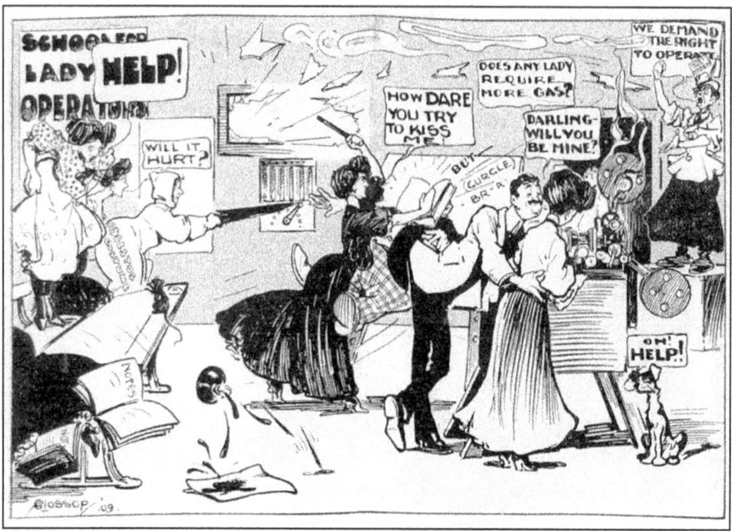

Fig. 3.2: Trade ridicule of the idea of women training to be projectionists in 1909.[351]

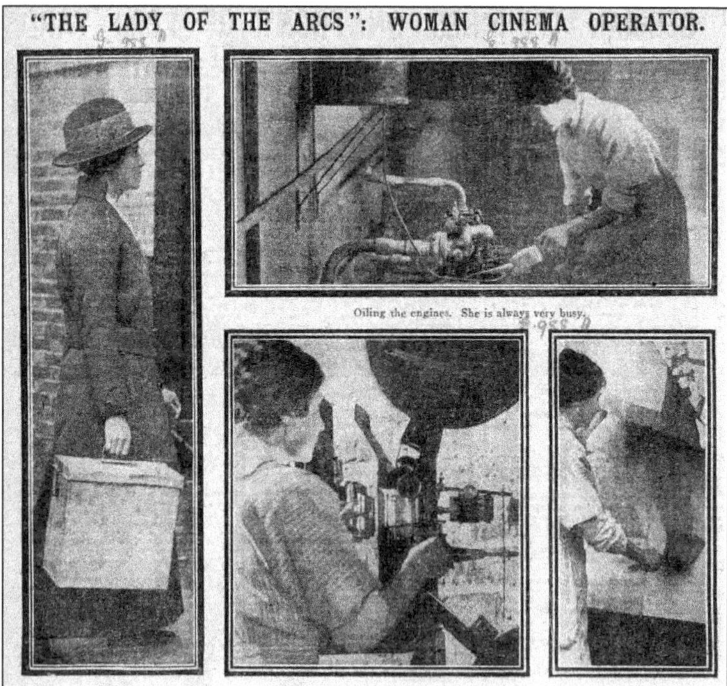

Fig. 3.3: Press interest in female operators during the Great War.[352]

351 'Grand Opening of the School for Lady Operators (We Don't Think)', *The Bioscope*, 24 June 1909, p. 7.

352 *Daily Mirror*, 17 June 1915, p. 4. See also 'Woman Cinema Operator', *Daily Record*, 15 April 1916, p. 1.

In an article dedicated to the subject of the film industry's employment of women during the First World War, David R. Williams reproduces further satirical cartoons published in the film industry trade press in 1915, which suggested that women lacked the necessary work ethic and powers of concentration, alongside a sceptical editorial comment concerning their ability to meet the physical demands of the job.[353] But the level of recorded objection was otherwise relatively modest.[354] In seeking Home Office advice about the safety implications of allowing women to enter the box, the London County Council explained that they did not see 'any reason why women should not be able to acquire the requisite degree of knowledge and skill and in the circumstances the Council is of opinion that no objection should be raised to the employment of competent women as cinematograph operators'.[355] (The outgoing Home Secretary, Reginald McKenna, agreed, though he felt compelled to warn that 'Women are more apt to lose their heads than men and cases have occurred when prompt action on the part of an operator has prevented serious consequences.'[356]) After it was misreported by journalists that McKenna's successor, Sir John Simon, wanted to encourage the employment of women as operators – when he had simply supported the position that no objection should be made[357] – there was a brief flurry of national press interest in the subject of female projectionists, which is typified by Fig. 3.3. We have found no estimates of the number of women employed as operators at this time, though, and there is some evidence to suggest that the figure may not have been particularly large.[358]

As Lawrence Napper has pointed out, the idea of wounded Great War soldiers being retrained and discreetly returned to civilian life out of public sight in cinema projection boxes has increasingly come to exercise a significant hold on the imaginations of writers, dramatists and television documentary makers – albeit under the completely mistaken assumption that this programme was devised

353 David R. Williams, 'Ladies of the Lamp: The Employment of Women in the British Film Trade During World War I', *Film History*, 9:1 (1997), pp. 118-120.

354 The *Kinematograph and Lantern Weekly*'s technical expert supported the employment of women, though he worried that too few of them had both nerve and imagination, rather than one or the other: Colin N. Bennett, 'The Right Sort of Lady Operator', *Kinematograph and Lantern Weekly*, 21 March 1918, p. 101.

355 Letter from the LCC to the Home Office, 10 May 1915, NA HO45/20876. The only caveat expressed concerned the perceived 'element of danger in the use by women operators of such dress materials as cotton and flannelette'.

356 Minutes of Home Office meeting, 12 May 1915, NA HO45/20876.

357 See unidentified press clipping, 14 July 1915, and accompanying comments in NA HO45/20876.

358 In later years, it was claimed that in the city of Southampton, which was the central UK hub for troop movements, and boasted around nineteen cinemas, only one woman entered this line of work during the '14-'18 conflict: 'Women Kinema Workers at Southampton', *Kinematograph Weekly*, 23 October 1941, p. 29.

for the benefit of veterans with disfiguring facial injuries.[359] The Cinematograph Trade Advisory Committee (Disabled Sailors and Soldiers), formed in partnership between the government and the film industry in 1917, actually came into being with the primary aim of providing work for men who had suffered leg amputations.[360] It organised what was arguably the most ambitious scheme of intensive projection training that Britain would ever see. The courses lasted for thirteen weeks, with thirty hours of classes per week. Projection training centres were established in Birmingham, Cardiff, Glasgow, Leeds, Liverpool, London, Manchester, Newcastle, Nottingham and Bournemouth. Against the wishes of the Cinematograph Exhibitors' Association (CEA), the Ministry of Labour invited representatives of both NATE and the ETU – despite the fact that both had very few projectionist members at this point in time – to sit on the technical committees for each regional training centre.[361] Their aim in this was specifically to try and ensure that the number of men trained did not exceed the level that could be realistically absorbed by employers in each area, and thereby avoid any possibility of creating future competition and conflict in the job market with conscripted operators, once the latter were discharged from the armed services.[362]

It was claimed in 1917 that sufficient openings existed for a minimum of 1,000 disabled soldiers to be trained as projectionists, though there was also a confident expectation than 2,000 men could ultimately be accommodated.[363] In practice, only 318 men completed the training, and the decision was taken in February 1919 to stop further recruitment because of severe difficulties experienced in finding employment for them.[364] By this point, it was being reported that eight out of ten graduates of the scheme could not get jobs in cinemas.[365] A stunned official from the

359 Lawrence Napper, 'Disabled Operators: Training Disabled Ex-servicemen as Projectionists During the Great War', *Journal of British Cinema and Television*, 15:1 (2018), pp. 104-105.

360 Letter from Paul Kimberley to Major Robert Mitchell, 16 August 1918, NA LAB/2/624/TDS5896/1919. The logic here does seem somewhat puzzling; projecting films involved constant standing, and it was suggested in 1920 that 'in Britain the proportion of operating rooms where an operator's stool will be found is by no means large' (Colin N. Bennett, 'Projection Points', *Kinematograph Weekly*, 15 April 1920, p. x).

361 Draft report of Ministry of Labour with reference to the regulations approved by the Cinema Trade Advisory Committee (Disabled Sailors and Soldiers) for the training of disabled men as cinematograph operators and to be submitted to the Ministry of Pensions, April 1917, NA LAB/2/624/TDS5896/1919.

362 Instructions issued by the Ministry of Pensions to regulate the training of disabled men as cinematograph operators, 22 August 1917, NA LAB/2/624/TDS5896/1919.

363 J. St. G. Heath, 'Reports Upon Openings in Industry Suitable for Disabled Soldiers and Sailors. No. III. The Cinematograph Industry', April 1917, NA LAB/2/624/TDS5896/1919.

364 'The Disabled Soldier Operator', *Kinematograph and Lantern Weekly*, 20 February 1919, p. 73; letter from William Johnson to Major Roger Mitchell, 20 February 1919, NA LAB/2/624/TDS5896/1919.

365 Report on a meeting of the National Cinema Trade Advisory Committee held at Montagu House, 20 February 1919, NA LAB/2/624/TDS5896/1919.

Ministry of Pensions noted that this was 'the first instance of a T.[rade] A.[dvisory] C.[ommittee] concluding its functions owing to lack of employment facilities'.[366] All of which begs the question: how did things go so wrong? By way of explanation, Napper quotes a public statement made by the CEA in April 1919, in which they claimed that the industry could not take any more disabled veterans because of the volume of demobilised men who were now demanding their former jobs as operators back.[367]

This was also the excuse that the exhibitors presented in private correspondence with the Ministry of Labour. The chairman of the CEA told L.C. Bell-Cox, the co-ordinator of the Trade Advisory Committee programme, that

> The slightest pressure on my part to train men against the firm and unanimous resolutions addressed to me by the two Trade Unions which control my labour would inevitably and quickly have put me in the position of the pitting of disabled trainees against qualified and unemployed trade unionists.[368]

As a result of his direct Committee dealings with NATE and the ETU, however, Bell-Cox had become all too aware that both of the unions were entirely 'dormant', as far as projectionists were concerned, and thus had zero negotiating strength within the industry.[369] Following further investigation, he was able to explain to his colleagues the real – scandalous – reason why the scheme had failed:

> during 1915 and 16 when many of the operators had to join the Colours, youths of between 16 and 20, owing to the shortage of labour, though they were no more than reel winders, were allowed under the circumstances to go into the boxes as operators, with the result that at the present time, no [sic] only the discharged disabled trained men, but the demobilised operator cannot find work, as Proprietors of Circuits and individual Picturedromes, are only too willing to exploit a cheap form of labour as long as they possibly can.[370]

In the aftermath of the Armistice, the correspondence pages of the film industry trade press and local newspapers received many letters from angry able-bodied ex-servicemen who found themselves unable to regain their old projection jobs. A small number blamed their situation on competition from women,[371] but most complained that they had been displaced by cheap teenage

366 Handwritten note by Captain R. Gery, 4 March 1919, NA LAB/2/624/TDS5896/1919.

367 Napper, 'Disabled Operators', p. 111.

368 Letter from F.R. Goodwin to L.C. Bell-Cox, 4 June 1919, NA LAB/2/624/TDS5896/1919.

369 Letter from L.C. Bell-Cox to F.R. Goodwin, 12 June 1919, NA LAB/2/624/TDS5896/1919.

370 Letter from L.C. Bell-Cox to Captain Telford-Hewson, 21 November 1919, NA LAB/2/624/TDS5896/1919.

371 E. Martin, 'Incompetent and Underpaid Operators', *Kinematograph and Lantern Weekly*, 22 May 1919, p. 104.

labour.[372] It was frequently alleged that weekly salaries in the range of £1-5-0 to £2-10-0 for chief and assistant operators were now commonplace throughout the country.[373] This was consistent with wage levels reported before the war, but the cost of living in Britain had doubled by the end of the conflict, and the national average wage paid in 1918 to ordinary labourers in the engineering industry, for example, was £3-14-0.[374] The prevalent use of poorly-trained youths provoked other concerns. It was repeatedly alleged that projection standards had suffered a dramatic deterioration over the course of the war, resulting in numerous presentational faults and programme interruptions.[375] Licensing authorities became deeply concerned about the safety implications of having teenagers running projection boxes, and a marked rise in film ignition incidents in Birmingham cinemas was attributed to their employment.[376]

Ministry of Labour officials began to openly suggest that legislation might be necessary to regulate employment practices in cinemas, but they ultimately settled on a covert course of action by encouraging the ETU to try and take the industry in hand. '[I]f the E.T.U. could only get the skilled Operators to join their Union, I feel this would make a great difference as then with a powerful Body behind them, the Operators could insist upon their rights and once and for all get rid of "Boy" labour', Bell-Cox wrote to the secretary of the union's Manchester branch in the early summer of 1919.[377] The ETU did not need government prompting to renew its interest in the film industry, having already reopened its sub-branch for operators in Manchester, along with a new branch in Dundee, and also held an open recruitment meeting for London projectionists by the middle of May 1919.[378] This was a period of aggressive

372 See, for example, 'Boys as Operators', *ibid.*, 23 January 1919, p. 32; 'A Soldier's Grievance', *ibid.*, 20 February 1919, p. 80; 'The Operators' Union', *ibid.*, 10 April 1919, p. 95; 'Why Unions Succeed', *ibid.*, 9 December 1920, p. 85; 'The Cinema Operator', *Nottingham Evening Post*, 15 May 1919, p. 3; 'The Cinema Operator', *ibid.*, 21 May 1919, p. 3; 'The Cinema Operator', *ibid.*, 23 May 1919, p. 3; 'The Cinema Operator', *ibid.*, 26 May 1919, p. 3.

373 'Operators' Work', *ibid.*, 6 December 1917, p. 90; George Aitken, 'Operators and Operating', *ibid.*, 10 January 1918, p. 73; 'Operators and Unions' *ibid.*, 3 April 1919, p. 101; 'Wages of the Cine', *John Bull*, 5 April 1919, p. 3; letter from F. Taylor to L.C. Bell-Cox, 7 July 1919, NA LAB/2/624/TDS5896/1919.

374 Alastair Reid, 'The Impact of the First World War on British Workers', in Richard Wall and Jay Winter (eds), *The Upheaval of War: Family, Work and Welfare in Europe, 1914-1918* (Cambridge: Cambridge University Press, 1988), pp. 221-233.

375 For example, Lance-Corporal F. Petherick, 'An Operator on Service', *Kinematograph and Lantern Weekly*, 16 August 1917, p. 103; 'Unskilled Operators', *ibid.*, 2 January 1919, p. 58; 'Certificates for Operators', *ibid.*, 27 February 1919, p. 82.

376 'Young Operators in Kinemas', *ibid.*, 12 December 1918, p. 76. The LCC passed a resolution on 31 October 1916 prohibiting anyone under the age of 18 from being left in charge of the box; see NA HO45/20876.

377 Letter from L.C. Bell-Cox to F. Taylor, 23 June 1919, NA LAB/2/624/TDS5896/1919.

378 J. Slater, 'The K.O.U.', *Kinematograph and Lantern Weekly*, 8 May 1919, p. 110; 'London Operators Join the E.T.U.', *ibid.*, 15 May 1919, p. 66.

expansion for the union more generally. Between 1918 and 1920, the national membership rose from 20,621, organised in 165 branches, to 57,292 in 403 branches.[379] As well as projectionists, the ETU also (briefly and unsuccessfully) tried to sign up film renters' employees, as well as photographic laboratory technicians, to a separate 'Film Workers' branch.[380] This would have given them the ability to starve exhibitors of films as well as projection labour, if employers took a bellicose approach in negotiations; part of the ETU's pitch to projectionists was that it could enforce their demands by calling electrical sub-station workers out on strike with them, thereby closing cinemas down in one fell swoop.[381] By September 1919, it was claimed that 100% of operators in London cinemas had joined the union, making for a membership total of over 800 in the five metropolitan sub-branches, according to one source.[382] By the end of the year, 160 men had been signed up in Manchester – a city with 68 cinemas – plus 75% of all the operators in the Birmingham area.[383]

This recruitment drive brought the ETU into direct conflict with NATE, and a bitter war of words duly ensued.[384] Such was the ETU's irresistible momentum at this stage, however, that in January 1920 NATE backed down from arguing that it had an exclusive claim upon operators, and agreed to sign a pact by which both unions agreed 'to recognise each other's membership card in the Entertainment Industry' and vowed 'not to induce a member of the other Union to leave one Union for the other'.[385] The CEA's response to the unionisation of projectionists on a hitherto unprecedented scale was distinctly mixed. Some of the regional branches were exceptionally hostile. Leeds exhibitors condemned the clauses outlined in the ETU's opening set of demands 'as a step in the direction of Soviet government'.[386] Edward Hewitson – who would be elected as the national CEA chairman in 1927 – tried to

379 Anon., *The Story of the E.T.U.: The Official History of the Electrical Trades Union* (Bromley, Kent: E.T.U., 1952), pp. 88, 115.

380 'Film Workers' Meeting', *Kinematograph Weekly*, 4 March 1920, p. xxv; 'Film Workers Organise', *ibid.*, 15 July 1920, p. xix.

381 J. Slater, 'The E.T.U. and its Critics', *Kinematograph and Lantern Weekly*, 5 June 1919, p. 78.

382 'London Branch Meeting of E.T.U. (Operators)', *ibid.*, p. 95; 'E.T.U. Operators' Branch', *Kinematograph Weekly*, 3 June 1920, p. xix. (A later source claimed that London membership peaked at 729: 'The Observation Window', *ibid.*, 22 July 1926, p. 51.)

383 'Manchester Operators' Meeting', *ibid.*, 4 December 1919, p. xxiii; 'E.T.U. Organises Birmingham Operators', *ibid.*, 18 December 1919, p. 93. The Birmingham figure was said to have risen to 98% by March 1920: 'The E.T.U. and Recognition', *ibid.*, 11 March 1920, p. 108.

384 'Kinema Operators' Union, E.T.U.', *Kinematograph and Lantern Weekly*, 12 June 1919, p. 60; 'E.T.U. Defies N.A.T.E.', *Kinematograph Weekly*, 6 November 1919, p. xxi.

385 'Agreement Between E.T.U. & N.A.T.E.', *ibid.*, 1 January 1920, p. 124.

386 'The Operators' Demands', *ibid.*, 4 March 1920, p. 109.

persuade fellow Birmingham cinema owners that they should on principle refuse to recognise the legitimacy of any trade union.[387]

Hewitson's stance was denounced in the trade press as 'wholly misguided and woefully behind the spirit of the times'.[388] The view that unions could no longer be ignored was also shared within the CEA's General Council. The First World War – as many recognised – had constituted a watershed moment for the British labour movement. Unions had been accorded a new national importance in facilitating the creation of an industrial economy geared to the conflict, and their parliamentary wing, the Labour Party, had replaced the Liberals as the main party of opposition. It was widely believed that Labour would be able to win a General Election within the next decade.[389] In 1917, the chairman of the CEA's London branch, F.R. Goodwin, wrote a series of articles advocating a post-war alliance with the Labour Party; it was the ideal political partner to protect the industry's interests, he argued, because the latter provided entertainment predominantly for the working classes. He also suggested that in order to clear the path for such a pact, the sector would need to 'put its own house in order' by co-operating with the industry unions to 'purge away all sweated and underpaid conditions of the workers'.[390] Goodwin backed up his convictions by entering and concluding negotiations with the ETU very briskly; an operators' rate card for London cinemas was agreed in January 1920. By the end of that year similar agreements were reached between the ETU and more than half of the 22 CEA branches: Aberdeen, Birmingham, Bradford and Leeds, Bristol, Glasgow, Hull, Leicester, Liverpool, Manchester, Northern, Sheffield and Sussex. The ability of the CEA's national executive to bend the regional branches to its will was notoriously limited, but there was a key supplementary factor that helped the progressive viewpoint to win favour: cinemas enjoyed unprece-

387 'The E.T.U. and Recognition', *ibid.*, 11 March 1920, p. 108.

388 'Midland & S.W. Supplement', *ibid.*, p. 118.

389 Chris Wrigley, 'Trade Unions and Politics in the First World War', in Ben Pimlott and Chris Cook (eds), *Trade Unions in British Politics* (London and New York: Longman, 1982), pp. 79-81, 86-89, 93-95.

390 F.[rederick] R.[ice] Goodwin, 'The Need for Unity in the Trade', *Kinematograph and Lantern Weekly*, 5 July 1917, p. 77; Goodwin, 'A Pact with the Labour Party', *ibid.*, 12 July 1917, p. 79. The CEA attempted to demonstrate its commitment to good industrial relations in 1918 by agreeing to help form and run a Joint Industrial Council (JIC) for the entertainment industry, following the recommendations of a landmark 1917 report produced by John Henry Whitley, MP, on 'The Relations of Employers and Employees'. The JIC in question consisted of representatives of employers and employees from the cinema, legitimate theatre and music hall industries, and proved to be an abject failure. Its chair conceded in 1921 that 'the Council is not doing and is not expected to do all that it might for the benefit of the Industry, whilst the thing which it is expected to do, namely, procure the complete gratification of a number of diametrically opposed interests, is quite impossible. The Council is composed of organised bodies who are in conflict with one another over their special interests' (transcript of address by Sir Oswald Stoll, 1 July 1921, NA LAB/2/485/HQ12269/2/1018). The CEA's damning verdict on the JIC is reported in 'Annual Report of the C.E.A.', *Kinematograph Weekly*, 17 February 1921, p. 88.

dented levels of popularity in the immediate aftermath of the Armistice, and some circuits experienced a rise in profits of over 500%.[391]

The ETU deals all contained very similar clauses, and the Manchester rate card might be taken as typical. The working week was to be capped at 48 hours, with double time paid for work undertaken after 11pm. One week's holiday with pay was to be granted every twelve months for all grades of operator employed for over six months. 'No other work to be recognised as operators' work', stated one clause, except projection, equipment maintenance and the collection, care and despatch of films. All cinemas had to employ an assistant or apprentice alongside a chief. Salaries were calculated according to whether a cinema was classed as First Grade (over 600 seats or having maximum admission charges of 9d. or above) or Second Grade, and followed the district rate paid to journeyman electricians. The minimum wage for adult operators was to be £4-10-0 per week at First Grade halls, and £3-10-0 at the smaller cinemas. It was agreed that wages would rise or fall in relation to changes in the local electricians' rate. In order to manage previous abuses around the employment of teenagers, operators between the ages of sixteen and 21 were to be classed as apprentices and had to serve five years before they could be promoted to chief. Women already engaged as operators could keep their jobs, but it was stipulated that 'no more females' should be engaged in future.[392]

Several minor incidents of industrial action by ETU operators attended the refusal of some cinemas in these districts to observe the agreed conditions, but it was generally perceived that the union passed its first 'trial of strength' with ease.[393] However, this new era of effectively organised projectionists did not last long. ETU membership statistics from 1921 to 1923 have been preserved, and these record a sudden precipitous decline in subscriptions. This began in 1921, when the union's branches for operators in Cardiff, Portsmouth, Plymouth, Sheffield and Southampton were all closed down. Membership in London and Manchester dropped to 412 and 41, respectively. At the close of that year the total number of operators enrolled in special ETU branches stood at 1,155. By the end of 1922 the figure was 359, and it fell again to 282 over the following twelve months.[394] The question of why projectionists

391 Burrows, *The British Cinema Boom*, pp. 117-118.

392 ETU Working Rules of the Cinema Operators, Assistants and Apprentices. Manchester and District, 9 February 1920, NA LAB/83/3320.

393 'Northern Supplement', *Kinematograph Weekly*, 3 June 1920, p. 135; 'Midland and S.W. Supplement', *ibid.*, 25 November 1920, p. 110.

394 ETU annual reports for 1922 and 1923, TU.ELEC.1.1, ETU Archive, Working Class Movement Library, Salford (hereafter WCML).

abandoned the union in droves almost immediately after it secured significant improvements in pay and conditions was never posed in the pages of the film industry trade press at the time. Retrospective explanations were occasionally hinted at in later years. The district secretary of the London ETU branch claimed in 1926 that projectionists collectively stopped paying their subs out of a naïve sense of complacency: 'the operators felt their position was secure; their wages and conditions were, in future, to be looked after and protected by the E.T.U., and, as a consequence, there was no further need to pay contributions to the Union'.[395] A subsequent brief account published in 1935 similarly accused the operators of straightforward disloyalty in 'not standing solidly with the union', though it noted that, after good wage agreements had been secured, 'The depression, which is now being overcome, naturally affected the Trade'.[396]

The reference here is not simply to the Great Depression of 1929-1933, but also to the global financial crash of 1920-1921, increasingly referred to by American historians as the 'Forgotten Depression',[397] which produced a large spike in unemployment levels. It has been argued that Britain did not recover from this financial downturn until the end of the Great Depression.[398] The effects of the earlier crash were particularly heavily felt by the British cinema industry in 1921, and it was generally acknowledged that film exhibitors experienced 'the worst slump in the history of the business' in that year as admissions nosedived.[399] The salary scales negotiated by the ETU were linked to changes in the cost of living, and when this fell in 1921, exhibitors were quick to demand wage cuts.[400] In a more extreme move, the London branch of the CEA voted to cancel its ETU agreement altogether in light of the difficult trading conditions being experienced.[401] It is possible that the newly-unionised projectionists became quickly disenchanted with the ETU because their much-vaunted pay increases were so short-lived. One should also note that the 1921 depression had a negative impact upon union subscriptions across all forms of industry. Chris Wrigley points out that national trade union mem-

395 W.J. Webb, 'Operators and the E.T.U.', *Kinematograph Weekly*, 5 August 1926, p. 52.

396 'E.T.U. Want 48-Hour Wage Agreement', *ibid.*, 27 June 1935, p. 8.

397 James Grant, *The Forgotten Depression: 1921, the Crash that Cured Itself* (New York: Simon & Schuster, 2014).

398 Harold L. Cole and Lee E. Ohanian, 'The Great U.K. Depression: A Puzzle and a Possible Resolution', *Review of Economic Dynamics*, 5:1 (January 2002), pp. 19-44.

399 Frank A. Tilley, 'The Story of the Year', in *Kinematograph Year Book 1922* (London: Kinematograph Weekly, 1922), p. 1.

400 'North Staffs', *Kinematograph Weekly*, 16 June 1921, p. 52; 'Long Shots', *ibid.*, 30 June 1921, pp. 28-29; 'Wage Reductions', *ibid.*, 18 August 1921, p. 45; 'Wages Reduction', *ibid.*, 29 September 1921, p. 59; 'Operators' Wages', 27 October 1921, p. 60.

401 'The E.T.U.', *ibid.*, 3 February 1921, p. 91.

bership fell from 8,253,000 in 1920 to 5,382,000 by 1923.[402] Projectionists lacked effective union representation for the remainder of the decade. After the Birmingham ETU branch was closed in 1922, the typical salary scale for operators in that district suffered a further contraction, which apparently left it in the £1-10-0 to £2-0-0 range.[403] The *Kinematograph Weekly*'s chief technical correspondent Colin N. Bennett launched a rare diatribe against cinema owners in 1924, suggesting that 'The whole feeling in the Trade on the subject of operators is wrong and rotten', and condemning their designation as 'cheap labour' paid with 'starvation wages'.[404]

Organisation Without Unions

As we have explained in Chapter One, the introduction of synchronised sound equipment in British cinemas from 1929 onwards changed the job of projection in several respects. Presenting a successful show became a significantly more difficult task, and the responsibilities of equipment maintenance were expanded and grew more exacting. The number of operators needed in a single cinema increased, and, in taking over from musicians the responsibility of delivering sound accompaniment, they now more firmly constituted 'the heart and soul of the theatre', as one commentator put it.[405] One might reasonably expect that improved terms and conditions of employment would follow such a considerable enlargement of duties, but, for the most part, this did not happen.

The small number of positive developments for employees that did accompany the transition to sound were confined to particular regions and ended up being short-lived. It had long been argued that the persistent 'price-cutting' that kept operators' salaries low was directly linked to the 'haphazard system of engaging and training newcomers' followed throughout most of the sector.[406] It was therefore broadly welcomed that the new challenges of mastering sound equipment led to the inauguration of a small number of substantial training initiatives. Several leading American distributors – Paramount-Famous-Lasky, Jury-Metro-Goldwyn, Fox, First National-Pathé, United Artists, Universal and Warner Brothers – joined forces to fund a training facility in London for teaching operators how to handle sound films.[407] Twenty-five hours of instruction were intensively packed into a two-week

402 Chris Wrigley, *British Trade Unions Since 1933* (Cambridge: Cambridge University Press, 2002), p. 7.

403 'Operators and the E.T.U.', *Kinematograph Weekly*, 30 August 1923, p. 71.

404 Colin N. Bennett, 'Projection Points, *ibid.*, 10 April 1924, p. 54.

405 H.L. Overend, 'Reproduction Quality', *ibid.*, 18 August 1932, p. 48.

406 Sidney J. Ottaway, 'Close the Door!', *ibid.*, 29 April 1926, p. 72.

407 'The Booth – Not the Box-Office', *ibid.*, 24 October 1929, p. 25.

course, on which forty students were enrolled at a time, with classes taking place in the mornings before cinema opening times.[408] Certificates were awarded to successful graduates, and the editor of the *Kinematograph Weekly* predicted that 'Exhibitors ... will not be slow in showing their appreciation of an operator who carries this hall mark'.[409] However, despite reports of there being long waiting lists of keen applicants to the scheme, only 277 projectionists were given training during its lifespan, and it was wound up within a year.[410] The experiment was not repeated anywhere else in England at this time. Places advertised for a similar training enterprise set up by the North West branch of the CEA were oversubscribed by 150%, but it did not get off the ground.[411] The anticipated rise in salaries never materialised, despite a significant expansion of working hours. A correspondent signing himself 'A Slave of the Lamp' claimed in a letter to the leading trade paper that he had 'been over twenty years in the operating-box under all sorts of conditions right from the penny show up to the super kinema of 1930, and I can truly say that never in my whole experience have I ever known conditions so appalling as they are at the present moment'.[412]

The ETU began a new recruitment campaign at this point, 'following upon complaints from talkie theatre operators, in regard to long hours'.[413] The union's revivified Manchester branch claimed that the standard rate of pay for operators in the district was now £1-4-0 to £2-0-0 for 60-75 hours of work per week.[414] A combination of negative coverage of cinema employment practices in the local press and a short strike action by unionised operators succeeded in bringing the Manchester CEA branch to the negotiating table, and in October 1930 they signed a new agreement with the ETU.[415] Working hours were capped at 48 per week again, and the minimum salaries for chief operators were fixed at £4 (Grade A halls), £3-10-0 (Grade B) and £3 (Grade C). Second assistant operators were to be paid 66.66% of the chief's wage, and a minimum of three operators were to be employed if sound equip-

408 'Sound-Film Training', *ibid.*, 12 December 1929, p. 21; 'The Observation Window', *ibid.*, 16 January 1930, p. 73.

409 'Efficiency', *ibid.*, 1 May 1930, p. 23.

410 'Sound Committee's Swan Song', *ibid.*, 4 December 1930, p. 29.

411 'Talkie Classes', *ibid.*, 16 January 1930, p. 62; 'Operators' Classes', *ibid.*, 27 February 1930, p. 57.

412 ''Operators Hours and Conditions', *ibid.*, 20 November 1930, p. 66.

413 'Operators' Problems', *ibid.*, 19 June 1930, p. 37.

414 'Operators' Threat', *ibid.*, 24 July 1930, p. 29.

415 'Manchester Operators' Grievances', *ibid.*, 31 July 1930, p. 27; 'Operators' Dispute', *ibid.*, 2 October 1930, p. 23.

ment was installed.[416] Without having to resort to industrial action, the ETU also managed to secure an agreement with the Glasgow and West of Scotland CEA branch along similar lines.[417] There were other advantages to being an operator in Glasgow in the early sound era. The local cinema owners decided to emulate the renters' sound equipment training classes in 1929 in collaboration with the Glasgow Education Authority.[418] This initiative was so successful that it subsequently evolved into a very substantial three-year projection apprenticeship course at the Stow College of Engineering, with 26 weeks of classes per year.[419] The Glasgow CEA branch continued to organise and subsidise this scheme – as a joint effort with the ETU – through to 1940. The issue of why Glaswegian exhibitors seem to have taken projection standards more seriously than the rest of their British peers can only be a matter for speculation. It is likely that their enlightened stance was a direct product of the worst disaster in British cinema history, which had taken place right on their doorstep in December 1929. Smoke from a burning film canister in a Paisley cinema's rewind room entered the auditorium, causing a panicked stampede and crush, which resulted in the deaths of 69 children.[420] A more conscientious approach to the recruitment, training and retention of projection staff was probably considered essential to make sure that no similar tragedy was ever repeated, and in order to help restore public trust locally.

Manchester and Glasgow would prove to be the only successful campaigning grounds for the ETU during the transition to sound. The London and Home Counties CEA branch straightforwardly refused to recognise their right to represent operators.[421] Lightning strikes held at a dozen cinemas in Liverpool caused minimal disruption and made little impression upon the North-West CEA members,[422] and this gave other large provincial branches the confidence to be bullish in their response to ETU demands. The Birmingham CEA declared the second Lancashire 'talkies strike' a

416 Electrical Trades' Union (Manchester District Committee) Working Rules for Cinema Operators and Assistants, NA LAB/83/3320.

417 'An Agreement with the E.T.U.', *Kinematograph Weekly*, 26 March 1931, p. 53.

418 'To Educate Sound Operators', *ibid.*, 24 October 1929, p. 37. The Edinburgh CEA branch followed Glasgow's lead and set up its own 'talkie' classes for operators, in conjunction with the Caledonian Wireless College. This course consisted of 22 hour-long lectures: 'Edinburgh Operators' Classes', *ibid.*, 28 November 1929, p. 77.

419 'Scottish Branch and E.T.U.', *ibid.*, 8 February 1934, p. 11.

420 Trevor Griffiths, *The Cinema and Cinema-going in Scotland, 1896-1950* (Edinburgh: Edinburgh University Press, 2012), pp. 82-83.

421 'Operators' Unrest', *Kinematograph Weekly*, 25 September 1930, p. 27.

422 'E.T.U. Challenge to Exhibitors', *ibid.*, 30 October 1930, pp. 26-27; 'Liverpool Projectionists', *ibid.*, 20 November, p. 36.

'fiasco', and claimed that, rather than joining the ETU, operators in the West Midlands were 'flocking into the Guild of British Projectionists and Technicians'.[423]

The Guild of British Kinema Projectionists and Technicians – its full title – was an organisation formed in the summer of 1929, in response to the introduction of synchronised sound. Amongst the initial aims of the Guild were provision of a forum for operators to discuss ideas and problems concerning sound equipment, and the creation of a framework for disseminating information about subsequent technological innovations.[424] From November 1932 onwards, it published a monthly magazine: the *Projectionists' Journal*. The founding executive argued that a new approach to projection was needed, and the slogan 'One hundred per cent. efficiency in the projection-room' was adopted as a primary campaigning objective.[425] The Guild's adoption and promotion of the term 'projectionist' in its title was a fundamental part of its mission to change perceptions of, and attitudes towards, the job, and in this it probably deserves a significant amount of the credit due for the fact that the word 'operator' was largely superseded within the British film trade over the course of the 1930s. Sixteen separate branches, or Guild Courts, were established – all in England – and their most conspicuous group activities consisted of Sunday lectures, visits to equipment manufacturing works and seasonal balls.

The Guild was not a trade union, but it replicated certain facilities and behaviours associated with unions: services such as an employment bureau, plus pension, sickness and unemployment benefit schemes were experimented with, and it participated in arbitration talks with employers. In this respect, the Guild was open to the criticism that, in competing with existing forms of labour representation in the field, it further fragmented an already divided sector. One disillusioned Guild member voiced such concerns at the 1939 AGM over the damage caused by having 'three bodies all catering for the projectionist, all at loggerheads, to the detriment of the projectionists'.[426] The main threat that the Guild posed to the two established trade unions for projectionists was not primarily that of direct competition, however; contrary to what the Birmingham CEA suggested, none of the provincial courts were very large, and national membership peaked around the 800

423 'E.T.U. Allegations', *ibid.*, 27 November 1930, p. 23.

424 'Projectionists in Council', *ibid.*, 12 September 1929, p. 40.

425 'Guild Slogan', *ibid.*, 18 June 1931, p. 69.

426 'Guild Annual Meeting', *ibid.*, 23 February 1939, p. 50.

mark.[427] The specific form of disruption presented by the Guild was more that of a major public relations headache. In 1930 the CEA chose to recognise the Guild over NATE and the ETU as its preferred consultation partner for all matters affecting projectionists. This enabled the cinema owners to pay public lip service to the idea that projectionists were 'entitled to some sort of organisation', without having to make the kinds of concessions that negotiation with a trade union would entail.[428] The CEA's endorsement of the Guild was also problematic because it granted increased legitimacy and exposure to an organisation that was not only *not* a union, but was also actively hostile to basic union aspirations. The secretary of NATE alleged that 'One of the obvious objects of the Guild is to prevent, or to destroy, the possibility of trades unionism, as such, amongst projectionists'.[429]

An editorial in the Guild's in-house journal warned that 'no good came of belonging to a trade union', and went so far as to praise the CEA as 'a fine body of business men'.[430] When CEA branches conducted consultation exercises with Guild representatives, the latter conveyed the message that their members were 'generally satisfied with the [working] conditions prevailing'.[431] The Guild's position on labour organisation can be usefully compared to the historical reluctance of white collar workers to unionise. This has conventionally been explained as a result of the fact that white collar workers typically do not wish to be identified with manual workers, in order to maintain a sense of social distinction, and believe that their aims and interests are more closely aligned with those of management.[432] The executive officers of the Guild demonstrated a very similar attitude. Its secretary, F.H. Woods, argued that the projectionist 'ranks in a class above the ordinary labour field'.[433] R. Howard Cricks, who vociferously championed the Guild as editor of the *Ideal Kinema* magazine, and was a member of the London court, suggested in 1936 that

> It is all very well for an electrician or a doorman to belong to a trade union, to threaten to walk out if he doesn't get an expected rise, and to kick if he is asked to work a few minutes overtime without pay.

427 R. Howard Cricks, 'Trade Unionism and the Guild', *ibid.*, 13 January 1938, p. 36; see also 'London Members Discuss Hours', *Projectionists' Journal*, June 1933, p. 8.

428 'The Projectionists', *Kinematograph Weekly*, 11 December 1930, p. 37.

429 'The Guild and the N.A.T.E.', *ibid.*, 30 August 1934, p. 7.

430 'Not a Trade Union', *Projectionists' Journal*, February 1934, p. 1.

431 'C.E.A. Proceedings', *Kinematograph Weekly*, 12 May 1932, p. 38.

432 Seymour Martin Lipset and Noah M. Meltz, with Rafael Gomez and Ivan Katchanovski, *The Paradox of American Unionism* (Ithaca, NY: Cornell University Press, 2004), pp. 128-129.

433 F.H. Woods, 'The Projectionists' Guild and Trade Unionism', *Kinematograph Weekly*, 20 January 1938, p. 68.

> The projectionist, particularly of a large show, has a job of especial responsibility, and must be a 'master's man.' The first projectionist is, after all, in the position of a foreman, and trade unions recognise that the foreman is a 'master's man,' and do not expect him to carry his union card. This applies with particular force to the chief projectionist. There is an important distinction nowadays made in a few super-kinemas between the first projectionist, who is in immediate charge of the projection room, and in the position of a foreman, and the chief projectionist, who has more of an executive post, of the nature of that of a works manager.[434]

Third and fourth projectionists were debarred from joining the Guild.[435] The fact that only 6% of all British projectionists belonged to the organisation was not perceived as the product of deficient recruitment efforts, for it was claimed that 'there are few projectionists now outside the ranks of the Guild whose capabilities and status make them desirable as members'.[436] Stanley Perry, the Guild's president (and chief projectionist at one of the country's most luxurious and prestigious cinemas, the Empire, Leicester Square) contended that his members were 'receiving salaries above the level being demanded by other organisations and enjoy excellent conditions of employment'; some of them, he said, earned £6 a week.[437] This perhaps suggests that the Guild's subscribers primarily consisted of chief projectionists who worked for the larger circuits like Odeon, ABC and Gaumont-British. It was generally claimed that pay and conditions for employees of the big three circuits – which collectively owned less than a quarter of all British cinemas – were superior to the arrangements at most independently-owned theatres.[438]

The Guild straightforwardly did not believe in the principle that projectionists should be entitled to a minimum salary rate. As Cricks explained, 'instead of demanding a minimum wage for everybody, regardless of his capabilities, the Guild method is to make a man worth more than the minimum wage'.[439] It was a fundamental creed within the Guild that employers were not to blame for the low salaries paid to most projectionists. Instead, those projectionists who complained about their pay and conditions were deemed at fault, because – it was argued – they delivered such a poor standard of projection that they made themselves unworthy of better remuneration. 'To ask for the general recognition of the

434 R. Howard Cricks, 'The Projectionist and His Career', *Ideal Kinema*, 13 August 1936, p. 42.

435 R. Howard Cricks, 'Staffing the Projection Room', *ibid.*, 11 April 1935, p. 39.

436 R. Howard Cricks, 'The Guild's Most Urgent Need', *ibid.*, 16 August 1934, p. 29.

437 'E.T.U. Want 48-Hour Week Agreement', *Kinematograph Weekly*, 27 June 1935, p. 8.

438 'Labour To-day', *ibid.*, 29 July 1937, p. 4; see also James Benson, 'Employers and Employed – Independent and Circuit Conditions', *ibid.*, 5 August 1937, p. 27.

439 R. Howard Cricks, 'Projectionists Taking Armament Jobs', *ibid.*, 7 October 1937, p. 41.

projectionist as a first-class workman when it is well-known that large numbers are not worthy of that recognition is a waste of time', according to the secretary of the Devon and Cornwall court.[440] Instead, it was argued that the onus was on projectionists 'to prove their mettle before getting their wages'; by showing 'our employers and managers that we really are craftsmen, we shall be treated as such'.[441]

In many respects, the Guild was effectively reviving the spirit of NACO, the original trade alliance for projectionists, which had similarly presented itself as a craft association rather than a militant trade union. The fact that the film exhibition industry in interwar Britain consisted of many diverse forms of corporate organisation – from small private companies formed before the First World War to large conglomerates floated on the Stock Exchange[442] – created stark disparities in conditions of employment. Whilst some big purpose-built city centre cinemas had extremely spacious projection boxes, and provided dedicated retiring rooms and shower facilities for projectionists, workspaces elsewhere were so cramped that some equipment manufacturers catered to customers who could only squeeze in two projectors if they were fixed on a single stand.[443] Just as NACO had sown divisions between veteran operators and newcomers in the 1910s, the Guild positioned itself as the preserve of elite artisans only, and set projectionists who had respectively enjoyed greater or lesser degrees of fortune in their employment histories against each other. We previously suggested that NACO's public denigration of the operators who remained outside its sphere may have served to embolden employers in their determination to keep wages at a depressed level, and the Guild's constant intimations that the vast majority of projectionists were incompetent no doubt had the same effect. Ironically, it was a paid officer of NACO's parent union, NATE, who delivered the most withering assessment of the Guild's impact:

> A Guild of 'selected' projectionists, of an 'hierarchy,' so to say, of a little inner circle of the 'upper ten' will not be of the slightest use to the trade, nor solve the projectionists' problems on a national scale.

440 Arthur E. Battrick, 'The Profession and the Man', *Projectionists' Journal*, August-September 1939, p. 1.

441 Arthur E. Battrick, 'Guild and Mutilation', *Kinematograph Weekly*, 10 March 1932, p. 85; '"Rear Shutter" Replies to "Jack, a Dull Boy"', *Ideal Kinema*, 12 July 1934, p. 43.

442 Data presented in Burrows, *The British Cinema Boom*, pp. 111-112, reveals that 547 cinema companies established before 1915 continued trading into the 1930s and beyond; 390 of these were still extant in the 1940s. The levels of capital which supported the main exhibition circuits in the '30s is outlined in F.D. Klingender and Stuart Legg, *Money Behind the Screen: A Report Prepared on Behalf of the Film Council* (London: Lawrence and Wishart, 1937), pp. 24–25, 30, 46–48.

443 Details provided, respectively, in 'Typical Projection Equipment 9. – The Plaza, London', *Kinematograph Weekly*, 12 May 1927, p. 76; 'Two Prices Only', *ibid.*, 19 January 1928, p. 55; 'The Double Ernemann', *ibid.*, 14 April 1927, p. 64.

> Nor will it be of any avail to regard those thousands of other men and women working in the Industry as 'untouchables'.[444]

Industrial Conflict

NATE, or NATKE (the National Association of Theatrical and Kine. Employees), as it was renamed in February 1937, enjoyed a progressive growth in both subscriptions and influence upon the film trade over the course of the 1930s. The main factor behind this rejuvenation was the appointment of Tom (later Sir Thomas) O'Brien as general secretary in 1932 – a role he held for the next 38 years (juggled alongside a career in Westminster as a Labour MP between 1945 and 1959). O'Brien – a Welshman of Irish parentage – ascended, aged 31, to the position of the youngest general secretary of any national trade union, after only ten years of service as a full-time NATE officer.[445] He brought considerable energy and stamina to the job, and a distinctive gift for flamboyant campaign rhetoric, but also a shamelessly opportunistic streak. In 1934, for example, when presenting a case to the Conservative government's Home Secretary, Sir John Gilmour – a harbourer of fascist sympathies, according to one modern historian[446] – for the need to add statutory employment regulations to the Cinematograph Act (1909), O'Brien brazenly deployed classic anti-Semitic conspiracy tropes. After declaring that 'Many of the most prominent magnates in the [film] Trade are Jews', intent on monopolising the industry through 'International financial interlocking and control', he urged the Secretary of State to assist in 'rescuing the workers of this industry from the tentacles of an ever growing and powerful octopi'.[447] A couple of years later, however, O'Brien can be found urging the National Joint Council of Labour (an anti-fascist campaign organisation) to throw its weight behind NATE's cause on the basis that 'the attitude adopted by important sections of the Cinema industry is one that is calculated to encourage the forces of fascism in Great Britain'.[448]

It was another act of cynical opportunism on O'Brien's part that led to a new phase of destructive conflict between NATE and the ETU. In the years immediately prior to O'Brien's appointment as its national organiser, NATE sought to forge campaigning alliances with the ETU. In November 1929, the two unions signed an

444 'The Guild and Trade Unionism', *ibid.*, 3 February 1938, p. 48.

445 'O'Brien's 25 Years as N.A.T.K.E. Official', *ibid.*, 18 September 1947, p. 7; 'Obituary: Sir Tom O'Brien', *The Times*, 6 May 1970, p. 12.

446 Martin Pugh, *'Hurrah for the Blackshirts!' Fascists and Fascism in Britain Between the Wars* (London: Pimlico, 2006), pp. 58-59.

447 Tom O'Brien, Case in Support of Resolution 29 Brighton Conference, 11 January 1934, MSS.292/675.1/1, TUC Archive, MRC.

448 Letter from Tom O'Brien to Sir Walter Citrine, 28 July 1936, MSS.292/54.731/4, TUC Archive, MRC.

agreement in which they vowed to conduct future negotiations with the CEA on a collective basis; there should be no attempt by one union to encroach on the membership of the other, it was stated, and there was also a proviso which granted to the ETU 'the first preference and a free field to organise the Operators who are not yet organised'.[449] All of these clauses were repeated and ratified in a new agreement signed by both parties in February 1934.[450]

By this stage, NATE and the ETU had been collaborating for 21 months in discussions conducted within the framework of a Joint Conciliation Board for London cinemas and cinema workers. This had been set up at the instigation of the London Trades Council – the federated body representing trade unions in the capital. After over two years of difficult and protracted negotiations with the London and Home Counties branch of the CEA, the Board stood on the verge of collapse, without any likelihood of an agreement being reached. NATE was the first union to declare time on the exercise, passing a resolution at its annual conference in July 1934 that it could not accept the CEA's proposals on minimum wages and working hours, and vowing to campaign henceforth for legislative regulation of the industry.[451] The London Trades Council then announced that they could not recommend the CEA's offer to cinema workers, and that they would ask the government to set up a national inquiry into the trades' employment practices.[452] The CEA's representatives on the Board subsequently came back with an improved wages offer which outlined a minimum wage for chief projectionists of £5-5-0 at 'AA' halls (those which earned more than £1,000 per week in takings), £4-0-0 at 'A' halls and £3-10-0 at 'B' halls; for any chief not working in the West End, or at a super-cinema, this was still a lower rate than that agreed for London cinemas by the ETU in 1920.[453] The major sticking point, though, was that the CEA was unwilling to budge on their stipulation that sixty hours of work per week could be required from employees (or 55 hours at cinemas that traded on all seven days of the week). The ETU continued to insist that they could not accept a maximum working week longer than 48 hours, as had been agreed fifteen years earlier, and also refused to endorse the agree-

449 Joint Recommendation arrived at by the Representatives of the Executive Committee of the E.T.U. and N.A.T.E. on November 16 1929, MSS.292/85/98, TUC Archive, MRC.

450 Excerpt from Minutes of Joint Sub-Committee of the E.T.U. and the N.A.T.E., held at 34 Little Newport Street, on Tuesday, 6th February, 1934, at 4-15pm, MSS.126/TG/1725/1, TUC Archive, MRC.

451 'N.A.T.E. Rejects Schedule of Conciliation Board', *Kinematograph Weekly*, 26 July 1934, p. 5.

452 'The Next Step in the Wage Dispute', *ibid.*, 9 August 1934, p. 3.

453 Joint Statement of the Conciliation Board, 15 July 1935, MSS.292/54.731/5, TUC Archive, MRC; 'London and Home Counties', *Kinematograph Weekly*, 15 January 1920, p. 127.

ment.[454] NATE suddenly decided to break ranks, however, and their assent to the working hours clause allowed a deal to go through in July 1935.

At NATE's annual conference that year, the union's assent to a sixty-hour working week was justified – with a dig at the ETU – on the basis that 'any attempt to operate the organisational methods normally applicable in productive industry to that of entertainment would be a purely reactionary policy unworthy of the combined intelligence of the trade union movement'.[455] But these were not working conditions that were widely replicated around the industrialised world. In the US, the National Recovery Agency's Motion Picture Code had capped the working week for cinema employees at forty hours from 1933 onwards.[456] This fact had been well publicised in Britain, as had agreements established in several other countries to keep working hours between forty and 49 per week.[457] The only obvious conclusion to be drawn here is that Tom O'Brien completely reversed his union's negotiating stance because he saw a chance to gain a competitive advantage over the ETU – by demonstrating to the CEA that NATE was a better and more pliant partner to do business with. At the TUC's 1935 Annual Congress he 'defended exhibitors', when blocking a motion proposed by the ETU to have the Congress denounce the cinema business as a 'sweated industry'.[458]

O'Brien was ultimately rewarded for this conciliatory approach to the CEA when a number of the latter's regional branches agreed to open talks with him – whilst steadfastly refusing to acknowledge the ETU – in order to formulate new wage agreements modelled on the London covenant. Ten such deals were concluded over the course of 1937. O'Brien's crowning achievement during this spell of diplomatic appeasement came on 26 November of the same year, when the CEA's national General Council voted 'to recognise the N.A.T. & K.E. as the Trade Union for the purposes of the negotiation of wages and working conditions of the employees of kinema exhibitors', and called upon all those branches who had yet to begin talks to now do so.[459] This 'landmark' moment in the

454 'E.T.U. Want 48-Hour Week Agreement', *ibid.*, 27 June 1935, p. 8.

455 'N.A.T.E. Discusses Quota and Wages', *ibid.*, 25 July 1935, p. 5.

456 'Code of Fair Competition for the Motion Picture Industry as approved on November 27 1933 by President Roosevelt', US Federal Documents, University of Florida Digital Collections, ufdc.ufl.edu/AA00006594/00001, accessed on 13 November 2017.

457 R. Howard Cricks, 'The Battle of the Standards', *Ideal Kinema*, 7 June 1934, p. 41; 'Payment for Operating Staffs', *Kinematograph Weekly*, 18 July 1935, p. 45.

458 'E.T.U. Attack Defeated', *ibid.*, 12 September 1935, p. 13.

459 'Official C.E.A. Recognition of N.A.T.K.E.', *ibid.*, 2 December 1937, p. 8; Hector A. McCullie, 'Kinema Labour Shakes Hands with Capital, *ibid.*, 13 January 1938, p. 44.

history of cinema labour relations was not simply NATKE's reward for helping to salvage a positive outcome from the London Conciliation Board. It was, in fact, a calculated effort to enlist O'Brien's help in protecting the CEA from a new threat of public opprobrium.

Since the late 1920s, repeated calls had been made for the government to conduct a full investigation of wages and working conditions within the cinema industry. Margaret Bondfield, the Minister for Labour in Ramsay MacDonald's second administration, announced in August 1930 that she planned to commission a comprehensive survey, but the collapse of the minority Labour government a year later stymied its progess.[460] Following a series of articles in the national press throughout the decade alleging 'Scandalous Cinema Conditions',[461] plus persistent questions in parliament on the subject tabled by the Labour MP Harry Day (himself a former cinema owner), the Ministry of Labour did finally conduct a detailed survey, via circulated questionnaires and follow-up visits to cinemas, in October 1937. By this means, information was compiled concerning 97% of cinemas in England, Scotland and Wales, and the 59,875 workers they employed.

The civil servants who tabulated the data observed that some of the findings were not as bad as had been feared. Most Gaumont-British cinemas were found to be paying their chief projectionists higher wages than agreed union rates (though they also typically paid lower ranking projectionists less than the approved minimum).[462] And it was noted that – although poorly paid – part-time employment as cinema cashiers, usherettes or cleaners in many cases 'provides a convenient resource for women who, for one reason or another, are not available for work at ordinary working hours'.[463] Relief was expressed privately that the results did not 'suggest the existence of a social evil so serious as to demand statutory interference',[464] but it was nonetheless conceded that there were some 'really appalling figures' in the report.[465] The worst of these related to the employment of boys under the age of eighteen. Four thousand, two hundred and eighty-eight teenagers

460 'Kinema Wages', *ibid.*, 7 August 1930, p. 21. See also John Izod, 'Empowering Cinema Operators in the USA and UK, 1927-1933', *Music, Sound, and the Moving Image*, 12:2 (Autumn 2018), pp. 231-233.

461 See, for example, 'Entertainment Industry Wages', *Manchester Guardian*, 18 December 1933, p. 11; 'Girls Must Work 70-Hour Week for 18/-', *Daily Herald*, 2 July 1934, p. 3; 'Beauty Parade to Keep Their Jobs', *ibid.*, 9 July 1937, p. 5. The Ministry of Labour compiled a clippings file of such items, preserved in NA LAB/98/29.

462 Memorandum from R.B. Ainsworth to E.C. Ramsbottom, 10 February 1938, NA LAB/10/83.

463 Memorandum from G.B. Hawkins to F.W. Leggett and G.H. Ince, 12 July 1938, NA LAB/10/83.

464 *Ibid.*

465 G.B. Hawkins, 'Cinema Investigation Summary', n.d., NA LAB/10/83.

in this age group were employed in cinemas (of whom 57% worked as projectionists); 32% of these boy projectionists worked more than 54 hours per week. There were 2,525 projectionists aged between 18 and 21, and although 68% of them worked for 48 hours or more per week, 87% of these youths earned less than £2. The median weekly wage for all full-time projectionists was £3 per week. Forty-eight per cent of full-time adult projectionists (aged over 21) earned less than £3. Looking for an apt standard of comparison, the report used figures collated in a 1929 investigation of the licensed catering trade – which was dominated by casual, unskilled workers – and observed that only 4% of men working in catering earned less than 9d per hour, whilst 17% of adult projectionists were paid below this rate.[466]

The report was not published, and no figures from it were ever disclosed. The principal reason for this was that NATKE gave their consent for it to be buried. Though the findings were never shared with the ETU, they were shown to Tom O'Brien. He judged that 'it was favourable to the workers' point of view' and potentially 'of considerable value to his Association'. However, he informed Frederick Leggett, the head of the Ministry of Labour's Industrial Relations department, that 'his Association would not have hesitated to ask for publication if they were not at present engaged in negotiations with the Cinematograph Exhibitors' Association ... [and] did not want anything to be done which might raise difficulties or delay progress'.[467] By granting recognition to NATKE a matter of weeks after the survey data was collected, and thereby demonstrating to the Ministry that it was putting its house in order, the CEA had acted to protect itself from any further government action. Leggett duly informed Ernest Brown, the Minister for Labour, that, because negotiations were well underway between the CEA and NATKE ,'the information [in the report] is not now up to date, having regard to the action which has taken place since the figures were collected'.[468]

The CEA's general council rewarded NATKE for its co-operation and discretion by exerting pressure upon the regional branches to facilitate the swift negotiation of wage agreements. Between November 1937 and May 1939, 33 such agreements (including sub-agreements within individual CEA branches that covered both rural and urban areas) were signed, affecting 2,040 cinemas. O'Brien claimed that these deals secured an aggregate increase in

466 'Report on the Enquiry into Wages and Hours in Cinematograph Theatres', Ministry of Labour, Statistics Branch, n.d., NA LAB/10/83.

467 Report of meeting between F.W. Leggett and NATKE, 3 November 1938, NA LAB/10/83.

468 Memorandum from F.W. Leggett to A.E. Brown, 14 November 1938, NA LAB/10/83.

wages of £55,000.[469] These achievements had a substantial impact upon union recruitment. Over the same period, 15,514 new subscribers joined NATKE.[470] Total annual membership had only been 8,421 in 1936, and 10,352 in 1937.[471] It's impossible to say what proportion of these numbers were theatre workers, or indeed how many projectionists were amongst the new recruits, but it seems reasonable to assume that this growth was primarily achieved amongst a variety of cinema workers influenced by their employers' recent endorsement of NATKE.

One factor behind the ETU's aforementioned decision to instigate large-scale industrial action in April 1938 was undoubtedly a perceived need to try and counteract NATKE's growing momentum, by demonstrating to projectionists that better, fairer agreements could be achieved by different methods. Their big show of strength was organised on three fronts – London, Manchester and Hull – that each had distinct grievances. It may be safely assumed that the controversial London Conciliation Board agreement of 1935 had done very little to recommend NATKE to projectionists in the capital, since by 1938 1,362 of them had joined the ETU; this figure was said to represent 95% of all unionised projectionists in the metropolitan area.[472] London was thus chosen as a key battleground because of the volume of workers that could be mobilised there, and because resentment at having a 55-hour working week ratified in a covenant approved by a member of the TUC still burned strong. Ever since the so-called 'talkies strike' of 1930, the Manchester CEA branch had continued to negotiate working agreements with the ETU, and the local projectionists' branch had over 250 members.[473] Manchester projectionists had thereby come to know a 48-hour maximum working week as the norm. But at the end of March 1938, Manchester's cinema owners voted to cancel their most recent agreement with the ETU, because of the fact that so many other CEA branches were signing rate cards with NATKE that allowed exhibitors to demand 55/60 hours of work from their employees.[474] The ETU projectionists therefore voted to strike to try and force the exhibitors to honour their existing deal. There was no agreed rate card in Hull, but the projectionists there were livid when their local CEA branch invited Tom O'Brien

469 'C.E.A.'s Happy Relations with N.A.T.K.E.', *Kinematograph Weekly*, 11 May 1939, p. 5.

470 'N.A.T.K.E. Reports Great Strides During 1938-9', *ibid.*, 13 July 1939, p. 3.

471 'N.A.T.K.E.'s Growing Power in the Trade', *ibid.*, 21 July 1938, p. 3.

472 *The Film Strike: The Projectionists' Case* (London: Farleigh Press, 1938), p. 6; copy in MSS.15X/2/148/; J. Rowan, 'Electrical Trades Union. Cinema Projectionist-Electricians', August 1938, MSS.126/TG/1725/1, TUC Archive, MRC.

473 *Ibid.*

474 'Manchester's Drastic Move', *Kinematograph Weekly*, 7 April 1938, p. 7.

to negotiate salary levels – this despite the fact that 90% of Hull projectionists were ETU members, and NATKE had none.[475] So, in addition to their grievances about pay and conditions, Hull's ETU chapter voted to go on strike to defend the principle that 'they should have a choice in the union they join and not be herded into [NATKE]'.[476] (ETU members in Birmingham, Bolton and the North East were also asked to consider strike motions, but voted against them.[477])

The strikes began on 15 April, the day before Good Friday. Surviving ETU committee minutes and correspondence in the TUC Archive reveal that the plan was to achieve a quick victory by disrupting business during what was then the most profitable period in the industry calendar: the Easter weekend.[478] The CEA refused to blink, however, and, despite not anticipating a long battle, the ETU decided that it should continue picketing rather than signalling for an early retreat. A long and bitter war of attrition followed, accompanied by claims that projectionists who crossed the picket line were assaulted, cinemas stink-bombed and projection equipment sabotaged, plus numerous arrests.[479] As we noted at the start of this chapter, the strike lasted for six weeks in Manchester and London, and dragged on for over 36 weeks in Hull. Despite this level of commitment, the union barely landed a glove upon its opponent, with no cinemas being forced to close.[480] The peace process was equally humiliating. No concessions were won in London, other than an assurance that the striking workers would get their jobs back; but, as of December 1938, 131 of these men were still unemployed.[481] The resolution of the Manchester dispute was publicly labelled a victory, with suggestions that the rate card guaranteeing a maximum 48-hour week would be restored. However, in October the Manchester

475 'New Wage Schedule for Hull Projectionists', *ibid.*, 30 December 1937, p. 8; 'Hull to Meet N.A.T.K.E. on Labour Talks', *ibid.*, 27 January 1938, p. 10; 'Strike Threat by Hull Projectionists', *ibid.*, 24 February 1938, p. 5; 'N.A.T.K.E. Well Received at Hull', *ibid.*, p. 8; 'Hull Refuses Recognition of E.T.U. Strikers', *ibid.*, 28 April 1938, p. 8.

476 R. Howard Cricks, 'Union Threats in London and Hull', *ibid.*, 31 March 1938, p. 55.

477 Minute 150, meeting of 5 May; minute 291, meeting of 16 May, in minutes of ETU sub-executive council meetings, April-June 1938, TUC.ELEC.2.B.88, ETU Archive, WCML.

478 Minute 28, meeting of 11 April 1938, *ibid.*; memorandum of interview with James Rowan, 3 May 1938, MSS.292/253/23/1, TUC Archive, MRC.

479 'Court Sequel to Strike Demonstration', *Kinematograph Weekly*, 21 April 1938, p. 5; 'The Aftermath of the Strike', *ibid.*, 28 April 1938, p. 35; 'Echo of Kinema Strike', *ibid.*, 5 May 1938, p. 6; 'Three London Operators Attacked', *ibid.*, 12 May 1938, p. 5; 'Strike Drags on Without Hope of Agreement', *ibid.*, 19 May 1938, p. 3; 'Strikers Bound Over', *ibid.*, 2 June 1938, p. 3; 'Projectionists Bound Over', *ibid.*, 7 July 1938, p. 14; interview with David Robson, conduced by Allan Lawson, 25 March 1998, BECTU Oral History Project interview no. 431, https://historyproject.org.uk/content/0431, accessed 20 November 2017.

480 Memorandum of interview with James Rowan, 3 May 1938, MSS.292/253/23/1, TUC Archive, MRC.

481 Minute 623, meeting of 19 December, minutes of ETU sub-executive committee meetings, October-December 1938, TUC.ELEC.2.B.90, ETU Archive, WCML.

CEA members voted to sign a new agreement with NATKE, rather than the ETU, because the former were willing to accept longer working hours.[482] The Hull dispute ended without any compromise from the local CEA branch concerning its refusal to recognise the ETU. In a final ironic twist, the ETU passed a resolution to blacklist all Hull cinemas – which deeply angered the striking projectionists, because it meant that they were prohibited from attempting to reclaim their jobs.[483] The union subsequently had to secure them other forms of work within the electrical industry in the district.[484]

This was the only defeat suffered by the ETU in the 1930s, which was a decade of militant campaigning activity for the union.[485] Several of its branches passed motions condemning the national executive committee for perceived incompetence.[486] The London Station Engineers No. 4 branch went so far as to suggest that the union had demonstrated its 'inability to cater for this class of worker', and called for all the projectionists to be transferred to NATKE.[487] Given the ETU's strong representation at cinemas in the three affected cities and – as we noted earlier – the marked appetite that the national press had for stories about exploited cinema workers, it requires further digging to explain why things went so badly wrong.

At a meeting of projectionists left without jobs by the strike, the view was expressed that the executive's 'inexperience and lack of knowledge' concerning the industry had been a key factor.[488] Tom O'Brien told the TUC leadership that he thought the ETU had made a tactical mistake by concentrating their picketing efforts upon cinemas that belonged to the larger circuits. In doing so, he suggested, they had underestimated the ease with which these circuits could bring in replacement labour from their other provincial cinemas, and had overlooked the greater vulnerability of independent cinemas – which constituted by far the largest block

482 'Manchester Faces T.U. Problem', *Kinematograph Weekly*, 3 November 1938, p. 7.

483 Minute 73, meeting of 9 January, minutes of ETU sub-executive committee meetings, January - March 1939, TUC.ELEC.2.B.91, ETU Archive, WCML.

484 'E.T.U. Calls Off Hull Strike', *Kinematograph Weekly*, 5 January 1939, p. 17; ETU annual report for 1939, TU.ELEC.1.2, ETU Archive, WCML.

485 Anon., *The Story of the E.T.U.*, p. 154.

486 For example, there were votes of censure passed in Tooting (minute 497, meeting of 23 June, minutes of ETU sub-executive committee meetings, April - June 1938, TUC.ELEC.2.B.88), Widnes (minute 260, meeting of 11 August), Blaenavon (minute 501, meeting of 22 September minutes of ETU sub-executive committee meetings, July - September 1938, TUC.ELEC.2.B.89, ETU Archive, WCML).

487 *Ibid.*

488 Minute 623, meeting of 19 December, minutes of ETU sub-executive committee meetings, October-December 1938, TUC.ELEC.2.B.90, ETU Archive, WCML.

of CEA members.[489] In much of its campaign propaganda, the ETU had sought to emphasise that 'the fight of the projectionists has a wider significance. Their struggle is against all those influences in British capitalism that are waging a consistent fight against the workers in every industry.'[490] Targeting the largest cinema companies made ideological sense in this context, but the most prolific and shameless offenders when it came to pay and conditions for employees were the independents. A few years later, O'Brien publicly declared that he wished J. Arthur Rank – owner of the Odeon and Gaumont-British circuits – would buy up every cinema in Britain, in order to eradicate the 'miserly, grabbing independent exhibitor[s]' who 'have no vision and are living in the Victorian era'.[491] O'Brien was probably right to suggest that the ETU had made a significant strategic error, but it is important to acknowledge the context in which he made this claim: it formed part of his defence against widespread allegations that NATKE was directly assisting the strike-affected cinemas by encouraging its own members to offer their services as blackleg labour! The CEA added fuel to these suspicions by openly thanking O'Brien for having 'been more than helpful' in the effort to keep cinemas open,[492] and a large number of municipal Trades Councils and other unions called – unsuccessfully – for NATKE to be expelled from the TUC.[493]

This painful defeat did not end the ETU's interest in projectionists, but membership seems to have plummeted as a direct consequence. By the end of 1938, the London branches had lost around 50% of their subscribers, and the Manchester branch was left with 86 adherents. The projectionists' branches in Birmingham, Newcastle, Sheffield and Sunderland all closed over the course of the year. By the end of 1939, national ETU membership amongst projectionists had shrunk by 505 since the previous year, to stand

489 Tom O'Brien, 'Organization of Cinema Employees. The Case for the National Association of Theatre and Kine Employees, Presented to the Trade Union Congress', 3 May 1938, MSS.292/253/23/1, TUC Archive, MRC.

490 *The Film Strike: The Projectionists' Case*, p. 13.

491 'Threat of Strike Overhangs C.E.A. Unless National Wage Scale is Agreed by July 16', *Kinematograph Weekly*, 11 July 1946, p. 11.

492 'C.E.A. and N.A.T.K.E. Statements on the Strike', Kinematograph Weekly, 21 April 1938, p. 5.

493 See, for example, letters to the TUC from Southall Labour Party and Trades Council (26 April 1938), Greenwich Trades Council (24 April 1938), Woodford and Wanstead Trades Council (26 April 1938), Bermondsey and Rotherhithe Trades Council & Borough Labour Party (27 April 1938), Transport and General Workers' Union (2 May 1938), MSS.292/253/23/1, TUC Archive, MRC. Whether or not NATKE was guilty of such an unprecedented violation of the code of conduct for trade unions – the TUC's investigation failed to find hard evidence – some of the behaviour it conducted in plain sight was almost as inflammatory: the Hull and District Trades Council complained that NATKE was 'discrediting the Trade Union movement' by conducting negotiations with the local CEA branch whilst there were ETU members out on strike. (Letter from J.D. Nicholson to Walter Citrine, 3 August 1938, MSS.292/253/23/1, TUC Archive, MRC).

at 1,119. The impact of wartime conscription helped to reduce it to 514 by December 1940.[494] Although the union remained strong and influential within the film exhibition sector in Glasgow, it was otherwise never again a significant force within the British film industry.[495]

National Agreements

During the Second World War, NATKE consolidated its position as the primary trade union for cinema workers, and by the end of the conflict it had been recognised by the TUC as one of the 25 largest unions in the country across all spheres of industry.[496] In a bid to augment its appeal to projectionists, NATKE negotiated an amalgamation with the Guild of British Kinema Projectionists and Technicians, effective from January 1943. This was the third approach that NATKE had made to absorb the Guild, having been firmly rebuffed in 1938 and 1941.[497] Only nine months before the merger was agreed, a majority of members in the London court had indicated in a ballot that they would prefer to join forces with the ETU rather than NATKE.[498] NATKE was seen as less desirable specifically because it represented all classes of cinema workers, and thereby lumped projectionists together with unskilled employees like doormen and usherettes. National Guild membership had fallen to 120 after the first two years of the war, however, and NATKE's offer came to be seen as its only chance of avoiding an ignominious dissolution.[499] Despite its puny size, the idea of an association with the Guild presumably retained some value to Tom O'Brien because it represented a means of demonstrating that NATKE respected the claim of projectionists to distinct status and entitlement. A new projectionists' section of the union was formed called the Kinema Projectionists and Engineers Association (KPEA), which continued publication of the Guild journal and housed its technical library.[500] At the inauguration of the KPEA, it was claimed that NATKE had around 3,000 projectionists on its books.[501]

494 ETU annual reports for 1939 and 1940, TU.ELEC.1.2, ETU Archive, WCML.

495 There was one legacy of the ETU's historic strength in Manchester that subsequently proved an irritant to local exhibitors. In 1940 Labour councillors in the city blocked the Manchester CEA's attempts to secure permission to open on Sundays in response to wartime demand because of the latter's ongoing refusal to recognise the ETU: 'Industrial Council Suggested', *Kinematograph Weekly*, 11 April 1940, p. 5.

496 'O'Brien Wants One Film Trade Union', *ibid.*, 13 September 1945, p. 3.

497 'Trade Unionism and the Guild', *ibid.*, 10 February 1938, p. 52; 'Guild Rejects Trade Union Affiliation', *ibid.*, 29 May 1941, p. 3.

498 'Guild Decision on Union Status', *ibid.*, 5 March 1942, p. 35.

499 'Guild Discusses Delivery Delays', *ibid.*, 3 July 1941, p. 22.

500 'N.A.T.K.E. Absorbs the Guild', *ibid.*, 21 January 1943, p. 5.

501 R. Howard Cricks, 'Guild and Union Wedded', *ibid.*, 11 February 1943, p. vii.

With NATKE's ascendancy over the ETU firmly established, O'Brien became outwardly more bullish in his dealings with cinema owners. Having previously gone out of his way to accommodate the special demands of the CEA's regional branches and sub-branches, by arranging 43 separate wage agreements,[502] he now demanded the right to negotiate directly with the CEA General Council for the prompt and nationwide implementation of war bonuses, to compensate for spiralling inflation and regular increases in the cost of living. It took a year to achieve this objective, though, and the victory was ultimately not accomplished by O'Brien's own hand. In July 1941 Odeon shocked its peers by announcing that it would award a 17.5% bonus to all employees across its circuit. In response, the CEA changed tack and announced that all its members would award a 12.5% bonus and that future pay adjustments would be negotiated as national agreements.[503]

Odeon took this unprecedented step, and the CEA followed its lead without too much internal dissension, because it was increasingly recognised that the industry was encountering a major recruitment crisis. The problem was essentially twofold. Jobs had become abundant in industries that directly contributed to the war effort, and the pay they offered made the rewards of a career in film projection pall by comparison.[504] Furthermore, the competition for labour was intensifying as the available pool dwindled because of conscription. The challenges of staffing projection boxes were exacerbated by the legacy of decades of underpaying, undertraining and generally undervaluing projectionists. For the duration of the war, chief projectionists aged 25 and above were exempt from enlistment. Second projectionists in the same age group were placed on the list of reserved occupations until September 1941, when the reservation age was raised to 35; this limit was subsequently increased every month, by one year, from January 1942 onwards.[505] When preparing to lobby the Ministry of Labour for the continued protection of particular grades and age groups, the CEA undertook a detailed census to ascertain the age range of British projectionists. Only 4,957 – i.e., 40% of the total number of projectionists recorded in the Ministry's 1937 survey of the industry – were aged 25 or over. A mere 610 projectionists were over 40 years old.[506] The industry was overwhelmingly reliant upon young men to staff its projection boxes, which dramatically

502 'The Odeon Agreement on Second War Bonus', *ibid.*, 17 July 1941, p. 5.

503 'A National War Bonus Settlement', *ibid.*, 21 August 1941, p. 3.

504 R. Howard Cricks, 'Projection Staffs During Wartime', *ibid.*, 7 December 1939, p. ix.

505 'Reservation of Projectionists', *ibid.*, 18 December 1941, p. 3.

506 'New C.E.A. Appeal for Reservation of Operators', *ibid.*, 7 March 1940, p. 3.

magnified the impact of conscription. Several commentators noted that it only had itself to blame for this.[507] As the chief projectionist of the Odeon, Peterborough, explained:

> The type of youth engaged as assistant operator in the silent days, and in more recent years, was not expected to stay in the job for any length of time, and as soon as he could obtain a better paid job as a 'sweeper-up' in a factory or something similar he quit the Trade for good. This explains the shortage of middle aged projectionists to-day, and shows the folly of the Trade in the 1920s in not taking the projectionist more seriously. Had the position been made worth while in those days, there would be little staff shortage now, as many practising projectionists would be over military age.[508]

The challenge of adequately replacing the conscripted men was exacerbated by the lack of any established training infrastructure, and envious eyes were directed towards an intensive three-week scheme of training for substitute cinema projectionists that had been quickly organised, on a national scale, in Nazi Germany.[509] The first demographic group that exhibitors turned to in searching for a source of stand-in labour was women – primarily those already employed in cinemas as usherettes and cashiers. The use of so-called 'projectionettes' in British cinemas (Fig. 3.4) during the Second World War has been the subject of quite extensive research within the last couple of years, and there would be limited value in revisiting here the contemporary range of opinion (of which some was very positive and supportive) published within the contemporary film industry trade press concerning the suitability of women for projection work, given that this has already been studied in some detail.[510] There are two broad assumptions made in recent scholarship on this topic that we think are worth pausing over and querying, however. Rebecca Harrison has suggested that we should understand 'women's employment as projectionists [as] being anathema to men working in the cinema industry'; Richard Farmer similarly argues that 'exhibitors fought so hard and for so long to keep hold of their operators' because they dreaded the prospect of having to replace them with women.[511] Although there were pockets of opposition to the idea, the major trade organisations and most prominent commentators on projection issues were actually strongly in favour at the outset.

507 See, for example, James Benson, 'Depleted Projection Boxes', *ibid.*, 18 September 1941, p. 34.

508 R. Howard Cricks, 'Shortage of Capable Projectionists', *ibid.*, 9 September 1943, p. ix.

509 R. Howard Cricks, 'Emergency Training of Projectionists', *ibid.*, 14 March 1940, pp. xiv-xv.

510 See Richard Farmer, *Cinemas and Cinemagoing in Wartime Britain, 1939-45: The Utility Dream Palace* (Manchester: Manchester University Press, 2016), pp. 137-141, 147-155; Rebecca Harrison, 'The Coming of the Projectionettes: Women's Work in Film Projection and Changing Modes of Spectatorship in World War II British Cinemas', *Feminist Media Histories*, 2:2 (April 2016), pp. 47-70.

511 *Ibid.*, p. 50; Farmer, *Cinemas and Cinemagoing in Wartime Britain*, p. 138.

The CEA began advocating the use of female projection labour in the first week of the war, and NATKE promptly seconded this.[512] The Guild and R. Howard Cricks subsequently voiced their agreement.[513] The reasoning behind these endorsements was entirely pragmatic: it was assumed that women would have no interest in staying on in the box beyond the end of the war, and therefore the bitterly resented difficulties that had been experienced in accommodating decommissioned projectionists in 1918-19 – which had consequently driven them into the arms of the ETU – might be more easily avoided. There was no shortage of men in the industry determined to argue that women would not be capable of covering the duties of a chief projectionist,[514] but, as one journalist observed, the classification of this rank as a reserved occupation 'simplifies the problem of training of substitutes, especially women, confining these to the lower grades'.[515]

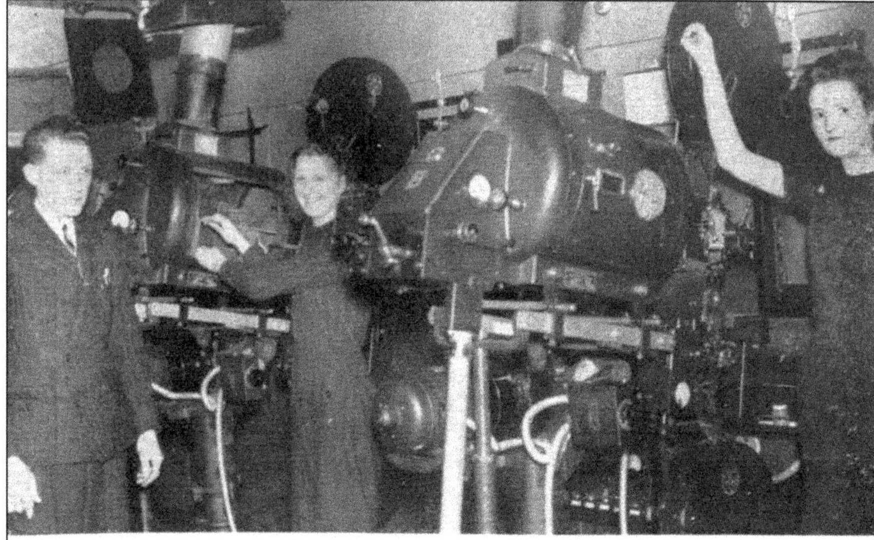

Chief projectionist, P. E. Gough, with projectionette staff at the Odeon, Bury, where B.T.-H apparatus provides both sound and picture.

Fig. 3.4: 'Projectionettes' on duty as operators at the Odeon, Bury in 1942.[516]

512 'C.E.A. Urges Employment of Women Projectionists', *Kinematograph Weekly*, 7 September 1939, p. 3; 'N.A.T.K.E. Recognition for Women Projectionists', *ibid.*, 14 September 1939, p. 3.

513 'Projectionists Discuss Policy', *ibid.*, 16 November 1939, p. 27; 'Guild Discusses Admission of Service Members', *ibid.*, 5 June 1941, p. 22; R. Howard Cricks, 'Emergency Training of Projectionists', *ibid.*, 14 March 1940, pp. xiv-xv.

514 'The Projectionist Problem', *ibid.*, 7 December 1939, p. 7; R. Howard Cricks, 'Projection Staffs During Wartime', *ibid.*, p. ix.

515 'Operators Reserved Above Age 25', *ibid.*, 2 May 1940, p. 3.

516 'This Week's Projection Room', *Ideal Kinema*, 15 January 1942, p. xvi.

Another supposition that needs to be handled with care is the idea that female projectionists were ubiquitous during the war, based on the assumption they represented the only available option for replacing conscripted men.[517] No attempts were made to survey or estimate the numbers of women who became projectionists at this time. Between 1939 and 1941 it was reported that efforts to recruit and train female projectionists had been set in motion by Gaumont-British in London, Glasgow, Birmingham and Liverpool and by the CEA in Bristol; vaguer details of equivalent efforts were also publicised by Odeon and ABC.[518] The most ambitious of these – and certainly the one reported upon in most detail – seems to have been Gaumont's Birmingham scheme. It involved two weeks of school training assessed by a preliminary examination, which preceded two-to-three months of practical training at a cinema work placement, followed by a further two weeks of advance teaching and a final examination. The first four students were admitted in October 1941, and by May 1942 it was reported that a combined total of 60 women (out of 65 entrants) had passed the examinations.[519] However, in July 1942 the Ministry of Labour cancelled the deferment from service of women under 24 years of age, so that they could henceforth by conscripted into jobs that directly supported the war effort. Exhibitors expressed 'considerable indignation' at what they felt had been a waste of time and money in training young women whom they now had little chance of retaining.[520] The Birmingham scheme was immediately scrapped, and there are no further reports of any comparable circuit training initiatives for women.[521] In January 1945, a survey of projection standards in '30 to 40' Birmingham cinemas found that women were employed in the box 'only in a few instances'.[522] Enquiries by NATKE revealed that only three female projectionists were working in Edinburgh at the end of 1943.[523] These figures may be atypically low, and independent cinemas would undoubtedly have recruited women through their own individual efforts

517 Harrison, 'The Coming of the Projectionettes', pp. 50, 52.

518 'Projectionists Discuss Policy', *Kinematograph Weekly*, 16 November 1939, p. 27; 'Apprentices as Operators', *ibid.*, 29 February 1940, p. 15; 'Bristol Selects 20 Women Operator Trainees', *ibid.*, 23 May 1940, p. 3; 'Women as First and Second Operators', *ibid.*, 23 October 1941, p. 8; 'Projectionist Trainees', *ibid.*, 6 November 1941, p. x; 'G.-B. Glasgow Course for Women Operators', 20 November 1941, p. 10; 'North Western Plans a Training Scheme', *ibid.*, 18 December 1941, p. 24. Richard Farmer notes that ABC claimed to have trained 200 women as projectionists by May 1941: *Cinemas and Cinemagoing in Wartime Britain,* p. 151.

519 'Birmingham's Training Course', *Ideal Kinema*, 14 May 1942, p. x.

520 'Women Call-Up Crisis', *Kinematograph Weekly*, 16 July 1942, p. 3.

521 'School for Women Operators', *ibid.*, 23 July 1942, p. 3. The North Staffordshire CEA branch announced a scheme to train girls aged 17-18 in 1944; it was conditional upon guarantees that they would spared from conscription, and it does not seem to have proceeded: 'Girl Trainees for the Box', ibid., 20 April 1944, p. 29.

522 J.M. Cannon, 'Film Damage: A Call to the Renters', *ibid.*, 11 January 1945, p. 55.

523 'Wages of Women Operators', *ibid.*, 2 December 1943, p. 47.

and organised in-house training on the job. The balance of available evidence suggests, though, that the main drive to recruit female projectionists was concentrated within a fairly short window of time, from October 1941 to July 1942, and it's quite possible that national numbers of projectionettes peaked in the hundreds rather than the thousands.[524]

If cinemas progressively abandoned the idea of training women as projectionists during the second half of the war, this obviously begs the question of how they managed to cover for conscripted employees and stay open for business. The answer appears to be that they primarily reverted to the same policy practised during the First World War: the hiring of boys (and some girls) aged between 14 and 17. Teenagers under 18 were said to be 'installed in most cinemas' even before female projectionists were taken off the list of reserved occupations.[525] Beginning in 1942, licensing authorities relaxed their rules about the employment of youths in projection boxes, even to the extent of allowing under-16s to work as assistant operators when 'A' certificate films were being screened.[526] In 1943 the *Kinematograph Weekly* launched a monthly 'Jottings for Juniors' column within its technical supplement, specifically aimed at the new influx of unskilled teenaged projectionists.[527] In another manifestation of the trade's habitually inconsistent and uncoordinated approach to projection training, a few local clusters of exhibitors established classes for juniors in Nottingham, Derby and Paisley (see Fig. 3.5).[528]

524 Although the actual number of women projectionists recruited during wartime remains unclear, there is no doubt about the fact that female employment in projection boxes was not confined to the war years. Various articles and letters in the trade press document the existence of female labour in some projection boxes during the interwar period. For example, a 1929 article about the Picturedome Cinema, Lancaster's conversion to sound noted that Miss Constance Haddart had become the first 'female talkie operator' ('A Talkie Record – First Female Operator', *Kinematograph Weekly*, 10 October 1929, p. 42). The projection box certainly did not revert to being an exclusively masculine space after the conclusion of World War Two. In 1955 it was reported that the Odeon and Gaumont circuits had arranged for fifty female projectionists that they collectively employed to attend a two-week refresher training course in London's West End ('Kirkcaldy Projectionist in London', *Fife Free Press and Kirkcaldy Guardian*, 28 May 1955, p. 7). There were a number of chief projectionists who were women working in the industry by the mid-1960s. A 1966 edition of the *Mining Review* newsreel included a feature on 'Dorothy', a chief working in Bishop Aukland. Although the commentary characterises her as 'probably the only woman chief projectionist in the business', we know of at least one other – Florence Barton – who was working as a chief in the Midlands (and later in Kent) during this period. Women projectionists at a more junior level were more common, and increasingly so in the multiplex era. For more on the employment of women as projectionists outside of wartime see Richard Wallace, Rebecca Harrison and Charlotte Brunsdon 'Women in the Box: Female Projectionists in Post-war British Cinemas', *Journal of British Cinema and Television*, 15:1 (January 2018), pp. 46-65.

525 'Reasons for Film Damage', *Kinematograph Weekly*, 19 March 1942, p. 45.

526 '16 Year Olds as Operators', *ibid.*, 16 April 1942, p. 5; 'More Child Employees in Kinemas', *ibid.*, 5 November 1942, p. 20.

527 'Jottings for Juniors', *ibid.*, 10 June 1943, p. xiv.

528 'Technical Training in the Midlands', *ibid.*, 3 August 1944, p. 34; 'Training Junior Projectionists', *ibid.*, 19 October 1944, p. 3; 'The Observation Window', *ibid.*, 11 January 1945, p. 30.

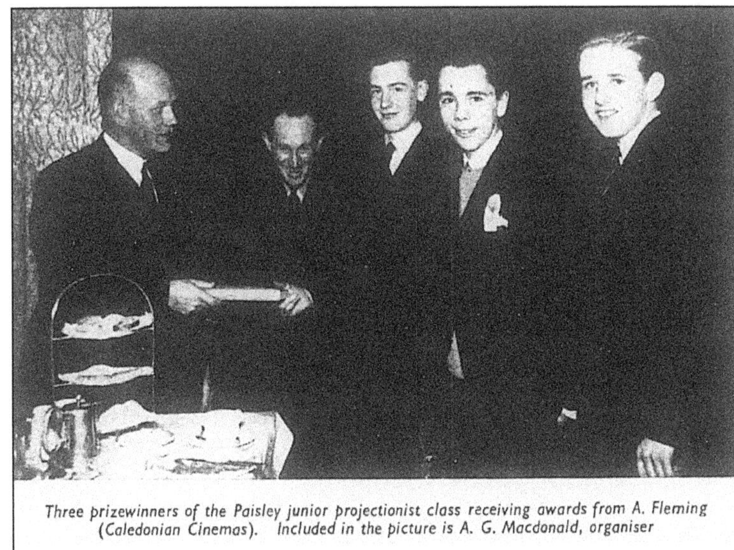
Three prizewinners of the Paisley junior projectionist class receiving awards from A. Fleming (Caledonian Cinemas). Included in the picture is A. G. Macdonald, organiser

Fig. 3.5: The training of teenage projectionists during World War Two.[529]

The industry's increasing reliance upon teenage projection labour was most frequently discussed (and lamented) in connection with a perceived epidemic of film mutilation problems. Wartime restrictions on the use of raw film stock were undoubtedly a factor here, by necessitating that prints stayed in circulation for longer.[530] 'Reduced or non-existent maintenance' of projectors was also highlighted in the discussion.[531] But it was generally agreed that the overriding issue was that prints were being carelessly handled by the large influx of casual junior staff.[532] In Derby, Nottingham, Leicester, Birmingham and Grimsby, local film distribution branches went to the lengths of establishing Film Damage Advisory Committees to try and trace the offending cinemas, so that they could be pressured into taking remedial action. The CEA sponsored the production of a short instructional film called *Better Projection*.[533] The prevalence of boy labour, and its associated problems, led to the *Kinematograph Weekly* commissioning a series of cartoons called 'Our Boy', satirising the failings of teenage projectionists, which ran for several years (see Fig. 3.6).

529 'Paisley Juniors Receive Class Awards', *ibid.*, 10 May 1945, p. xxv.

530 R. Howard Cricks, 'Enemies of Film Stock Economy', *ibid.*, 11 March 1943, p. ix.

531 R. Howard Cricks, 'Film Economy and Print Condition', *ibid.*, 8 April 1943, p. vii.

532 See, for example, R. Howard Cricks, 'Kinema Technique and Equipment', *ibid.*, 8 June 1944, p. ix; 'Straight Talk on Film Damage', *ibid.*, 7 December 1944, p. 11; J. Whitnall, 'Where Does Film Damage Arise?', *ibid.*, 18 January 1945, p. xxix.

533 James Benson, 'The "Better Projection" Film', *ibid.*, 22 June 1944, p. 37.

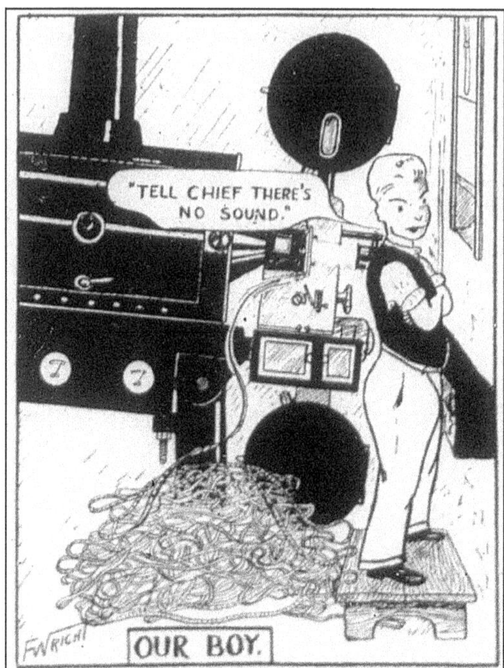

Fig. 3.6: The alleged incompetence of teenage projectionists satirised in the 'Our Boy' cartoons.[534]

When it became apparent that there would probably be insufficient single women available to supply the industry's personnel needs, the CEA also dedicated a considerable amount of energy to the development of another approach. In a further echo of trade policy during the previous war, it was proposed once again that injured ex-servicemen should be trained as projectionists.[535] Ambitious plans for nine-month apprenticeships were developed, which were to involve three months of teaching at extensively-equipped training centres, and six months spent in supervised work placements.[536] Government support was very confidently anticipated, so when the Ministry of Labour ultimately announced that it would not fund the programme, a sense of great outrage was expressed, along with accusations that promises had been broken.[537] (Perhaps someone in the Ministry remembered all too clearly how they had been undermined and embarrassed when penny-pinching cinema proprietors scuppered the First World War scheme for rehabilitating disabled soldiers as projectionists.)

534 'Our Boy', *ibid.*, 13 June 1946, p. xxvii.

535 'London Exhibitors' Contact with Local Authorities', *ibid.*, 23 September 1943, p. 13.

536 'Managers' Complicated Status', *ibid.*, 4 November 1943, p. 18; 'Training Ex-Servicemen as Projectionists', *ibid.*, 20 July 1944, p. 38.

537 James Benson, 'Training Disabled as Projectionists', *ibid.*, 21 September 1944, p. 35.

The end of the Second World War did not straightforwardly alleviate the challenges of adequately staffing cinema projection boxes. By the Spring of 1946 it was being widely reported that large numbers of pre-war projectionists did not want to return to their former jobs after being released from military service. As one such individual explained:

> Among former 'civvy street' operators whom I have met while serving in the Navy there seems to be a definite trend toward 'keeping clear' of projection rooms and all they entail. I have met many such fellows whose only aims are to get 'demobbed' and then, in their own words, 'find some other job'; they set their post-war aims in many directions, but very few in the direction of a kinema. The majority of my acquaintances openly state that for them projection is definitely 'out,' or, at the most, they will only return until something better comes along.[538]

Several readers confirmed that they knew lots of men who felt the same way. Having broadened their skills and employability prospects in the armed forces, they were not prepared to return to poor wages and long, unsociable, working hours.[539] It was subsequently suggested that for many projectionists who did return to their old positions in expectation of better conditions, 'Disillusionment has bred disappointment and dissatisfaction, so much so that there has been a drift away from the box, and, in many cases, the same crews are carrying on that got by during the war.'[540] The CEA was forced to plead with licensing authorities to maintain special wartime permissions they had granted allowing youths aged under 16 to be employed in the box.[541]

Cinema box office earnings in Britain reached an all-time peak in 1946,[542] and the combination of this level of prosperity with a skilled labour shortage theoretically offered propitious conditions for the officially recognised union to push for significant improvements in pay and working conditions. Meaningful *symbolic* concessions were certainly achieved in this year. NATKE got the CEA to agree that there should be a single national framework to set all terms and their future improvement, rather than dozens of individually negotiated branch settlements. As part of this national agreement, the maximum working hours per week were finally restricted to 48. New wage scales were agreed by consolidating pre-war basic district rates of pay with the wartime bonuses that

538 P.G. Canham, 'Staffing the Projection Room', *ibid.*, 14 March 1946, p. xxxv.

539 'Staffing the Projection Room', *ibid.*, 16 May 1946, p. xxxi.

540 Percy Pilgrim, 'It's the Searcher for Knowledge Who Will Succeed', *ibid.*, 18 December 1947, p. 218.

541 'The Employment of Under 16s in the Projection Room', *ibid.*, 20 June 1946, p. 47.

542 H.E. Browning and A.A. Sorrell, 'Cinema and Cinema-Going in Great Britain', *Journal of the Royal Statistical Society. Series A (General)*, 117:2 (1954), p. 134.

had been awarded (which for weekly salaries between £2 and £3 had involved a 38.33% increase, and a 29% increase for wages over £3),[543] and adding a further 10% increase for wages above £2-10-0 and 15% for those below.[544] Thus, a chief projectionist in a class 'A' hall in London would now earn £5-13-5, his second would get £4-0-4, and his third £2-7-2.

Tom O'Brien heralded the national agreement as a landmark moment in the history of the British film industry, and craved indulgence for the signatories to 'blow their own trumpets' concerning this 'great achievement'.[545] It effectively represented the final nail in the coffin as regards the ETU's ambitions for cinema projectionists. The electricians' union suffered the loss of its last negotiating foothold within the film exhibition industry when the Glasgow and West Scotland CEA branch cancelled its rate card with the ETU in favour of the NATKE deal.[546] Just under a year later, the ETU signed a peace treaty with NATKE, in which it recognised the latter's 'domination of the general kinema employment market', in return for the right to claim sole dominion over film studio electricians.[547]

The significance of the national agreement was less clear-cut in other respects, however. Two weeks before it was signed and sealed, O'Brien announced that he was set to call his members out on strike because there were too many independent exhibitors who would not give assent to the deal.[548] And yet, once both parties shook hands, local CEA branches could not disguise their relief that 'considering the general trend in wages and terms of conditions ... they had not done too badly in the agreement'.[549] There is considerable room for suspicion here that O'Brien concocted the strike threat as a piece of sham theatre in order to give his members the impression that he had forced their employers into making much greater concessions than they wanted to.

In the broader context of that 'general trend in wages' across the British economy as a whole, this was not a particularly generous settlement. Between October 1938 and July 1945, wage rates in the industrial sector had already risen by 51%. The average wage of a coal miner in 1945 was £5-7-0, and amongst all grades of railway

543 'New War Bonus Rates Settled', *Kinematograph Weekly*, 15 June 1944, p. 3.

544 'C.E.A. and N.A.T.K.E. Reach Wages Agreement', *ibid.*, 18 July 1946, p. 3.

545 Tom O'Brien, 'The National Agreement', *ibid.*, 25 July 1946, p. 12.

546 'New Dispute Between Unions Over Staff Wages Pact', *ibid.*, 19 September 1946, p. 22.

547 '50,000 Film Workers Involved in New Agreement between Three Trade Unions', *ibid.*, 26 June 1947, p. 3.

548 'Threat of Strike Overhangs C.E.A. Unless National Wage Scale is Agreed by July 16', *ibid.*, 11 July 1946, p. 11.

549 'Ratification of Wages Agreement Postponed for Study', *ibid.*, 1 August 1946, p. 22.

workers the typical weekly pay packet was £5-16-10.[550] Rumblings of discontent over the terms that O'Brien had negotiated led to various manifestations of insubordination from the NATKE membership. The Nottingham branch passed a vote of no confidence in O'Brien in 1947, and its committee was duly suspended by the executive in retaliation.[551] One irate member from Southsea insisted that 'Not until NATKE says to the industry "we are *going* to give the workers a square deal and not *may* we," will membership increase and give the union a 100 per cent. backing'.[552] Subsequently, O'Brien comprehensively revised his own assessment of the national agreement as a triumph, and withdrew NATKE's support for it, declaring that 'The present wages structure is a disgrace to the industry and a disgrace to the country'.[553] A new offer that was negotiated with the CEA in 1949 of 12.5% pay rises for workers on £3-£5 per week and 5% for those earning more than £5 was acknowledged by the union to be 'unsatisfactory', but was recommended to NATKE members as the best deal possible.[554] The complaint of one 'Third Operator' that O'Brien's rhetoric too often boiled down to 'Marge today and butter tomorrow, perhaps', would be repeatedly echoed in the remaining decades of his reign.[555]

Certification and Apprenticeships

The post-war labour shortage became even more serious during the 1950s as the metaphorical chickens that years of low pay and poor working conditions had created in the industry came home to roost. *Kinematograph Weekly* addressed the unfolding crisis in articles with titles such as '"Disastrous" Absence of Incentive', 'Where are the Boys?' and 'Staff Shortage Threat', and suggested various ways of combatting the problem, including the adoption of a two-shift working system to address the anti-social hours, and offering those interested the opportunity to take on managerial responsibilities.[556] In June 1951, regular columnist 'The Manager'

550 'Workers' Earnings', *The Economist*, 2 March 1946, p. 350.

551 'No Confidence Vote in Tom O'Brien', *Kinematograph Weekly*, 14 August 1947, p. 15; 'Notts N.A.T.K.E. Row over S.O.: All Officials Suspended', *ibid.*, 25 September 1947, p. 7.

552 R. Talbot, 'NATKE Must Give Us a Fair Deal First', *ibid.*, 2 September 1948, p. 22.

553 'NATKE to Scrap Wages Agreement with CEA', *ibid.*, 16 September 1948, p. 3.

554 'CEA-NATKE Agree New Wages Pact', *ibid.*, 12 May 1949, p. 3; 'Union Men Considering Wages Plan', *ibid.*, 2 June 1949, p. 10.

555 'Disgusted with NATKE "Misleaders"', *ibid.*, 16 June 1949, p. 17.

556 'In and Out of "The Box": "Disastrous" Absence of Incentive: Conditions Have Improved', *Kinematograph Weekly*, 13 September 1951, p. 34; 'The Projectionist', 'Where are the Boys?', *Ideal Kinema*, 8 November 1951, p. 19; 'The Projectionist', 'Staff Shortage Threat', *ibid.*, 13 May 1954, p. 18; 'The Manager', 'A Two-Shift System to Ease Projection Staff Problems', *Kinematograph Weekly*, 21 June 1951, p. 27; 'Letter: Projectionists: Give them An Incentive: By One Who is Now a Manager', *ibid.*, 6 September 1951, p. 13. See also: "The Projectionist", 'Recruits Wanted', *Ideal Kinema*, 13 January 1955, p. 31; 'Projectionists: O'Brien Warns the Exhibiting Industry', *Kinematograph Weekly*, 20 January 1955, p. 4.

addressed the impending crisis, noting that 'The shortage of projectionists becomes more acute', and that it was generally agreed 'that conditions of employment, as much as standards of wages, frighten potential candidates away from this interesting work'.[557] In February 1953, the same paper's 'The Chief' characterised the junior projectionist as 'becoming an extinct species', and noted that 'the few surviving specimens in captivity have a scarcity value. From what I hear I should say that 75 per cent. of the boxes in this country are either understaffed for lack of a junior or badly staffed because of his inefficiency'.[558]

The primary solution identified to address this labour shortage – and the trade's concomitant reliance upon teenage labour – was a formalised apprenticeship scheme for projectionists. It was increasingly felt that systematic training would provide a clear sense of long-term career progression and in so doing raise the standards – both actual and perceived – of the profession and encourage recruitment. This was not a new idea. Earlier attempts to devise a system of qualifications for projectionists by NACO (examinations) and the Guild of British Projectionists (a correspondence course) had been dismal failures. Certain more substantial programmes that we have mentioned previously were either very short-lived or remained regional anomalies. Developed by NATKE and the CEA, with the input of the British Kinematograph Society (BKS) and the Ministries of Labour and Education, the new proposed national scheme had an extremely lengthy and protracted gestation. The reasons for this are revealing, and help to explain why its eventual realisation did not fulfil the desires of any of the interested parties, and also how it came too late to have any meaningful industry-wide benefit.

The 1946 National Agreement had committed employers to ensuring that their junior projectionists attended technical classes that were to be organised by NATKE,[559] but, despite much noise on the subject, no meaningful progress was made until the following decade.[560] In May 1951 the front page of *Kinematograph Weekly* proclaimed, 'All Projectionists With Certificates by 1955' and set out the contents of a draft memorandum, 'which, it is expected,

557 'The Manager', 'A Two-Shift System to Ease Projection Staff Problems', *Kinematograph Weekly*, 21 June 1951, p. 27.

558 'The Chief', 'The Problem of the Junior', *Ideal Kinema*, 12 February 1953, p. 15.

559 R. Howard Cricks, 'A Study of the National Agreement', *ibid.*, 12 September 1946, p. xiv.

560 With the exception, once again, of Scotland, where formalised classes began in Aberdeen in September 1949 (National Association of Theatrical and Kine Employees [Aberdeen Branch], MS 2642.2, University of Aberdeen Special Collections), followed with courses run in Glasgow, Dundee, Fife and Greenock by 1952 ('Classes for Scottish Projectionists', *Kinematograph Weekly*, 28 December 1950, p. 22; 'Classes for Operators', *ibid.*, 25 January 1951, p. 36; 'The Projectionist', 'About Projection', *Ideal Kinema*, 14 February 1952, p. 17).

will be adopted by the majority of CEA branches in Great Britain subject to minor alteration'.[561] The educational syllabus and examination was to be developed by a sub-committee of the BKS and 'The Ministry of Labour and the Ministry of Education will advise, from a national level, for suitable instructional classes to be given in every CEA branch area for projection room trainees.' The planned apprenticeship now involved the following:

> Apprenticeship for four years, which is binding on the student.
>
> Administration by a joint local committee.
>
> Apprentices must be between 16 and 17.
>
> Transfer of employment can be only with the consent of the local committee.
>
> The Ministry of Labour will arrange for deferment from national service until after the period of training, providing national defence demands make this possible.
>
> There will be three examinations for various grades of employment.
>
> All existing projectionists over 21 and with five years' experience shall be given a second projectionist certificate on passing an examination. With six years' experience, they can take a test for chief projectionist.
>
> The joint local committee has power to take away certificates.[562]

Despite pressure from NATKE that all projectionists – and not just apprentices – should be certified, the CEA suggested that it was not likely that this could be accomplished 'until 1954 or 1955' at the earliest. [563]

One trade editorial commented that 'the men who work in this nerve centre of every theatre have seldom been regarded as any more than "the man who turns the handle"', but the proposals meant that 'we are on the threshold of a new period in kinema operation'.[564] The planned scheme was seen to demonstrate clear benefits for both the CEA and NATKE: 'For the union the award of certificates to a trained man will help in recruiting and in negotiating for new wage and conditions agreements', whereas 'if every projectionist has a certificate, the exhibitor is given adequate protection from the inefficient workman who, by his laziness, can bring no credit to his colleagues, no satisfaction to himself and certainly nothing but loss of business and prestige to the industry'.[565]

561 'All Projectionists With Certificates by 1955', *Kinematograph Weekly*, 24 May 1951, p. 3.

562 *Ibid.*

563 *Ibid.*

564 'Skill to be Rewarded', *ibid.*, 24 May 1951, p 4.

565 *Ibid.*

R. Howard Cricks described the scheme as 'the most important thing that has ever happened to projectionists in this country. Once it comes into operation it will provide an assured status for the craft'.[566] The CEA's technical advisor Leslie Knopp proclaimed that the draft apprenticeship agreement that had been developed by the association's Sussex branch should be adopted by all branches of the CEA,[567] and that both the examinations and certificates 'must be the same all over the country if they are to be of any value'.[568]

However, almost immediately the realisation of the plan began to falter. Only a few months after the publication of the proposals, NATKE were complaining about implementation delays, with Tom O'Brien claiming that 'a few CEA branches had agreed schemes, but other branches were trying to make unsuitable variations of the proposed draft or were showing little or no interest in apprenticeships'.[569] Two specific issues relating to certification became major sticking points as discussions developed. The first concerned the bodies that would be signatories to the certificates; the second, whether certificates should be a requirement at all. NATKE was particularly keen to stake its claim to oversee the certification system, by suggesting that 'there are plenty of members of the union competent to adjudicate on the ability of their fellow members, and that the award of certificates should be left to them'.[570] The CEA rejected this outright, raising concerns that the presence of the signature of a NATKE official was symbolic of the union's objective 'towards a "closed shop," whereby no projectionist other than a union member can obtain a certificate'.[571] This was a key concern of the Manchester branch, which worried that 'once accepted, the certificate might be demanded as a condition of one's licence' and that 'there will follow acceptance of certificates an authoritative demand for the employment of certificated projectionists only'.[572] The CEA's counter proposal – that certificates should be replaced with a letter written by an apprentice's employer – was abhorred by NATKE, who argued that a letter 'might give the exhibitor power to retain youths for the full period of training at a time when it is difficult to engage staff, yet gives no guarantee that individual employers will see that adequate training

566 'The Training and Apprenticeship Scheme Approved', *Ideal Kinema*, 14 June 1951, p. 15.

567 'The South Leads Branches in Talks for Apprenticeship Schemes', *Kinematograph Weekly*, 24 May 1951, p. 15.

568 'Apprenticeship Scheme must be National', *ibid.*, 7 Jun 1951, p. 7.

569 'NATKE Wants Action on Apprenticeships', *ibid.*, 27 Sep 1951, p. 3.

570 R. Howard Cricks, 'Getting Down to Certification', *Ideal Kinema*, 11 October 1951, p. 11.

571 'Apprentices: CEA Oppose NATKE', *Kinematograph Weekly*, 21 February 1952, p. 7.

572 'Firm Stand Against O'Brien's Move to Certificate Trained Projectionists', *ibid.*, 27 Mar 1952, p. 16.

is given during this period'.[573] Although R. Howard Cricks's view that the BKS was 'the only truly independent and technically qualified body in the industry, and the only body whose certificate will command universal respect' was sensible, it did not assuage either of the two main parties' concerns.[574]

The inability to formalise agreements worsened the recruitment crisis. In April 1952, with discussions on the verge of collapse, the CEA reported that 'Ministry of Labour employment offices are telling youths not to take up jobs as kinema projectionists, and will continue to do this until the CEA has agreed a nation-wide apprenticeship scheme.'[575] In this context, the CEA's general council felt that the association 'was not in a tenable position to further resist the NATKE being a signatory to the certificates'. Furthermore, NATKE had begun to show some flexibility by agreeing that 'if general certificates ever came into force all operators who had fulfilled the conditions laid down in the national agreement would automatically be entitled to a certificate, for which it would not be necessary for them to apply through NATKE', thus deflecting the fears over a 'closed-shop' future. Nevertheless, progress remained slow and the Ministry continued their policy of discouraging youths from becoming projectionists well into 1953.[576]

Negotiations were not helped by two concurrent developments that had a direct bearing on the national apprenticeships. In July 1951, the Circuits Management Association Limited (CMA) – the company formed by the merger of the Odeon and Gaumont circuits[577] – announced the development of an internal training programme for its projectionists.[578] The first stage of the scheme was a series of refresher training courses for chief projectionists to take place at the Gaumont State, Kilburn, to be followed by the development of a training centre in London for young projectionists.[579] The latter was 'fully operational' by February 1953, and worked as follows:

> The youngster who ... is led to apply for a job at a CMA theatre and who is successful in his application, first spends a short time in the projection room. If in due course he is found suitable for the job and

573 'Apprentices: CEA Oppose NATKE', *ibid.*, 21 February 1952, p. 7.

574 R. Howard Cricks, Technical Department', *Ideal Kinema*, 13 March 1952, p. 13.

575 'Ministry Telling Youths Not to Work in Kinemas', *Kinematograph Weekly*, 17 April 1952, p. 10.

576 'Apprenticeship Scheme Delay is Impeding Projectionist Intake', *ibid.*, 18 September 1952, p. 18; 'No Projection Recruits Until Scheme Agreed', *ibid.*, 21 May 1953, p. 3.

577 Allen Eyles, *Odeon Cinemas 2: From J. Arthur Rank to the Multiplex* (London: Cinema Theatre Association, 2005) pp. 31-32.

578 'CMA Training For Its Own Projectionists', *Kinematograph Weekly*, 12 July 1951, p. 7.

579 'C.M.A.'s New Training Scheme', *Ideal Kinema*, 12 Jul 1951, p. 17; 'C.M.A. Training Scheme', *ibid.*, 11 October 1951, p. 18.

> if he wishes to continue in it, he goes to a training sub-centre, of which there are 12 throughout the country – each of them one of the key theatres of the group ... At the end of six months juniors found suitable for the job are indentured for a period of five years. At this stage they spend three weeks at the main training centre at Haverstock Hill, in North-West London ... Before leaving Haverstock Hill the student takes an examination and then returns to his base theatre.[580]

The apparent success of these arrangements meant that one of the key stakeholders in the CEA had little reason to press for the rapid implementation of the CEA-NATKE scheme, and indeed may even have had reasons to delay things further to prolong the recruitment problems of their competitors.

The other major hindrance was a generally unfavourable response to the draft syllabus for the taught components of the CEA-NATKE apprenticeships published by the BKS. In October 1951, a committee including members from the BKS, NATKE, the CEA and the Ministry of Education had been convened to discuss a suitable syllabus, and this was eventually published in August 1952.[581] The course needed to be sufficiently broad and rigorous to meet the approval of the Ministry of Labour, and thereby qualify for deferment from National Service, but there was a widespread view that the content was too theoretical, and would 'discourage youths from undertaking the course, or that too many will fail to complete it'. One commentator also noted that the nature of the proposed teaching meant that there was 'a realistic probability' that, once trained, apprentices might leave the industry having gained the necessary skills for more lucrative employment elsewhere.[582]

The BKS agreed to some further amendment of the syllabus in response to the CEA criticisms. Although it did not appease all dissenting branches of the CEA, the final version published in June 1953 did encourage those that were positively inclined towards the proposals – including the London and Home Counties branch – to ratify agreements with NATKE and the Ministry of Labour and begin localised apprentice schemes.[583] It was announced that the London branch would become 'the first in England to have made arrangements to put the training and apprenticeship scheme into

580 R. Howard Cricks, 'This is the Form for Tomorrow's Technicians', *Kinematograph Weekly*, 12 February 1953, pp. 9, 11.

581 'NATKE Consulted on Projection Syllabus', *ibid.*, 25 October 1951, p. 9; The Syllabus of Training Projectionists Under the CEA-NATKE Apprenticeship Scheme', *Ideal Kinema*, 14 August 1952, p. 16.

582 W. G. Altria, 'This in Theory is the Way it is Proposed to Train Projectionists Tomorrow', *ibid.*, 14 August 1952, p. 3.

583 'School Begins', *ibid.*, 8 October 1953, p. 17.

operation', and teaching began for the first group of fifteen apprentices at the Wandsworth Technical Institute in September 1953.[584]

The modest scale of this first cohort was an immediate cause for concern. The columnist known as 'The Projectionist' noted that many more candidates than this had been nominated by exhibitors, and felt that 'unless the immediate intention of limiting the class to such a few is reconsidered, or other classes are initiated in other London boroughs, the disappointment of the boys who were weeded out may easily have the effect of causing them to look to other trades for employment'.[585] Even for those who were selected, the wages on offer did not offer much of an incentive to stay the course: starting at £2 15s per week, the salary was to progressively rise throughout the four-year apprenticeship to a level of £4 10s upon completion. Some felt that it was doubtful 'that many boys will be prepared to work until they are 19, maybe older, at these rates, when industries which require less skill are offering higher pay'.[586]

With London leading the way, other CEA branches began to ratify their own local schemes, with the Nottingham,[587] Kent, Sheffield[588] and Notts and Derby[589] branches all making agreements with NATKE by the end of 1953, joined by the Newcastle upon Tyne branch the following year.[590] Despite this initial push, there was insufficient momentum for the scheme to progress further without a national agreement.[591] A sticking point for many exhibitors was the idea of attendance at all classes being compulsory.[592] Tom O'Brien accused the CEA of 'throwing out the whole idea of a national scheme merely because some exhibitors would do anything to prevent the union participating'.[593] As was the case with earlier wage negotiations, his ire was reserved for independent exhibitors, who, he felt, wanted 'to treat this matter as a political issue. They are concerned only with keeping NATKE out'.[594] In

584 Projection Trainee Classes in London', *Kinematograph Weekly*, 11 June 1953, p. 7; 'Projectionist Scheme to Start Sept.', *ibid.*, 9 July 1953, p. 13; 'School Begins', *Ideal Kinema*, 8 October 1953, p. 17.

585 'The Projectionist', *ibid.*, 13 August 1953, p. 13.

586 'School Begins', *ibid.*, 8 October 1953, p. 17.

587 Nottingham Courses for Projectionists', *Kinematograph Weekly*, 10 September 1953, p. 8.

588 'Apprenticeship Scheme Terms Agreed with NATKE', *ibid.*, 3 December 1953, p. 22; 'Recruits Wanted', *Ideal Kinema*, 11 March 1954, p. 19.

589 'Cost and Quality of Publicity Attached', *Kinematograph Weekly*, 1 April 1954, p. 31.

590 'Projectionists' Scheme Agreed in the North', *ibid.*, 29 July 1954, p. 25.

591 'Group Levy Idea Turned Down', *ibid.*, 4 February 1955, p. 28.

592 '...CEA Delegates Anxious for Agreement', *ibid.*, 10 February 1955, p. 29.

593 'O'Brien Puts All Blame on CEA', *ibid.*, 27 January 1955, p. 9.

594 'NATKE Warns Exhibitors on Training', *ibid.*, 20 January 1955, p. 3; 'Projectionists: O'Brien Warns the Exhibiting Industry', *ibid.*, 20 January 1955, p. 4.

March 1955, NATKE made what it described as 'very major concessions' by withdrawing their requirement for certificates to be signed by a union officer and instead suggesting that 'on completion of the apprenticeship the indenture shall be suitably endorsed by the employer and the chairman of the local joint committee', which the union agreed should be set up in each region to administer the scheme. The trade-off for this concession was holding firm on the view that 'we cannot agree that attendance at classes should be haphazard', and that 'An apprentice should be released without loss of pay for one day or two half-days ... for attendance at technical classes arranged by the local joint committee with the local education authority'. It was also felt that 'it would be too much to ask local committees to inaugurate these schemes and to administer them with any effect and efficiency without some kind of national overseership', and it was proposed 'that some small and national joint advisory committee should be appointed'.[595]

NATKE's movement on the issue led to a breakthrough at the end of April 1955, when the CEA and the union agreed a framework for a national apprenticeship scheme that would be 'administered by a National Joint Apprenticeship Council composed of representatives of CEA and NATKE operating through local joint committees in each branch area'.[596] Attendance at technical classes was mandatory 'Where these are provided', but it was felt that 'if it is found difficult to arrange classes, a correspondence course could be used' to satisfy the requirements of the Ministry of Labour.[597] The Ministry duly conferred deferment from National Service for participating trainee projectionists in December 1955.[598]

The initiation of a nationally agreed apprenticeship programme should have been a very significant step forward. However, its flaws were many, and serious. NATKE's failure to convince the CEA that apprenticeships should be compulsory meant that decisions to implement the scheme were deferred to individual branches, and those that did take them were under no obligation to force new recruits through the accreditation process.[599] Some of the more militant regional offices of NATKE boycotted the apprenticeships because – to quote the Manchester branch – 'as the

595 'NATKE "Major Concessions" on Training', *ibid.*, 24 March 1955, p. 3.

596 'CEA-NATKE Agreement on Training', *ibid.*, 28 April 1955, p. 3; 'Training: It's Up to the Branches Now', *ibid.*, 19 May 1955, p. 23.

597 'CEA-NATKE Agreement on Training', *ibid.*, 28 April 1955, p. 3.

598 'Training: It's Up to the Branches Now', *ibid.*, 19 May 1955, p. 23; 'Apprenticeship', *ibid.*, 22 December 1955, p. 10.

599 'Training: It's Up to the Branches Now', *ibid.*, 19 May 1955, p. 23.

scheme is run on a voluntary basis, [union members] have no desire to serve on any [joint] committees', and it was still inactive in this area two years later.[600]

Many local schemes struggled to recruit sufficient trainees for courses to proceed. This problem was compounded by very low levels of unemployment across the country; in 1955, the unemployment rate was 1.2%, the lowest figure for any year of the 20th century outside of wartime.[601] Take-up in Portsmouth was poor because the city 'had reached a state of full employment';[602] a recruitment drive in Sheffield attracted only twelve potential apprentices;[603] in South Wales a low number of applications for the course at Cardiff Technical College made it unviable.[604] In March 1957, a meeting of the National Joint Apprenticeship Council noted that it was 'generally speaking, satisfied, with the progress of the scheme in Scotland and the London areas' but that 'in the outlying areas ... the council would like to see much more rapid progress'.[605] By August 1957, it was estimated that there were 115 apprentices training in the London area, but that the total across the rest of the country only amounted to 200, and that in most areas 'there are too few apprentices to justify training arrangements'. In a rare ray of light for the scheme, the CMA had agreed to link its training to the national apprenticeship agreement so that 'all apprentices enrolled in future by the group will be indentured under the national scheme'.[606] The central role that the major circuits played in the upkeep of the scheme can be seen in reports from Liverpool the following September where it was stated that eighteen of the twenty apprentices attending classes in the city were from either CMA or ABC cinemas.[607]

By 1958, there was a general feeling that 'the overall picture was gloomy' for the programme.[608] The following year, the North West CEA branch proposed that it should be scrapped entirely. The cost of the scheme was questioned, with one member noting

600 Projectionists "No" May Stop Training', *ibid.*, 28 July 1955, p. 22; 'Apprenticeship Plan's Progress in Manchester', *ibid.*, 2 May 1957, p. 9.

601 James Denman and Paul McDonald, 'Unemployment Statistics from 1881 to the Present Day', *Labour Market Trends*, 104 (1996), pp. 6-7.

602 'Syllabus Will Scare Boys Away', *Kinematograph Weekly*, 4 August 1955, p. 20; 'Branch Talks with NATKE on Apprenticeship Classes', *ibid.*, 3 May 1956, p. 107.

603 'Apathy Over Apprentice Classes', *ibid.*, 29 September 1955, p. 21.

604 'Too Few Students for Training Session', *ibid.*, 4 August 1955, p. 10.

605 'Apprenticeship Progress Slow in Country', *ibid.*, 21 March 1957, p. 3.

606 R. Howard Cricks, 'Talking Technically', *Ideal Kinema*, 15 August 1957, p. 25.

607 'New Rules Allow Roll Tickets', *Kinematograph Weekly*, 18 September 1958, p. 26.

608 'CEA General Council Meeting', *ibid.*, 26 June 1958, p. 25.

that 'The association was spending £2,000 a year on the scheme' and yet 'Many of the boys at present employed in operating boxes were apprenticed to other trades and worked in the operating boxes in the evenings to earn extra money'.[609] It was increasingly recognised that the correspondence course was extremely ineffective and poorly supervised,[610] and and at a meeting of the CEA General Council in 1961, it was decided that this element of the scheme should be discontinued'.[611]

By this point in time, attempts to get a sustainable apprenticeship system off the ground had been ongoing for well over a decade, without any broad success. The non-compulsory nature of the CEA-NATKE scheme meant that it did not fulfil either party's desires. Without universal uptake, a minimum standard of quality projection could not be guaranteed. With no wholesale increase in projection standards, the dream of increased leverage in wage negotiations did not materialise. The scheme also failed to provide anything like the numbers of recruits to projection boxes that had been hoped for.

Although some blame for the latter could be placed on the difficulty of the syllabus, it also seems clear that the industry had failed to satisfactorily improve the poor pay and working conditions that had always characterised the British film exhibition industry. The introduction of the CEA-NAKTE National Agreement did streamline the process of wage negotiations, and although there were occasional moments of tension, these were generally finalised without any protracted drama.[612] However, difficulties faced by the industry at a wider level meant that these negotiations rarely resulted in significant improvements for projectionists. The continued presence of Entertainment Tax (eventually abolished in 1960) and the imposition of the Eady Levy (introduced in 1950 and made compulsory by legislation in 1957) on the exhibition of all films shown in the UK meant that a larger percentage of exhibitors' profits was being returned to the UK government and the produc-

609 'Support for Levy Investigation', *ibid.*, 9 November 1959, p. 7; 'Bid to Discontinue the Apprenticeship Scheme', *ibid.*, 31 December 1959, pp. 6-7.

610 'Apprentices Don't Want to Learn', *ibid.*, 13 October 1960, p. 8; 'CEA General Council Meeting', *ibid.*, 22 September 1960, p. 30.

611 'CEA General Council Meeting', *ibid.*, 16 March 1961, p. 25.

612 In 1954 a dispute between the CEA and NATKE about wages was referred to the Ministry of Labour, with the union seeking arbitration, though an agreement was eventually reached before any significant industrial action was initiated ('NATKE Seeks Arbitration on Wages', *ibid.*, 15 July 1954, p. 3; 'Bid to End CEA-NATKE Deadlock', *ibid.*, 22 July 1954, p. 3). In 1958 the union proposed that negotiated wage increases should only apply to union members, which, although initially accepted by the exhibitors, drew criticism for another perceived attempt to initiate a closed shop ('NATKE Pay-Agreement Problems', *ibid.*, 25 September 1958, pp. 3, 10; 'CEA General Council Meeting', *ibid.*, 16 October 1958, p. 10).

tion arm of the industry.[613] On top of this, wider societal changes, particularly the expansion of television, led to a steep decline in cinema attendance. From the high of 1.6 billion admissions in 1946, attendance declined steadily to 1.1 billion in 1956 before falling more rapidly to around 0.5 billion in 1960, with numbers continuing to fall into the 1980s.[614] As the apprenticeship programme was being rolled out nationally in 1956 and 1957, 417 cinemas were simultaneously closing their doors, with the loss of 250,000 seats, in a situation that Conservative MP Raymond Gower described in the House of Commons as 'a desperate battle';[615] around 1,500 cinemas closed in total between 1950 and 1960.[616]

It is hardly surprising, given this broader context, that CEA members were reluctant to grant projectionists any significant wage increases. Although the National Agreement was periodically renewed, wage rises regularly failed to keep up with increasing living costs, and attempts to couple the negotiations of wages and conditions were repeatedly denied, as were efforts to raise the wages for those dealing with 3-D and 'special widescreen processes.'[617] As one commentator opined, 'at present the end product for a student projectionist is not good enough'.[618]

Long and anti-social work schedules also remained a bitterly contentious issue. One projectionist decried 'the average crazy arrangement of working hours', and another felt that

> Men are leaving the trade because they find that family life and all the other incidentals of normal civilised life are denied them. ... It is

613 Margaret Dickinson and Sarah Street, *The Cinema and State: The Film Industry and the Government 1927-84* (London: BFI, 1985), pp. 206-211, 219-226; James Fenwick, 'The Eady Levy, "The Envy of Most Other European Nations": Runaway Productions and The British Film Fund in the early 1960s', in I. Q. Hunter, Laraine Porter and Justin Smith (eds.), *The Routledge Companion to British Cinema History* (London; New York: Routledge, 2017), pp. 191-199; Jonathan Stubbs, 'The Eady Levy: A Runaway Bribe? Hollywood Production and British Subsidy in the Early 1960s', *Journal of British Cinema and Television*, 6:1 (2009), pp. 1-20.

614 Hanson, *From Silent Screen to Multi-Screen*, p. 93. For a more detailed discussion of the decline of cinema attendance during the 1950s and 1960s see Sam Manning, *Cinemas and Cinema-Going in the United Kingdom: Decades of Decline, 1945-65* (London: University of London Press, 2020).

615 HC Deb (25 March 1958) vol. 585, col. 198-9. Available at https://hansard.parliament.uk/Commons/1958-03-25/debates/1071b824-f0e3-48c3-86d0-44e6bcd10bd4/EntertainmentsDuty(Cinemas), accessed 3 February 2020.

616 '200 MPs Expected to Hear Tax Plans', *Kinematograph Weekly*, 27 March 1958, p. 3; Ernest Betts, *The Film Business: A History of British Cinema 1896-1972* (London: George Allen & Unwin LTD, 1973), p. 227.

617 'Increases Less Than Cost of Living Rises', *Kinematograph Weekly*, 26 March 1953, p. 18; 'O'Brien Doubts on Wage Talks', *ibid.*, 27 November 1952, p. 3; 'Conditions Are Out of NATKE Wage Talks', *ibid.*, 15 January 1953, p. 3; 'This is Our Biggest Opportunity', *Ideal Kinema*, 9 July 1953, p. 18; 'CEA Hears NATKE 3-D Wage Plea', *Kinematograph Weekly*, 6 August 1953, p. 8; 'NATKE Wants Rates for New Techniques', *ibid.*, 1 April 1954, p. 7. In 1963 it was agreed that Cinerama projectionists 'in the provinces' would be given 'a similar increased ratio of salaries to those in London' ('More Pay for Cinerama Projectionists', *ibid.*, 15 August 1963, p. 3).

618 'Too Few Students for Training Session', *ibid.*, 4 August 1955, p. 10.

> admitted that late hours and holiday work are incidental and unavoidable in the amusement industry, but surely there should be some compensation for this! Instead, we have the 48-hour week, the longest in any trade. The audience, for who we work to amuse, mostly has a 40- or 44-hour week ... A start should be made by reducing our week to 44 hours with a view to a further reduction to 40 in a five-day week.[619]

Although various suggestions for two-shift working patterns were proposed, nothing concrete materialised.[620] Modest reductions in working hours were eventually introduced by the end of the decade. NATKE negotiated a 44-hour working week in 1958. This was further reduced to 43 hours in 1960, though this was at the expense of the '15-minute supper break', which was transferred from the employers' to the employees' time.[621] It was not until the 1971 agreement that the working week was finally reduced to 40 hours.[622]

There was also a growing unease about the expansive scope of the job and the impact of the wide variety of non-projection-specific labour upon the image of the profession. We have covered these duties elsewhere in this book (see Chapter One), but discussions about their relationship with the status of projectionists became intertwined during the labour shortages of the 1950s. In November 1956, the *Ideal Kinema*'s 'Projectionist' columnist made the following argument, which is worth quoting at length:

> With but few exceptions, senior projectionists have long since realised that the words 'projection' and 'projectionist' have greater meaning and cover a far wider field of work than is normal. In simple language, the work of projection in a cinema is that directly connected with the principle of showing pictures, and the projectionist is the person who applies his ability in doing so. In many ways, unfortunately, and largely due to the manner in which cinema technical work has developed, both words generally mean a very expansive general ability. Instead of 'projecting' pictures we find ourselves stoking the boilers, cleaning the flues, carting the ash, and we also run the heating and ventilation plant. We find ourselves at times acting as stage managers, dressing the stage, hanging the drapes. As a diversion we, also, are expected and often do, carry out the work of electrical contractors complying with a stringent set of regulations, and coping with minor tasks such as the unstopping of drains and

619 H.H. Allen, 'Letter: Crazy Working Hours', *Ideal Kinema*, 17 June 1954, p. 59; 'WPL' (Work-Plus-Leisure), 'Letter: Bad Conditions Make Staff Shortages', *ibid.*, 17 June 1954, p. 59.

620 "The Projectionist", 'Two Schemes for Shifts', *Ideal Kinema*, 14 July 1955, p. 13.

621 'CEA General Meeting', *Kinematograph Weekly*, 18 September 1958, p. 25; 'More Pay and Shorter Hours for NATKE', *ibid.*, 26 May 1960, p. 3.

622 'National Agreement Between The Cinematograph Exhibitors' Association of Great Britain and Ireland and The National Association of Theatrical, Television and Kine Employees', *National Agreement between the CEA and NATTKE, 1971 & Memorandum of Agreement between the Kent County Branch of the CEA and NATKE, 1964*, MSS.437/NATKE/9/1, MRC, p. 3.

> replacing of washers. Occasionally, we have shown our opposition to this wide scope of labours. The issue has been raised during CEA/NATKE agreement negotiations but all to little or no purpose. So we go on as operators, projecting ourselves into glorified handymen. We older ones are, in the main, so used to it that in a sense we have become indifferent, but is it a good thing for the up-and-coming youngsters that these attitudes to ourselves and our work should persist? I do not think it is! We must consider the matter very broadly. In the first instance do we think it desirable that projectionists should confine their exertions to projecting pictures, doing nothing else than to carry out the mechanics of the post, or do we think the work should include the care and maintenance of only those items of equipment which are immediately and directly connected with the job of projecting pictures? What is probably most important is: do the apprentices and juniors want to become the general factotums that the Chiefs now are? I don't think they do, and furthermore I am of the opinion that, unless there is a very pronounced change of direction in the way of our future projectionists, the job will not hold them.[623]

To add to this observer's concerns, the practical conditions of cinema projection were also changing during this time, with the introduction of projection technologies that required new skills and more technical knowledge, but for little advancement in status or pay. The most notable of these were widescreen and 3-D projection, but cinemas were also interested for a time in screening live television broadcasts.[624] Two cartoons published by the *Ideal Kinema* highlight the increasingly labour-intensive working environment of the mid-1950s projection box. In the first (Fig. 3.7), a fresh-faced recruit responding to a job advertisement – 'Rewind Boy Wanted' – is interviewed by a second projectionist who asks, 'Of course, I assume that you are fully conversant with CinemaScope, 3-D presentation, wide-screen, stereophonic sound and TV projection, and that you have taken your BSc. degree.' The cartoon speaks to the broadening expertise demanded of projectionists, whilst at the same time lampooning the perceived difficulty of the C.E.A.-N.A.T.K.E. apprenticeship syllabus. In the second cartoon (Fig. 3.8) another second projectionist writes to the editor of the *Ideal Kinema* to announce his solution to 'the problem of the

623 "The Projectionist", 'What Do You Want Your Future to Be?', *Ideal Kinema*, 8 November 1956, p. 15.

624 For historical and aesthetic overviews of widescreen and 3-D cinema see: Dan Adler, Janine Marchessault and Sanja Obradovic (eds), *3D Cinema and Beyond* (Bristol: Intellect, 2013); Charles Barr, 'CinemaScope: Before and After', *Film Quarterly*, 16:4 (Summer 1963), pp. 4-24; John Belton, *Widescreen Cinema* (Cambridge, MA; London: Harvard University Press, 1992); Harper Cossar, *Letterboxed: The Evolution of Widescreen Cinema* (Lexington, KY: University Press of Kentucky, 2011); Yong Liu, *3D Cinematic Aesthetics and Storytelling* (Cham: Palgrave Macmillan, 2018); Miriam Ross, *3D Cinema: Optical Illusions and Tactile Experiences* (Basingstoke: Palgrave Macmillan, 2015); Owen Weetch, *Expressive Spaces in Digital 3D Cinema* (London: Palgrave Macmillan, 2016); Tana Wollen, 'The Bigger the Better: From CinemaScope to Imax', in Philip Hayward & Tana Wollen (eds), *Future Visions: New Technologies of the Screen* (London: BFI, 1993), pp. 10-30; Ray Zone, *Stereoscopic Cinema and the Origins of 3-D Film, 1838-1952*, (Lexington, KY: University Press of Kentucky, 2007); Ray Zone, *3-D Revolution: The History of Modern Stereoscopic Cinema* (Lexington, KY: University Press of Kentucky, 2012).

shortage of projectionists'. This, the image reveals, is due to the employment of a large octopus which is shown to be simultaneously tending two projectors and a sound rack, changing the non-sync music, rewinding a reel and delivering a cup of tea to the correspondent.

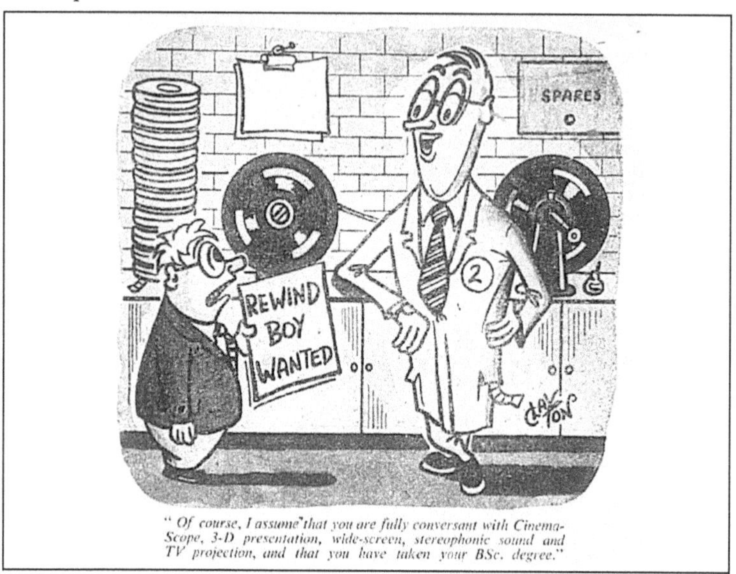

Fig. 3.7: The Ideal Kinema satirises the increased technical expertise required in the 1950s projection box ...[625]

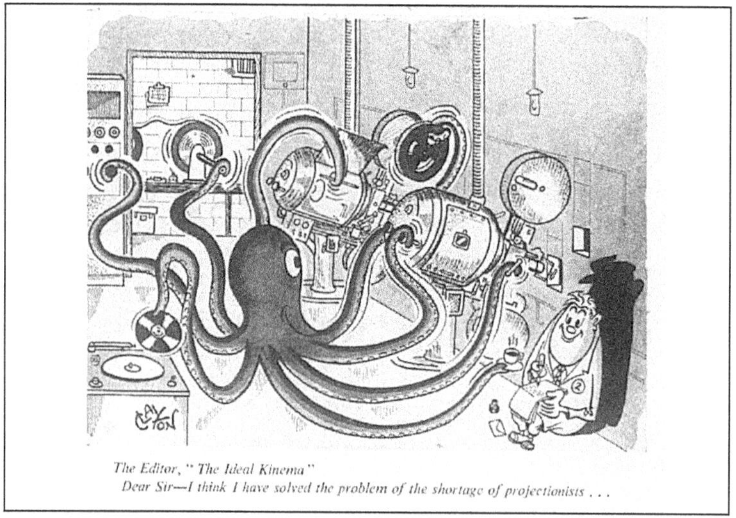

Fig 3.8: ... and takes the impact of the labour shortages to their logical conclusion.[626]

625 *Ideal Kinema*, 11 March 1954, p. 21.

626 *Ibid.*, 9 September 1954, p. 23.

Any hope that the scope of the job would be reduced was never likely to be met, and the move to single-manning (see Chapter One) that swept across the exhibition sector at the end of the 1960s actually served to exacerbate many of these pressures for those who remained in the box. To add to the sector's woes, Harold Wilson's government introduced the Selective Employment Tax in 1966, which was designed to subsidise, and stimulate recruitment in, the manufacturing industries by placing a levy on every service industry worker employed in Britain (encompassing entertainment industries such as the cinema).[627] This would have a direct impact upon projection boxes, on top of the fact that 'the invention of safety film and new safeguards and the installation of limited automation', collectively reduced the number of projectionists required to safely conduct screenings.[628]

In 1946, the Essoldo chain spent £25,000 to begin developing their own automation system as a response to 'the acute shortage of skilled projectionists, and the difficulty of recruiting youths to the industry'.[629] Although one might presume that any such attempt to reduce the necessary man-power in the projection box would have met with strong union resistance, the widespread labour shortages meant that NATKE had very little leverage when it came to such issues. Indeed, the union initially voiced strong support for the use of automated projection equipment. Tom O'Brien argued in 1955 that 'if the device had been likely to injure the interests of projectionists, NATKE would have opposed it', but instead he saw the system 'as a means of solving one of [the industry's] main problems'. Showing a stunning lack of foresight, he contended that the Projectomatic system 'was not going to be an excuse for exhibitors to sack anyone or cut down the staff in the box; it would be used by exhibitors, in co-operation with the union to ease the problems of projectionists to-day'.[630] In a foreshadowing of the kind of rhetoric that accompanied the introduction of digital projectors in cinemas (see Chapter Four), R. Howard Cricks supported O'Brien's position, suggesting that the union leader was 'working for the best advantage of his members', and that 'the installations of devices such as the Essoldomatic will have the effect of reducing the projection-room staff to perhaps two; but these will need to be highly skilled men, able to cope with the complex technicalities of all automated devices'.[631]

627 'Payroll Tax Will Hit Production', *Kinematograph Weekly*, 12 May 1966, p. 3.

628 Harry Roelich, 'Where Do We Go From Here…?', *ibid.*, 26 May 1966, p. 4.

629 'Projecting Without a Projectionist', *ibid.*, 28 January 1954, p. 7.

630 R. Howard Cricks, 'Talking Technically', *Ideal Kinema*, 19 April 1956, p. 23.

631 R. Howard Cricks,' 'Talking Technically', *ibid.*, 6 October 1955, p. 15.

This was not to be the case. O'Brien's view on automation shifted quickly, and by the middle of 1957, 'Projectionist members of the union ... were becoming increasingly disturbed at the tendency to use Projectomatic to cut down the number of projectionists employed in the operating box', which he felt 'threatened serious breaches of the projectionist clauses in the CEA/NATKE agreement that laid down the number of projectionists to be employed'.[632] Cricks rebutted these claims, using O'Brien's earlier arguments in favour of automation against him:

> I find it a little unrealistic of Sir Tom O'Brien that, after having welcomed Projectomatic because it would ease the job of the Projectionist and improve his conditions of employment, he is now objecting that it may lead to a reduction in projection staffs. I am sure exhibitors would be willing to employ as many competent projectionists as NATKE can supply – but Sir Tom knows full well that competent projectionists simply cannot be secured in sufficient numbers.'[633]

NATKE continued to stipulate a minimum number of projectionists that were required 'to provide the adequate and efficient running of the projection boxes to fulfil the normal working week', and the 1964 National Agreement specified these in relation to cinema sizes:

> Grade AA Five projectionists, one of whom may be a probationer or apprentice.
>
> Grade A Four projectionists, one of whom may be a probationer or apprentice.
>
> Grade B Three projectionists, one of whom may be a probationer or apprentice.
>
> Grade C Two projectionists, one of whom may be a probationer or apprentice.[634]

From the 1968 agreement onwards, however, these requirements were replaced by a statement about single-manning, noting that 'the recommendation is now that C.E.A. members should not in future start to operate single manning until the Head Office of C.E.A. had been advised and agreement reached between the exhibitor concerned' and NATKE.[635] In its failure to address the labour shortages through the negotiation of competitive improvements in wages and conditions and the creation of an effective

632 'NATKE Concern at Growth of Part-Time Work', *Kinematograph Weekly*, 18 July 1957, p. 3.

633 R. Howard Cricks, 'Talking Technically', *Ideal Kinema*, 15 August 1957, p. 25.

634 'National Agreement Between The Cinematograph Exhibitors' Association of Gt. Britain and Ireland and The National Association of Theatrical and Kine Employees', *Cinema Staff, Agreement Between CEA and NATKE*, MSS.333/1/V/3.4, MRC, p. 12.

635 'National Agreement Between The Cinematograph Exhibitors' Association of Great Britain and Ireland and The National Association of Theatrical, Television and Kine Employees', *National Agreement between the CEA and NATTKE, 1971 & Memorandum of Agreement between the Kent County Branch of the CEA and NATKE, 1964*, MSS.437/NATKE/9/1, MRC, p. 11.

apprentice scheme, the union opened the door for the recruitment crisis to be used as a tool by exhibitors to further erode the position of the projectionists by significantly reducing their number.

Membership of NATKE (or NATTKE – the National Association of Theatrical, Television and Kine Employees – as it was renamed in 1970) fell from 30,726 in 1950, to almost half that number by 1971.[636] Following the death of Sir Tom O'Brien in 1970, various cinema workers interviewed by Michael Chanan later in the decade made 'virtually unprintable' accusations concerning the union leader's allegedly corrupt and overly accommodating relationship with the CEA.[637] Although about half of the projectionists we interviewed noted that they were members of the union (and its direct successors the Broadcasting and Entertainment Trades Alliance [BETA; 1984-1991] and the Broadcasting, Entertainment, Cinematograph and Theatre Union [BECTU; 1991-present]) in the post-O'Brien era, there is still a general feeling expressed that there were very few visible benefits to membership, beyond the renegotiation of wage agreements. Later documentary evidence continues to paint a picture of an ineffectual union that regularly failed to provide robust support to its members. In 1977 a projectionist approached the Organisation of Industrial Relations Department of the TUC, concerned about his cinema's move to single-manning and stating explicitly that 'I dont [sic] trust my Union to find me employment ... I didn't get any Union help or concern over finding a Job When Penge Odeon Closed. Neither did anyone else there.'[638] In 1982, A. W. Fuller, a projectionist at the ABC, Edgeware, Middlesex complained to the TUC of 'some events to [sic] many to mention here some of which are degrading and serious enough for me to have written to N.A.T.T.K.E. the union I belong to asking them to help me, having written twice and having had no reply to date I feel there must be some thing wrong'.[639] After being referred back to the union and involving his local MP, he followed up his complaint to the TUC to make it clear that 'you would not believe that a member could be treated in such a manner by a union. If I could tell you I think you might even believe that nattke are not fit to be affiliated to you.'[640]

Although these are extreme cases, they tally with a broader perception conveyed to us that this was a union that increasingly took a

636 The National Association of Theatrical, Television and Kine Employees, 26 April 1972, MSS.292D/91/75: NATKE, 1970-1984, MRC.

637 Chanan, *Labour Power in the British Film Industry*, p. 48.

638 Letter from David Webb to The Secretary of the Organisation and Industrial Relations Department, TUC, 9 Feb 1977, MSS.292D/91/75: NATKE, 1970-1984, MRC.

639 Letter from A. W. Fuller to TUC, 26 April 1982, MSS.292D/91/75: NATKE, 1970-1984, MRC.

640 Letter from A. W. Fuller to TUC, 25 June 1982, MSS.292D/91/75: NATKE, 1970-1984, MRC.

hands-off approach when it came to cinema projection. A number of projectionists that we interviewed highlighted this feeling. Neil Thompson suggested that 'I don't think they did an awful lot for us, I don't think we had a good union myself.'[641] He left BECTU in 2000 because he felt that he didn't know 'if they're putting the money to good use', and his overall sense was of a weak union that was unable to stand up to the power of the major circuits. 'I think Rank got the better of them in the end', he argues.

These perceived failings were exacerbated during the multiplex era, where the influence of American conglomerates, often with anti-union proclivities, created a situation in which only two of the major UK circuits – Odeon and Cineworld – recognised BECTU as the appropriate trade union for projectionists. Even within the unionised chains, years of buy-outs and mergers had made arrangements complicated, and resulted in situations where individual chains were split between highly unionised cinemas and those which had a very weak union presence.[642] The Blackstone Group, for example, combined the highly unionised UGC/Virgin chain (one projectionist we interviewed suggested that 95% of UGC projectionists were members of BECTU) with non-unionised Cineworld cinemas to create – under the Cineworld name – a circuit with an imbalance of union representation.[643] The two parts of the company were kept financially distinct, in part to keep costs in the non-unionised sites down. This caused a clear split between the different groups of projectionists, with Ken Bagnall (a Cineworld projectionist) recalling that 'they probably had more hours, and their hours were protected. Their kit was arguably superior to ours.'[644]

Likewise, the merger of the UCI and Odeon chains initially led to a situation where different cinemas operating under the Odeon name had very divergent working practices. John Young (a former AMC and UCI projectionist) recalls discussing his experiences at a UCI site with colleagues at a nearby Odeon venue, where the technical manager 'couldn't believe that we had all the films plated off and ready and we left before the managers had left', whereas the Odeon team would 'stay 'til four [am] plating off the mov-

641 Interview with Neil Thompson, conducted by Richard Wallace, 11 November 2014.

642 For an overview of the various cinema mergers and buyouts in the UK, see Stuart Hanson, *Screening the World: Global Development of the Multiplex Cinema* (Cham: Palgrave Macmillan, 2019), pp. 118-129.

643 Interview with Chris Tweddell, conducted by Richard Wallace, 12 November 2014. Mick Corfield, a former Virgin cinemas projectionist and BECTU officer, recalls that the UGC cinemas were referred to as 'BECTU sites' within internal correspondence. Interview with Mick Corfield, conducted by Richard Wallace, 3 August 2015.

644 Interview with Ken Bagnall, conducted by Richard Wallace, 17 September 2015.

ies'.[645] Upon further investigation, it became clear to Young that the former AMC projectionists were paid single time for any overtime worked, whereas the Odeon projectionists got double time for anything after midnight. This kind of discrepancy 'caused a lot of problems in meetings ... when we amalgamated and had to put the two teams together under a single contract'.

Not everyone lost faith in the importance of, and necessity for, union representation. Brad Atwill notes that

> I still see the importance of a union ... especially if you're working for any sort of chain of cinemas ... [I]t's a business at the end of the day and it's a business with a lot of people that can quite easily cut back a lot and don't want to pay a great deal. ... I think a lot of [cinema workers] from management down are underpaid for the amount of work that they do ... [T]here's a lot of stress involved and there's a lot of, you know, running to times and a lot of plate spinning, and I think that isn't really taken into account. ... So, I think across the board pay needs to be assessed really, but I think that's across the country as a whole, you know ... [F]ront of house, often, at most sites can get a bit of a raw deal and ... I've done it myself – it's not fun being floor staff, especially not in kids' holidays where your day is basically wandering round cleaning up puke all day ... and you're getting paid minimum wage and no money for your break and stuff. So, yeah, I think it's important to have that sort of strength of a union behind you, at least for support, you know; contract change comes in, you're not having to worry about what things mean, somebody can look at it and tell you what it means and say whether it's fine.[646]

Despite his idealism, the picture Atwill paints of the average multiplex worker's situation is one of low pay and poor conditions, suggesting that the main issues facing the various projectionists' trade unions and their different iterations (whether NACO, ETU, NATE, NATKE, NATTKE or BECTU) have remained largely the same for over 100 years.

Perhaps the union's biggest intervention in the affairs of projectionists since the end of the 1950s came in response to another wave of technical changes, when the era of film projection gave way to the screening of digital film files. The fragmented nature of union representation caused some significant issues during this period for BECTU negotiators, especially when conducting redundancy discussions. The impact of digital technologies – and the union's response to them – will be dealt with at length in Chapter Four. However, it is worth noting here that the challenges of organising a co-ordinated militant response amongst a deeply fragmented workforce remained as difficult to overcome as it had in previous crises faced by the profession. Although BECTU made

645 Interview with John Young, conducted by Richard Wallace, 5 February 2015.

646 Interview with Brad Atwill, conducted by Richard Wallace, 10 November 2014.

attempts to mobilise its projectionist members in the face of digitalisation, this was countered by arguments made throughout the 2000s by cinema exhibitors (and repeated by trade organisations) that cinemas would still require skilled technicians to maintain digital projectors in the future. Ultimately, the union was able to mount only limited resistance to the digitalisation of projection boxes, leading to the concomitant near-extinction of the projectionist that is documented in the final chapter of this book.

Chapter Four

Digital Projection(s)

In 2003 Eastman Kodak ran a promotion in the British trade journal *Cinema Technology* advertising their new Digital Cinema Operating System (Fig. 4.1). The advertisement asked the reader to 'Imagine a pre-show that's as entertaining for [the audience] as it is profitable for you', and suggested that the Kodak digital system has 'all the scheduling, storage, and playback capability a cinema will ever need'. Splashed across the centre of the page is an image of a bored-looking man in his early 30s, sitting in the centre of a row of cinema seats, eating popcorn, with an empty popcorn tub that has been fashioned into an approximation of the Kodak Digital Cinema logo placed on his head. Ostensibly selling a product to enhance the audience's experience of the period prior to the start of a film, the advertisement concludes with the eye-catching statement: 'So you and your audience can sit back, relax, and enjoy the show, even before it begins.' This line seems to be addressing two different potential beneficiaries of the technology: the cinema manager responsible for the financial success of their venue, and the projectionist, whose labour is so alleviated by the pre-programmed digital projection system that he has been granted a holiday from his projection duties – a notion literalised by the lei around the man's neck. The advert thus gives the suggestion that three distinct individuals – the film viewer; the manager; the projectionist – could, with the help of digital projection, become one-and-the-same person.

In the context of its 2003 publication, the advert holds in tension a number of different elements that are central to this book's concerns. A reduction in projection labour is posited as the direct result of the technological advances offered by Kodak, and this is a rhetorical device that belongs to a long line of historical adverts and cartoons, such as Fig. 1.4 in Chapter One, where the anticipated introduction of long-running film reels promised an imagined future in which pipe-smoking projectionists could recline in easy chairs as the film played. In both instances, the exaggerated ironic rhetoric proved to be inaccurate. The technical advances of the 1950s didn't lead to a relaxed working environment, but to the rationalisation of the projection team; less work overall, but more for each individual. For the 21st century projectionist, the eventual removal of analogue film – the feature of the exhibition process that most of all required specialist expertise – meant that the single-manned multiplex projection box became a 'zero manned' digital operation.[647]

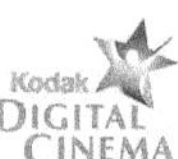

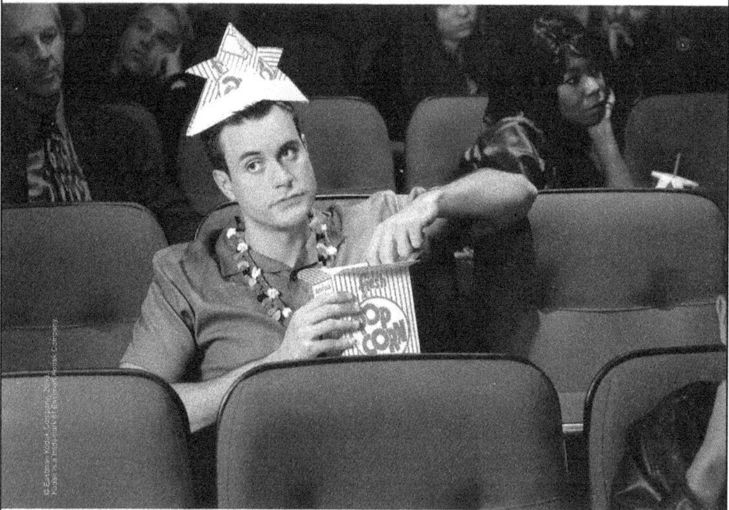

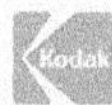

Fig. 4.1: Advert for KODAK Digital Cinema Operating System imagines a projectionist in the digital age.[648]

647 Mark Buck, Technical Manager of Vue, Hull, quoted in Jim Slater, 'Nationwide Success for CEA Digital Roadshow', *Cinema Technology*, 22:3 (September 2009), p. 23.

648 'Advert: KODAK Digital Cinema Operating System', *Cinema Technology*, 16:2 (June 2003), p. 7.

The Kodak advert is prescient, however, in predicting the amalgamation of the positions of cinema manager and projectionist into a single entity. As we will show, the reformulation of labour enabled by digital projectors led to a rapid reduction in the processes required to get a film onto cinema screens. This initiated a mass programme of redundancies amongst existing projection staff, and technical responsibilities have largely been subsumed within managerial roles. Those former projectionists still employed in cinemas often share any remaining projection duties with work on the cinema floor selling tickets and confectionery, managing duty rotas and answering emails.

In this chapter we will address the digital transformations in cinema exhibition and the impact that this has had on the work of projectionists. Inevitably, discussions of deskilling and redundancy will dominate our account of the digital transition. However, this is only part of the wider picture. Digital projectors did not arrive overnight, and consequently many projectionists had plenty of time – often a number of years – to acclimatise to the new technology and gain experience of working with it. Furthermore, although the cinema projectionist in the UK is severely endangered, they are not totally extinct. Independent and arts centre venues often employ technicians to oversee their audio-visual operations, and so there is scope to give a sense of what the job as it has been reformulated entails. Unsurprisingly, the new projection processes are substantially different to those outlined in Chapters One and Two, but they do exist and are worth exploring alongside the broader narrative of institutional and industrial change.

Digital Developments: Image, Standards, Finance

The Kodak advert's imagined digital future is one in which there are still projectionists present in mainstream cinemas, and in this it replicates a broader industrial rhetoric around the uptake of digital projection equipment prior to 2007. The move to digital was not an inevitability, and we can see a great deal of tension – and a strong sense of uncertainty – across the industry as to if, when, and how any such conversion might take place. Initially, these uncertainties centred around a combination of issues – concerning image quality, digital standards and funding – that created an overall sense within the projectionist community that the digital transition need not be a source of concern.[649] This view was supported by the trade press and professional associations linked to the exhibition sector,

649 For a more detailed overview of early digital exhibition see Richard Wallace, 'Going Digital: The Experience of the Transition to Digital Projection in UK Cinemas', *Journal of British Cinema and Television*, 15:1 (January 2018), pp. 6-26.

including the British Kinematograph Sound and Television Society (BKSTS) and their quarterly organ *Cinema Technology*, which was widely read by projectionists.

Image quality was the initial obstacle. Discussions of digital projection technologies took place within trade papers, cinema expos and training schemes during the late 1990s and were visible to any projectionist paying attention to the wider industrial debates. Phil Fawke – a projectionist since the 1940s – recalls that he 'knew it was coming', and that although 'it was experimented on for a number of years', the industry 'hadn't got it completely perfect'.[650] With a sense of stoical scepticism, John Young recalls an even longer history of such speculation: 'when I first started at Cannon [in 1973] they were all saying, "It's going to be video projectors and there's not going to be projectionists." And then about 25 years later, "Oh, it's not going to be video, it's going to be digital."'[651] Young visited the newly opened UCI cinema at the Printworks in Manchester in late 2000 (a 20-screen cinema that contained the UK's first digital projector outside of the West End) to view a demonstration of their digital equipment.[652] 'This won't work', he recalls saying, 'because every circle was oval ... because you haven't got enough pixels'. From this, Young 'knew it would take a good few years to come'.

The trade press expressed similar views, focusing especially on the divergent requirements of audiences and filmmakers. At a BKSTS event in May 2000 it was argued that although 'the consumer is quite happy with what he sees in the prototype projections', digital projection would only arrive 'when we can say to a film maker that it is capable of doing everything that film can do and more'.[653] Colour intensity was a particular issue, and one commentator suggested that 'the digital versus film comparison was like comparing plastic with leather – the new medium has less life and less vibrancy'.[654] It was not until 2008 that Jim Slater, the Managing Editor of *Cinema Technology*, felt able to make the claim that 'the public wouldn't be able to see the difference'.[655]

Format standardisation also took many years to be resolved. In 1999 the Society of Motion Picture and Television Engineers

650 Interview with Phil Fawke, conducted by Richard Wallace, 4 December 2014.

651 Interview with John Young conducted by Richard Wallace, 5 February 2015.

652 'The Printworks and thefilmworks – Far More Than A Cinema or Twenty', *Cinema Technology*, 14:2 (June 2001), p. 25-26.

653 John Croft, 'Electronic Cinema – What Next?', *ibid.*, 13:3 (September 2000), pp. 21-22.

654 Jim Slater, 'BARCO Brings D-Cinema to BAFTS', *ibid.*, 14:2 (June 2001), p. 13-14.

655 Jim Slater, 'Digital Awareness Day – Projectionists Face up to the Challenge of Digital Cinema', *ibid.*, 21:3 (September 2008), pp. 44-45.

(SMPTE) had formed a 'task force to look into standards'.[656] Although some progress had been made by mid-2004, BKSTS Fellow David Bancroft argued that 'it isn't happening fast enough for some', and that 'There is currently only partial ... congruence between the European and North American perspectives'.[657] He raised the inarguable point that 'The film industry starts from a unique base, with 35mm release prints setting the excellent precedent of a single standard with worldwide compatibility ... What everyone in the film business ideally needs is a digital equivalent'.[658]

The digital uptake was also slowed because of an initial failure to agree a suitable funding model for the digital infrastructure. The most significant savings would be made by studios and distributors, and, in a startling presentation given in 2006, Hamish McAlpine – the chairman of Tartan Films – estimated that for a film shown at 100 sites, the distributor would save around £58,000 by using digital files instead of 35mm film prints.[659] However, in order to make these savings for distributors, exhibitors would potentially have to take the financial hit of buying and maintaining expensive digital projectors, and thereby replace extremely durable mechanical equipment with devices that had built-in obsolescence. According to one commentator, 'Whilst a classic film projector lasted at least 20 years, the new ones – costing up to five times as much ... have to be replaced within 2-3 years. And their IT structure needs to be updated too.'[660] Leeds-based projectionist Alan Foster noted that 'the life of a digital projector is about ten years. ... At ten years, a 35-mill projector is a baby, it's hardly got warmed up, you know?'[661] Given these issues, it was unsurprising that exhibitors needed persuading to replace a reliable system, with one that (from their perspective) had little aesthetic or financial benefit, and Jim Slater stated in 2008 that

> The delays in adoption so far have generally come down to the difficulties in making a good business case for the transition from a long-established and reasonably-profitable industry based on 35mm film and straightforward electromechanical projection equipment which is known to last for decades.[662]

656 Ray Clipson, 'Cinema Technologies Old and New Come Face to Face at ITEA Technical Seminar', *ibid.*, 12:4 (September 1999), p. 18.

657 David Bancroft, 'Digital Cinema Standards', *ibid.*, 17:2 (June 2004), pp. 18, 19.

658 *Ibid.*, p. 18.

659 Jim Slater, 'The Digital Cinema Experience So Far', *Training for Digital Projectionists*, 1 (June 2006), p. 8. The average cost of a film print was determined as £700, and that of a digital file – including the initial encoding process – at around £115.

660 Werner Eymann, 'Digital Cinema: Guarding the Jewels', *Cinema Technology*, 16:1 (March 2003), p. 1.

661 Interview with Allan Foster conducted by Richard Wallace, 16 September 2015.

662 Jim Slater, '2008 – The Real Start for UK Digital Cinema?', *Digital Cinema* supplement to *Cinema Technology*, 21:1 (March 2008), p. 35.

One semi-successful attempt was made to break this funding deadlock quite early on. In July 2003 the UK Film Council (UKFC) announced its intention to cover the cost of installing 250 digital screens across 150 UK sites by mid-2005.[663] Although characterised at the time as 'a few digital drops in an ocean of celluloid', the UKFC project – known as the Digital Screen Network (DSN) – was a psychological step forward, if not an overwhelmingly transformative one.[664] The DSN's objective was not the complete digitalisation of the UK exhibition sector. Rather, it was an attempt to 'extend access to film and [engage] the widest possible audience for non-specialist film'.[665] A report published at the time of the network's launch found that 'access to specialized film is restricted across the UK' because of the prohibitive cost of producing sufficient film prints.[666] The installation of nationwide digital infrastructure was seen as a means of overcoming this problem, and it was intended that 'In return for the UK Fim Council's financial contribution towards the equipment, cinemas will devote a set percentage of playing time to specialised programming'.[667] The installations were completed in April 2007,[668] and it was reported that the number of specialist films grossing over £1 million had thereby tripled, from eleven (2000-2003) to 33 (2004-2007).[669]

Gillian Doyle *et al.* have argued that by 2007 'the UKFC had finally moved digital to the mainstream of its strategic thinking'; however, the broader questions around funding had still not been resolved.[670] At the end of that year, 97% of UK cinema screens still used 35mm film,[671] and in 2008 cinema consultant Anthony Williams characterised the UK industry as being located in '"the chasm" between successful early adopter stage and the situation where the major market exhibition players seriously adopt'.[672] BFI

663 'Advert: Introduction to Digital Cinema', *Cinema Technology*, 16:4 (December 2003), p. 29.

664 Joost Hunninger, 'The CILECT Workshop: Exploring Digital Cinema', *ibid.*, p. 30.

665 Gillian Doyle, Philip Schlesinger, Raymond Boyle and Lisa W. Kelly, *The Rise and Fall of the UK Film Council* (Edinburgh: Edinburgh University Press, 2014), p. 113.

666 'UK Film Council's Digital Initiative', *Cinema Technology*, 17:1 (March 2004), p. 10.

667 *Ibid.*

668 'Digital Screen Network Delays', *ibid.*, 18:1 (March 2005), p. 10; 'Arts Alliance Digital Cinema to Manage World's First Large Scale Digital Screen Network...BKSTS to Help with Projectionist Training', *ibid.*, 18:2 (June 2005), p. 4; 'DSN Complete', *Digital Cinema* supplement to *Cinema Technology*, 20:3 (September 2007), p. 25.

669 *Ibid.* There is reason to doubt the success of the scheme, however, given that the only individual films mentioned in this report were digital re-releases of *Casablanca* (USA, Michael Curtiz, 1942) and *Goldfinger* (UK, Guy Hamilton, 1964), hardly the 'specialised product' the UKFC would have had in mind.

670 Doyle *et al.*, *Rise and Fall of the UKFC*, p. 122.

671 Jim Slater, '2008 – The Real Start for UK Digital Cinema?', *Digital Cinema* supplement to *Cinema Technology*, 21:1 (March 2008), p. 35.

672 Jim Slater, 'Independents' Day', *Cinema Technology*, 21:2 (June 2008), p. 14.

statistics show that after a 100% increase in digital take-up between 2006 and 2007 (from 4.1% to 8.2% of UK screens – presumably a direct result of the DSN initiative), the following year saw this momentum stagnate, barely rising to a total of 8.5% of UK screens.[673]

The major financial breakthrough came with the development of the Virtual Print Fee (VPF) model, which was outlined to *Cinema Technology* readers in 2007 by Arts Alliance Media (AAM), the company responsible for installing the DSN's equipment:

> The basic premise is that a third party (i.e. AAM) pays up front for the equipment, and then recoups the cost of the equipment over time, through payments from distributors (who pay the majority of the cost) and exhibitors ... [T]he idea behind it is that the distributors save money by shipping digital, rather than 35mm, prints, and so these savings are used to contribute towards the cost of the equipment.[674]

Although the VPF was not without its critics, it succeeded in shifting the financial burden away from exhibitors and towards those making the biggest savings, and made the mass conversion to digital financially viable.[675] By 2011 digital projection was available in more than 50% of UK cinema screens. Another major factor was the intense, if relatively short-lived, wave of new-generation 3-D films, spearheaded by James Cameron's *Avatar* (USA, 2009), which required digital presentation, and which David Bordwell has characterised as digital projection's 'Trojan Horse'.[676] This was the final encouragement that the exhibition sector needed and by 2014, 100% of the UK's cinema screens had digital capability, with film as a distribution format for mainstream cinemas being all-but-dead.[677]

Discourses of Instability

The lengthy delay between the initial digital installations and universal adoption of the format served to dampen expectations that this outcome was unavoidable. It also prolonged uncertainty as to how digital projection would affect the employment of

673 British Film Institute (BFI), *Statistical Yearbook 2015* (London: British Film Institute, 2015), p. 12. Also available at https://web.archive.org/web/20190821135626/https://www.bfi.org.uk/sites/bfi.org.uk/files/downloads/bfi-exhibtion-2015-11.pdf, accessed 21 August 2019.

674 Arts Alliance Media, 'The Virtual Print Fee – Arts Alliance Answer the Questions', *Digital Projection* supplement to *Cinema Technology*, 20:3 (September 2007), p. 31.

675 For a more detailed overview of the limitations of the VPF, see Doyle *et al.*, *Rise and Fall of the UK Film Council*, pp. 118-122 and Jim Slater, 'EDCF Workshop', *Digital Projection* supplement to *Cinema Technology* 21:2 (June 2008), pp. 36-39.

676 David Bordwell, *Pandora's Digital Box: Films, Files, and the Future of Movies* (Madison, WI: The Irvington Way Institute Press, 2012), p. 75.

677 BFI, *Statistical Yearbook 2015*, p. 12.

projectionists, and during this period there was general (public) agreement that although the job would be subjected to significant reformation, projectionists would remain a vital part of the exhibition sector.

In 2000, Paul Schofield, Technical Manager of Odeon UCI Cinemas, made it clear that 'the role of a projectionist in the future is going to be different if film does bite the dust', and that 'being computer literate will almost certainly be mandatory'.[678] He continued:

> Downloading the data streams of movies, adverts and trailers will almost certainly take up a lot of time as well as organising the information into separate programmes for each set of equipment. It's true to say that the role could become less labour intensive. The time he or she would have spent lumping heavy and bulky film canisters around making up programmes and winding them onto platters could in future be spent at a keyboard and monitor, arranging downloaded commercials and trailers into complete programmes alongside the feature.[679]

Schofield even suggested that 'The need for a more technically competent projectionist could also put further pressure on the industry to ensure that operators have recognised vocational qualifications. Something which has been lacking for years.'[680]

Similar predictions of the projectionist's continued usefulness were expressed throughout the decade. In 2004 it was reported that 'there will still be a need for skill and attention in the projection booth to ensure that the promise and capability of digital projection is delivered to the paying audiences'.[681] Although a panellist at a 2008 Digital Awareness Day organised by the BKSTS gave the 'honest' view that savings could be made 'from a reduction in the number of technical people', this was tempered by the general view that 'Projectionists won't lose their jobs if they remain flexible enough to cope with more and different product', which 'could increase revenues and make all our jobs more secure in the long term'.[682] In 2009, it seemingly remained the consensus industry view that projectionists would 'have an absolutely key role to play' in the delivery of digital cinema content.[683] This repeated message

678 Paul Schofield, 'Electronic Cinema – Tomorrow's World?', *Cinema Technology*, 13:3 (September 2000), p. 25.

679 *Ibid.*

680 *Ibid.*, p. 26.

681 Denis Kelly, 'Projectionist Training Day at Digital Test Bed', *ibid.*, 17:2 (June 2004), p. 22.

682 Jim Slater, 'Digital Awareness Day', *ibid.*, 21:3 (September 2008), p. 52.

683 Jim Slater, 'Calling All Digital Projectionists', *ibid.*, 22:3 (September 2009), p. 8.

convinced many projectionists that their jobs would be secure if they were willing to retrain.[684]

Following the announcement of the Digital Screen Network, the BKSTS became more focused on the practicalities of this re-training. In December 2004 Jim Slater highlighted the scale of the work as he perceived it:

> The cinema exhibition industry will be faced with a situation where virtually all of its current technical staff (who have generally been trained in the electro-mechanical techniques used for current 35mm film projection) require new training in the operations and maintenance of the digital projection equipment and its complex ancillaries, including computers, servers, decoders, receiving equipment etc.[685]

This assessment was made within the context of a feature highlighting the BKSTS's intention to launch a quarterly publication that would 'build into a technical reference guide to Digital Cinema',[686] and the first issue of *Training for Digital Projection* was published in June 2006 as a supplement to *Cinema Technology*.[687] Training programmes run by the BFI and the BKSTS highlighted the impending need for the large-scale re-training of projectionists. An advert for the BFI's 'Demystifying Digital' event for projectionists in 2007 made it clear that 'you can't just rely on your 35mm preparation and display skills, but must adapt and learn new engineering skills'.[688] The following year an advert for the BKSTS's 'Digital Cinema Awareness Day' included the eye-catching headline: 'Digital Cinema is Coming – be aware!'[689]

In contrast, the exhibitors themselves seemed reluctant to address projectionist training. In early 2005, Odeon's Burton-on-Trent

684 At the same time as the message about the continued need for projection staff was circulated, there was a less visible – but still present – debate about the design of future cinema buildings in the digital age, with some commentators proposing the possibility that digital cinemas would no longer need projection rooms because of the compact design of the projectors. This raised the question of where projectionists would be working and what they would be doing in these cinemas. Odeon's Paul Schofield quelled such concerns by arguing that the buildings into which most digital projectors were to be installed would already have been built *with* projection boxes (Paul Schofield, 'Electronic Cinema: Tomorrow's World?', *ibid.*, 13:3 (September 2000), p. 25). Nevertheless, by the end of the decade there were a number of 'boothless cinemas' operating in the UK, including the the Lexi, Kensal Rise and the HMV, Wimbledon (Bill Chew, 'Boothless Cinemas – Is Less More, Part 1?', *ibid.*, 25:3 [September 2012], pp. 14-22; Jim Slater and Man-Nang Chong, 'The Rise of Boothless Cinemas', *ibid.*, 25:3 [September 2012], pp. 24-25; Bill Chew, 'Boothless Cinemas – Is Less More, Part 2?', *ibid.*, 25:4 [December 2012], pp. 18-20; Owen Williams, 'The Cinema of the Future', *Empire*, 302 [August 2014], pp. 72-73).

685 Jim Slater, 'UK Film Council Cash for Mags for Asian Cinema, Niche Films and Screenwriters – But Nothing so far for Projectionist Training', *Cinema Technology*, 17:4, (December 2004), p. 32.

686 Jim Slater, 'Editorial', *Training for Digital Projection*, 1 (June 2006), p. 3.

687 The supplement was short-lived. Its name was changed to *Digital Projection* after four issues when it also moved from a stand-alone publication to one contained within the pages of *Cinema Technology* itself. The final issue was published in June 2008.

688 'Demystifying Digital – The BFI Southbank Multimedia Box Training Course', *Cinema Technology*, 20:3 (September 2007), p. 48.

689 'Digital Cinema is Coming – Be Aware!', *ibid.*, 21:2 (March 2008), p. 29.

training centre for projectionists was closed,[690] and, despite initial reports to the contrary, Paul Schofield made it clear that there was 'no current plan to open up another training school' in its place. Instead, existing 35mm training was to be provided on an ad hoc basis 'using the extensive current knowledge of our Chiefs and Booth Managers'.[691] Digital training was to be provided in a similar manner, because 'Until more digital equipment is installed in our cinemas, it may just be a little too early to start digital cinema training sessions for projectionists'.[692] The situation was unchanged in 2008, and there was no longer any suggestion of awarding the 'vocational qualifications' that Schofield had spoken of six years earlier.[693]

The responsibility for training was instead taken up by various trade associations (BFI, BKSTS), contractors (Arts Alliance, Sound Associates) and projector manufacturers (Christie, Barco). Arts Alliance ran compulsory two-day workshops for DSN members that covered 'the basics of loading programme content into the equipment and building up shows', 'The operation of the projection and storage equipment', and 'basic troubleshooting techniques and tasks like changing lamps'. This was followed up with a further session at the trainee's cinema 'whilst the equipment is being installed'.[694] By March 2007, more than 275 projectionists had taken part in the scheme as part of the DSN rollout.[695] Digital projectionists whose theatres were not part of the initial DSN scheme had to stay abreast of industrial developments by attending various external training events or reading up on the new technology themselves. In 2005, Jim Slater suggested that as it stood, 'Formal training on this new "digital" kit has often been restricted to hands-on one-to-one training by the installation engineers, backed up by a sophisticated emergency help-line'. He continued:

> as anyone who 'plays' with computers knows, it is only by determined efforts to get to know the capabilities of such kit that you really become confident in its operation. Many of the projectionists I have met have told me that they have put in a lot of their own time to learn about the computer kit, and I have been impressed by just how competent they have become.[696]

690 'Odeon Projectionist's Training School Closed', *ibid.*, 18:1 (March 2005), p. 9.

691 Jim Slater, 'A Vision of the Future', *ibid.*, 19:1 (March 2006), p. 35.

692 *Ibid.*, p. 36.

693 Jim Slater, 'Digital Awareness Day', *ibid.*, 2:3 (September 2008), p. 51.

694 Jim Slater, 'The Digital Cinema Experience So Far', *Training for Digital Projection,* 1 (June 2006), p. 5; Fiona Deans, 'So You Want to Be A Digital Projectionist', *ibid.*, p. 22.

695 Jim Slater, 'It's Systems and Scalability That Will Determine the Future of Digital, say Arts Alliance', *ibid.,* 4 (March 2007), p. 17. Projector manufacturer Barco also established the Digital Cinema Certified Partner programme, though this prioritised the training of service engineers responsible for the conversion process itself (Jim Slater, 'Digital Projection ... and So Much More', *Cinema Technology*, 22:2 [June 2009], p. 16).

Alan Foster's account of his attitude towards the new digital projector arriving at the Hyde Park Picture House in Leeds exemplifies Slater's view:

> when digital came out ... it was the time to take stock and see whether my aged brain could actually understand how this works ... and the way I've often done things was to sit down on my own with it on a Saturday afternoon when there was nothing on. So, we had a kids' show in the morning and then I just sat, and fortunately it went in and I didn't have a problem with it.

Ewan Dunford, technical manager at the Watershed, Bristol, suggests that some projectionists 'may have sat on their laurels' as the digital transition approached, but he recalls thinking that he'd 'better crack on' and 'learn a bit more about this'.[697] He also suggests that the changing technological landscape with digital meant that there was a constant sense of having to renew his expertise:

> It's only just been rushed in and there's no one ... not even the Head of Department ... that already knows about it and can talk about the equipment and fix it ... The new world of IT infrastructure is kind of like the technical projectionist starting again in a way. Well, I remember the first time I went in a projection room ... and I remember just hours and hours of lacing film up and getting it right ... I think that's probably the type of hours that I need to put towards the new way of being a new style projectionist. ... So, we spent ... all this time and effort putting [the digital projectors] in and it's like we've got to start over again, like we're 18 again, you know?

The focus on on-the-job training is perhaps best demonstrated by Mark Buck, the technical manager of the UK's first all-digital multiplex, the Vue cinema in Hull which opened in 2007. At a CEA Digital Roadshow event in 2009 it was noted that 'His training consisted of two days at Dolby, during which he had learned a vast amount, but he said that his best training had come from being on his own with ten projectors and having to make the whole site run!'[698] Although it is tempting to argue that this lack of action on the part of the exhibitors themselves suggests that they had prior knowledge of the drastic reduction in projectionist numbers to come, the failure to apportion resources towards digital training is also entirely in keeping with the industry's perennial shoddy record on projectionist training, as outlined in the previous chapter.

The opening of the aforementioned Vue, Hull, was described by Vue Entertainment CEO Tim Richards as paving 'the way for the

696 Jim Slater, 'Training for the Ever Changing Projection Room', *ibid.*, 18:1 (March 2005), p. 12.

697 Interview with Ewan Dunford, conducted by Richard Wallace, 26 August 2015.

698 Jim Slater, 'Nationwide Success for CEA Digital Roadshow', *Cinema Technology*, 22:3 (September 2009), pp. 22-23.

future of cinema',[699] and Buck characterised the experience as 'totally different' to running a projection team: 'I have ten screens, ten digital projectors, no projection team, indeed no projection staff apart from myself ... and I spend most of my time in the cinema foyer managing cash tills and staff, in the office arranging staff rotas, and even deputise for the Manager in his absence'.[700]

Buck described the operation of the projection box as 'Zero-manning',[701] and argued that the digital system's reliability was exemplified by his presence at the CEA Digital Roadshow event 'whilst the cinema projection equipment was running unmanned 250 kilometres away to a schedule which had been arranged a week earlier'.[702] Slater described this as 'a pointer to the way in which cinemas of the future are likely to operate, having achieved massive efficiencies in staff and enormous flexibility.'[703]

Earlier in the year, Slater had expressed surprise when visiting the projection box at the Cineworld cinema in Sheffield, because, having heard of the cinema's plans to replace *and remove* one of their 35mm projectors, he had made the assumption, 'quite wrongly, as it turned out', that 'this must be because they were short of space'. Instead, Cineworld's digitalisation strategy was to completely remove thirty of their 35mm projectors as a cost-saving measure by lowering maintenance costs on unused equipment. Slater wondered 'what price you would put on retaining the flexibility to be able to show anything that comes along for the next few years'.[704] This view, which was shared by many in the industry, demonstrated a continued belief that there would still be people working in projection boxes in the future with the skills to run 35mm equipment, and embodies the general assumption of the projectionist community that their digital skills would be needed *in addition to, rather than instead of,* their existing mechanical skills. However, it is clear from Cineworld's digital rollout, Vue's all-digital cinema plans, and Odeon's reluctance to formalise training, that this was not an underlying priority for the exhibitors themselves.

This displacement of skills was clearly signalled by a change in nomenclature. Just as the terms used to address those working with cinema projection equipment in the first half of the 20th century

699 'No Film at all at Vue's £5m Prince's Quay, Hull Multiplex', *Digital Projection* supplement to *Cinema Technology*, 20:4 (December 2007), p. 41.

700 Slater, 'Nationwide Success for CEA Digital Roadshow', p. 22

701 *Ibid.*, p. 23.

702 *Ibid.*

703 *Ibid.*, p. 22.

704 Jim Slater, 'A Whole New World as Cineworld Goes Digital and 3D', *ibid.*, 22:2 (June 2009), pp. 36, 38.

had shifted from 'operator' to 'projectionist', in order to characterise the skill level that the work demanded (see Chapter Three), the change from 'projectionist' to 'technician', for those still occupying projection-related roles in the digital age, reflects the dispersal of these skills into a more generalised form. Brad Atwill suggests that 'we're not really projectionists anymore, we're technicians now, and we do a whole plethora of other things'.[705] Mark Cosgrove, the film curator at the Watershed in Bristol, offers a particularly clear example of how stark the transition from 35mm projectionist to digital technician had been over the first decade of the 21st century:

> we needed to appoint a new member of staff ... The job descriptions hadn't been dusted down for quite a while and [at the] head of the job description was, 'has to be able to strip down and do all that stuff with a projector, make and break films ... run changeovers, run a box,' all the sort of mechanical and electrical skills that you would expect. And being able to deal with 35, 16, super-8 [film] because we've got all those formats. And I think at the bottom we said 'some digital', because we do a lot of conferencing and a lot of events ... When I ... did an audit of skills for the projectionist, data handling was the headline one ... and at the bottom of the job description was 'don't worry about 35, 16, we'll train you up' ... That was probably seven or eight years ago ... and that was a slap in the face as it were for me [that] the world's changed.[706]

This shift of requirements from practical, mechanical and electrical expertise to digital skills is a testament to the ways in which day-to-day work patterns had changed in the industry by the early 2010s. Vue, Hull pointed the way for the average digital projection box in the UK, with the digital uploading and programming of films considerably reducing the amount of time required to prepare and schedule film programmes. Furthermore, the replacement of the film print with the film file and the reduction in agency afforded by the projection equipment meant that maintenance and dust reduction also became less of an issue.[707]

During a digital 'roadshow' event organised by the CEA, Stuart Hudson, Technical Manager at the Odeon, Bayswater, gave a sense of the path that the film file takes on its way into and out of the projection box:

> digital film material arrives on hard drives from the distributor and then has to be 'ingested' into the server via USB. The Key Delivery Messages [KDMs - necessary to match the file to a specific cinema

705 Interview with Brad Atwill, conducted by Richard Wallace, 10 November 2014.

706 Interview with Mark Cosgrove, conducted by Richard Wallace, 26 August 2015.

707 For a conceptual discussion of the move from the film print to the film file see, André Gaudreault and Philippe Marion (trans. Timothy Barnard), *The End of Cinema? A Medium in Crisis in the Digital Age* (New York: Columbia University Press, 2015), pp. 6-7.

> and prevent unauthorised screenings] that accompany each movie are generally received via an email message and then transferred to a USB memory stick which is used to plug the KDM into the server. ... [T]he ingestion process takes between one and two hours to transfer the 200 GBytes or so of data from the hard drive to the server, with digital trailers taking only about 5 minutes.[708]

Paul Oliver, the Technical Manager at the Odeon, Hatfield, suggested that on top of this loading time it then takes 'about half an hour to copy a movie ... to the server in each required screen'.[709] Although this might seem like a time-consuming process, Hudson made it clear that 'the ingestion process can take place even when the projector is playing out another movie', so 'You don't have to stand there and wait', and 'you can go off and do other tasks around the projection room' while the file transfers are taking place. Hudson suggested that these other jobs might include an element of 'regular "housekeeping"', such as 'tidying up the content on the various hard drives and deleting unwanted material to free up space for new content', or one of a small number of infrequent maintenance tasks, including lens cleaning and lamp changes. Indeed, Hudson suggested that the only clearly identifiably 'new' task was that 'the filters on the digital projectors need cleaning every 500 hours', though these were also 'replaced when lamps are changed', combining two jobs into one process.[710]

At the BKSTS's Digital Awareness Day in 2008, Oliver gave a sense of how these jobs might translate into a projectionist's weekly schedule:

> On Fridays the adverts playlist is changed, the availability of all the next week's movies is checked and all KDMs are loaded and checked. Hard drive housekeeping takes place as necessary. Over the weekend test runs are carried out as needed, and the used hard drives are made ready for return to the distributor on the Monday. On Tuesday the dates for all the KDMs are checked – they like to have ten days of availability. Wednesday sees test runs and Thursdays meter readings are taken from all the digital projectors and recorded, advert listings are checked, and yet more checks are made to see that all the films for the next week are available.[711]

Although Jim Slater noted that Oliver's account 'left us with the impression that work in a digiplex is much like a normal projectionst's work, but with much of the physical humping around of film replaced by "drag and drop" on a computer screen', there is very little hands-on work involved in running a digital screen, especially given that many of the smaller jobs could be attended to

708 Slater, 'Nationwide Success for CEA Digital Roadshow', p. 21

709 Slater, 'Digital Awareness Day', p. 50.

710 Slater, 'Nationwide Success for CEA Digital Roadshow', p. 21

711 Slater, 'Digital Awareness Day', p. 50.

during the ingestion process.[712] In Chapter One we identified the wide range of activites undertaken by a projectionist that were occluded by Florence Barton in her use of the term 'normal projection duties'. In the digital projection box, almost every single one of these activites has been replaced by a pre-existing digital playlist template into which each week's films are dragged and dropped, and the weekly schedules can be contructed in a matter of minutes. John Neal, a projectionist at the Curzon cinema, Clevedon descibes the running of a digital print as 'trivial' in comparison to film projection.[713]

Returning to the question of training, it is clear that one reason why exhibitors were reluctant to spend large amounts of time and money developing in-house training schemes was because there was very little training required. In 2006 a glossary published in *Training for Digital Projection* listed the following under its entry for 'Guide to Playing a Digital Show':

> Step One: Load Content
>
> Step Two: Build the Show. Drag and drop on the computer screen to assemble Ads, Trailers, Movies, and Cues. Load movie. Load license [sic]
>
> Step Three: Play the Show. Press Play to start show manually or schedule an automated show using the digital cinema system or existing automation.[714]

This marks a drastic reduction in the amount of work needed to get a film onto the screen, and so naturally the amount of specialised training required to undertake this labour was also reduced. Brad Atwill highlights the discrepancy between his training as a film projectionist at a Cineworld multiplex in 2007 and the situation when he left in 2011: 'When I started there in projection, it was the best part of six months before I did a shift on my own', but 'in the space of three years the training ... that you got went from being months and months to a few hours fitted in in a week, at the most if you stretched it out'. As the number of digital projectors increased, and projectionists became familiar with the equipment, the quantity of training required was reduced to the point that it could be delivered in-house, in much the same way that Atwill describes.

712 *Ibid*. Slater appears to be using the term 'digiplex' as shorthand for digital multiplex. Charlotte Brunsdon has written evocatively about the physical strain involved in moving film prints as being characteristic of the profession (Charlotte Brunsdon, '"This is not a cinema': the projectionist's tale", *Screen*, 60:4 [Winter 2019], pp. 232-234).

713 Interview with John Neal, conducted by Richard Wallace, 15 January 2015.

714 'Glossary', *Training for Digital Projection*, 1 (June 2006), p. 23.

Redundancy

Given the radical reduction in projection-related work engendered by digital, it may seem – in hindsight – unsurprising that mass redundancies were one major consequence. This was particularly the case in the multiplex sector, where 'zero-manning' became the preferred operational model for all of the major chains, with one person responsible for overseeing the technical requirements of the venue as a small part of their weekly routine, the majority of which was spent on the floor undertaking less skilled work such as selling tickets and dispensing refreshments.

It has been argued elsewhere that the experience of redundancy for multiplex projectionists was one of uncertainty as the initial slowness of the uptake in digital projection equipment gave way to a much more rapid transition as the 2000s drew to a close.[715] The persistence we have documented of a 'cinemas will always need projectionists' rhetoric provided a misleadingly reassuring message, which meant that some projectionists were given a false sense of security about their future employment prospects. This created a disunity amongst unionised projectionists that, to some extent, mirrored the longer history of ineffective trade union struggle, bedevilled by multiple parties acting at cross purposes, discussed in Chapter Three. Mick Corfield, a former projectionist and National Official for BECTU, recalls this period being particularly frustrating because his attempts to mount union resistance at an early stage were thwarted by the members' belief in these assurances. 'Projectionists disappointed me', he recalls,

> they kept saying over and over ... 'my job's going to be so [much] easier.' And I'd go, 'You're not going to have a job. They're not going to pay you £13 an hour to watch the cricket ... They're not going to do this anymore. They're looking at ways of getting you out of the door because that's how they'll make the cost savings on this.'[716]

Corfield began proactive union consultation very quickly once it became clear that zero-manning was likely to become the industry standard. By the end of 2009 he had formed a working group 'to examine the future for cinema projectionists' and explained to *Cinema Technology* that

> BECTU is under no illusion that things can stay the same for projectionists, recognises that the future is inevitably digital, and is striving to find a path via which projectionists can develop their careers into new areas, for the benefit of both projectionists and the cinema industry.[717]

715 Wallace, 'Going Digital', pp. 10-14.

716 Interview with Mick Corfield, conducted by Richard Wallace, 3 August 2015.

717 Jim Slater, 'BECTU Looking into the Future of Projectionists', *Cinema Technology*, 22:4 (December 2009), p. 20.

Whilst at this stage the clear aim was to develop a 'proposed new role profile, discussing what part the projectionist of the future ... will play in the overall work of a cinema', there was an acceptance that the labour of projection alone was not enough to sustain this role. Initial thoughts were 'that current staff could be trained to carry out many of the servicing tasks that are currently done by hired-in outside contractors'.[718] These tasks would include projector maintenance, screen management around the cinema, the overseeing of alternative content and conferencing, alongside some of the traditional projectionist tasks such as heating and air conditioning maintenance that had been stripped away from the job during the era of single-manning.

Although clearly hopeful that there would be some continuation of his role in the digital era, Corfield seems to have been one of the few people actively confronting a less optimistic outlook on projection, and there were suggestions that part of the function of the working group was to lay the groundwork for future redundancy negotiations. One of the key questions that the group would address was 'Are significant job losses a necessary consequence of digital projection?', and another core aim was 'to persuade its own members to accept change'.[719] Corfield's task, then, seems to have been to balance the interests of a labour force that variously held four distinct positions: those who considered digital a fad and that their jobs would be safe and largely unchanged; those who thought their jobs would be safe, but substantially easier; those who thought their jobs would be safe, but substantially different (and require retraining); and 'an undercurrent of traditionalists who, in their hearts of hearts, think that digital projection kit has been welcomed into projection rooms rather like a "trojan horse", and they are genuinely fearful for the future'.[720]

This latter view emerged in response to general trends in installation that occurred across the industry, with most cinemas installing a single projector (often as part of the DSN initiative) before going on to change the rest of their screens some years later. The installation of these initial projectors was time and labour intensive. Neil Thompson recalls that the first one in his cinema was installed in 2009, and that it 'took about a month or two to get installed', and Chris Blower notes that 'they basically bought an army of technicians in to set it all up'.[721] This single installation

718 *Ibid.*, pp. 20, 21.

719 *Ibid.*, p. 21.

720 *Ibid.*

721 Interview with Neil Thompson, conducted by Richard Wallace, 11 November 2014. Interview with Chris Blower, conducted by Richard Wallace, 11 August 2015.

was viewed with a certain amount of suspicion and bemusement by a number of projectionists, including Corfield himself, who recalls that 'They put one in my cinema ... as a union man it was interesting, I couldn't say no, but at least I could keep my eye on it'. The notion of 'keeping an eye' on the alien technology is echoed by others. Chandra Makwana recalls looking at the newly installed NEC projector as 'something strange [coming] into our building', and Blower notes that when the first digital projector arrived at his cinema in 2004 'we weren't allowed to touch it because ... we got no idea what it was like, some kind-of-like future technology we'd never seen before'.[722]

Corfield's response went far beyond suspicion. 'I knew straight-away that we would be finished', he remembers, 'there was no two ways about this'. This was confirmed to him when the projector broke down and a mechanic was able to repair and restart the equipment remotely: 'So, that was when it was pretty straightforward that we knew that we were on our way out.' In September 2010, *Cinema Technology* reported on a meeting between Corfield's team and the senior management of the Cineworld chain, arguing that 'BECTU and its members understand only too well that the rapid pace of technological development is certain to have a negative impact on staffing levels and BECTU is trying to engage with the company in a serious and meaningful way in order to minimise job losses.'[723]

Corfield suggests that part of the thinking behind this shift in strategy was that having developed a job description that took in 'maintenance of escalators, maintenance of lifts, maintenance of air filters, changing the lamps', he quickly realised that 'we were being fobbed off', and that the various chains 'led us on for quite a while'.[724] Corfield's statement of intent in regard to these potential job losses was both measured and strong:

> The union's aim is to protect the interests of those staff that want to remain part of the digital future of cinema, whilst ensuring that those that don't see their future in the industry are properly rewarded for their years of service to the cinema industry. It is not acceptable to the union that its members be thrown on the scrapheap where there may be potential to avoid this, but it is recognised that redundancies are inevitable. It is against this background that BECTU seeks to ensure the best possible severance terms for staff that are made redundant.[725]

722 Interview with Chandra Makwana, conducted by Richard Wallace, 16 March 2015.

723 Mick Corfield, 'Digitalisation and the Impact on Projectionists', *Cinema Technology*, 23:3 (September 2010), p. 35.

724 Interview with Mick Corfield.

725 Corfield, 'Digitalisation and the Impact on Projectionists', p. 35.

A key aim of the negotiations, therefore, was agreeing a voluntary redundancy package that the union felt 'should be a long way in excess of statutory redundancy terms'. This turn towards a dual approach to negotiations – attempting to shape the future role for any technical jobs that might remain, whilst also planning for redundancies – became a key strategy. Corfield also revealed that 'meaningful talks' with the Apollo chain were ongoing, and he encouraged other circuits to engage with BECTU's negotiators in a similar spirit. Nevertheless, there is the suggestion that the union intended to escalate its pressure on cinema management:

> BECTU intends to step up its campaign to ensure that its projection and technical members in Cineworld achieve the best possible outcome in terms of pay and benefits, job security and job satisfaction for its members in the digital future and for a just settlement for its members that will not be part of that future.[726]

However, the fact that the initial digital installations weren't immediately followed by the conversion of the other screens led many projectionists to become complacent. Brad Atwill expresses this view when he suggests that he began to feel 'that it would never go, and all our jobs would be fine'. Corfield has criticised the continued practices of industry groups such as the BKSTS during this cross-over period (around 2009-2011), whose training events continued to focus heavily on the projection of film:

> I had gone to many events that were organised by the BKSTS ... where they were doing projectionist training, and the projectionist training was how to splice a film, how to do this and do that ... when I got the opportunity [to speak], [I] kept saying, 'I don't understand why you're doing this, because you're training people for jobs that are non-existent. If ... 95% of your job is handling film and there is no film, what are you going to do?'[727]

This, combined with 'their mantra' that 'they're always going to need a projectionist' led to resistance from union members. 'We weren't listened to,' Corfield recalls. Chris Tweddell, who was also involved in the Cineworld negotiations, recalls that 'the attitude for a lot of people was head in the sand, you know, it's years away, it's never going to happen', and that as a result, his job 'was trying to make people understand that it's going to happen. It is going to happen. Now you have to deal with it, you now have to move with

726 *Ibid*. It appears that some circuits felt threatened by BECTU's pressure and in 2013 a BECTU circular encouraging recruitment and distributed with the latest issue of *Cinema Technology* appears to have been removed by cinema managers before being passed on to projection staff. The letter was reprinted in the following issue. Mick Corfield, 'BECTU letter', *Cinema Technology*, 26:2 (June 2013), p. 59.

727 As an example, the BKSTS's 'Best Practice for Projectionists' training scheme held in Sheffield (October 2009), Glasgow (December 2009), Swindon (January 2010) and London (March 2010) included overview sessions on digital projection and 3D, but focused much of the day on 35mm, including sessions on film handling, projector maintenance and xenon lamps ('Projection Training Nationwide', *ibid.*, 23:1 [March 2010], p.10).

the times and stay in it and learn about the technology or you're going to have to think, "What am I going to do next?"'[728]

It is for this reason that Corfield recognised the clear importance of persuading BECTU's own members of the imminent threat to their jobs alongside negotiating with the employers. The process of persuading projectionists that there was little hope was not an easy one. 'I insisted ... that we should go back while we have the strength to discuss a redundancy package', Corfield suggests, recalling that a key line of argument was that 'they've already got half your screen as digital ... if you try and [negotiate] afterwards you'll have no power'. This attitude was shared by Tweddell, who acknowledges that although 'everybody had fight in them' to resist the redundancies, the situation meant that he 'was very much of the opinion that we need to do it while we've got power'. Timing was a key issue, but Tweddell's argument to dissenting projectionists was that 'once they can replace you by somebody pressing a button, it doesn't matter what you do, you don't have any power. You can't go on strike and close the cinemas because they can get anybody to do it.'

Corfield led the negotiations, which he suggests took eight months and were 'horrendously long, horrendously complicated', in part because the status of unionised workers across the various cinema chains was a complicated one. Only the Odeon and Cineworld chains recognized BECTU as the appropriate trade union for projectionists, and Corfield characterised chains such as Empire and Apollo (now part of the Vue circuit) as 'anti-union'. As we noted in the previous chapter, even within the unionised chains, years of buy-outs and mergers meant that the terms of workers within the same company differed from site-to-site, union representation was not organized uniformly, and it was often the case that individual cinemas followed the precedents set over time by their previous corporate owners. Nevertheless, Corfield was pleased with the eventual settlement that was reached for Cineworld workers, recalling that the majority of projectionists took voluntary redundancy when offered because the package was perceived to be a good one.

BECTU's attempt to pre-emptively negotiate redundancy terms was far-sighted. Although the initial installation of single digital projectors was a time- and labour-consuming process, this was not the case for the subsequent wholesale conversion to digital, which Ken Bagnall describes as being 'all a bit of a blur' due to its speed.[729] Atwill recalls that when the remaining screens at his cinema

728 Interview with Chris Tweddell, conducted by Richard Wallace, 12 November 2014.

729 Interview with Ken Bagnall, conducted by Richard Wallace, 17 September 2015.

received their new projectors 'they all arrived at once and they were all just eerily standing in bubble wrap around the projection booth, knowing that they were going to replace everything else that was there'. From this point on 'it was only two or three days that they made the final push and that was it'.

Chris Blower remembers there being an air of secrecy around the transition that matches the general lack of clear information provided to projectionists at a site-specific and industry-wide level. He received a phone call in the middle of 2011 from the projectionist at another cinema in the same chain. 'I hear you're next for the digital installation', he recalls them saying:

> [We] were like, 'Are we? We've heard nothing about that at all.' So, we did a bit of digging and we found out we were ... From the time we got the phone call to the complete installation it was about a month ... The people that did the installation just worked overnight, they ripped everything out, put the digital projector in two screens at a time overnight. So, we'd show the same film in 35mm one day and then exactly the same film in digital the day after in the same screen ... It was a really quick turnaround.

The bulk arrival of projectors was inextricably linked to the redundancy process. Brad Atwill recalls that the inevitability of the situation 'didn't really sink in until ... probably about a month before, [when] we started to action end of the line stuff ... putting dust covers on things and saying, "Shit, these are actually getting taken out"'. Thompson's account of the arrival of the digital equipment is especially moving and is worth quoting at length because of the way in which his redundancy is addressed by proxy through his account of the final 35mm show at the Empire, Newcastle, and his own fate seems implicitly intertwined with the treatment of the obsolete 35mm equipment:

> the digital got changed more or less overnight before we left. There was about eight screens to do ... All the digital equipment arrived one night and it was all just standing, waiting to be put in. And within two days all the projectors and Cinemeccanica stuff had been pushed to one side, and the digital machines had been put in. All the plugs were ready just to put into the wall, they had all been rewired weeks before. ... I was the last one to lace up a 35mm projector in that place. And the lads were just standing, watching me as I was lacing up and I said, 'When this has finished you're carting this out aren't you?' And he said, 'Yeah, as soon as that's finished we'll be getting rid of [it].' And there was a digital projector right behind, ready to put in its place. Once the film finished, I went down the bottom end [of the projection box] to do something, [and] when I came back it was all just pushed out the place, four of them just got hold of it and pushed it to one side, the plinth, the lot, the projector. And the digital was in its place and that was the last one to go in, and I just thought 'My god,' you know? I just couldn't believe it. They had it all wired up

> ready and they said, 'Right, just check it and on the next show you can go ahead.' I said, 'What, already?' And he says, 'Oh yeah, it's ready.'

In most cases, the mass removal of 35mm projectors was followed by the mass redundancy of their operators. Although many took the opportunity to accept redundancy pay, there was also a certain amount of staff reshuffling that took place during this period, when the reconfiguration of technical labour was still uncertain. Chandra Makwana recalls getting a letter about a month after the digital projectors were installed in his cinema, 'offering voluntary redundancy or you can keep your job with lower pay, but you have to work in the office. Well, I'd got no idea in the office.' Chris Blower recalls that he'd 'heard stories from other cinemas [that] as soon as digital came in all the projectionists were gone and the management ran all the shows. So, I thought that was what was going to happen to us.' However, when his multiplex eventually went fully digital, 'our old technical manager decided to take voluntary redundancy ... [H]e was there for two weeks after we went digital and he left. ... So, his job became vacant and I applied for it and got the job.' Blower adds that when he saw the job advertisement for a technical manager 'I thought, well if there's still going to be a technical manager there's still going to be a projection department', but that only two months after successfully getting the job 'we started hearing about redundancies'. Although Blower acknowledges that he was offered a new position – 'a combination of manager and technical manager' – it paid 'considerably less' than he was getting as a technical manager and he eventually took voluntary redundancy. 'We were just waiting to be made redundant for about a year', he recalls, 'so it wasn't a very nice time at all.' The false sense of security felt by some of those in managerial positions is clearly conveyed in a number of the interviews. Mike Marshall experienced a similar set of circumstances at the Odeon, Glasgow Quay. 'We were told because we were technical managers we were quite safe', he recalls, 'but it never worked out that way'.[730]

Part of the redundancy talks in some cinemas involved undertaking working time studies to itemise the skills required by the job in the digital age, and Chris Tweddell suggests that 'it very quickly became evident [that Cineworld] didn't need any of the projection skills but ... the stuff that projectionists do in the cinema that aren't recognised, they still need that'. From Tweddell's point of view, then, the management 'recognised that they still needed people but didn't need projectionists, so it was a new job you're talking about', that was, by implication, 'no longer as skilled as it would have

730 Interview with Mike Marshall, conducted by Richard Wallace, 22 June 2015.

been'. Some projectionists, including Tweddell himself, were able to stay on in these newly-created managerial jobs. 'I wanted to stay in the industry, so I had to apply for one of these jobs', he recalls, adding that 'I applied and got a job as a manager in the cinema, and that's primarily what I'm doing now ... [T]he job changed totally into more of a management job with some AV on the side'.

This was not the case for the majority of projectionists, however, and Tweddell is clear that 'most people I know who used to work in the industry are driving buses, trains, working for alarm companies, all over the country doing different things'. Chandra Makwana suggests that 'I feel sorry for a lot of people that have lost their job. I mean redundancy, yes, okay, they took the money and gone, but what are you going to do? ... I'm a film technician ... I got films in my mind; that's locked in and it's not going away.' Some of the older projectionists who were not yet at retirement age have, perhaps inevitably, struggled to find work since being made redundant, given that their particular skillset is not easily transferrable. Brad Atwill began his projection career at the start of the digital transition, in the knowledge that he would be making up the shortfall in staffing that resulted from the take-up of the voluntary redundancy packages. He suggests that he

> hated it because it was something that I really cared about, and a job that I loved ... but you couldn't help feel even worse for the two guys who'd been doing that job for ... the best part of 30 years, and all of a sudden the rug's been pulled, and it's not certain, because they had to then apply for jobs downstairs at the cinema they'd been at since it opened, and it was just... yeah, it did feel a bit callous and cold.

Loss of Agency

Not every projectionist left the industry at this point. As Tweddell notes, there were some managerial positions that incorporated the technical upkeep of the cinema, and the retention of a dedicated technician (and sometimes even a small team of them) was quite normal in independent cinemas. However, the reduction of technical expertise of the average digital projectionist that was a consequence of the limited training opportunities provided went hand-in-hand with a loss of control over the projection equipment. There are two parallel arguments that can be made about the long-term evolution of cinema projection technology as it relates to the projectionist. There is the economic argument: that most technological advances reduce the amount of work required by the projection team, ultimately reducing the number of projectionists employed by any one cinema, with the savings being passed on to the exhibitors. We can see this in the relaxation of safety regulations once acetate safety film replaced nitrate, in the arrival of automation systems allowing the projection box to be left legally unattended for the first time, and in the non-rewind platter systems facilitating the single-manned multiplex (see Chapter One). Digital represents the final stage in this process of evolving the projectionist out of the cinema projection ecology. To return to a concept we first introduced in Chapter One, around the turn of the 21st century, film became the latest 'reverse salient' in the technological system of cinema projection, and in overcoming it the projectionist was no longer a requirement of the reformulated system.

This obsolescence can also be linked to an argument about the aesthetic development of the projection apparatus presented in Chapter Two. We suggested here that a mediating human presence orchestrating the entertainment was once considered essential to the experience of cinema, whilst – paradoxically – the virtual erasure of this presence was simultaneously heralded throughout the history of the medium as the apogee of good projection. The exclusion of human agency in the digital box reduced both the potential for human error to creep into the projection process and the opportunity for the contaminating touch of the projectionist to degrade the print through handling. This has occurred through the literal reduction of fragile materials and human agents, but also through the security features put in place around the digital film file. This is, perhaps, the ultimate example of the projectionist's agency being removed from the projection process.

Even if there is a projectionist present in the projection box, the systems are deliberately designed to preclude the temptation to intervene. This has both a practical and an aesthetic dimension. As early as 2002, the removal of human judgement from the digital presentation process was being reported in the trade press. Writing about the London premiere of *Star Wars: Episode II – Attack of the Clones* (USA, George Lucas, 2002), Jim Slater noted that

> if I had been in control I would have 'wound the brightness up' a little – there wasn't a single 'high-key' shot in the film. Interestingly, the projection team too had had similar thoughts, but had been assured that one of the true benefits of the completely digital cinema process was that Director George Lucas could be sure that the film would be displayed exactly as he wanted it – and that was what we saw at Leicester Square.[731]

This fixity of the digital image removed the possibility of the rogue 'remixing' of films that we discussed in Chapter Two. The *Star Wars* example demonstrates clearly how even the most experienced projectionists – those of London's showcase West End cinemas – might hold different aesthetic values to the filmmaker, and how

731 Jim Slater, 'TI Shows *Star Wars* Using DLP', *Cinema Technology*, 15:3 (September 2002), p. 5.

the digital systems prevented the resulting human instinct to 'correct' perceived flaws in the film.

Such loss of control over the aesthetic aspects of the projected image speaks to a more general 'locking out' of projectionists from projection technology. 'The film projector is like a steam locomotive,' Alan Foster suggests, when setting out the differences between film and digital projectors. 'Something might go wrong, but you'll still get home. You won't get home as fast as you would have done normally, but it keeps going.' Neil Thompson suggests something similar, arguing that 'at least with film ... if it was crippled you could more or less try and get to the end of the show. Even if the light wasn't so good or the sound lost a channel you could just deliver it to the one speaker and you could get away with it.' Ray Reed talks of trying to 'squeeze it through' if a film projector failed, and there are numerous accounts of on-the-fly bodges being made by quick-thinking projectionists.[732] Ken Bagnall remembers that if a platter motor failed 'we'd have somebody literally pushing the platter all the way through', and Chris Tweddell recalls having to stand with his finger held over an LED sensor to avoid a projector shutdown during the final minutes of an interlocked screening.[733] Perhaps most spectacularly, Phil Fawke recalls that on older projectors 'the take up used to go', and the projectionist would 'put a screwdriver in the spool and do a whole spool' by standing beside the projector and holding the screwdriver in place as an axel around which the film reel would rotate.

Foster argues that 'digital is a totally different ball game', and that 'If something goes wrong, at the end of the day it's a "switching it off and rebooting it" ... situation, and then hope that it will come on right and carry on its merry way.' Neil Thompson agrees, arguing that digital 'either works or it doesn't, there's no in between'. Peter Howden suggests that 'you used to get more problems on 35mm projectors than you do on digital', but that 'if we get a problem on digital there's not a lot we can do about it except stare at it'.[734] There are a number of reasons for this paralysis. Firstly, the diagnostic process is not straightforward or transparent. As Adrian Pearce notes, 'if something does go wrong with it, it's hard to know *what* is wrong with it. [With] 35mm you can see

732 Interview with Ray Reed, conducted by Richard Wallace, 5 February 2015.

733 An interlocked screening used a single print to feed two projectors at the same time, each projecting into a different screen.

734 Interview with Peter Howden, conducted by Richard Wallace, 13 November 2014. This does not mean that there were no teething problems with the digital technology. However, by and large these had been overcome by the point of digital's dominance in the exhibition sector. For discussion of some of these issues in the trade press, see Jim Slater, 'Everything Isn't Always Perfect First Time', *Training for Digital Projection*, 3 (December 2006), p. 15; Slater, 'Nationwide Success for CEA Digital Roadshow'; Slater, 'Digital Awareness Day'.

exactly what has gone wrong because you can see all the moving parts'.[735] Brad Atwill emphasises that this in turn prevents any preparatory or evasive measures being taken, because 'you can't see a problem as far off as you could [with 35mm]'. He specifies that 'if you can see there's some damage to [a 35mm print], you know it's not going to look quite right' and that there are measures that can be taken to mitigate this. With digital,

> I've had a file corrupt with absolutely no warning until you go to play it and you have this screen full of people and you've gone through the ads and all of a sudden it's stuttering on screen, it's just not working and there's no visible reason why it's not. You can try ... working through problems, [but] it gets to the point where you're like, 'I can't actually do anything about this.'

Even if a problem can be diagnosed, the security features of digital projection equipment preclude all but the most experienced engineers from conducting internal maintenance and repairs. These locks stop the projectionist from tampering with the internal working of the projectors and are in part the result of wider industrial concerns about digital piracy. 'They'll not let you do anything with the servers because of security', Ray Reed notes, adding that the studios are 'shit scared' of films being copied during the projection process.

The encryption on the electronic data is achieved through the use of Key Delivery Message (KDM) files, which are loaded onto the server separately to the film file, unlocking the digital encryption and allowing the film to be played within certain restricted parameters, usually limited to a specified number of screenings or a particular timeframe. However, digital piracy can still take place at the point at which the data is processed and so physically securing the projection apparatus prevents anyone from intercepting the digital signal from within the system. As one commentator outlined in 2006, 'physical security can be used to prevent access to any parts of the circuit where value [sic] movie data is processed'. Such measures also included 'logging of attempts to disassemble or otherwise attack the unit'.[736] This security set up naturally has implications for the projectionist's ability to maintain and programme the digital equipment. Brad Atwill suggests that 'there's so many anti-tamper switches that as soon as you try to undo a screw, it then won't turn on, and you have to call an engineer out who will have to come and put the screw back in and tell it it's okay'.

735 Interview with Adrian Pearce, conducted by Richard Wallace, 20 October 2014.

736 Xavier Varians, 'Protecting Content', *Training for Digital Projection*, supplement to *Cinema Technology*, 19:3 (September 2006), p. 15.

Peter Howden describes his particular frustration with this policing of technical labour: 'The film business – being a paranoid business – will not let you do anything without making sure that it's you that's doing it'. This created a particularly frustrating relationship with digital security infrastructures that all 'have different passwords ... It's the one thing about setting up all these things on Friday ... [Y]ou could do the thing in half the time if you didn't have to keep putting in the bloody password'.

In some rare cases, attempts have been made to develop and retain expertise within projection teams. At the Watershed, Bristol, Ewan Dunford has created an online Wiki that provides an overview of all of the apparatus, and their maintenance requirements, because 'the technician, projectionist, should know absolutely everything about their own environment'. He describes the process of creating the Wiki as being 'a bit like an MRI scan' in that 'I just stood there with an A4 piece of paper ... and everything that I saw – the air conditioner ducting, the line of circuit breakers, the CD player, absolutely everything – [I recorded] the model numbers and ... if there are spares associated with it'.

The Watershed also has its own YouTube channel which houses instructional videos. 'It's a legacy', Dunford suggests, noting that for the 35mm projectors 'all the bits and bobs that I've got for it can go on for hundreds of years, so if I said, "Well I've had enough, I'm leaving now," ... you want to pass that information on'. Dunford's processes are very much the exception, however, and in general the lack of agency that governs the operation of digital projectors also means that the expertise required to keep the cinema programme running is no longer part of the exhibition sector's institutional knowledge; 'that knowledge isn't in cinemas anymore', Chris Tweddell states. Andrew MacLean seconds this sentiment, suggesting that 'with the digital stuff that whole kind of physical thing's gone ... the ability to hold your nerve and put your hand in the machine'.[737]

Deskilling

The mainstream tendency towards removing technological and aesthetic agency from those still responsible for cinema projection is emblematic of the deskilling that has accompanied the long-term evolution of projection technology. As previously argued, the move between different projection arrays resulted in a reformulation of the expertise needed to prepare, show and maintain film prints. However, the introduction of platters and automation systems meant that projectionists were no longer regularly using skills

737 Interview with Andrew MacLean, conducted by Richard Wallace, 25 August 2015.

that would have been par for the course for their professional forbears: for instance, the careful handling of nitrate film, the rhythm of the 20-minute change over, or the process of replacing carbon rods in arc lamps. Rather than viewing the transition to digital as a drastic change, we can see it as the ultimate move in a much longer process of de-skilling and agency removal that has been occurring for as long as the role of projectionist remained a viable career.

The removal of professional expertise that the digital turn signifies is mourned in a particularly direct and forceful way by some of the projectionists that we interviewed. We have already noted the projectionist's loss of agency when it comes to addressing faults with the digital projector. Ray Reed extends these observations to make a wider point about the deskilling of projectionists in the digital era when he suggests that being 'on the phone to a guy in London who gets into the projector via his laptop' means that '[y]ou're just standing there totally useless'. The notion that these highly skilled electricians and technicians find themselves to be 'totally useless' in a digital world – even if they have the skills to do the work – speaks to the ways in which the projectionist's status has fallen from the most important and highly-paid non-managerial position in the building, to a mostly-dispensable commodity.

Those projectionists still employed in technical roles spoke with great clarity about the impact that the move away from physical, manual work to computerised data management has had on their experience of the job. Frank Gibson suggests that although he believes that digital is 'much better' in terms of the image quality it affords, from a labourer's perspective

> it's not like having that proper hands-on [experience], not like on film ... I've got no time for it, because it's just like putting an ordinary DVD on ... once it's all downloaded, that's it, you're not actually working. You're keeping the projector running, [making] sure it goes alright ... but it's not the same. I like to have hands-on.[738]

Chandra Makwana agrees that with digital 'you don't do anything', and Reed points out that 'for me, it's boring'. He speaks towards a generational divide in the modern projection room, suggesting that 'The kids love it because they're used to computers, they've probably had laptops since they were five year olds so they love the technology. They love messing about with it.' This move to computerised film presentation marks a key break from Reed's perception of what it means to be a projectionist. He describes it as 'a totally different world', and suggests that 'it's not projection anymore'. Instead of the manual, practical and creative labour that we

738 Interview with Frank Gibson, conducted by Richard Wallace, 14 October 2014.

outlined in Chapters One and Two, Reed describes the modern projection process as 'administration', noting that 'the kids upstairs' are

> chasing films by email, they're chasing KDMs by email, they're emailing clients for private hires; it's an office job. ... That's what's happened, it's become an office job and an IT management job. ... It's still skilled but skilled in admin and IT management. So, the skills have just become different.

Chris Tweddell echoes Reed's sentiments: 'I think people do still recognise the skill I've got, but that's kind of a side-line, it's not that important' as part of the modern cinema environment.

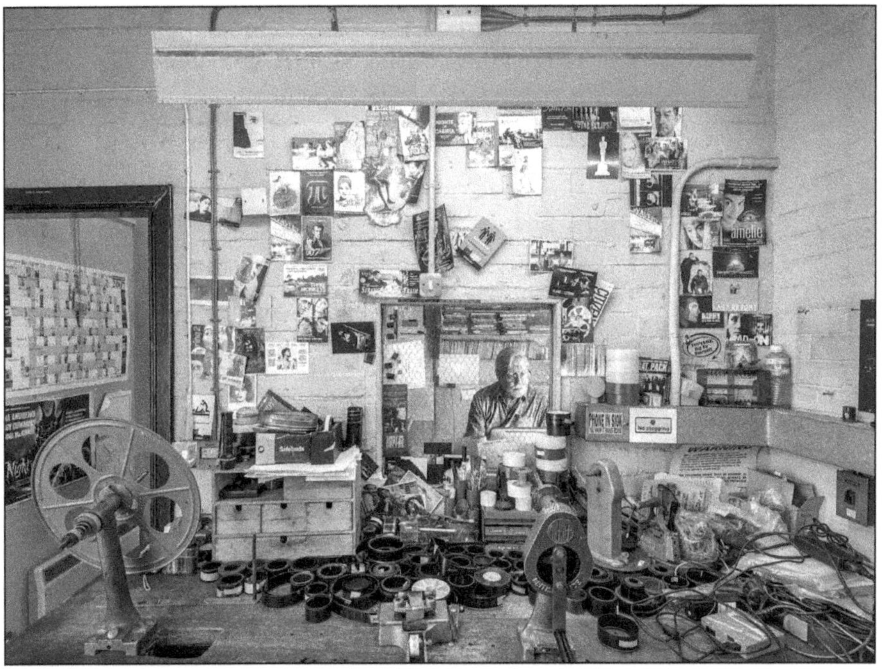

Figure 4.2: Richard Nicholson's photographic portrait of Peter Howden, projectionist at the Rio cinema, Dalston doing digital projection by answering his emails. Image © Richard Nicholson.

A particularly stark example of the digital transformation of projection expertise can be seen in Richard Nicholson's photograph of Peter Howden, projectionist at the Rio cinema in Dalston, which was displayed as part of his 2016 exhibition 'The Projectionists' (Fig 4.2). Although Nicholson's photographs are not candid pictures of projectionists at work, but carefully staged arrangements, they capture the essence of the job – and the spaces in which the labour takes place – in a dynamic and truthful way. Whereas most of the photographs show projectionists engaging with 35mm film equipment as a means of showing the projectionist 'at work', the photo of Howden is perhaps the most revealing, given that in preparatory discussions Howden revealed that he spent most of his time when the film was running at his computer answering emails. Howden's portrait, then, depicts a modern cinema projectionist at work, sitting at a computer in the former rewind-room answering emails, in contrast with the rarely used rewind bench which dominates the foreground of the image, and which stands in for all of the mechanical and physical labour that has been displaced in the digital world. Meanwhile, the digital projector continues its pre-programmed routine out of shot and unattended.

Like Howden, Reed acknowledges that 'I can probably sit at a desk now with a mouse and a keyboard and that could be it for a couple of hours.' This relaxation in the physical intensity of the labour also means that, before his retirement, more of Reed's time was spent around the cinema

> doing bits and pieces of repairs, or sorting problems around the building. ... I think when you're out of the projection room [and] you're working round the building, you're more just a skivvy, you know, you're just running around here, you see wiping arse, you know what I mean, it's all you do.

Reed makes it clear that he doesn't feel any less valued, but that he has been de-skilled. As he argues, 'running 35mm was a skill. Running digital is skilled but not for me, more for the young kids who are doing more admin work ... I'm not at their level, so basically I've been de-skilled. That's probably the way I feel ... My skills are not needed in projection.' This view is echoed by Simon Allen, a former projectionist at the National Film Theatre, who argues that 'the depressing thing about digital was ... you could see your skill set going out the window and you were being presented with this new set of challenges that were not very interesting. So, that's when I was thinking, "Oh, I think I'd like to retire now."'[739]

Although these processes of deskilling can be seen as the latest step in a longer process of change within the vocation, rather than a fundamental break, this argument does risk underplaying the significance of digital projection. It is clear that ultimately this *is* different to each of those earlier examples of deskilling and erosion of agency, because – to a great extent – this transformation is final, and has resulted in the loss of the majority of projectionists from the industry. Although some, like Reed and Allen, were able to time their retirements with the digital transition, many projectionists were not so lucky. The removal of agency in terms of keeping the digital show running has also had significant implications for the presentation of digital films, and in these final sections we

739 Interview with Simon Allen, conducted by Richard Wallace, 8 March 2016.

address the experience of digital cinema with, and without, the projectionist.

The Cinema Experience in the Digital Age

As we have shown, much of the rhetoric around digital projection concerns the ease with which films can now be distributed and exhibited by cinemas without the need for the mediating figure of the projectionist. From such views we might conclude that the entire labour process of the projectionists – in other words everything that we described in Chapters One and Two – has been replaced by the electronic processes enacted by the digital projector, server and programming software. However, as we also argued in Chapter Two, cinema presentation in the modern era is significantly different to that found throughout the first two-thirds of the 20th century. To some extent, changes such as the removal of masking and curtains, and the creative use of coloured lights can be accounted for by the gradual deskilling and destaffing of projection boxes during the multiplex era, where curtains were removed as a cost-saving exercise, and the manual 'live' performances were replaced by pre-programmed automation systems.

However, even though most of the mechanical processes have been digitalised, the same is not necessarily true of the instinctual and aesthetic thought processes of the skilled projectionist that were once considered so vital. As such, there are certain aspects of the modern experience of cinema presentation that seem specific to digital projection. One notable example is the drastically different way in which cinema lighting is orchestrated. Instead of the carefully configured and gradual movement into the film cued by the lighting that we described in Chapter Two, Frank Gibson notes that his local Odeon shows 'the adverts with the house lights up'. At the other end of the performance, Chris Tweddell acknowledges the suddenness with which the pre-programmed lights are typically turned *on* at the end of the feature, suggesting that instead of a carefully timed fade 'now it just goes bang, there you go, it's on, stunned'.

That this is such a widespread experience in digital theatres might suggest that it is an inherent feature of the digital apparatus; like the projector itself, the lights are either on or they're not. However, this is not the case, and whilst the practical aspects of the job may have been competently replaced by machines, it appears that for many cinemas the psychological aspects underpinning the projectionist's mood work have not been so easily digitalised. Brad Atwill suggests that 'the argument with digital is that ... anyone can do it because you just need to know the software'. He argues against the simplicity of this view by acknowledging the aesthetics of cinema exhibition: 'I still argue that there is a craft to it, and it's care in the presentation side.'

Rachel Dukes seconds this view, suggesting that 'the biggest problem with digital projection' is that 'people thought that all we did was press "play"'.[740] However, she emphasises that 'to get to the point of pressing "play" you have to do a lot of other things'. Alan Foster reiterates this by pointing out that the projector 'knows what to do, but only because we've told it'. For Atwill there is such a thing as digital presentation, and that

> it's easy to knock together a playlist, but it's difficult to get your timings right, to know how long the lights in that screen take to come down, because every dimmer's slightly different ... to make sure that that's also enough time for you to change any aspect ratios that you need to do.

Playlists, therefore, can be carefully built to accommodate the nuances of individual screens, individual projectors and individual film files.

What is clear from the interviews with those projectionists still involved in hands-on cinema projection – usually in independent cinemas or arts venues – is that there are ways in which the projectors can be programmed to replicate the aesthetic experience of the pre-digital era, but that the absence of a dedicated technical person *with an aesthetic eye for detail* – and the desire from senior management – means that this is rarely done in mainstream venues. As Mike Marshall surmises: 'anything you want, you can put it in. You can put an interval in; if you want a curtain to go in you put a curtain in. ... It's nothing to do with technology it's just all down to money.' The emphasis on quality and care is congruent with the ethos of the independent and arts centre venues where the last remaining projectionists are still employed. It is possible that such venues consider the continued employment of a technical team a literal price worth paying to maintain this distinction from their mainstream rivals, a visual signifier of 'caring' about the film presentation that is both different to the customer's experiences of a multiplex and, ironically, at odds with the projectionist's status as an invisible figure (see Chapter Two).

Nevertheless, there is clearly something substantial to the assertions that more care could be taken with digital projection than is widely accepted by the industry. Peter Howden argues that 'things are much less fixed on digital than on 35mm in terms of ratio, and labels have even less to be believed than they were on film cans'. The question of standardisation does not seem to have been en-

740 Interview with Rachel Dukes, conducted by Richard Wallace, 19 December 2014.

tirely resolved, and Howden puts this down to the possibility that the producers of digital cinema prints are not specialists in cinema projection in the same way that those working in film laboratories would have been: 'I suspect these days, people make DCPs [Digital Cinema Package] and could be making Blu-Rays or whatever. ... [T]he volume levels are up here, there and everywhere ... there are much greater variations on things than there ever used to be with film'. This necessitates an additional level of checking that is missing from most cinemas. Alan Foster echoes these sentiments, noting that the pre-built programmes don't always accommodate the specifics of the individual film print received, and that for the creation of a perfect presentation, a laborious process of checking should still be taking place. Each of the prints 'has to be checked to make sure that it's going to work right on the day' and that 'if it's a little bit black at the end of the film' the tab closing point 'needs adjusting and taking into account so that they still close at the end of the film'. Small tweaks are made to the pre-set programme on an individual basis and although such processes do not fit within the workload and expertise available to the multiplex, they are still accommodated within some cinemas in the independent sector. Although Atwill admits that these matters are 'little nuances', and that focusing on such details might be an 'old school view' of cinema presentation, he argues that it is, ultimately, these nuances that 'give people a reason to come out of the house' and justify spending their money at the cinema. This has become even more pertinent in the wake of the COVID-19 pandemic, where the exhibition industry faces the greatest existential threat in its history, as distributors and audiences question how much supplementary merit lies in retaining the theatrical window of film consumption and the 'added value' of visiting a cinema venue.

Given the transformations that have taken place within the projection box at a technological and human level, one might expect the projectionists we interviewed to hold strong negative views about the status and quality of digital projection. It is unsurprising that some projectionists feel that the contrast and colour of digital files do not match the richness of film. John Neal, for example, argues that it is still the case that film presents the extremes of the colour spectrum more dramatically – '35mm will present black and white, whereas digital will present dark grey and slightly off white' – and Andrew MacLean suggests that the colour is not as vibrant on digital: 'certainly from the projection room, the reds aren't the same, you know'. One thing that surprised us as we began to research this book, however, was that there was a predominantly positive response to the technical qualities of the digital image from projectionists, with the majority citing a preference for it over film.

Mick Corfield suggests that 'a good 35mm print in pristine condition, that's presented well has far more depth to it than a digital picture, *far* more depth, and I would still prefer that'. However, he qualifies this statement by acknowledging the imperfections of the average projectionist, arguing that 'projectionists weren't all singing and dancing and wonderful ... I've scratched films ... [T]here have always been poor projectionists'. The sheer number of accounts of problems both within and outside of the projectionist's control that have been shared by the interviewees and that are apparent in the trade press are testament to the fact that not every projectionist met their own standards 100% of the time, and, as Corfield notes, many were not aiming for especially high standards to begin with. Furthermore, for Corfield it isn't the case that *any* 35mm print is superior to a DCP, but specifically 'a good 35mm print in pristine condition'. This is – and always has been – a rare commodity. As we have seen throughout this book, a huge amount of time and effort was given over by projectionists in their attempts to put on the perfect show. On the one hand, this involved attempting to adhere to certain aesthetic standards of presentation through the enacting of a series of learned manual processes, guided by an instinctual idea of what looked 'good'. At the same time, much of the cleaning and maintenance work outlined in Chapter One was designed to eliminate dirt and dust from the projection equipment, keep the film free of scratches and blemishes, and in turn reduce the amount of on-screen noise. The latter was a battle that could never be entirely won, and over time it was inevitable that no matter how well it was cared for, the fact of a film print's passing through the projector, in contact with the rollers, gates and sprockets, meant that deterioration was inevitable. This is not an issue with a digital image, and, as Adrian Pearce notes, 'you show it once, you show it a thousand times, it's exactly the same'.

The replicability of the digital experience was a key selling point for digital projection from the beginning and is, perhaps, the most admired aspect of digital as far as the projectionists we interviewed were concerned. Phil Fawke, for example, recalls that

> I thought digital [was a] load of bunkum, you know. I thought that [the] quality would never, ever be as good but ... I've seen it and I've got to agree it's not just good, it's better. Plus, the fact you don't get all the scratches. I mean, some of the 'Sunday stuff' we used to get: there was so many joins in it. Well, it was an insult to charge people to watch it really.

The aged prints often shown as part of Sunday matinees are widely regarded as the nadir in terms of projection quality, often having been in circulation for many years, and thus a meaningful comparator for how digital's longevity outlasts the fragility of celluloid, at least as far as the initial theatrical run is concerned.[741]

The repeatability of the digital print is not the only positive aspect of the digital film experience articulated by projectionists. Fawke acknowledges that with digital prints 'you don't get racks' and 'you can't miss a changeover', and Atwill suggests that because digital doesn't 'depend on the operator when it comes to picture quality and sharpness and fitting the screen right' that the overall image is far more stable once it has been finalised: it's 'set up by an engineer and it doesn't shift from that, you know. Your focus is always going to be right, so long as they've done it right in the first place. Your framing is always going to be right ... [I]t's a smaller margin of error on that presentation side'. Ray Reed appreciates the 'nice still picture' and the lack of distortion that you find with digital sound: 'the sound is always spot on, because with 35mm once a print had been round for a while the soundtrack would become damaged and therefore the sound was crap'. Neil Thompson describes digital as 'absolutely fantastic', and his admiration for digital's clarity is evident: 'it's just like looking out of a window at a scene, it's clean, it's unobtrusive and it's just perfect ... [W]hen film's running you do get a bit of judder because it's a moving image. Whereas with digital it's just completely still'. This prioritisation by projectionists of clarity and stability of the image over all else is not new, and recalls the challenge to established projection standards posed by the introduction of the softened style of cinematography in the 1920s, which we discussed in Chapter Two.

Despite Thompson's overriding admiration for the sharpness of the digital image, there is an element of scepticism to be found within his assertion that the digital image is in some ways 'too good'. This is a view shared by Chris Tweddell, who describes the digital image as 'soulless' when compared with film. Ironically, he cherishes some of the flaws that have been eradicated in the digital era, arguing that 'you can sense movement on film, you can see grain on your film, you know, there's some heart and soul'. However, he also acknowledges that 'people are used to digital now, they're used to that rock steady [picture]', and that 'most paying public in a commercial cinema don't notice the difference; they wouldn't have a clue'. Brad Atwill typifies this nuanced ambivalence towards digital as follows:

> from an audience perspective, it is great. I mean it does look brilliant and done properly it does look great. Sound quality as well is far superior. But, at the same time, it comes down to would you rather

741 Charlotte Crofts has addressed the other side of this debate, arguing that the preservation of digital materials is no less perilous than analogue film prints, and that in the long run their survival may even be harder to sustain (Charlotte Crofts, 'Digital Decay', *The Moving Image*, 8:2 [Fall 2008], pp. xiii-35).

> listen to a great digital recording of your favourite song, or would you rather have it on vinyl and it's very much a personal preference ... and it's very similar ... There's a lot more warmth to film, and certain films look better on print and certain films look better in digital and it's not black and white ... People prefer different things. I slide between the two ... I think red's the perfect colour for film, whereas blue is the perfect colour for digital. I think blues and blacks look beautiful in digital, reds and nice warm oranges and things look far superior in print, to me anyway.

What we find articulated time and time again in the interviews is the description of a (digital) cinema image that seems to accord almost completely with the kind of perfect image that the projectionist in the analogue projection box had strived so tirelessly to achieve for over a century. It is not, then, difficult to understand the industry-wide acceptance of digital projection by projectionists and audiences alike.

What is lamented by projectionists, however, is the loss of humanity from the spaces of film projection, and the sense that, with the removal of people from the exhibition workflow, there is nobody left to care for the way a film is presented. Atwill makes it clear that projecting film correctly is something he really cares about, and that the arrival of digital displaced these acts of caring on to a series of inflexible digital processes. He notes with sadness that the loss of projection as a key job in the cinema industry meant 'knowing that that level of care wouldn't be there anymore ... which sounds stupid to get annoyed by but ... I know how this cinema is, and as much as I love the people downstairs, their jobs are already busy and stressful enough as it is without them having to worry about this, so they're not going to'.

This loss of the human element can, perhaps, be felt most intensely in the clinical environment of the digital projection box. Mike Marshall argues that 'Nothing's the same at all. There's no moving parts, there's nothing. All you hear is fans. That's all.'[742] Atwill similarly recalls that 'the biggest thing that I missed when I went back to Cineworld when they'd completely got rid of the 35mm and opened the door into projection and it being silent was so unnerving'. He remembers that 'that was when it really hit home', because he was

> used to ... there being a bit of music playing and ... you could see the guy at the other end just kind of sat there ... and you'd hear that whirring and the ticking and you knew that things were running. It

742 The sonic environment of the analogue projection box has been explored in some detail by Michael Pigott, both in writing and in Pigott's artistic work (the latter under the name Michael Lightborn). See: Michael Pigott, 'Sounds of the Projection Box: Liner Notes for a Phonographic Method', *Journal of British Cinema and Television*, 15:1 (2018), pp. 27-45; Michael Lightborne, *Sounds of the Projection Box* (Gruenrekorder, 2018), https://www.gruenrekorder.de/?page_id=16703, accessed 17 September 2020.

> felt alive, it felt like a sort of living entity in itself. To then open the door and nobody be there ... it lost it then. I think that's when it felt cold ... And it was all because the business end of the projector wasn't clicking away and sounding beautiful.

The sense of humanity attached to the 'alive' 35mm projectors in contrast to the 'cold' digital projectors can also be seen in the way projectionists engaged with the mechanical machines. Neil Thompson recalls that the three Cinerama projectors that he used at the Queen's Cinema, Newcastle in the 1970s were given the names Able, Baker and Charlie (replicating the military alphabet put in place by the Combined Communications Board during the Second World War), and Atwill argues that the technical flaws exhibited by certain projectors became endearing characteristics. He recalls the removal of 'our beloved broken screen ten' being particularly emotional because 'nobody ever knew what was wrong with it'. The final screening using that projector was accompanied by a short, but 'profound', eulogy directed towards the machine itself; 'sort of "we'll miss you the most"', Atwill recalls. 'As much as it was the biggest nightmare day-to-day ... it was the most missed projector because it had character'. Within these accounts, the removal of the anthropomorphised machines is configured as being part of the dismantling of what Atwill characterises as 'a little group like a little sort of family, a close-knit group of mates', of which the projectors were a part.

Although some projection teams made attempts to personalise the digital machines – and the act of 'ingesting' digital files already confers a level of anthropomorphism on the content-hungry projectors – these accounts show that their glitchy and impersonal nature were often ironically highlighted. One of Atwill's former colleagues attached images of 'famous crashed computer screens' to their digital projectors, including HAL from *2001: A Space Odyssey* (UK-USA, Stanley Kubrick, 1968), the computer terminal from *The Matrix* (USA, Lana & Lilly Wachowski, 1999), and the wagging-fingered caricature that rogue computer operator Dennis Nedry (Wayne Knight) uses to lock down the systems in *Jurassic Park* (USA, Steven Spielberg, 1993). Other sites of minor resistance include the Hyde Park Picture House in Leeds, where projectionist Alan Foster has wired the digital projector up to a spare button on one of the remaining 35mm projectors, so that he can start the digital programme using the analogue equipment. Mike Marshall recalls that before leaving the projection room at the Odeon, Glasgow Quay, he was able to use the redundant film projectors that remained in situ to revitalise the sterile atmosphere: 'We used to just put the projector on so you could hear the projector running,' he recalls, 'just make a wee loop [of film] up and let it run so there was a sound all the time. You would hear the projector instead of all the fans'.

Of course, the greatest loss of 'humanity' from the projection box is that of the projectionists themselves. Despite their general admiration for the digital image, the projectionists are quick to make the link to their own circumstances and that of the wider labour force, something pithily articulated by Frank Gibson when he states that 'digital looks better, but it puts me out of business, that's all I've got against it'. However, there is general agreement that digital is better able to achieve many of the aims of the dedicated projectionist, particularly those pertaining to image quality, if not presentation standards, that underpin much of the labour detailed in Chapter One. Peter Howden is 'sorry it didn't happen 20 years ago', and offers some particularly articulate views on the relationship between digital projection and the historical aims of the projectionist: 'I'm in favour of actually being able to see everything that the film makers wanted you to see'. Most incisively, he reiterates the philosophy that we documented in Chapter Two that 'projectionists are traditionally completely invisible and the more invisible they are the better', adding that 'my argument for digital is that it makes it easier for the projectionist to be invisible'.

The idea of the projectionist as an invisible figure has been taken to its logical conclusion in the digital age, following their complete removal from the projection of theatrical feature films in mainstream cinemas. More optimistically, it has been argued that the digital turn has expanded cinema beyond the confines of cinema venues into galleries, nightclubs and public spaces, and that, viewed from this perspective, far from being a species on the verge of extinction, the projectionist is experiencing a phoenix-like revival.[743] However, as we have seen, cinema, as it is presented at the multiplex, is now almost completely devoid of a human mediator between machine and viewing experience. This is not solely the result of digitalisation, and we have argued throughout this book that the erosion of labour and agency has occurred across the whole history of the profession. John Douglas reminds us of this fact: 'When I started in 1953, [the] Chief said to me, "I don't know why you've come into this business; it's finished!"' Though this was obviously an overly-pessimistic view of the industry as it stood in the mid-1950s, Douglas concludes by suggesting that although the chief 'was a bit before his time ... it did finish. It's gone now. It's gone now.'[744]

743 Michael Pigott and Richard Wallace, 'A New "Wild West" of Projection', in Virginia Crisp and Gabriel Menotti (eds), *Practices of Projection* (Oxford: Oxford University Press, 2020), pp. 19-35.

744 Interview with John and Peter Douglas, conducted by Richard Wallace, 24 June 2015.

Afterword

In Love with Film Projection

Charlotte Brunsdon

> 'Since the change from film to digital projection in the mid-2000s, it has become harder and harder to project from film in a cinema. But there is a romance to film projection not shared with its contemporary replacement, and projecting film opens up new and broader programming opportunities.
> With dedication, commitment and the right advice, it is still possible to continue this 120-year-old tradition.'[745]

In October 2020, when the UK was poised between two periods of lockdown imposed in response to the COVID-19 pandemic, the Independent Cinema Office circulated its latest publication, *An Introductory Guide to Film Projection.* This clear and helpful guide, which is illustrated with often rather beautiful photographs, is addressed to a reader who might never have watched anything but a digitally projected film. It explains the mechanics of film projection, the different sorts of film, and gives advice on how to source equipment. It is also a bit in love with these old ways of projecting film. The epigraph above, with its reference to the 'romance' of film projection is taken from the email which was used to circulate the guide. Inside the guide, this romance is explained further: 'in a digitally dominated world there is also something magical about the mechanical process of projecting a film print – in essence, displaying captured light – that the cold steady pixels of digital cinema lack'.[746]

Whether you agree with this idea of the magic of film projection or not, the return to mechanical projection being advocated is a bit like the enthusiasm for vinyl which swept through the music industry after it too had gone digital. It is a consciously retro

745 Independent Cinema Office, 'A 120 Year Old Tradition', subscriber email 28 October 2019.

746 Dominic Simmons, *An Introductory Guide to Film Projection*, with photographs by Alexa Raisbeck and Dominic Simmons (London: Independent Cinema Office, 2020), p. 3; https://ico-assets-live.s3.eu-west-1.amazonaws.com/wp-content/uploads/2020/10/27080201/ICO_Online-Guide_Film-Projection_FINAL.pdf, accessed 26 January 2021.

embrace of a pre-digital form, like writers who insist on first drafts on typewriters, or film-makers who still want to edit on Steenbecks. The Independent Cinema Office is suggesting that, in 2020, small cinemas can extend their range and attract in new audiences with the special event of celluloid projection. A bit like an artisan baker, or a micro-brewery, this new retro-projection would contribute to a boutique cinema – analogue evenings, perhaps. Analogue life is seen as warmer and sensually richer even if also more flawed.

This book has documented the analogue life of film projection as it was lived the first time round. Magical the image may be, but the labour that projected it on to the screen was anything but magical. Dangerous, demanding, weighty, tedious – these are some of the ways in which the work of film projection can be described. Burrows and Wallace have tracked the whole 20th century story of film projection, from the mobile operators of the early days right up to the multiplexes. They provide an alternative history of the cinema, one which is made not by looking at the screen and describing the different types of films, or by researching the memories of audiences, but one which starts with the mechanics of projection, and how the image gets onto the screen in the first place.

Privately, I am a bit of a film-sentimentalist. I like celluloid – or the acetate- and polyester-based media we still call celluloid. I like its transparency, its slidiness, its sprocket holes, its smell. I was never the kind of film scholar who is enchanted by the glamour of the silver screen. I like the austere and joyous black-and-white film experiments of the 1920s. My scholarly interest in the medium developed in the context of ideas about 20th century modernism and demands that the artwork should attend to its own materiality. The later context of avant-garde and underground cinemas, the flourishing of film co-ops and workshops, the portability and accessibility of formats such as 16mm, provided alternative understanding of what film practices and film art might be. It wasn't about stars and spectacle and the big Hollywood studios for me. It was all scratches and loops and duration. The specificity of film to be found in its very materiality. I have loved films like Ken Jacobs' *Tom, Tom, the Piper's Son* (USA, 1969) in which a full-length feature is made from the re-filming of a 1905 silent short fragment, so that the action becomes abstracted and the grain of the film supersedes the progress of the narrative. Stan Brakhage's three-minute *Mothlight* (USA, 1963), in which the flicker of the film frames is enacted through the apparent flutter of the real mothwings caught on the film strip, enchanted me even as I mourned the moths. Annabel Nicolsons's *Reel Time*, a performance piece I saw at the London Film-makers' Co-Operative in the early 1970s, was witty and serious in its presentation of the combination of mechanical action, light, celluloid and duration as cinema. Nicolson sat amongst the spectators with a Singer sewing machine – very much the same generation of machine as an early projector – through which she ran a loop of film that was also passing through the projector. She, and the sewing machine, were, in a sense, the pick-up spool, and the image projected onto the screen changed as the film was increasingly punctured by the sewing machine needle.

I like the way film demands you treat it with respect. It will get scratched by dust (dust!) and becomes brittle if kept in the wrong conditions. It snaps if you don't lace it up correctly in the projector, and if you don't secure the end into the pick-up spool it bounds all over the floor. I loved the rituals of film projection, preparing the print, lacing the machines, checking all the pathways, and then the roar of power and the final adjustments to sound, focus, and racking as the image is thrown onto the screen.

As the presentation and distribution of film began to change, with the big cinema chains moving increasingly to multiplexes, and, as this book has shown, the labour of projection becoming increasingly automated, it became evident that the cinema of the 20th century was in transition. At the same time, there was a parallel increase in artist moving-image work, and film seemed to be moving out of cinemas and into galleries, where it was often very poorly presented. The skills of the cinema projectionists might be becoming redundant, but their knowledge certainly wasn't shifting sites to the new environments for projected film.

It was in these contexts that the idea for the project from which this book emerges took shape. As the film industry accelerated, in exhibition, the switch to digital which had already transformed film production, it became evident that the hidden figures of film exhibition, the projectionists, were likely to be evicted from cinema buildings, their labour now unnecessary. Their skill in handling the material of film, always most prized when most invisible, would be forgotten. What did projectionists think about what was happening? How did they think of their work? What were their views about the digital image and the new regimes of exhibition?

We were not the only group of film enthusiasts to see the timeliness of documenting the contribution of projectionists to what had been cinema, and the introduction to this book details some of the other photographic and oral histories. However, the combination of interests the team brought together meant that our enquiry rapidly expanded beyond our initial idea that we should record some projectionists talking about what they did. Jon Burrows' understanding of early cinema meant that he could counter any tendencies to apocalyptic interpretations of the present transition with an historical understanding of the ways in which cinema, in the early stages of its development, had moved from fairgrounds into fixed buildings. Richard Wallace was familiar with the complexity of the testimony produced in oral history interviews, the way in which time and memory work unpredictably to render the past in the present. My own interest in the materiality of film was matched by our colleague Michael Pigott's artistic practice and his commitment to projection events outside the cinema in both gallery and city. It was also clear that cinema itself has a long history of engagement with the figure of the projectionist, and that movies which feature projectionists are one of the ways in which the medium has reflected on itself. Claire Jesson joined us to research films with projectionist characters.[747] So the project expanded in both length and width, but at its core remained the desire to document the contribution of the projectionist to cinema.

When we started the Projection Project, a pervasive melancholy about the end of cinema was perceptible in both scholarly and popular discussions about the medium. The term cinephilia was used increasingly to designate a passionate attachment to a way of watching moving images which was becoming archaic as the new screens of the mobile phone and the computer became almost ubiquitous. Distinguished film critics recounted film-going autobiographies in which they remembered the atmosphere and even the smell of the cinemas of their youth. Did the transition to digital mean that cinema as we had known it was over?

Alongside the interviews with projectionists and the historical research that underpin this book, we undertook a programme of reading to map the contours of the debates about projection, the moving image, celluloid, theatrical exhibition, the digital image, digital delivery, and the nature of cinema. Our aim was to understand how the broader transition to digital should be understood in relation to cinema specifically. Was it, as some claimed, the end of cinema, in which that medium joined other art forms such as music in what was destined to be an endless cycle of remediation? Or was it an enormously significant transition that could nevertheless be understood within a cinematic continuum that had absorbed previous crises such as the transition to sound, the possibility of colour and the arrival of television? Did the coded pixels of the digital image produce a different relation to what film

747 Claire Jesson, *The Projectionist in Cinema and the Persistence of Film*, unpublished PhD thesis, University of Warwick, 2018.

studies scholars call 'the pro-filmic event' – what was in front of the camera? Had film lost its much debated imprint of the real, the indexical image, in the shift from analogue to digital? When people watched a movie on a mobile phone, was it still a movie in the same way as it was when people watched a movie in a cinema? Did it matter how it was originated – on celluloid or born-digital? And what about all that film-work that had so attracted me in its location of the specificity of the medium in the interplay between image, projection and the material support of celluloid. What did an avant-garde digital practice look like, and where did it take place?

We traced our way through these discussions about the nature of relationship between the image and the world and the significance of collective rituals of viewing. We considered the possibility that 20th century cinema was merely an electro-mechanical episode in the centuries-long history of projection. We worried over competing definitions of film and cinema, some of which emphasised medium, some practices of viewing and exhibition. We developed an understanding of our own project as a modest contribution to the history of 20th century cinema and its transitions in the early 21st century. In whatever different ways individuals in the group came to understand these larger ontological questions about cinema, together we could ensure that the hidden and soon to be forgotten practices of film projection were documented. Our research showed that cinema history from the point of view of projection could be periodised in a material way that counterpoints more familiar film-based accounts, as the first chapter explains. Using the notion of the array – a particular technological constellation of apparatus – dominant in each period, this periodization moves from the mobile array through nitrate and xenon arrays, through to the multi-screen array. These phases are defined through different criteria, with one key phase defined by film stock – nitrate – and the following by light source, xenon, while both the mobile and multiplex phases are defined by place and mode. This is in some senses a material history of cinema, onto which the labour of projecting the image onto the screen can be mapped in its own three phases. The projectionist comes into view, and then disappears. The operator of the mobile array loses his mobility in the shift to fixed exhibition venues, becoming the projectionist for the nitrate and xenon eras, slowly transitioning to the technician during the multiplex era, a transition only fully realised in the digital moment. 'Projectionist' as a job could be located as the central term within the historical chain operator-projectionist-technician.

What we did not anticipate, while preparing and undertaking the research that is presented in this book, was that our understanding of the nature and history of cinema would be interrupted by the world-wide closure of cinemas because of the COVID-19 epidemic. Cinema exhibition itself, in the early 21st century was already under siege from the increased availability of digital 'content', with the brand name Netflix coming to signify new modes of domestic consumption of movies and television series. Lockdown accelerated and reshaped shifts to digital viewing. It wasn't just cinema projectionists who were being made redundant. The low-pay, zero hours contracts that staff many front-of-house jobs in cinemas disappeared overnight. The partial reopening of British cinemas in summer 2020 was accompanied by new etiquettes. Venues, demanding online booking and contact details, showed little videos on their websites about how to behave in cinemas. The one thing you could no longer do was sit anonymous in a crowd of strangers to watch a movie.

At the time of writing, it is unclear how matters will develop in this continuing crisis. In relation to cinema, though, it is possible to make two observations. First, that the months of cinema closure have affected ideas of what the pleasures of watching films are and how we understand cinema. For me, this has meant reconsidering the importance of theatrical exhibition in any understanding of what cinema is. I have personally always chosen to try to see films first in a theatrical context, but, in a way, that is my job. I teach film, and I know that I'll often spend a good deal of time with particular films in a non-theatrical context – on DVD, or streamed, or in the seminar room. I still remember the enormous liberation of the 1980s availability of films on video tape, which meant I no longer had to spend hours in a little room at work with a projector or a Steenbeck, making notes on a film I wanted to teach or write about. I have been professionally dependent on the way that films persist across platforms and modes of delivery, even though there are vast variations in image and sound quality. My preference for first seeing movies in cinemas has been underpinned by a sense of that uninterrupted screening being somehow 'the real thing', as well as the recognition that this is the best way for me to watch difficult or upsetting material, far from the distractions of my own home. However, not being able to go to the cinema at all showed me that perhaps I had underestimated how important that going out in a crowd of strangers to watch the same film was to a definition of the medium. While we had, in the Projection Project, been much engaged with the question of what was at stake in digital delivery, as opposed to celluloid projection, having no access to cinemas has made this distinction seem less important. I now think that going to a public place and having the projected image in front of one on a big screen is more defining of cinema – as John Belton has argued – than I had grasped.[748] The materiality of film exists in more than one temporal plane, and the film in cinema performance is one. While all the presentational disappointments of automised digital projection, as explored in Chapter Four, continue to degrade much about the cinema experience, there is something about cinema as a public art form that is lost when you watch the same film, even if more comfortably, at home.

The other point is, as is always the case with cinema, there is no disentangling of the moving image from the industry and financial instruments that produce, distribute and exhibit it. The response of the film industry to the increased incursion of internet viewing on their audiences this century has led to a marked bifurcation within film exhibition, with multiplexes concentrating on big budget blockbusters – often running in more than one screen simultaneously – while independent and arthouse venues have developed a more curated, boutique programme. Within the first year of Covid, when most cinemas closed in March 2020, the studios delayed the release of the scheduled summer blockbusters, including the symbolically British contribution, the new James Bond film, *No Time to Die* (UK-USA, Cary Joji Fukunaga, 2021). Further delay was announced in October when James Bond was postponed again, and the Cineworld chain announced that it would be closing its doors after the limited summer re-openings. Vue, one of the other leading British chains, immediately also announced that many of their cinemas would only be open from Fridays to Mondays. British news media erupted into a tumult of 'end of cinema' opinion pieces. However, as Danny Leigh pointed out in the *Financial Times*, Cineworld and Vue were propagating a very particular view of cinema, which was blockbuster-driven.[749] Far from there being no films, there were plenty of mid and small budget films available – it's just that the business model of the multiplex chains were now so imbricated with a blockbuster model that the chains' cry of 'no films' rendered these more modest productions even more invisible.

This could be the moment when the prospects of independent cinemas and arthouses improve. Smaller venues, curated programmes, a lot of attention to front-of-house hosting and super-

748 John Belton, 'If film is dead, what is cinema?' *Screen*, 55:4 (Winter 2014), pp. 460-470. Drive-in cinemas during a pandemic are an interesting case here, as I discovered at a Luna Cinema screening of *Cool Runnings* (USA, Jon Turteltaub, 1993) at Warwick Castle in July 2020. Because car windows must be kept shut against contagion, despite being outside in a public place (a field), with a big screen in front of you, the experience is more like watching television as your car becomes your living room.

749 Danny Leigh, 'Cinemas are dead. Long live the movies', *FTWeekend*, 10/11 October 2020, p. 2.

vised social distancing may prove more attractive to film lovers.[750] Some of the projectionists' contributions to this experience that this book has documented may re-emerge in these newly imagined cinemas. But this etiolated, boutique experience certainly won't be the public artform of the 20th century. When we began the Projection Project, we thought we were documenting the end of electro-mechanical skilled practices and a certain sort of analogue employment in the projecting of moving images in cinemas. We worked hard to avoid the way in which a project of this kind often has an in-built nostalgia. The colour richness and tonal resonance of celluloid is sometimes mourned as if it projected itself onto the cinema screen. Working as a projectionist involved terrible hours, often poor pay, and considerable loneliness. Our interviews with projectionists who had lost their livelihoods, but still considered the digital image superior, showed how complex this type of change is in practice. All the while that we were researching these transitions, we didn't anticipate that cinema itself, as a public art form, might be under threat by the time we finished the project. The technology business editor of the *Times* newspaper recently asked, 'If cinema chains were to go the way of Blockbuster, would we really mourn their passing?'[751] We say yes.

750 This may be a fond hope. Simon Duke argues that 'the march of progress won't spare the independent arthouse' ('Disney has to look at the bigger picture, in spite of our nostalgia for cinemas', *The Times*, 15 October 2020, p. 37).

751 *Ibid.* (Blockbuster was a chain of video rental shops ubiquitous on the high street in the 1980s and 1990s.)

Appendix

Details of Projectionists Interviewed for this Book

The table below contains the details of each interview conducted for this book. Unless otherwise stated the interview was conducted by Richard Wallace.

Table 1: Details of Projectionists Interviewed for this Book

Name	Year as a Projectionist	List of Cinemas / Chains	Interview Details
Simon Allen	1969-2011	Odeon, Cheltenham; Odeon, Torquay; National Film Theatre	08/03/2016
Brad Atwill	2009-	Cineworld, Boldon; Tyneside Cinema, Newcastle	10/11/2014
Ken Bagnall	1998-2011	Cineworld, Wakefield; Cineworld, Chesterfield; Cineworld, Bradford	17/09/2015
Chris Blower	2003-2012	Did not wish to disclose	11/08/2015
Martyn Butler	1970-mid 1980s	Dolman Theatre, Newport; Prince of Wales, Cardiff; Grand Pavilion, Llandrindod Wells; Warner Theatre, Leicester Square, London; Odeon, Marble Arch	25/08/2015
Mick Corfield	1989-2007	Showcase, Derby; The Cannon, Hagley Road, Birmingham; The Arcadian, Birmingham; Cineworld, Broad Street, Birmingham	03/08/2015
Mark Cosgrove	Film programmer with some experience of projection	Plymouth Arts Centre; Watershed, Bristol	26/08/2015
John Douglas	1953-1997	New Savoy, Glasgow; Odeon, Rutherglen; The Gaumont, Anniesland, Glasgow; Odeon, Renfield Street, Glasgow	24/06/2015
Peter Douglas	1953-1997	The Capitol, Ibrox; Odeon, Scotstoun, Glasgow; The Tivoli, Partick; The Gaumont, Anniesland; Odeon, Sauchiehall Street; Odeon, Renfield Street, Glasgow	24/06/2015
Rachel Dukes	1998–	Did not wish to disclose	19/12/2014
Ewan Dunford	2007–	Watershed, Bristol	26/08/2015
Paul Edmunds	1964-Not known	The Oak, Birmingham; The Grove, Birmingham; King's Norton, Birmingham; The Electric, Birmingham; Midlands Arts Centre (mac), Birmingham	02/12/2014
Philip Fawke	1940-2008	Regal, Leamington Spa; Regal, Coventry; Globe, Coventry; King's Norton, Birmingham; Midlands Arts Centre (mac), Birmingham	04/12/2014

Allan Foster	1959-	Marlboro', Bradford; Lyric, Leeds; Hyde Park Picture House, Leeds	16/09/2015
Frank Gibson	1956-2020	The Crown, Coventry; The Prince of Wales, Coventry; The Moulin Rouge, Oxford; University of Warwick, Coventry	14/10/2014
Peter Howden	1968-	Electric, Portobello Road; Everyman, Hampstead; Rio, Dalston	13/11/2014
Sam Lavington	Cinema manager with some experience of projection	Hippodrome, Ripley; Belper; Screen. Long Eaton; The Ritz, Burnham-on-Sea; The Phoenix, Spilsby	20/08/2015
Andrew MacLean	1977-	Aviemore Centre; Capitol, Aberdeen; Phoenix, Dingle, ROI; Watershed, Bristol; IMAX, Bristol; freelance projectionist	25/08/2015
Chandra Makwana	1977-2013	Northfield Odeon; Odeon, Richmond; Odeon, Kensington; Odeon, Haymarket; Odeon, Leicester Square; Odeon, Panton Street; Odeon, Wardour Street; Odeon, Streatham; Odeon, Uxbridge	16/03/2015
Mike Marshall	1971-	Curzon Classic, Glasgow (1971-); Classic Grand, Glasgow; The George, Bellshill; Glasgow Film Theatre (1974); Classic House (1974-75); ABC 2, Glasgow (1975-1977); Classic Grand (1977-1992); Odeon, Dundee (1993-1997); Odeon, Glasgow Quay (1997-2012); Premier Leisure, Saltcoats (2012-)	22/06/2015
John Neal	1996-	Curzon, Clevedon	15/01/2015
Chris O'Kane	2000-2013	Glasgow Science Centre; Premier Leisure, Saltcoats	23/06/2015
Adrian Pearce	2000-	Showcase, Coventry; Warwick Arts Centre, Coventry	20/10/2014
Joan Pearson	1947-1974	ABC Aston, Birmingham; ABC Bristol Road, Birmingham; Robin Hood, Birmingham; ABC Sparkbrook, Birmingham	21/07/2016
William Pearson	1946-1996	ABC Astron, Birmingham; ABC Sparkbrook, Birmingham; ABC Forum, Birmingham; ABC Royalty, Birmingham; Robin Hood, Birmingham; ABC Bristol Road, Birmingham; The Oak, Selly Oak; ABC, Coventry; Arcadian, Birmingham	21/07/2016
Ray Reed	1966-2015	The Tyneside Cinema, Newcastle (formerly The News Theatre); The Pavilion, Newcastle; Odeon, Biker; Odeon Pilgrim Street, Newcastle; Odeon, Gateshead	05/02/2015
Neil Thompson	1974-2014	Queens, Newcastle; Odeon Pilgrim Street, Newcastle; Odeon/Empire, Newcastle	11/11/2014
Chris Tweddell	1988-	AMC Metro Centre, Gateshead; Cineworld, Boldon Colliery	12/11/2014
Michael Williams	1956-1964	Olympia, Cardiff; Caste, Merthyr Tydfil	24/08/2015
John Young	1973-2012	The Classic, Low Fell; AMC, Milton Keynes; AMC, Metro Centre	05/02/2015

Notes:
John Douglas and Peter Douglas were interviewed at the same time.
Joan Pearson and William Pearson were interviewed at the same time by Richard Wallace and Rebecca Harrison.
Chris Tweddell was interviewed with Brad Atwill present.

Bibliography

Archives

Coventry Archives, Herbert Art Gallery & Museum, Coventry

Electrical Trades Union (ETU) Archives, Working Class Movement Library, Salford

Home Office (HO) and Ministry of Labour (LAB) records, National Archives, London

National Association of Theatrical and Kine Employees (NATKE) Aberdeen Branch papers, Special Collections, University of Aberdeen, Aberdeen.

Trades Union Congress (TUC) Archives, Modern Records Centre, University of Warwick, Coventry

Trade Periodicals

The Bioscope

Cinema Technology

Ideal Kinema

Kinematograph Weekly (1907-1919: *Kinematograph and Lantern Weekly*)

Optical Lantern and Cinematograph Journal

Projectionists' Journal

Articles and Books

Anon. [Arthur S. Newman], *The Modern Bioscope Operator* (London: Ganes, 1910).

Anon., *The Film Strike: The Projectionists' Case* (London: Farleigh Press, 1938).

Anon., *The Story of the E.T.U.: The Official History of the Electrical Trades Union* (Bromley, Kent: E.T.U., 1952).

Charles R. Acland and Haidee Wasson (eds), *Useful Cinema* (Durham, NC: Duke University Press, 2011).

Dan Adler, Janine Marchessault and Sanja Obradovic (eds), *3D Cinema and Beyond* (Bristol: Intellect, 2013).

Dudley Andrews, *What Cinema Is!: Bazin's Quest and its Charge* (Chichester; Malden, MA: Wiley-Blackwell, 2010).

Philip Auslander, 'Musical Personae', *TDR (The Drama Review)*, 50:1 (2006), pp. 100-119.

Timothy Barnard, 'The "Machine Operator": *Deus Ex Machine* of the Storefront Cinema', *Framework* 43:1 (Spring 2002), pp. 40-75.

Timothy Barnard, 'Projectionists', in Richard Abel (ed.), *Encyclopedia of Early Cinema* (London; New York: Routledge, 2005).

John Barnes, *The Beginnings of the Cinema in England Vol. 2: 1897* (Exeter: University of Exeter Press, 1996).

Charles Barr, 'CinemaScope: Before and After', *Film Quarterly*, 16:4 (Summer 1963), pp. 4-24.

John Belton, *Widescreen Cinema* (Cambridge, MA; London: Harvard University Press, 1992).

John Belton, 'If Film is Dead, What is Cinema?', *Screen*, 55:4: (Winter 2014), pp. 460-470.

Ernest Betts, *The Film Business: A History of British Cinema 1896-1972* (London: George Allen & Unwin LTD, 1973).

David Bordwell, *Pandora's Digitial Box: Films, Files, and the Future of Movies* (Madison, WI: The Irvington Way Institute Press, 2012).

David Bordwell, Janet Staiger and Kristin Thompson, *The Classical Hollywood Cinema: Film Style & Mode of Production to 1960* (London: Routledge, 1985).

Raymond Boyle, 'Digital Divides? UK Film Council Strategy and the Digital Screen Network', *International Journal of Media & Cultural Politics*, 11:1 (2015), pp. 3-20.

David Breskin, 'Interview With David Lynch', in Richard A. Barney (ed.), *David Lynch: Interviews* (Jackson: University Press of Mississippi, 2009).

Ben Brewster, '*Traffic in Souls*: An Experiment in Feature-Length Narrative Construction', *Cinema Journal*, 31:1 (Autumn 1991), pp. 37-56.

British Film Institute (BFI), *Statistical Yearbook 2015* (London: British Film Institute, 2015).

H.E. Browning and A.A. Sorrell, 'Cinema and Cinema-Going in Great Britain', *Journal of the Royal Statistical Society. Series A (General)*, 117:2 (1954), pp. 133-170.

Kevin Brownlow, 'Silent Films – What Was the Right Speed?', in Thomas Elsaesser with Adam Barker (eds), *Early Cinema: Space, Frame Narrative* (London: BFI, 1990).

Charlotte Brunsdon, '"This is Not a Cinema": The Projectionist's Tale', *Screen*, 60:4 (Winter 2019), pp. 527-547.

Charlotte Brunsdon, Jon Burrows and Richard Wallace, 'Introduction', Journal of British Cinema and Television, 15:1 (January 2018), pp. 1-5.

Judith Buchanan, '"Now Where Are We?": Ideal and Actual Early Cinema Lecturing Practices in Britain, Germany and the United States', in Julie Brown and Annette Davidson (eds), *The Sounds of the Silents in Britain* (Oxford; New York: Oxford University Press, 2013).

Jon Burrows, 'Penny Pleasures: Film Exhibition in London During the Nickelodeon Era, 1906-1914', *Film History*, 16:1 (2004), pp. 60-91.

Jon Burrows, 'The 1909 Cinematograph Act: Some Myths Debunked', *Picture House*, 35 (2010), pp. 3-11.

Jon Burrows, *The British Cinema Boom, 1909-1914: A Commercial History* (Basingstoke: Palgrave Macmillan, 2017).

Jon Burrows, '"Certified Operators" versus "Handle-Turners": The British Film Industry's First Trade Union', *Journal of British Cinema and Television*, 15:1 (January 2018), pp. 73-93.

Lisa Cartwright, 'The Hands of the Projectionist', *Science in Context*, 24:3 (September 2011), pp. 443-464.

Francesco Casetti, *The Lumière Galaxy: Seven Key Words for the Cinema to Come* (New York: Columbia University Press, 2015).

Lucie Česálková, '"Feel the Film": Film Projectionists and Professional Memory', *Memory Studies*, 10:1 (January 2017), pp. 49-62.

Michael Chanan, *Labour Power in the British Film Industry* (London: BFI, 1976).

Michael Chanan, *The Dream That Kicks: The Prehistory and Early Years of Cinema in Britain* (London: Routledge & Kegan Paul, 1980).

Harold L. Cole and Lee E. Ohanian, 'The Great U.K. Depression: A Puzzle and a Possible Resolution', *Review of Economic Dynamics*, 5:1 (January 2002), pp. 19-44.

Harper Cossar, *Letterboxed: The Evolution of Widescreen Cinema* (Lexington, KY: University Press of Kentucky, 2011).

R. Howard Cricks, *The Complete Projectionist: A Textbook for all who Handle Sound and Pictures in the Kinema* (London: Kinematograph Publications, 1933).

R. Howard Cricks, *The Complete Projectionist: A Textbook for all who Handle Sound and Pictures in the Kinema*, 3rd edn (London: Kinematograph Publications, 1943).

R. Howard Cricks, *The Complete Projectionist: A Textbook for all who Handle Sound and Pictures in the Kinema*, 4th edn (London: Odhams Press, Ltd., 1949).

Virginia Crisp and Gabriel Menotti Gonring (eds), *Besides the Screen: Moving Images Through Distribution, Promotion and Curation* (Basingstoke: Palgrave Macmillan, 2015).

Virginia Crisp and Gabriel Menotti Gonring (eds), *Practices of Projection: Histories and Technologies* (Oxford: Oxford University Press, 2020).

Charlotte Crofts, 'Cinema Distribution in the Age of Digital Projection', *Post Script: Essays in Film and the Humanities*, 30:2 (Winter-Spring 2011), pp. 82-98.

Charlotte Crofts, 'Digital Decay', *The Moving Image*, 8:2 (Fall 2008), pp. xiii-35.

Sean Cubitt, *The Practice of Light: A Genealogy of Visual Technologies from Prints to Pixels* (London; Cambridge, MA: The MIT Press, 2007).

Sean Cubitt 'Projection: Vanishing and Becoming', in Oliver Grau (ed.), *MediaArtHistories* (London; Cambridge, MA: The MIT Press, 2014).

James Denman and Paul McDonald, 'Unemployment Statistics from 1881 to the Present Day', *Labour Market Trends*, 104 (1996), pp. 5-18.

Margaret Dickinson and Sarah Street, *The Cinema and State: The Film Industry and the Government 1927-84* (London: BFI, 1985).

Mary Ann Doane, 'The Location of the Image: Cinematic Projection and Scale in Modernity', in Stan Douglas and Christopher Eamon (eds), *Art of Projection* (Ostfildern: Hatje Cantz Verlag, 2009).

Stan Douglas and Christopher Eamon (eds), *Art of Projection* (Ostfildern: Hatje Cantz Verlag, 2009).

Gillian Doyle, Philip Schlesinger, Raymond Boyle and Lisa W. Kelly, *The Rise and Fall of the UK Film Council* (Edinburgh: Edinburgh University Press, 2015).

John Ellis, 'Filming for Television: How a 16mm Film Crew Worked Together', *VIEW: Journal of European Television History & Culture*, 8:15 (2019), pp. 91-110.

John Ellis, 'Why Hands on History Matters', in Nick Hall and John Ellis (eds), *Hands on Media History: A New Methodology in the Humanities and Social Sciences* (London; New York: Routledge, 2020).

Leo Enticknap, *Moving Image Technology: From Zoetrope to Digital* (London; New York: Wallflower Press, 2005).

Allen Eyles, *ABC: The First Name in Entertainment* (Burgess Hill: Cinema Theatre Association, 1993).

Allen Eyles, 'Classic Repertory Cinemas', *Picture House*, 45 (2020), pp. 3-51.

Allen Eyles, *Gaumont British Cinemas* (Burgess Hill: Cinema Theatre Association, 1996).

Allen Eyles, *The Granada Theatres* (London: Cinema Theatre Association, 1998).

Allen Eyles, *Odeon Cinemas 1: Oscar Deutsch Entertains Our Nation* (London: Cinema Theatre Association, 2002).

Allen Eyles, *Odeon Cinemas 2: From J. Arthur Rank to the Multiplex* (London: Cinema Theatre Association, 2005).

Richard Farmer, *Cinemas and Cinemagoing in Wartime Britain 1939-45: The Utility Dream Palace* (Manchester: Manchester University Press, 2016).

Charles Feinstein, 'New Estimates of Average Earnings in the United Kingdom, 1880-1913', *Economic History Review*, 43:4 (November 1990), pp. 595-632.

James Fenwick, 'The Eady Levy, "The Envy of Most Other European Nations": Runaway Productions and The British Film Fund in the early 1960s', in I. Q. Hunter, Laraine Porter and Justin Smith (eds.), *The Routledge Companion to British Cinema History* (London; New York: Routledge, 2017).

André Gaudreault and Philippe Marion (trans. Timothy Barnard), *The End of Cinema? A Medium in Crisis in the Digital Age* (New York: Columbia University Press, 2015).

James Grant, *The Forgotten Depression: 1921, the Crash that Cured Itself* (New York: Simon & Schuster, 2014).

Alison Griffiths, *Shivers Down Your Spine: Cinema, Museums, and the Immersive View* (New York: Columnbia University Press, 2008).

Trevor Griffiths, *The Cinema and Cinema-going in Scotland, 1896-1950* (Edinburgh: Edinburgh University Press, 2012).

Tom Gunning, 'The Cinema of Attractions: Early Film, Its Spectator and the Avant-Garde', *Wide Angle*, 8:3 (1986), pp. 63-70.

André Habib, 'Reel Changes: Post-mortem Cinephilia or the Resistance of Melancholia', in Santiago Hidalgo (ed.), *Technology and Film Scholarship: Experience, Study, Theory* (Amsterdam: University of Amsterdam Press, 2018).

Stuart Hanson, *From Silent Screen to Multi-Screen: A History of Cinema Exhibition in Britain Since 1896* (Manchester: Manchester University Press, 2007).

Stuart Hanson, *Screening the World: Global Development of the Multiplex Cinema* (Cham: Palgrave Macmillan, 2019).

Rebecca Harrison, 'The Coming of the Projectionettes: Women's Work in Film Projection and Changing Modes of Spectatorship in World War II British Cinema', *Feminist Media Histories*, 2:2 (Spring 2016), pp. 47-70.

Ben Highmore, *Cultural Feelings: Mood, Mediation and Cultural Politics* (London; New York: Routledge, 2017).

Bert Hogenkamp, 'Labor Movement: Europe' in Richard Abel (ed.), *Encyclopedia of Early Cinema* (London and New York: Routledge, 2005).

Everett C. Hughes, 'Good People and Dirty Work', *Social Problems*, 3:1 (1962), pp. 3-11.

Thomas P. Hughes, 'The Evolution of Large Technological Systems', in Wiebe E. Bijker, Thomas P. Hughes, and Trevor J. Pinch (eds), *The Social Construction of Technological Systems: New Directions in the Sociology and History of Technology* (Cambridge, Mass.: MIT Press, 1993).

Edward H. Hunt, *Regional Wage Variations in Britain 1850–1914* (Oxford: Clarendon Press, 1973).

Chrissie Iles, *Into the Light: The Projected Image in American Art 1964-1977* (New York: Whitney Museum of American Art, 2001).

John Izod, 'Empowering Cinema Operators in the USA and UK, 1927-1933', *Music, Sound, and the Moving Image*, 12:2 (Autumn 2018), pp. 217-240.

Claire Jesson, *The Projectionist in Cinema and the Persistence of Film*, unpublished PhD thesis, University of Warwick, 2018.

Matthew Jones, 'Memories of British Cinema', in I.Q. Hunter, Laraine Porter and Justin Smith (eds), *The Routledge Companion to British Cinema History* (London; New York: Routledge, 2017).

Matthew Jones, Melvyn Stokes and Emma Pett, *Cinema Memories: A People's History of Cinema-going in 1960s Britain* (London: Bloomsbury, 2022).

F.D. Klingender and Stuart Legg, *Money Behind the Screen: A Report Prepared on Behalf of the Film Council* (London: Lawrence and Wishart, 1937).

Annette Kuhn, *An Everyday Magic: Cinema and Cultural Memory* (London: I.B. Tauris, 2002).

Brian Larkin, 'The Politics and Poetics of Infrastructure', *Annual Review of Anthropology*, 42 (2013), pp. 327-343.

Bruno Latour, 'Where are the Missing Masses? The Sociology of a Few Mundane Artifacts', in Wiebe E. Bijker and John Law (eds), *Shaping Technology/Building Society: Studies in Sociotechnical Change* (Cambridge, Mass.: MIT Press, 1992).

Seymour Martin Lipset and Noah M. Meltz, with Rafael Gomez and Ivan Katchanovski, *The Paradox of American Unionism* (Ithaca, NY: Cornell University Press, 2004).

Yong Liu, *3D Cinematic Aesthetics and Storytelling* (Cham: Palgrave Macmillan, 2018).

Rachael Low, *The History of the British Film 1906-1914* (London: George Allen & Unwin, 1949).

Rachael Low, *Filmmaking in 1930s Britain* (London: George Allen & Unwin, 1985).

Sam Manning, *Cinemas and Cinema-Going in the United Kingdom: Decades of Decline, 1945-65* (London: University of London Press, 2020).

Michael Marder, *Dust* (London: Bloomsbury, 2016).

Thomas McLaughlin, *Street Smarts and Critical Theory: Listening to the Vernacular* (Madison, WI: University of Wisconsin Press, 1996).

Robert Murphy, 'Coming of Sound to the Cinema in Britain', *Historical Journal of Film, Radio and Television*, 4:2 (1984), pp. 143-160.

Lawrence Napper, 'Disabled Operators: Training Disabled Ex-Servicemen as Projectionists During the Great War', *Journal of British Cinema and Television*, 15:1 (January 2018), pp. 94-114.

Jan Olsson, 'Exhibition Practices in Transition: Spectators, Audiences and Projectors', in Santiago Hidalgo (ed.), *Technology and Film Scholarship: Experience, Study, Theory* (Amsterdam: University of Amsterdam Press, 2018).

Jussi Parikka, *A Geology of Media* (Minneapolis; London: University of Minnesota Press, 2015).

William Paul, *When Movies were Theater: Architecture, Exhibition and the Evolution of American Film* (New York: Columbia University Press, 2016).

Roberta E. Pearson and William Uricchio, 'Coming to Terms with New York City's Moving Picture Operators, 1906-1913', *The Moving Image: The Journal of the Association of Moving Image Archivists*, 2:2 (Fall 2002), pp 73-93.

Michael Pigott, 'Sounds of the Projection Box: Liner Notes for a Phonographic Method', *Journal of British Cinema and Television*, 15:1 (January 2018), pp. 27-45.

Michael Pigott and Richard Wallace, 'A New "Wild West" of Projection', in Virginia Crisp and Gabriel Menotti (eds), *Practices of Projection* (New York: Oxford University Press, 2020).

R. Pitchford and F. Coombs, *The Projectionist's Handbook: A Complete Guide to Cinema Operating* (London: Watkins-Pitchford, 1933).

Alessandro Portelli, 'What Makes Oral History Different', in Robert Perks and Alister Thomson (eds), *The Oral History Reader*, 3rd edn (London; New York: Routledge, 2016).

Martin Pugh, *'Hurrah for the Blackshirts!' Fascists and Fascism in Britain Between the Wars* (London: Pimlico, 2006).

Michael Quinn, 'Distribution, the Transient Audience, and the Transition to the Feature Film', *Cinema Journal*, 40:2 (Winter 2001), pp. 35-56.

John B. Rathbun, *Motion Picture Making and Exhibiting* (Chicago: Charles C. Thompson, 1914).

Alastair Reid, 'The Impact of the First World War on British Workers', in Richard Wall and Jay Winter (eds), *The Upheaval of War: Family, Work and Welfare in Europe, 1914-1918* (Cambridge: Cambridge University Press, 1988).

F. H. Richardson, *Motion Picture Handbook: A Guide for Managers and Operators of Motion Picture Theaters*, 2nd edn (New York: Moving Picture World, 1912).

Jeffrey Richards, *The Age of the Dream Palace: Cinema and Society in 1930s Britain* (London: Routledge & Kegan Paul, 1984).

David Rosenbaum, 'Trysting with Trolls', *Film Comment*, 11:3 (May-June 1975), pp. 36-37.

Miriam Ross, *3D Cinema: Optical Illusions and Tactile Experiences* (Basingstoke: Palgrave Macmillan, 2015).

Dominic Simmons, *An Introductory Guide to Film Projection*, with photographs by Alexa Raisbeck and Dominic Simmons (London: Independent Cinema Office, 2020).

Matthew Soar, 'The Beginnings and Ends of Film: Leader Standardization in the United States and Canada (1930-1999)', *The Moving Image*, 16:2 (Fall 2016), pp. 21-44.

Jackie Stacey, *Star Gazing* (London: Routledge, 1994).

Markus Stauff, 'Television's Many Technologies: Domesticity, Governmentality, Genealogy', in Annie van den Oever (ed.), *Techné/Technology* (Amsterdam: Amsterdam University Press, 2014).

Melvyn Stokes and Richard Maltby (eds), *Identifying Hollywood's Audiences: Cultural Identity and the Movies* (London: BFI, 2013).

Jonathan Stubbs, 'The Eady Levy: A Runaway Bribe? Hollywood Production and British Subsidy in the Early 1960s', *Journal of British Cinema and Television*, 6:1 (2009), pp. 1-20.

Charles S. Swartz's (ed.), *Understanding Digital Cinema: A Professional Handbook* (Oxford; Burlington, MA: Focal Press, 2005).

Frederick A. Talbot, *Moving Pictures: How They are Made and Worked* (London: William Heinemann, 1912).

Miles Taylor, 'The Beginnings of Modern British Social History', *History Workshop Journal*, 43 (Spring 1997), pp. 155-176.

Studs Terkel, *Working: People Talk About What They Do All Day and How They Feel About What They Do* (New York: New Press, 2004).

E. P. Thompson, *The Making of the English Working Class* (London: Gollancz, 1963).

Paul Thompson, *The Voice of the Past: Oral History*, 3rd edn (Oxford: Oxford University Press, 2000).

Frank A. Tilley, 'The Story of the Year', in *Kinematograph Year Book 1922* (London: Kinematograph Weekly, 1922).

Paolo Cherchi Usai, Spencer Christiano, Catherine A. Surowiec and Timothy J. Wagner (eds), *The Art of Film Projection: A Beginner's Guide* (New York: The George Eastman Museum, 2019).

Andrew V. Uroskie, *Between the Black Box and the White Cube: Expanded Cinema and Postwar Art* (Chicago; University of Chicago Press, 2014).

Lies Van de Vijer, 'The Cinema is Dead, Long Live the Cinema!: Understanding the Social Experience of Cinema-going Today', *Participations: Journal of Audience & Reception Studies*, 14:1 (May 2017), pp. 129-144.

Richard Wallace, '"We Might Go into Double Act Mode": "Professional Recollectors", Rehearsed Memory and its Uses', *Oral History*, 45:1 (Spring 2017), pp. 55-66.

Richard Wallace, 'Going Digital: The Experience of the Transition to Digital Projection in UK Cinemas', *Journal of British Cinema and Television*, 15:1 (January 2018), pp. 6-26.

Richard Wallace, Rebecca Harrison and Charlotte Brunsdon, 'Women in the Box: Female Projectionists in Post-war British Cinema', *Journal of British Cinema and Television*, 15:1 (January 2018), pp. 46-65.

Janet Wasko, 'The Future of Film Distribution and Exhibition', in Dan Harries (ed.), *The New Media Book* (London: BFI, 2002).

Owen Weetch, *Expressive Spaces in Digital 3D Cinema* (London: Palgrave Macmillan, 2016).

David R. Williams, 'Ladies of the Lamp: The Employment of Women in the British Film Trade During World War 1', *Film History*, 9:1 (1997), pp. 116-127.

Tana Wollen, 'The Bigger the Better: From CinemaScope to Imax', in Philip Hayward & Tana Wollen (eds), *Future Visions: New Technologies of the Screen* (London: BFI, 1993).

Chris Wrigley, 'Trade Unions and Politics in the First World War', in Ben Pimlott and Chris Cook (eds), *Trade Unions in British Politics* (London; New York: Longman, 1982).

Chris Wrigley, *British Trade Unions Since 1933* (Cambridge: Cambridge University Press, 2002).

G. M. Young (Annotated by George Kitson Clark), *Portrait of an Age: Victorian England* (London: Oxford University Press, 1977).

Ray Zone, *Stereoscopic Cinema and the Origins of 3-D Film, 1838-1952* (Lexington, KY: University Press of Kentucky, 2007).

Ray Zone, *3-D Revolution: The History of Modern Stereoscopic Cinema* (Lexington, KY: University Press of Kentucky, 2012).

Web

American Film Institute, 'Warren Beatty Introduces BONNIE AND CLYDE', https://www.youtube.com/watch?v=v3_i7w2XPIE, accessed 6 Mar 2020.

BECTU, 'Picturehouse cinema chain was the "Largest cinema workers strike in UK history"', https://web.archive.org/web/20181022025144/https://bectu.org.uk/news/2676, accessed 26 January 2021.

Paul Bradshaw, 'The Best Letters Film Directors Sent to Projectionists', https://www.denofgeek.com/movies/the-best-letters-film-directors-sent-to-projectionists/, accessed 26 August 2020.

Ambrose Heron, 'Letters to Projectionists', http://www.filmdetail.com/2011/06/26/letters-to-projectionists-kubrick-lynch-malick-bay/, accessed 10 July 2019.

Ryan Lamble, 'John Landis Interview: Monsters in the Movies, Genre Cinema, Political Zombies, Aliens, and More', https://www.denofgeek.com/movies/alien/18272/john-landis-interview-monsters-in-the-movies-genre-cinema-political-zombies-aliens-and-more, accessed 10 July 2019.

Walter Murch, 'Who Has Final Cut on the Film? The Projectionist!', https://www.webofstories.com/play/walter.murch/108;jsessionid=5D6DCEB9CF9A7FEF5975A1F7B1F9EFAC, accessed 10 July 2019.

'Planetary Projection', *caboose books*, https://www.caboosebooks.net/planetary-projection, accessed 25 January 2021.

The Projection Project, 'The Cinema Projectionist', https://cinemaprojectionist.co.uk/, accessed 25 January 2021.

Events

Richard Nicholson, *The Projectionists*, exhibition, The Gas Hall, Birmingham Museums and Art Gallery, 19–24 April 2016.

Other

Michael Lightbourne, *Sounds of the Projection Box* (Gruenrekorder, 2018), https://www.gruenrekorder.de/?page_id=16703, accessed 17 September 2020.

Index

A
ABC circuit, 128, 143, 157
ABC Edgware, Middlesex, 165
ABC Edgware Road, London (fig.), 44
Adelphi, Slough (fig.), 23
Allen, Simon, 29, 31, 33, 38, 39, 49, 56, 63, 64, 77, 92-93, 198
AMC Theatres, 167
Apollo Cinemas, 187, 188
Arts Alliance Media, 175, 178
Atwill, Brad, 48, 49, 50, 51, 52, 54, 61, 63-64, 92, 96, 167, 181, 183, 187, 188, 189, 191, 194, 199-200, 201, 203-204, 205
Auslander, Philip, 93
Aviemore Centre, Aviemore, 59
B
Bagnall, Ken, 52, 68, 77, 96, 166, 188, 193
Bancroft, David, 173
Barco Ltd, 178
Barnard, Timothy, 5, 16, 69-70, 76, 104
Barry Lyndon (UK-USA, 1975), 86
Barton, Florence, 57, 66, 144
Bay, Michael, 86
Bell-Cox, L.C., 117, 118
Belton, John, 97, 212
Bennett, Colin N., 72, 76, 123
Benson, James, 20
Billy Rose's Jumbo (USA, 1962), 64
Bioscope, The, 113, 114 (fig.)
Blackstone Group, 166
Blower, Chris, 39, 47, 61, 100, 185, 189, 190
Bomback, R.H., 44
Bondfield, Margaret, M.P., 133
Bonnie and Clyde (USA, 1967), 84
Bordwell, David, 175
Brewster, Ben, 72-73
British Film Institute (BFI), 178
British Kinematograph, Sound and Television Society (BKSTS), 172, 176, 177, 178, 187; *see also* British Kinematograph Society
British Kinematograph Society (BKS), 44, 150, 153, 154; *see also* British Kinematograph, Sound and Television Society
Broadcasting and Entertainment Trades Alliance (BETA), 165; *see also* Broadcasting, Entertainment, Communications and Theatre Union
Broadcasting, Entertainment, Communications and Theatre Union (BECTU)
  awareness of past history, 102
  founding of, 165
  response to digitalisation, 184-185, 186-187, 188; *see also* National Association of Theatrical and Kine Employees
Brown, Ernest, 134
Brownlow, Kevin, 70
Brunsdon, Charlotte, 1, 5
Buck, Mark, 179
Burrows, Jon, 210
Butler, Martin, 23-24, 30, 90
C
Cardiff Technical College, 157
Cartwright, Lisa, 97
Catlin, Edward S., 110
Česálková, Lucie, 7-8
Chanan, Michael, 102, 112
Chaplin, Charlie, 70
Christiano, Spencer, 3
Christie, 178
Cinemas
  conversion to digital, 174-175
  multiplexes, 43-56, 98-100

numbers of people employed by, 133
post-war decline of, 159
'tripling' of, 49
'twinning' of, 48-49
Cinema Technology, 172, 177
Cinematograph Act 1909, 16-17, 26, 107, 130
Cinematograph Exhibitors' Association (CEA)
annual conference of, 37
attitude concerning female projectionists, 142
attitude to unions, 119-120, 125-126, 127, 132, 134, 135, 147-149, 152, 155
attitude to working hours, 131, 147
involvement in training schemes, 116-117, 146, 150-158
itemisation of projection duties, 58-59
Cinematograph Trade Advisory Committee (Disabled Sailors and Soldiers), 116-117
Cineworld, Boldon Colliery, 49
Cineworld circuit, 166, 186, 188
Cineworld, Sheffield, 180
Circuits Management Association (CMA), 153, 157
Citizen Kane (USA, 1941), 85
Corfield, Mick, 184-186, 187, 188, 202
Cosgrove, Mark, 181
COVID-19 pandemic, 1, 201, 211-212, 213
Cricks, R. Howard, 19, 26, 46, 68, 78, 81, 82, 83, 87, 127-128, 152, 152, 163, 164
Crofts, Charlotte, 6
Cruel Sea, The (UK, 1953), 91
Cubitt, Sean, 4-5
Curzon, Clevedon, 41, 51
D
Daily Worker, 101
Day, Harry, M.P., 133
Depression of 1920-21, 122-123
Digital Screen Network (DSN), 174, 178
Douglas, John, 27, 31, 32, 33, 38, 56, 65, 91, 95, 206
Douglas, Peter, 27, 39, 43, 45, 52, 54-55, 56, 61, 62, 63, 65, 95, 96, 98
Doyle, Gillian, 174
Dukes, Rachel, 50, 96, 200
Dunford, Ewan, 179, 195
Dying of the Light, The (USA 2015), 5
E
Eady Levy, 158
Eastman Kodak, 169
Edmunds, Paul, 31, 88
Electrical Trades Union (ETU)
agreements with cinema owners, 120-121, 124-125
involvement in training schemes, 116, 125
position on working hours, 131
recruitment of projectionists, 113, 118-119, 148
relations with NATE, 119, 130-132, 148
strike actions organised by, 101-103, 124, 125-126, 135-138
subscription levels, 119, 121-123, 124-125, 135, 138-139
Electric, Notting Hill, London 38
Empire Cinemas, 188
Empire, Kilburn, London, 46
Empire, Leicester Square, London, 20
Empire, Newcastle, 189
Entertainment Tax, 158
Enticknap, Leo, 34, 38, 39-40
Essoldo circuit, 46, 163
Essoldomatic, 46-47 (fig.), 55, 163
Eyles, Allen, 94
F
Farmer, Richard, 141
Fawke, Phil, 22-23, 26, 27, 32-33, 38, 56, 62, 85, 91, 95, 172, 193, 202
Fight Club (USA, 1999), 82
Forum, Nottingham, 64, 91
Foster, Alan, 38, 52, 173, 179, 193, 200, 201, 206
Fuller, A.W., 165
G
Gaumont-British circuit, 128, 133, 143, 144, 153
Gaumont State, Kilburn, London, 153

Ghost of St. Michael's, The (UK, 1941), 91
Gibson, Frank, 26, 32, 33, 40, 61, 63, 65, 95, 196, 199, 206
Gilmour, Sir John, 130
Goodwin, F.R., 120
Gower, Raymond, M.P., 159
Graham, John H., 87
Guild of British Kinema Projectionists and Engineers
attitude concerning female projectionists, 142
attitude towards unionisation, 127-129, 139
condescension towards projectionists, 128-129
definition of projectionists' status, 67, 83, 127
formation of, 126
membership levels, 126-127, 128, 139
Gunning, Tom, 16
H
Haddart, Constance, 144
Harrison, Rebecca, 5, 141
Harry Potter and the Deathly Hallows - Part 2 (UK-USA, 2011), 85
Hudson, Stuart, 181-182
Highmore, Ben, 6-7, 9, 93
Home Office, 46, 115
Howden, Peter, 35, 38, 77, 95, 98, 100, 193, 194-195, 197 (fig.), 200, 201, 206
Hughes, Everett, 108
Hughes, Thomas P., 13-14
I
Independent Cinema Office, 207-208
Indiana Jones and the Last Crusade (USA, 1989), 85
Izod, John, 5, 20
J
Jesson, Claire, 210
J. Frank Brockliss Ltd, 94
Jurassic Park (USA, 1993), 205
K
Kinema Projectionists and Engineers Association, 139
Kinematograph Renters' Society, 71
Kinematograph Weekly, 144, 145, 149
Knopp, Leslie, 152
Kodak Digital Cinema Operating System, 169-171
Kubrick, Stanley, 86
Kuhn, Annette, 8
L
Larkin, Brian, 9
Last Projectionist, The (UK, 2011), 5
Latour, Bruno, 18
Lauste, Emile, 15-17
Lavington, Sam, 31, 61, 84, 93, 100
Leggett, Frederick, 134
Leigh, Danny, 213
Les Miserables (France, 1912), 73-74
London County Council, 21-22, 115
London Trades Council, 131
Lucas, George, 85
Lynch, David, 68-69, 85
M
McAlpine, Hamish, 173
McKenna, Reginald, 115
MacLean, Andrew, 29, 33, 51, 97, 98, 195, 201
Makwana, Chandra, 31, 49, 99, 186, 190, 191, 196
Malick, Terrence, 85
Marder, Michael, 60
Mason, Edward H., 109
Marshall, Mike, 32, 90, 93, 99, 190, 200, 204, 205
Master Brenograph, 90, 91 (fig.)
Matrix, The (USA, 1999), 205
Ministry of Education, 150, 151, 154
Ministry of Labour,
designation of reserved occupations in wartime, 58, 140, 143
involvement in projection training schemes, 116-117, 146, 150, 151, 153, 154, 156
surveys of cinema employment practices by, 21, 22, 133-134
Mothlight (USA, 1963), 208

Mulholland Dr. (USA-France, 2001), 85
N
Napper, Lawrence, 5, 115
National Association of Cinematograph Operators (NACO)
dissolution of, 112-113
formation of, 103-106
hostility to novices, 110-111
membership criteria, 106
reorganisation of, 111-112
similarities to Guild of British Kinema Projectionists and Technicians, 129
subscription levels, 111, 112; *see also* National Association of Theatrical Employees; National Association of Theatrical and Kine Employees
National Association of Theatrical and Kine Employees (NATKE)
attitude towards automation, 163-164
attitude towards female projectionists, 142
attitude towards Guild of British Kinema Projectionists and Technicians, 129, 139
attitude towards single manning 42, 164
establishment of operators' branch, 105
expansion of cinema branch membership, 112
involvement in training schemes, 116, 150-158
position on working hours, 131, 132, 136-137, 160
relations with CEA, 132, 134, 135, 138, 140, 147-149
relations with ETU, 119, 130-132, 138, 148
subscription levels, 135, 139, 165
National Association of Theatrical Employees (NATE); *see* National Association of Theatrical and Kine Employees
National Association of Theatrical, Television and Kine Employees (NATTKE); *see* National Association of Theatrical and Kine Employees
National Film Theatre, London, 198
National Joint Council of Labour, 130
Neal, John, 41, 51, 92, 183, 201
Nicolson, Annabel, 209
Nicholson, Richard, 197
No Time to Die (UK-USA, 2021), 213
O
O'Brien, Sir Thomas, 130, 132, 135, 137, 138, 139, 148, 149, 152, 155, 163, 164, 165
Odeon, Bayswater, London, 181
Odeon circuit, 128, 140, 143, 144, 153, 166, 177-178, 188
Odeon, Glasgow Quay, 190, 205-206
Odeon, Hatfield, 182
Odeon, Nottingham, 48-49
Odeon, Penge, London, 165
Odeon, Peterborough, 141
Odeon, Renfield Street, Glasgow, 65
Odeon, Sevenoaks, 53, 57, 66
Oliver, Paul, 182
Olympia Cinema, Cardiff, 61
Olsson, Jan, 73
Operators; *see* projectionists
P
Parikka, Jussi, 9
Paul, William, 86-87, 88-89
Pearce, Adrian, 49-50, 51, 54, 55-56, 60-61, 62, 193-194, 202
Pearson, Bill, 42
Pearson, Joan, 42
Perry, Stanley, 128
Philips Projectawind, 43-45
Pigott, Michael, 204, 210
Planetary Projection, 7
Point, The, Milton Keynes, 43
Projection
automation of, 45-48, 180
categorisation as a part of film production, 68-83
costs of analogue vs digital, 173-175
different technological arrays, 14
digitalisation of, 67, 169-206
faults, 99-100
introduction of sound, 19-22
'making-up' prints, 40-42, 53-55
mobile array, 15-17

multi-screen array, 43-56, 89
need for cleanliness, 20, 61, 209
nitrate array, 17-43
reel changeovers, 28-30, 72-83
showmanship and, 25-26, 87-100, 199-201, 204
significance of screen curtains, 87-89
sound volume control, 83-85
speeds in silent era, 69-72
xenon array, 35-43
Projectionists
age range of, 140
attitudes towards unions, 165-167
attitudes towards digital image quality, 201-204, 206
changes of job title, 13, 20-21, 180-181
cleaning responsibilities, 60-62
concern with visual clarity, 84-85, 192
deskilling through technological change, 195-199
disabled soldiers employed as, 115-117
equipment maintenance responsibilities, 62-64
goal of 'invisibility', 76-78, 97, 100, 206
grades of, 22-26, 56
impact of sound upon, 19-21, 27, 124, 126
loss of control with digital projection, 191-195
loneliness of, 54-55
mass redundancies of, 183-191
numbers employed nationally, 21-22, 144
pay and conditions, 101, 104, 106-110, 118, 121, 124, 128, 131, 133-134, 135, 140, 147-149, 155, 159-160
post-war shortage of, 147, 149-150
predicted role in digital era, 176-177, 182, 184-185
promotional responsibilities, 64-66
reputation for damaging prints, 79-82, 145
responsibility for non-synchronous sound, 89-90, 92
responsibility for screen lighting, 90-93
role of Chief, 24-26, 86
specialised cinemas and, 171, 191, 200, 201, 207-208
supplementary duties, 56-66
teenagers employed as, 117-118, 133-134, 141, 144-146, 147, 158
training of, 64, 123-124, 125, 143, 144-145, 150-158, 177-179, 183
women employed as, 113-115, 117, 141-144
workload of, 35-37, 43, 45-55, 160-162
Projection Project, The, 1, 7, 209-212, 214
Projectors
3-D and, 35, 98-99
'cakestand' system, 43-45, 49-52
carbon arc lighting, 31-33
breakdowns, 52, 55-56
difficulty fixing problems with digital, 193-194
digital, 169-171, 181-182, 192-195
gramophone attachments, 19
hand cranking of, 17-18
motorisation of, 17-18
personalisation of, 205
repairability of analogue, 193-194
safety features of, 26-28
safety film and, 34-35
security features of digital, 194-195
sounds of, 51, 204-205, 206
tower system, 39-40
widescreen and, 35
xenon lighting, 37-39, 55
Q
Queen's Cinema, Bayswater, London, 94 (fig.)
Queen's Cinerama Theatre, Newcastle, 93, 205
R
Rank, J. Arthur, 138
Rank Organisation, 64, 166
Reed, Ray, 31, 63, 64, 193, 194, 196, 198, 203
Reel Time (UK, 1973), 209
Regal, Coventry, 33

Regal, Edmonton, London, 90, 91 (fig.)
Regal, Leamington Spa, 22-23, 56
Regal, St Leonards-on-sea, 87
Richards, Tim, 179
Richardson, F.H., 13, 69, 72
Rio, Dalston, London, 197 (fig.)
Rosenbaum, David, 6, 76-77, 100
Ross Sceneograph, 90
S
Scala, Sheffield, 27
Schofield, Paul, 176, 178
Selective Employment Tax, 163
Showcase, Coventry, 49
Side by Side (USA, 2012), p. 5
Simon, Sir John, 115
Slater, Jim, 172, 173, 178, 180, 182, 192
Society of Motion Picture Engineers (SMPE), 78, 79
Society of Motion Picture and Television Engineers (SMPTE), 172-173
Sound Associates, 178
Sound technology; *see* Projection
Spielberg, Steven, 85
Standard Release Print, 78-79, 81
Stanley-Aldrich, W., 27
Star Cinemas, 55
Star Wars: Episode II – Attack of the Clones (USA, 2002), 192
Stauff, Markus, 13
Surowiec, Catherine A., 3
S
Thompson, Neil, 29, 31, 32, 39, 40, 43, 52, 62, 63, 68, 77, 93, 166, 185, 189, 193, 203, 205
Tom, Tom, the Piper's Son (USA, 1969), 208
Town Hall, Newmarket, 16
Trades Union Congress, 132, 138, 165
Traffic in Souls (USA, 1913), 73, 75
Transformers: Dark of the Moon (USA, 2011), 86
The Tree of Life (USA, 2011), 85
Tweddell, Chris, 40, 55, 77, 83, 99-100, 187, 188, 190-191, 193, 195, 197, 199, 203
2001: A Space Odyssey (UK-USA, 1968), 205
Tyneside Cinema, Newcastle, 63
T
UCI Cinemas, 166
UCI Printworks, Manchester, 172
UGC circuit, 166
UK Film Council (UKFC), 174
Uroskie, Andrew, 9
Usai, Paolo Cherchi, 3-4, 6
U
Variety Artistes Federation, 105
Virgin Cinemas circuit, 166
Vue, Hull, 179
W
Wagner, Timothy J., 3
Wallace, Richard, 210
Wandsworth Technical Institute, 155
Watershed, Bristol, 179, 181, 195
Welling Kinema, East Wickham, 27
Williams, Anthony, 174
Williams, David R., 5, 115
Williams, Mike, 28, 30, 41, 61, 62-63, 64-65, 77, 83, 88, 90, 96, 97
Williamson, W.A., 108-109
Woods, F.H., 127
Wrigley, Chris, 122-123
Y
Yates, David, 85-86
Young, G.M., 8
Young, John, 23, 63, 92, 93, 98-99, 166-167, 172